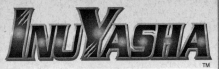

VOL. 28
VIZ Media Edition

Story and Art by
RUMIKO TAKAHASHI

English Adaptation by Gerard Jones

Translation/Mari Morimoto
Touch-Up Art & Lettering/Bill Schuch
Cover and Interior Graphic Design/Yuki Ameda
Editor/Ian Robertson

Managing Editor/Annette Roman
Editorial Director/Elizabeth Kawasaki
Editor in Chief/Alvin Lu
Sr. Director of Acquisitions/Rika Inouye
Sr. VP of Marketing/Liza Coppola
Exec. VP of Sales & Marketing/John Easum
Publisher/Hyoe Narita

© 1997 Rumiko TAKAHASHI/Shogakukan Inc. First
published by Shogakukan Inc. in Japan as
"Inuyasha." New and adapted artwork and text
© 2007 VIZ Media, LLC. All rights reserved.
The stories, characters and incidents mentioned in
this publication are entirely fictional.

For the purposes of publication in English, the artwork in this publication is printed in reverse from
the original Japanese version. No portion of this
book may be reproduced or transmitted in any form
or by any means without written permission from
the copyright holders.

Printed in the U.S.A.

Published by VIZ Media, LLC
P.O. Box 77010
San Francisco, CA 94107

VIZ Media Edition
10 9 8 7 6 5 4 3 2 1
First printing, January 2007

PARENTAL ADVISORY
INUYASHA is rated T+ for Older Teen. This
book contains violence. It is recommended
for ages 16 and up.

www.viz.com

store.viz.com

INUYASHA

VOL. 28

VIZ Media

May 28, 2010

NEW PORT
RICHEY PUBLIC
LIBRARY

YA F

INU YASHA

3228800123423

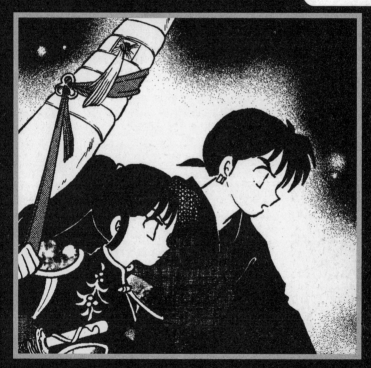

STORY AND ART BY
RUMIKO TAKAHASHI

CONTENTS

HE STORY THUS FAR

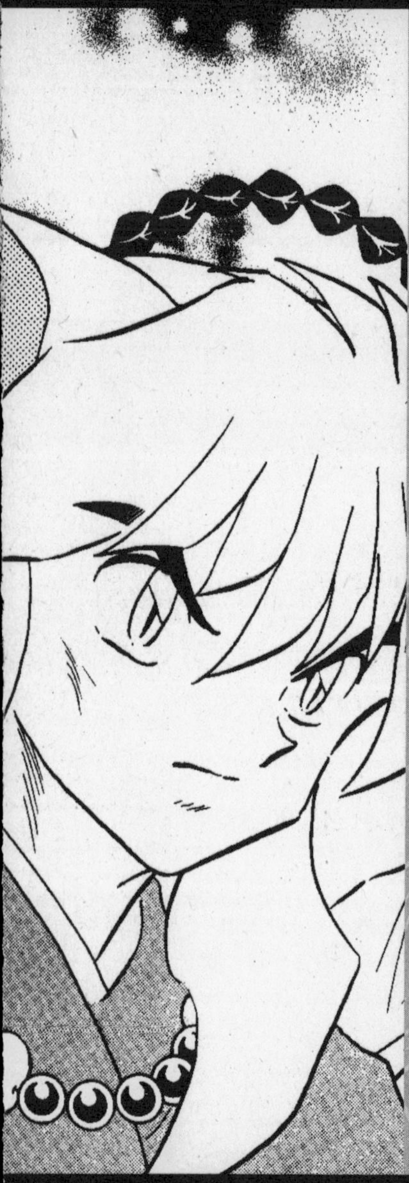

Long ago, in the "Warring States" era of Japan's Muromachi period (*Sengoku-jidai*, approximately 1467-1568 CE), a legendary dog-like half-demon called "Inuyasha" attempted to steal the Shikon Jewel—or "Jewel of Four Souls"—from a village, but was stopped by the enchanted arrow of the village priestess, Kikyo. Inuyasha fell into a deep sleep, pinned to a tree by Kikyo's arrow, while the mortally wounded Kikyo took the Shikon Jewel with her into the fires of her funeral pyre. Years passed.

Fast-forward to the present day. Kagome, a Japanese high school girl, is pulled into a well one day by a mysterious centipede monster and finds herself transported into the past—only to come face to face with the trapped Inuyasha. She frees him, and Inuyasha easily defeats the centipede monster.

The residents of the village, now 50 years older, readily accept Kagome as the reincarnation of their deceased priestess Kikyo, a claim supported by the fact that the Shikon Jewel emerges from a cut on Kagome's body. Unfortunately, the jewel's rediscovery means that the village is soon under attack by a variety of demons in search of this treasure. Then, the jewel is accidentally shattered into many shards, each of which may have the fearsome power of the entire jewel.

Although Inuyasha says he hates Kagome because of her resemblance to Kikyo, the woman who "killed" him, he is forced to team up with her when Kaede, the village leader, binds him to Kagome with a powerful spell. Now the two grudging companions must fight to reclaim and reassemble the shattered shards of the Shikon Jewel before they fall into the wrong hands...

S VOLUME Trapped inside the holy shield of Mount Hakurei, Inuyasha's demonic power has been stripped
/, leaving him vulnerable. Will Miroku's wind tunnel prove strong enough to break the barrier and free Inuyasha?
will Inuyasha's strength be enough to defeat the leader of the Band of Seven, who has absorbed the shikon
ds from his fallen comrades and become an even more formidable foe? A fierce battle is about to erupt—and
ku is about to make a shocking appearance!

CHARACTERS

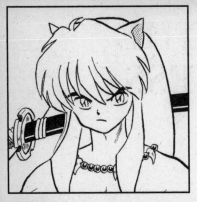

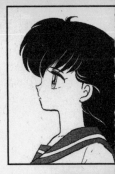

INUYASHA
Half-demon hybrid, son of a human mother and demon father. His necklace is enchanted, allowing Kagome to control him with a word.

KAGOME
Modern-day Japanese schoolgirl who can travel back and forth between the past and present through an enchanted well.

MIROKU
Lecherous Buddhist priest cursed with a mystical "hellhole" in his hand that's slowly killing him.

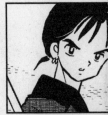

NARAKU
Enigmatic demon-mastermind behind the miseries of nearly everyone in the story.

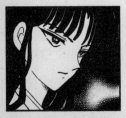

SANGO
"Demon Exterminator" or slayer from the village where the Shikon Jewel was first born.

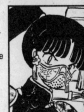

KOGA
Leader of the Wolf Clan, Koga is himself a Wolf Demon and, because of several Shikon shards in his legs, possesses super speed. Enamored of Kagome, he quarrels with Inuyasha frequently.

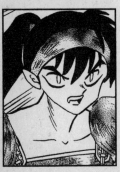

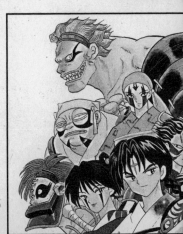

BAND OF SEVEN
A group of undead killers brought back to life by Naraku through the powers of the Shikon Jewel Shards.

SCROLL ONE

INSIDE THE DARKNESS

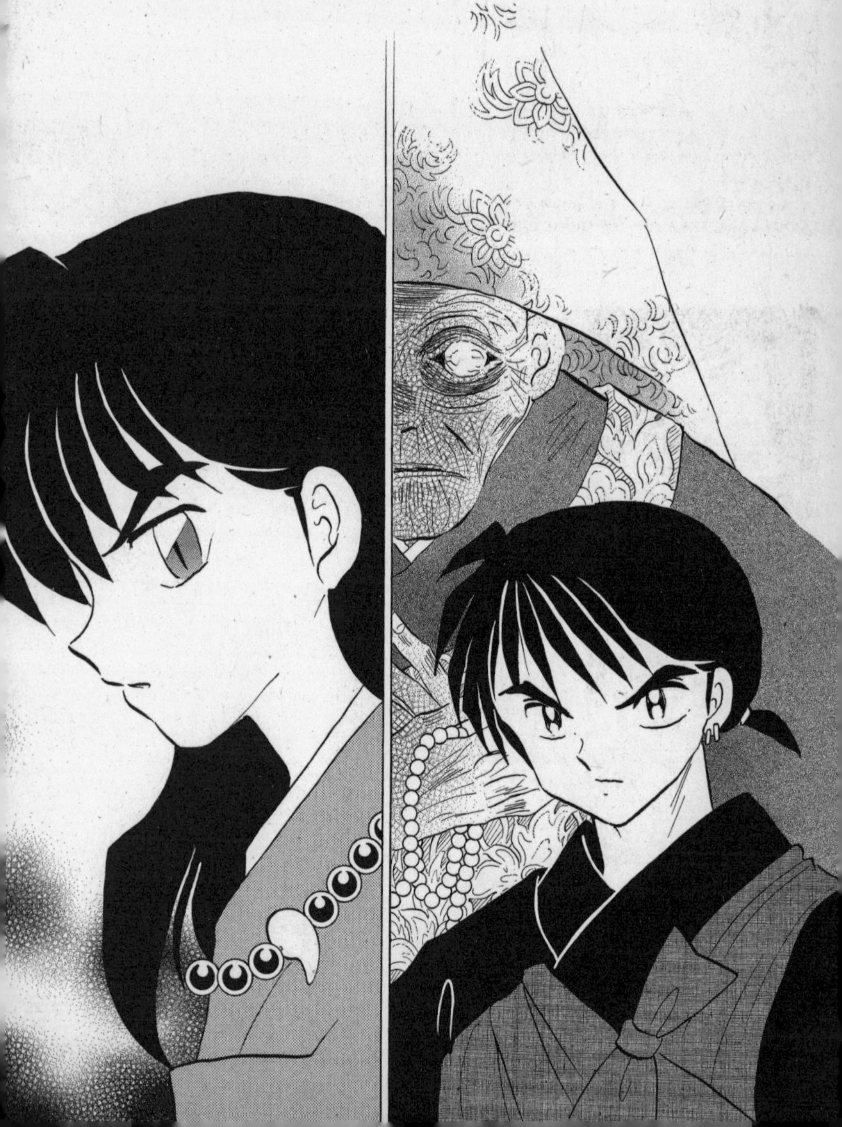

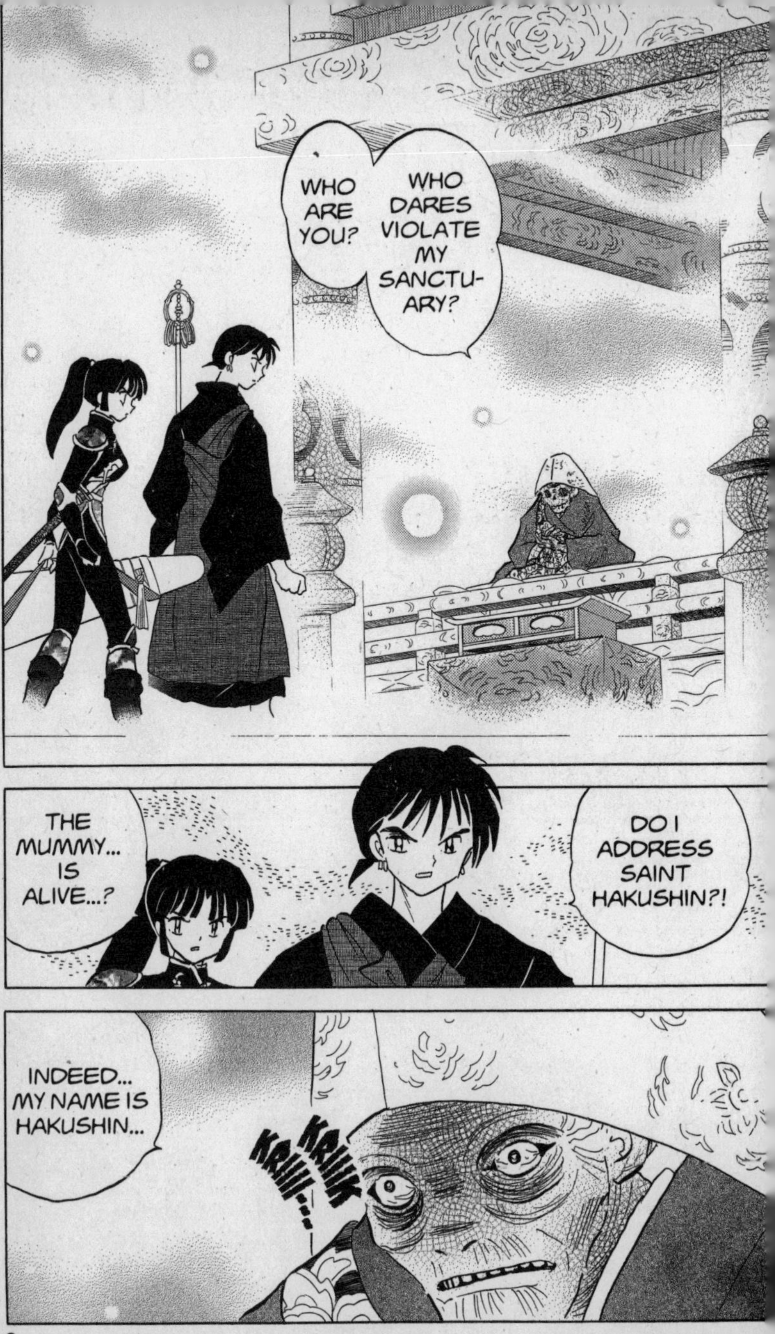
WHO ARE YOU?
WHO DARES VIOLATE MY SANCTUARY?
THE MUMMY... IS ALIVE...?
DO I ADDRESS SAINT HAKUSHIN?!
INDEED... MY NAME IS HAKUSHIN...
KRIIIII...
KRIIIK

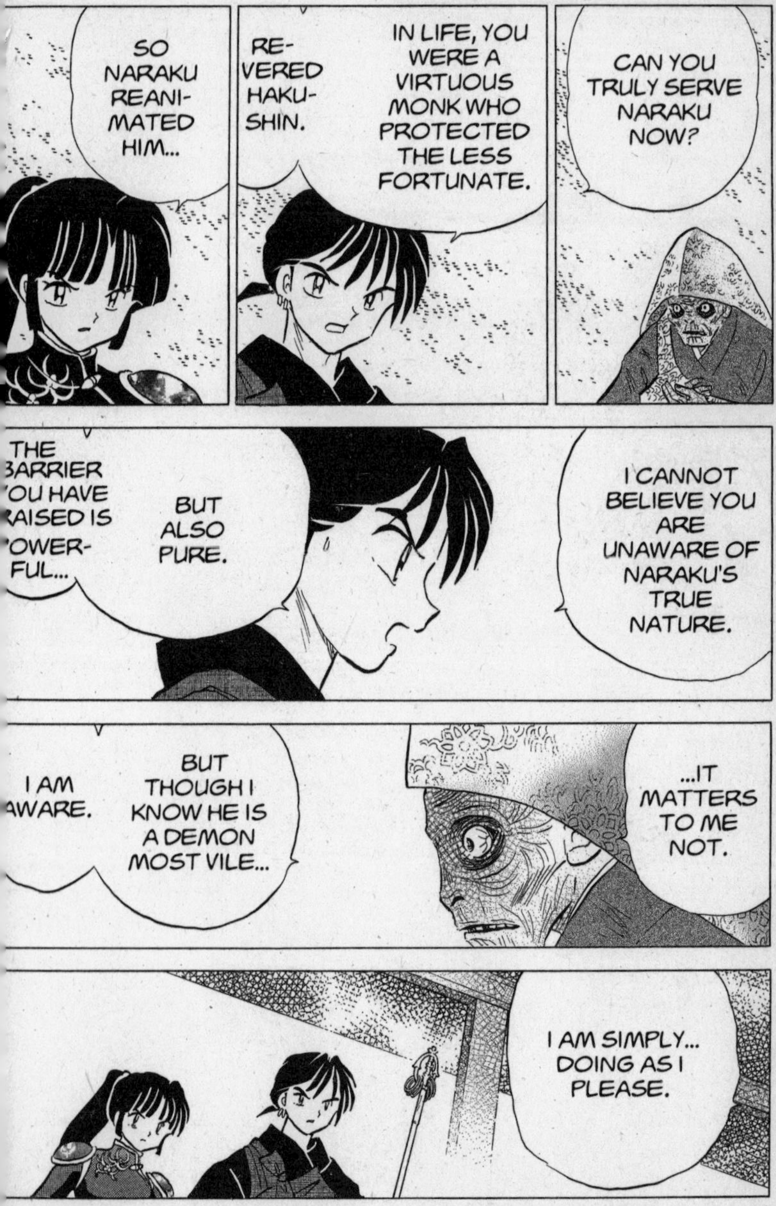
SO NARAKU REANIMATED HIM...
REVERED HAKUSHIN.
IN LIFE, YOU WERE A VIRTUOUS MONK WHO PROTECTED THE LESS FORTUNATE.
CAN YOU TRULY SERVE NARAKU NOW?
THE BARRIER YOU HAVE RAISED IS POWERFUL...
BUT ALSO PURE.
I CANNOT BELIEVE YOU ARE UNAWARE OF NARAKU'S TRUE NATURE.
I AM AWARE.
BUT THOUGH I KNOW HE IS A DEMON MOST VILE...
...IT MATTERS TO ME NOT.
I AM SIMPLY... DOING AS I PLEASE.

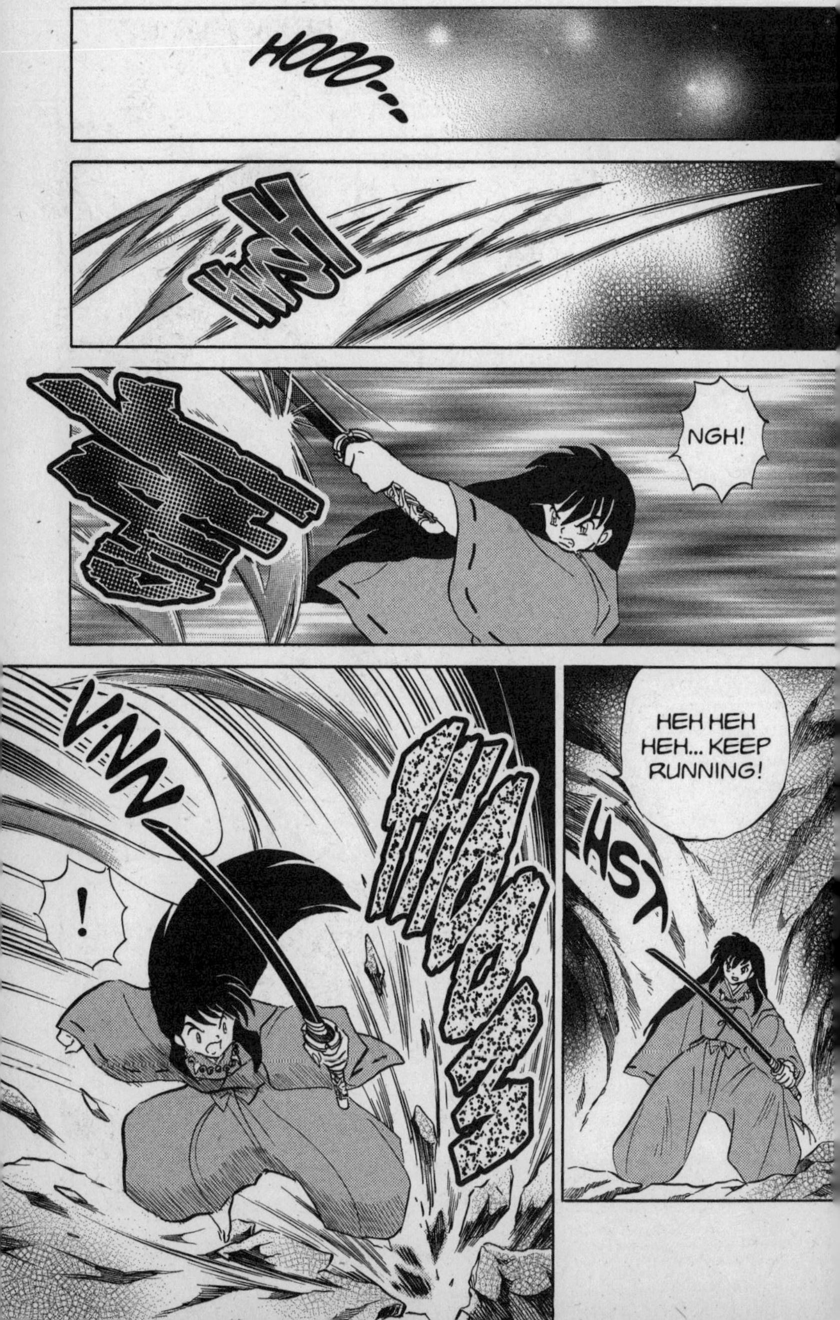
HOOO...
NGH!
!
HEH HEH HEH... KEEP RUNNING!

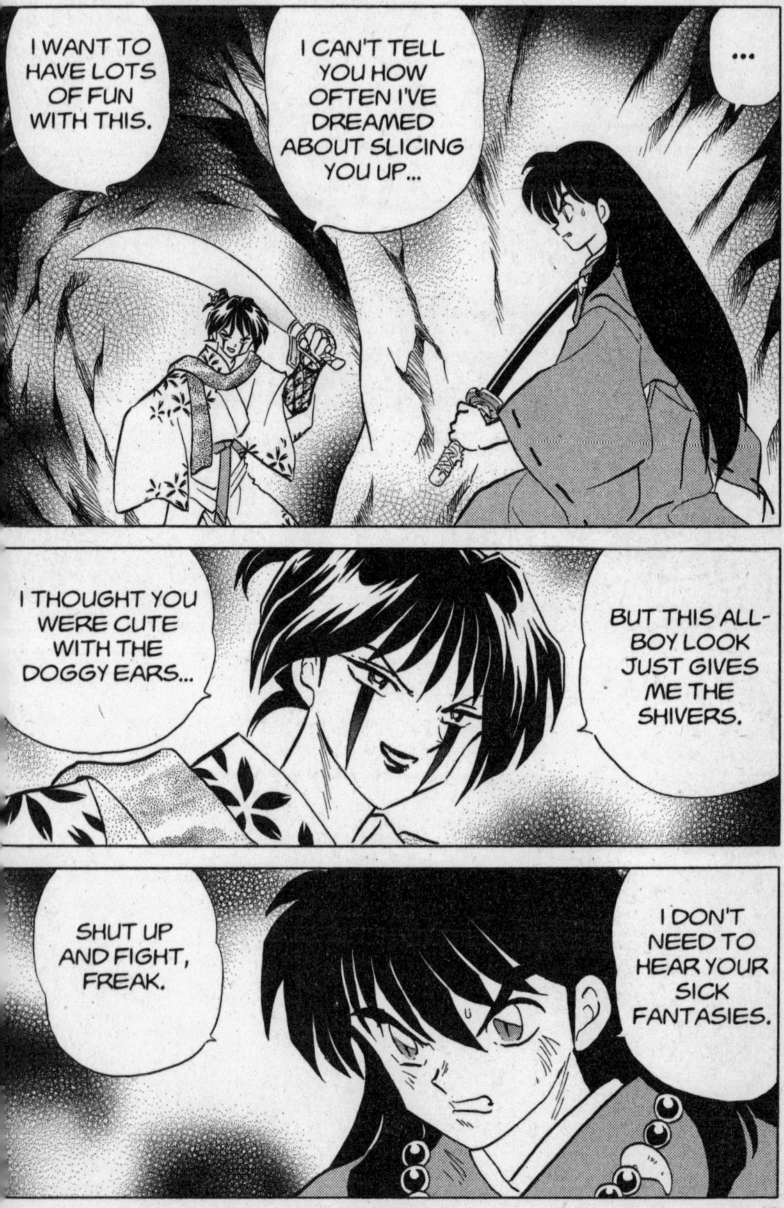
I WANT TO HAVE LOTS OF FUN WITH THIS.
I CAN'T TELL YOU HOW OFTEN I'VE DREAMED ABOUT SLICING YOU UP...
...
I THOUGHT YOU WERE CUTE WITH THE DOGGY EARS...
BUT THIS ALL-BOY LOOK JUST GIVES ME THE SHIVERS.
SHUT UP AND FIGHT, FREAK.
I DON'T NEED TO HEAR YOUR SICK FANTASIES.

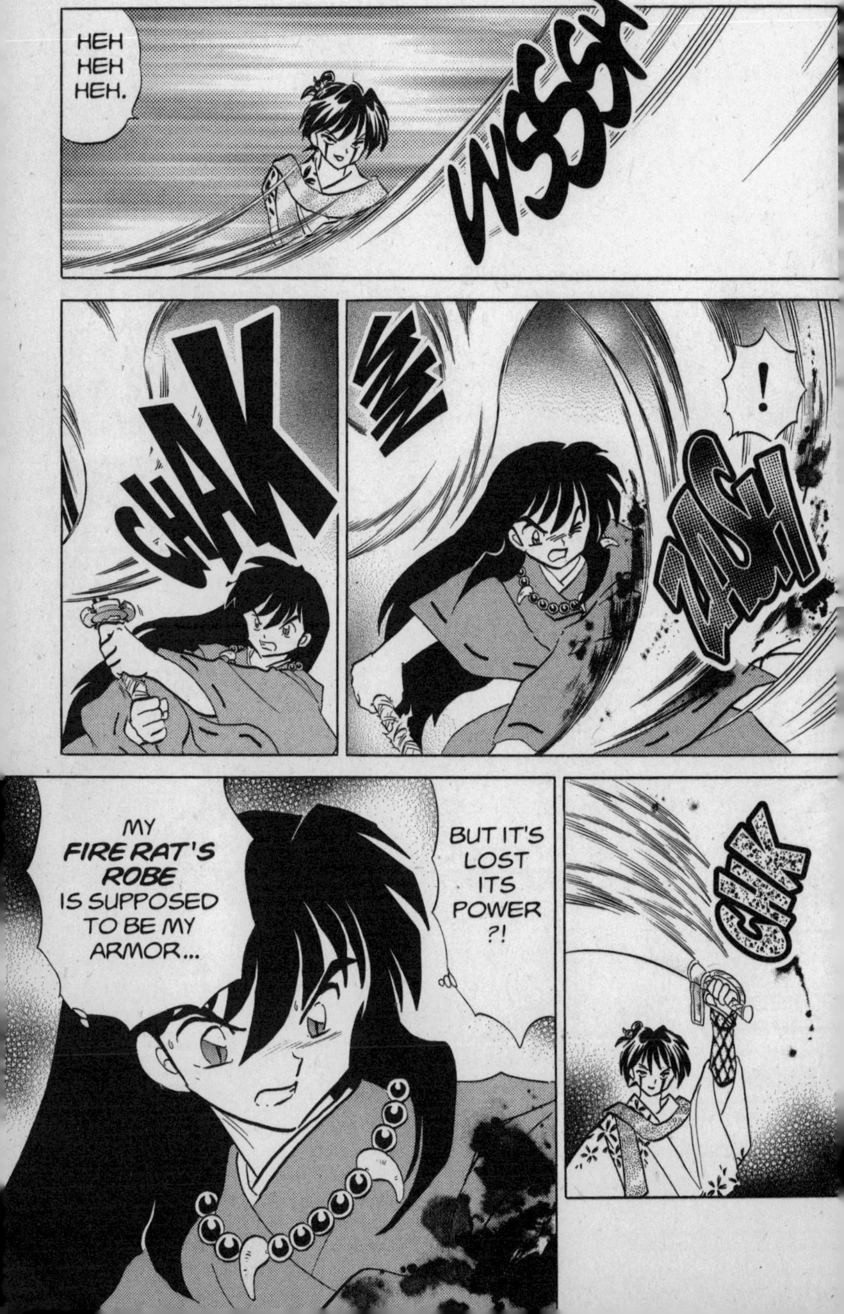
HEH HEH HEH.
WSSSH
CHAK
SW
!
ZASH
MY *FIRE RAT'S ROBE* IS SUPPOSED TO BE MY ARMOR...
BUT IT'S LOST ITS POWER ?!
CHAK

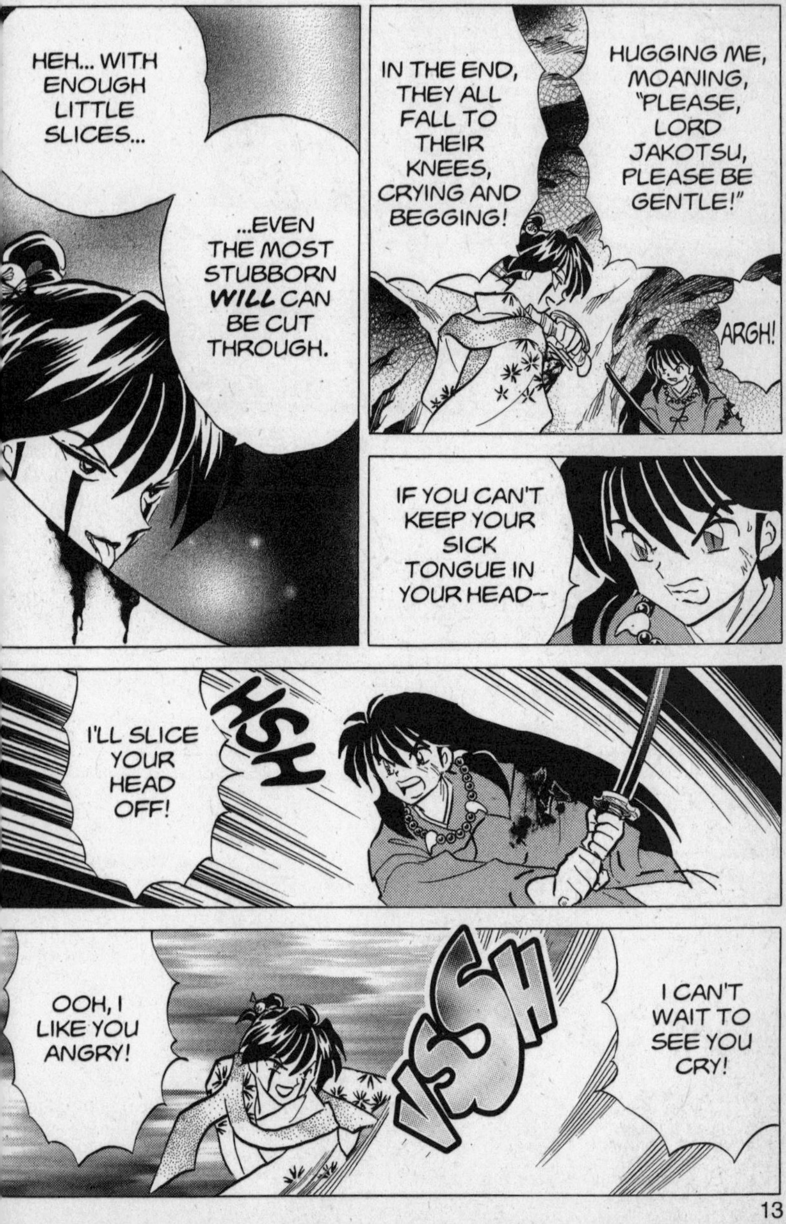
HEH... WITH ENOUGH LITTLE SLICES...
...EVEN THE MOST STUBBORN WILL CAN BE CUT THROUGH.
IN THE END, THEY ALL FALL TO THEIR KNEES, CRYING AND BEGGING!
HUGGING ME, MOANING, "PLEASE, LORD JAKOTSU, PLEASE BE GENTLE!"
ARGH!
IF YOU CAN'T KEEP YOUR SICK TONGUE IN YOUR HEAD--
I'LL SLICE YOUR HEAD OFF!
HSH
OOH, I LIKE YOU ANGRY!
VSSH
I CAN'T WAIT TO SEE YOU CRY!

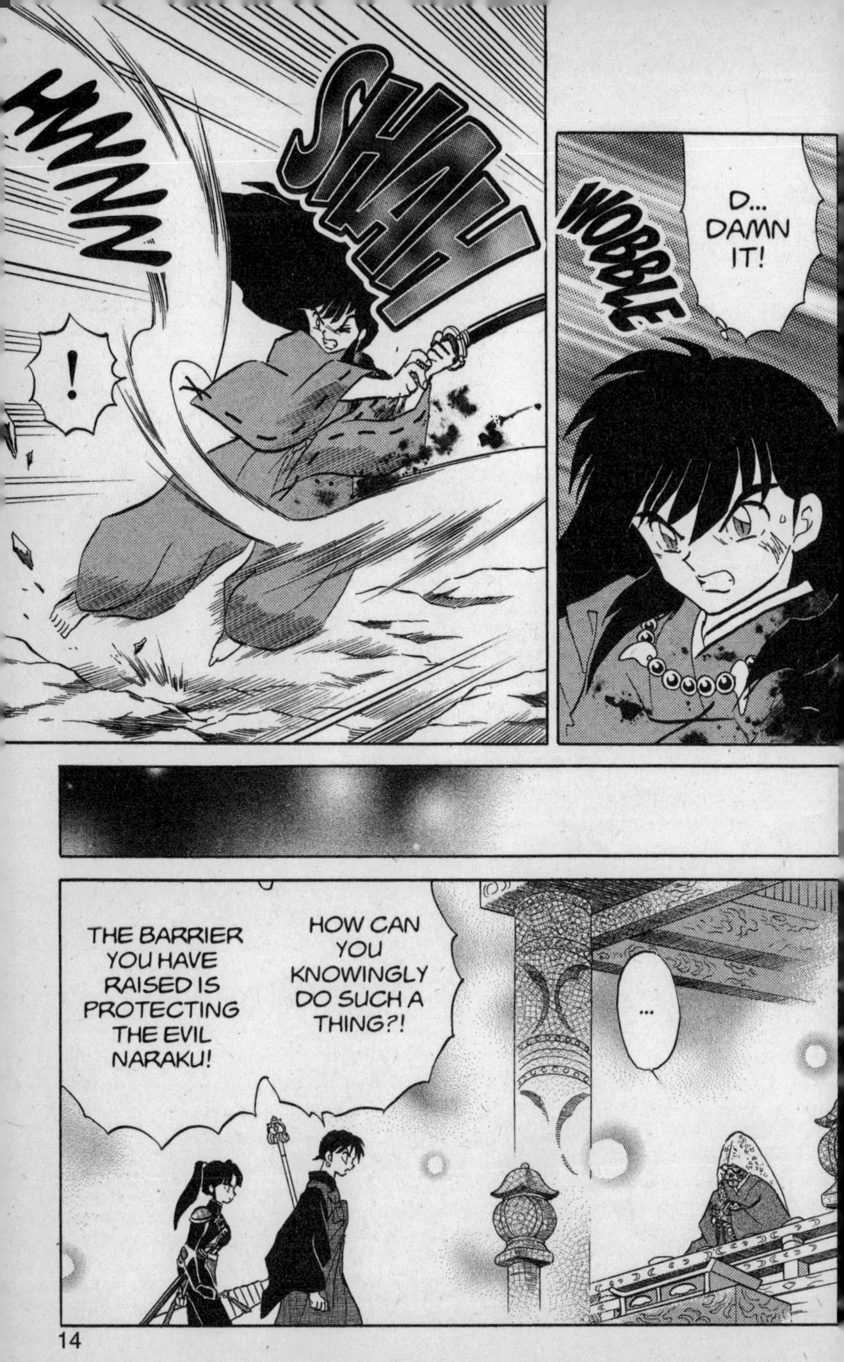
HWNNN
SHAH!
!
WOBBLE
D... DAMN IT!
THE BARRIER YOU HAVE RAISED IS PROTECTING THE EVIL NARAKU!
HOW CAN YOU KNOWINGLY DO SUCH A THING?!
...

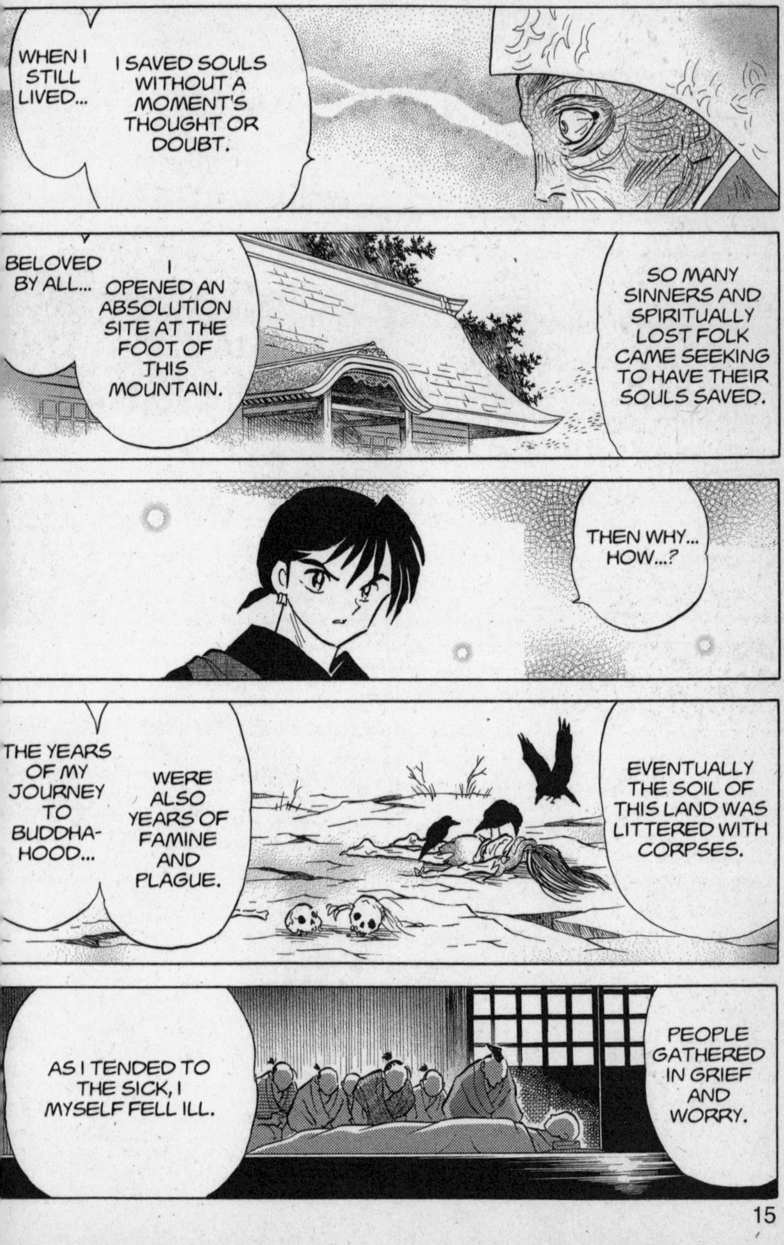
WHEN I STILL LIVED...
I SAVED SOULS WITHOUT A MOMENT'S THOUGHT OR DOUBT.
BELOVED BY ALL...
I OPENED AN ABSOLUTION SITE AT THE FOOT OF THIS MOUNTAIN.
SO MANY SINNERS AND SPIRITUALLY LOST FOLK CAME SEEKING TO HAVE THEIR SOULS SAVED.
THEN WHY... HOW...?
THE YEARS OF MY JOURNEY TO BUDDHA-HOOD...
WERE ALSO YEARS OF FAMINE AND PLAGUE.
EVENTUALLY THE SOIL OF THIS LAND WAS LITTERED WITH CORPSES.
AS I TENDED TO THE SICK, I MYSELF FELL ILL.
PEOPLE GATHERED IN GRIEF AND WORRY.

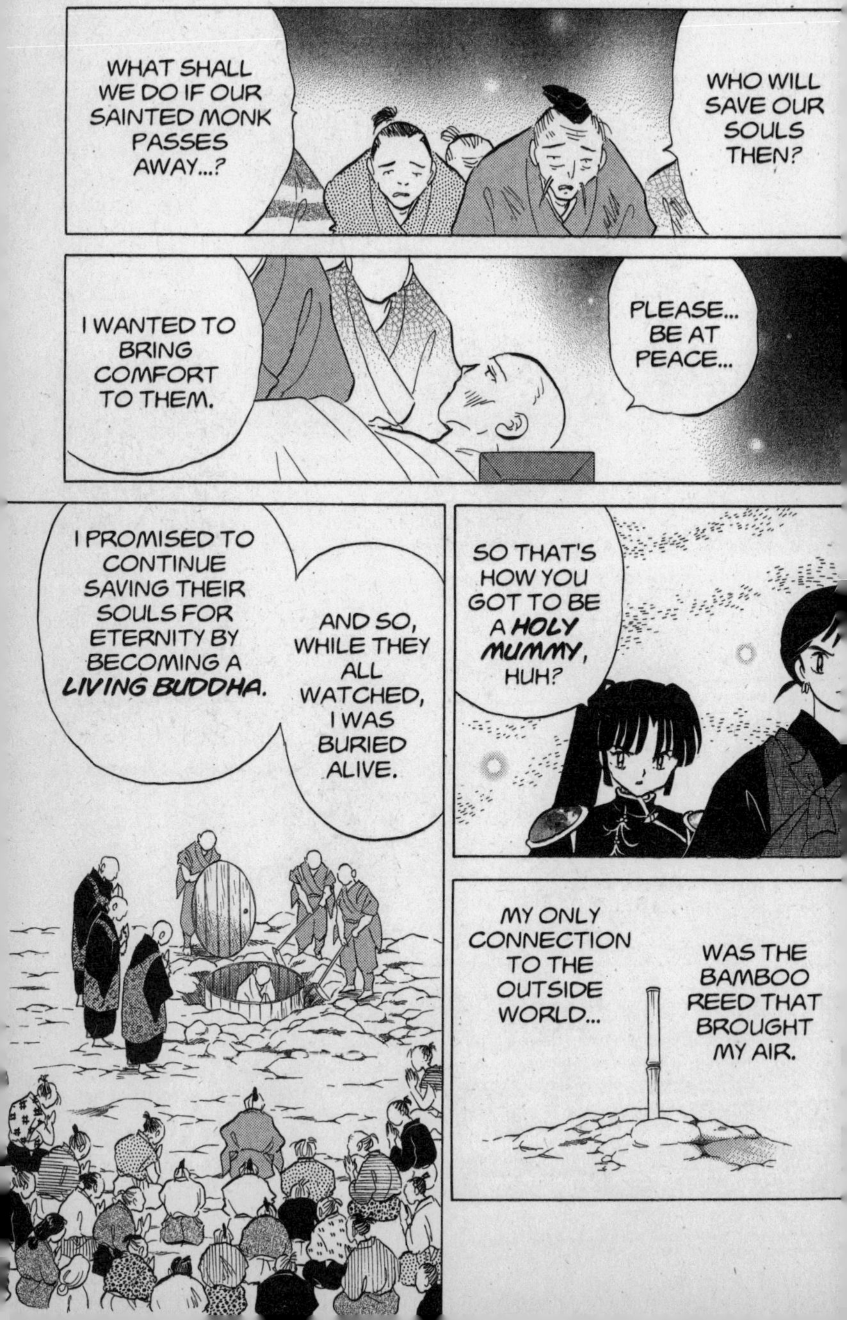
WHAT SHALL WE DO IF OUR SAINTED MONK PASSES AWAY...?
WHO WILL SAVE OUR SOULS THEN?
I WANTED TO BRING COMFORT TO THEM.
PLEASE... BE AT PEACE...
I PROMISED TO CONTINUE SAVING THEIR SOULS FOR ETERNITY BY BECOMING A *LIVING BUDDHA*.
AND SO, WHILE THEY ALL WATCHED, I WAS BURIED ALIVE.
SO THAT'S HOW YOU GOT TO BE A *HOLY MUMMY*, HUH?
MY ONLY CONNECTION TO THE OUTSIDE WORLD...
WAS THE BAMBOO REED THAT BROUGHT MY AIR.

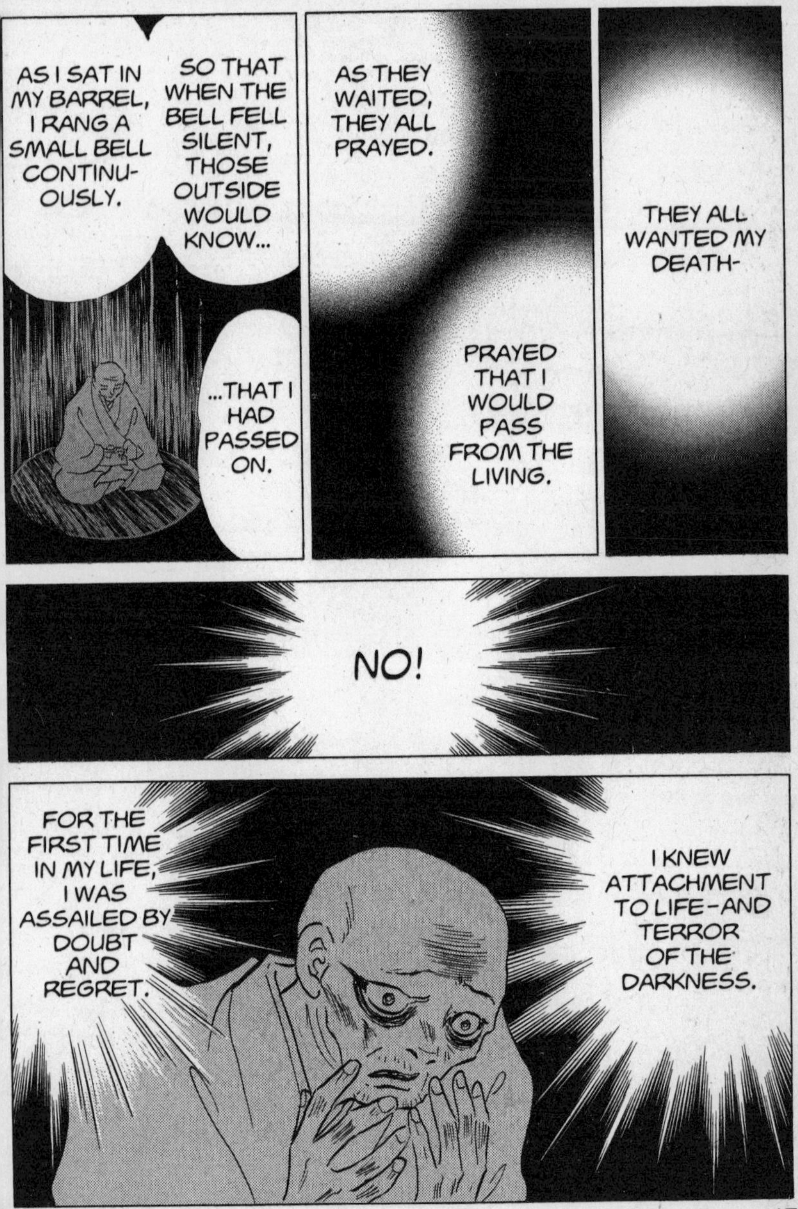
AS I SAT IN MY BARREL, I RANG A SMALL BELL CONTINU-OUSLY.
SO THAT WHEN THE BELL FELL SILENT, THOSE OUTSIDE WOULD KNOW...
...THAT I HAD PASSED ON.
AS THEY WAITED, THEY ALL PRAYED.
PRAYED THAT I WOULD PASS FROM THE LIVING.
THEY ALL WANTED MY DEATH-
NO!
FOR THE FIRST TIME IN MY LIFE, I WAS ASSAILED BY DOUBT AND REGRET.
I KNEW ATTACHMENT TO LIFE-AND TERROR OF THE DARKNESS.

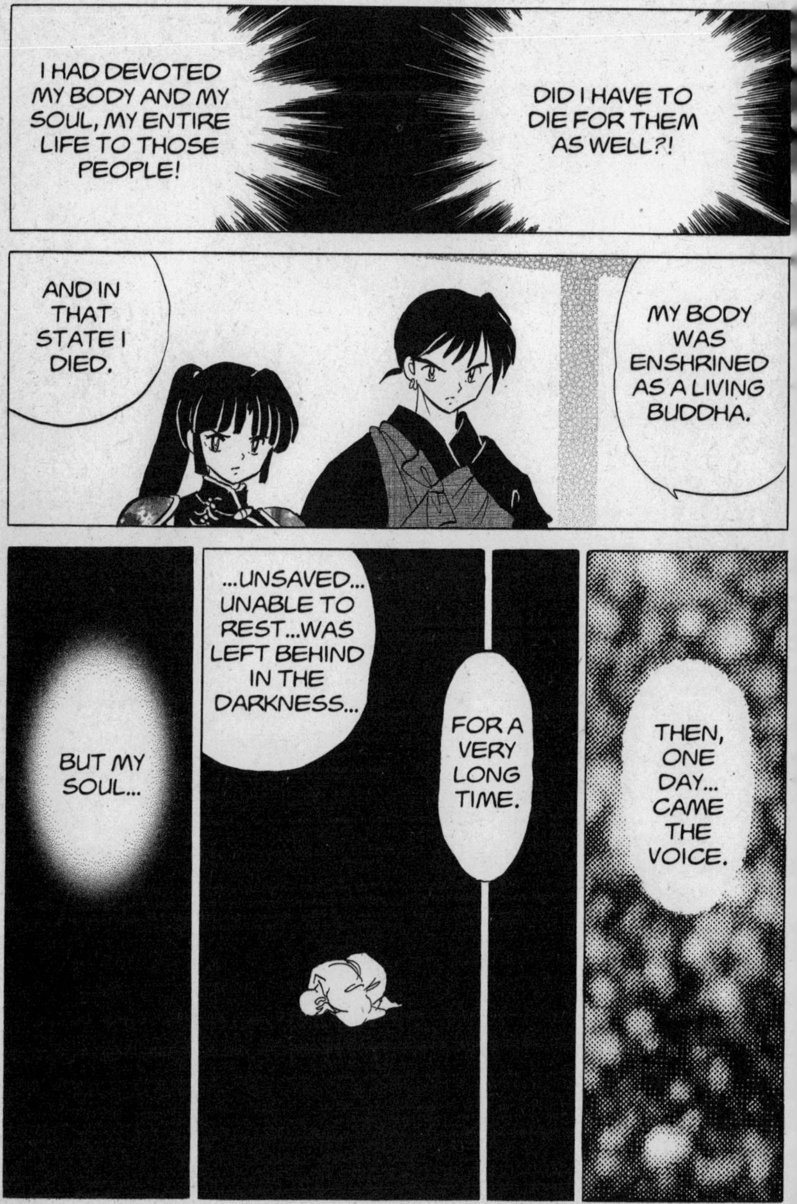
I HAD DEVOTED MY BODY AND MY SOUL, MY ENTIRE LIFE TO THOSE PEOPLE!
DID I HAVE TO DIE FOR THEM AS WELL?!
AND IN THAT STATE I DIED.
MY BODY WAS ENSHRINED AS A LIVING BUDDHA.
BUT MY SOUL...
...UNSAVED... UNABLE TO REST...WAS LEFT BEHIND IN THE DARKNESS...
FOR A VERY LONG TIME.
THEN, ONE DAY... CAME THE VOICE.

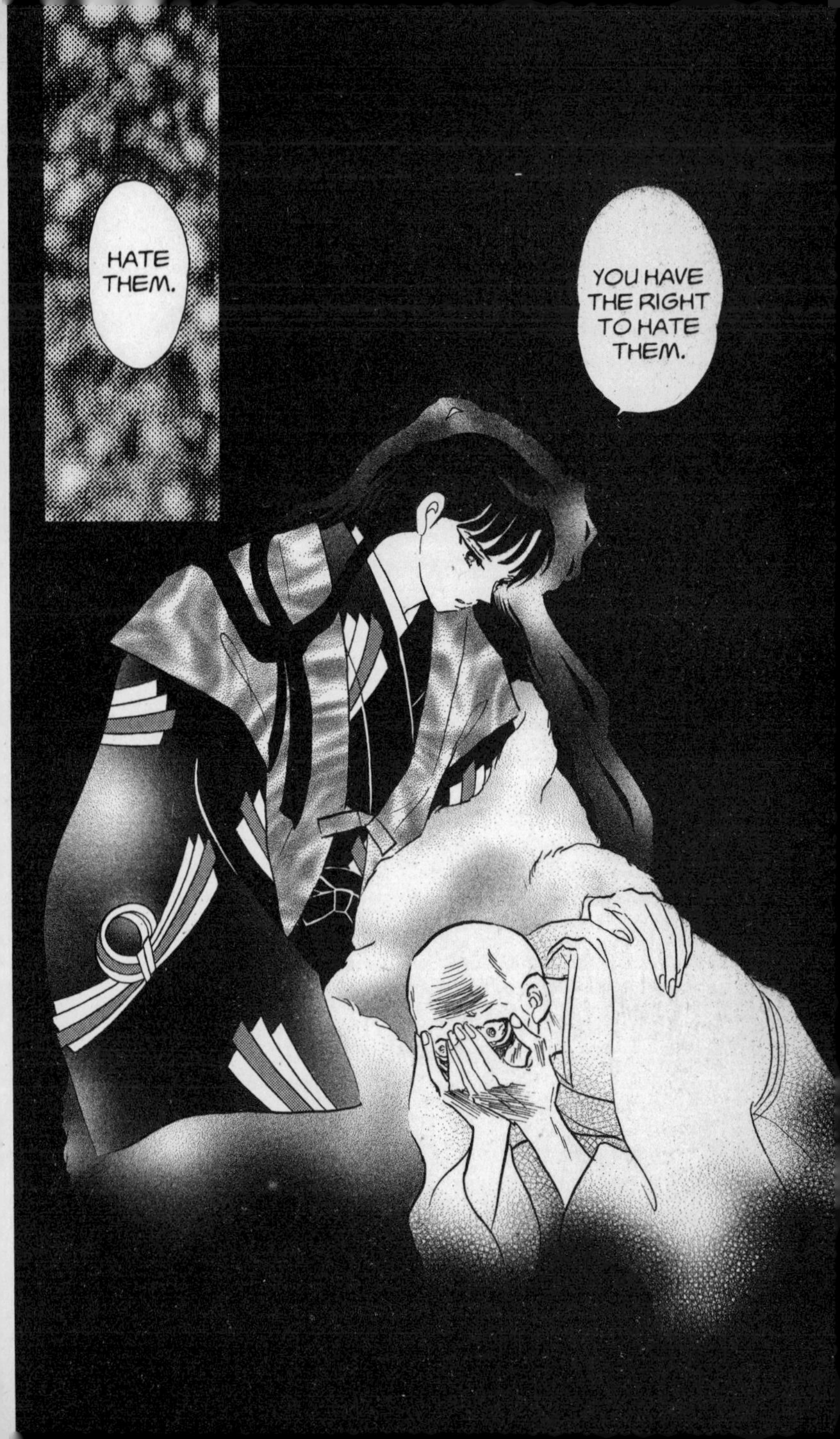
YOU HAVE THE RIGHT TO HATE THEM.
HATE THEM.

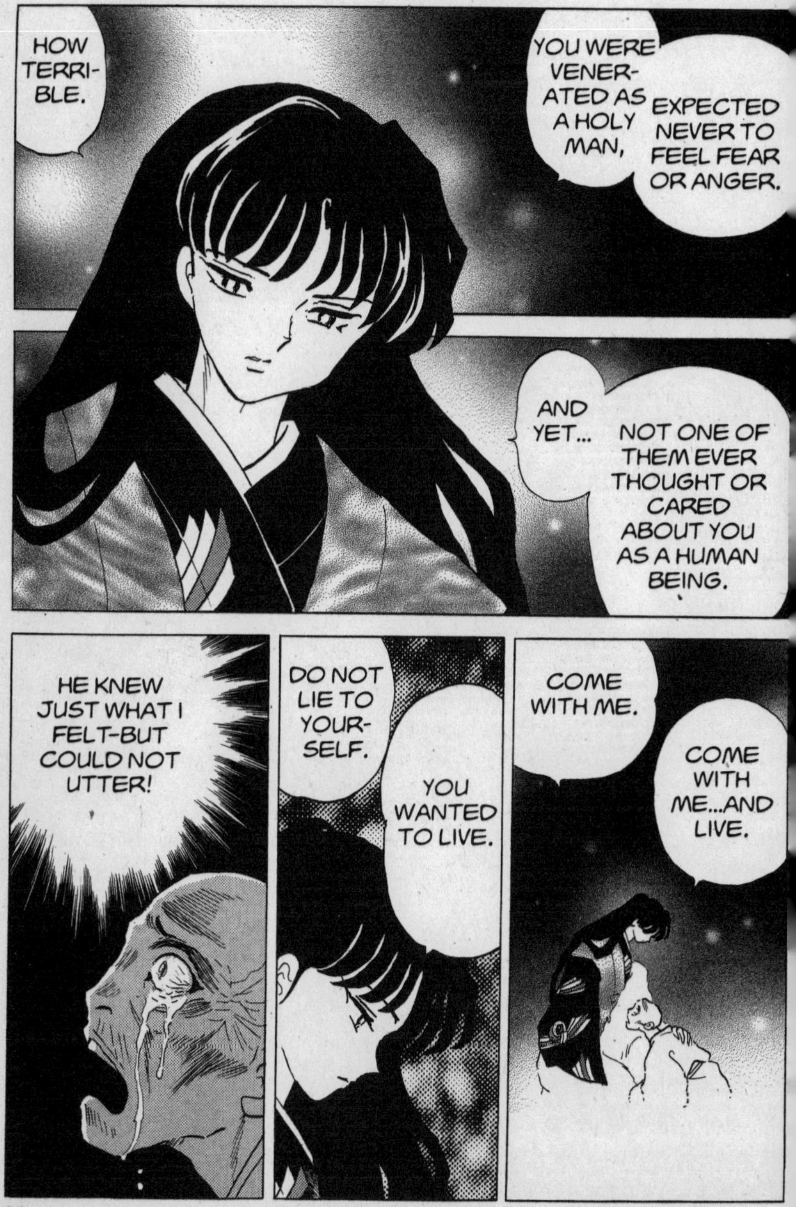
HOW TERRIBLE.
YOU WERE VENERATED AS A HOLY MAN,
EXPECTED NEVER TO FEEL FEAR OR ANGER.
AND YET...
NOT ONE OF THEM EVER THOUGHT OR CARED ABOUT YOU AS A HUMAN BEING.
HE KNEW JUST WHAT I FELT-BUT COULD NOT UTTER!
DO NOT LIE TO YOURSELF.
YOU WANTED TO LIVE.
COME WITH ME.
COME WITH ME...AND LIVE.

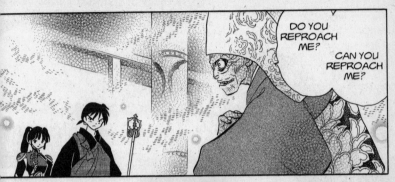

DO YOU REPROACH ME?

CAN YOU REPROACH ME?

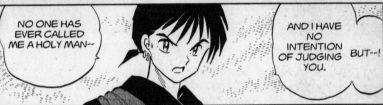

NO ONE HAS EVER CALLED ME A HOLY MAN--

AND I HAVE NO INTENTION OF JUDGING YOU. BUT--!

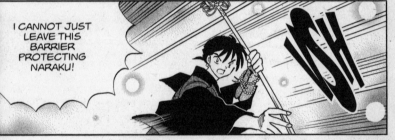

I CANNOT JUST LEAVE THIS BARRIER PROTECTING NARAKU!

VSH

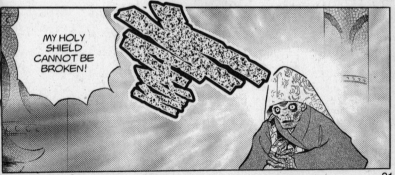

MY HOLY SHIELD CANNOT BE BROKEN!

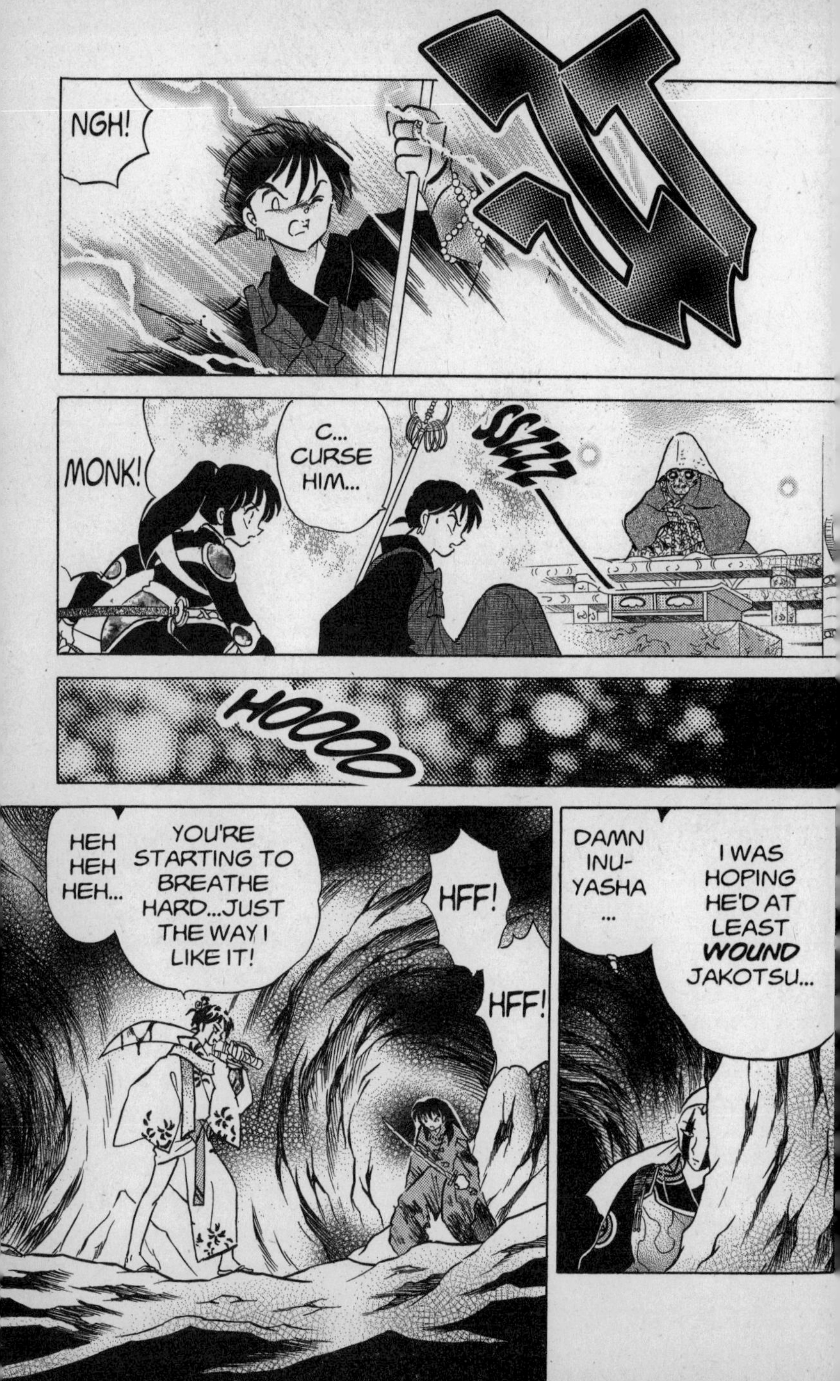
NGH!
MONK!
C... CURSE HIM...
HOOOO
HEH HEH HEH...
YOU'RE STARTING TO BREATHE HARD...JUST THE WAY I LIKE IT!
HFF!
HFF!
DAMN INU-YASHA ...
I WAS HOPING HE'D AT LEAST **WOUND** JAKOTSU...

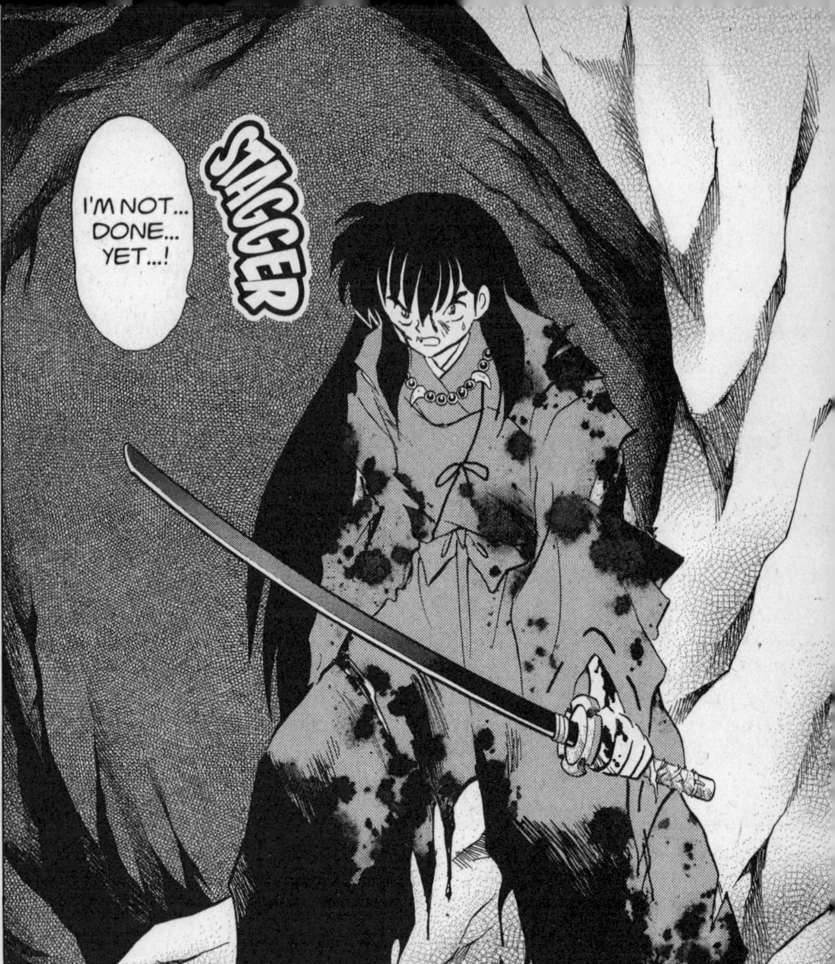
I'M NOT... DONE... YET...!
STAGGER
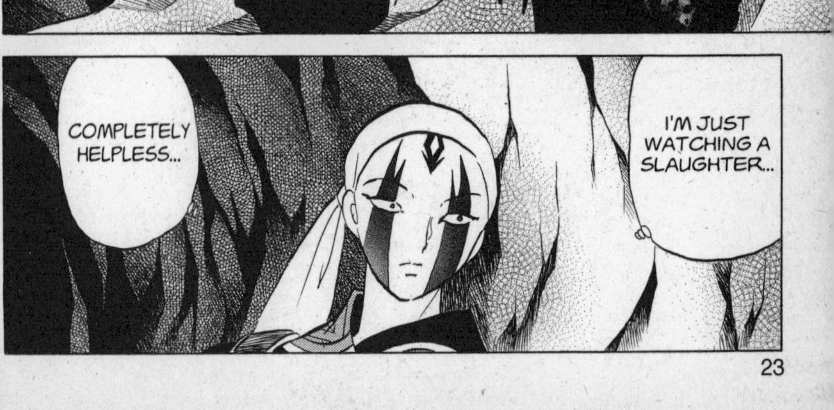
COMPLETELY HELPLESS...
I'M JUST WATCHING A SLAUGHTER...

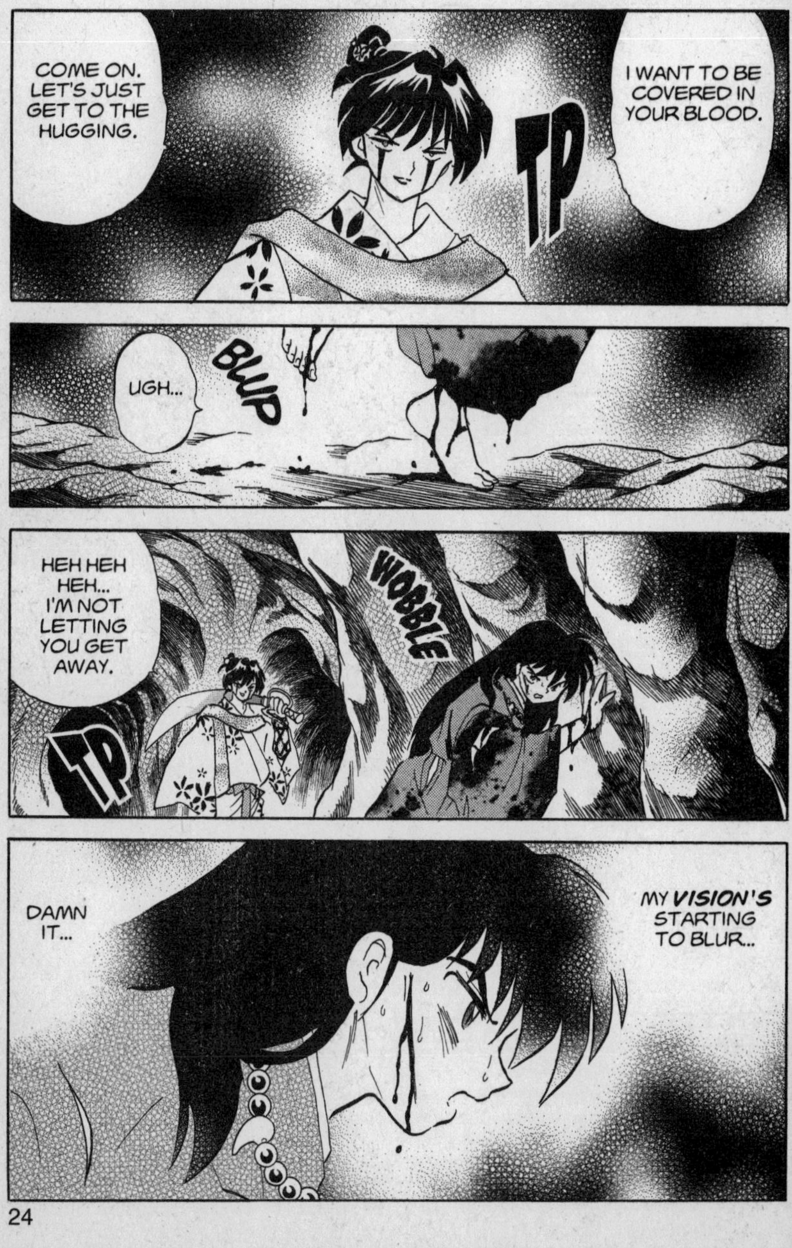
COME ON. LET'S JUST GET TO THE HUGGING.
TP
I WANT TO BE COVERED IN YOUR BLOOD.
UGH...
BLUP
HEH HEH HEH... I'M NOT LETTING YOU GET AWAY.
WOBBLE
TP
DAMN IT...
MY **VISION'S** STARTING TO BLUR...

SCROLL 2

THE MOUNTAIN CHANGES

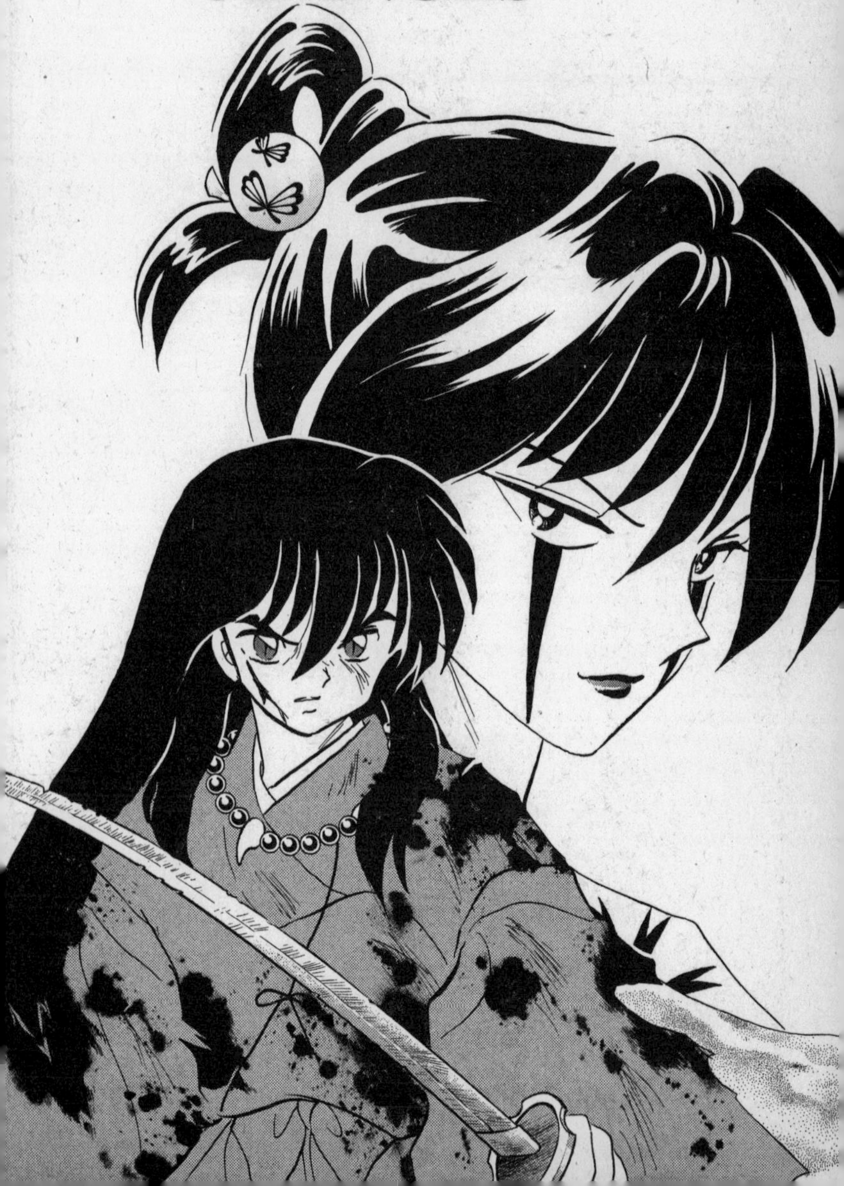

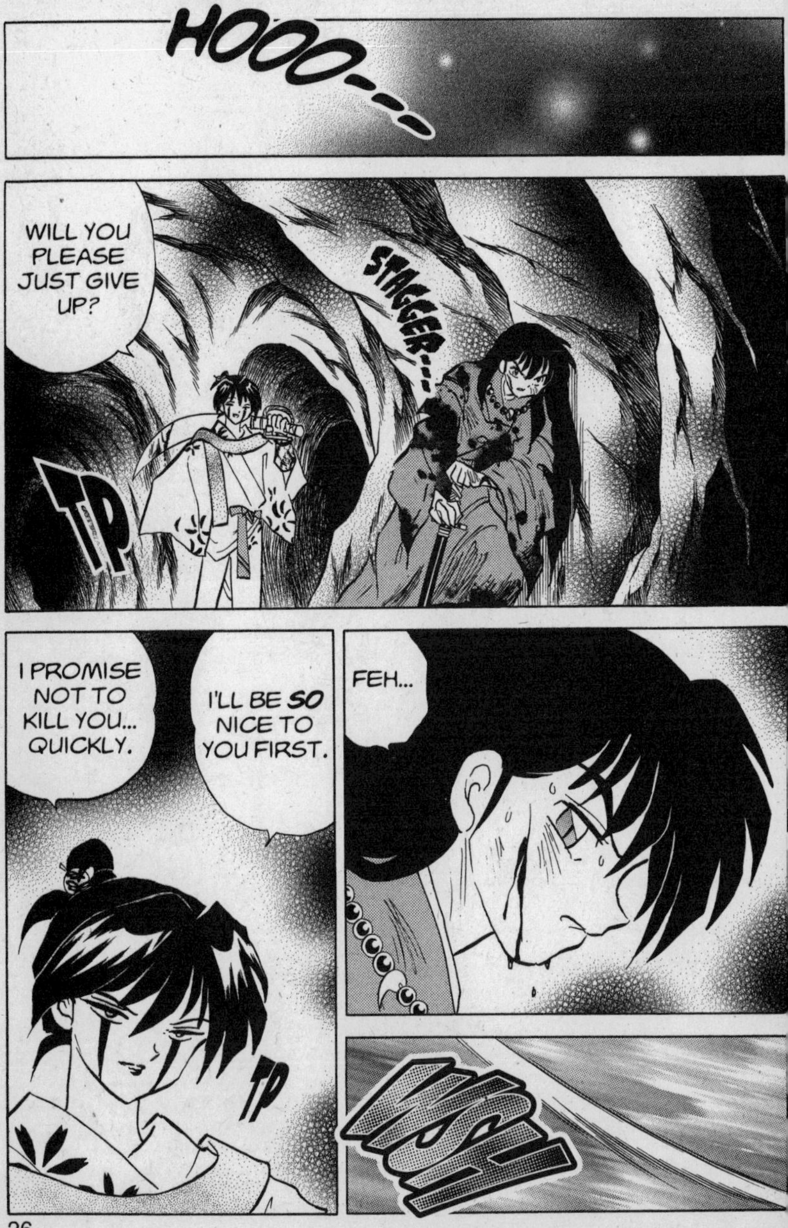
HOOO---
WILL YOU PLEASE JUST GIVE UP?
STAGGER...
TP
I PROMISE NOT TO KILL YOU... QUICKLY.
I'LL BE SO NICE TO YOU FIRST.
TP
FEH...
WSH

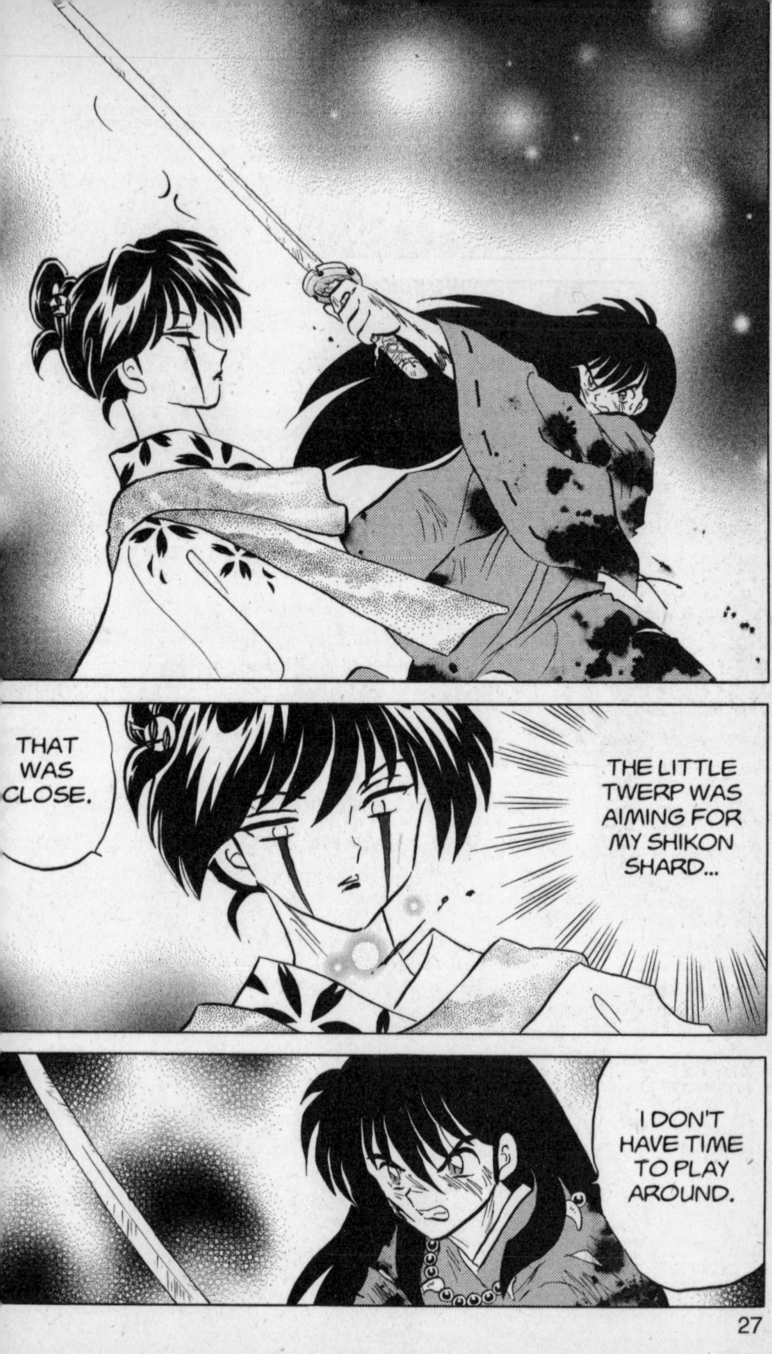

THAT WAS CLOSE.
THE LITTLE TWERP WAS AIMING FOR MY SHIKON SHARD...
I DON'T HAVE TIME TO PLAY AROUND.

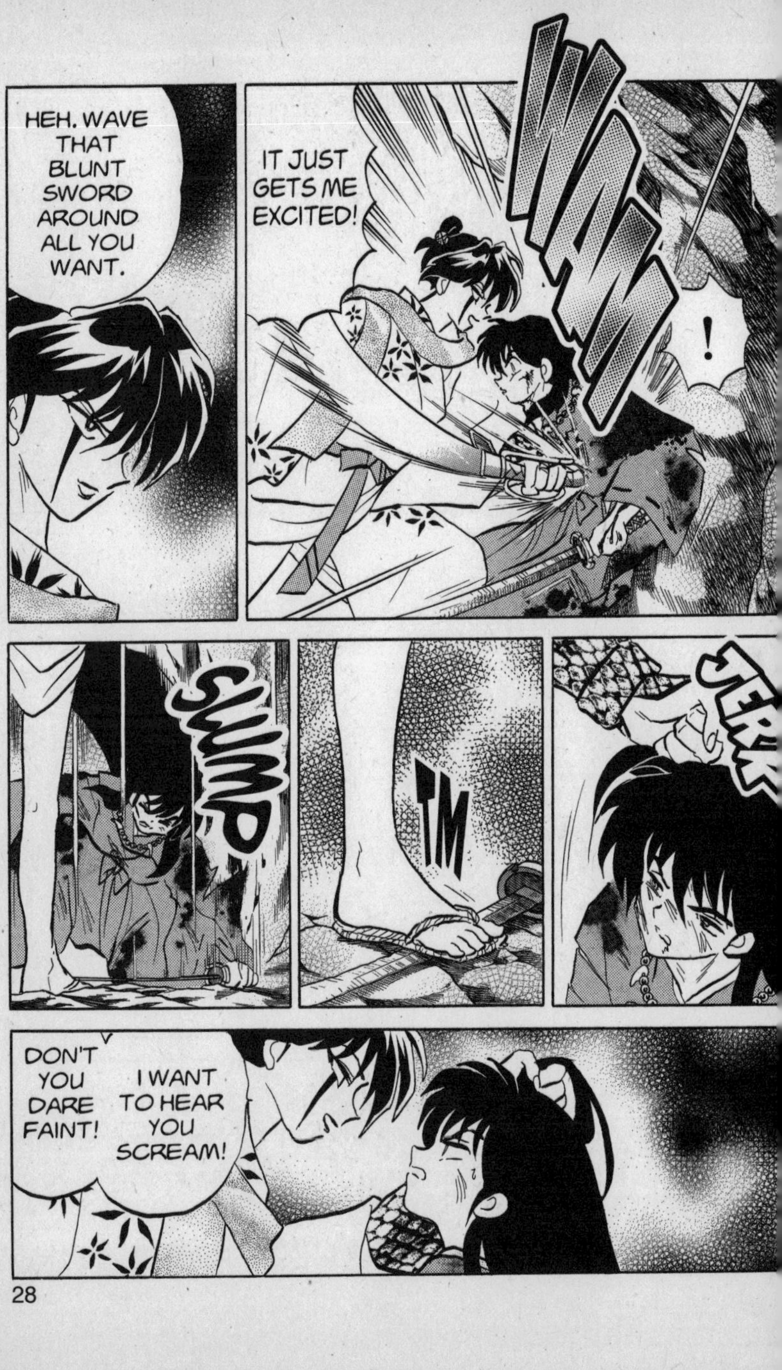
HEH. WAVE THAT BLUNT SWORD AROUND ALL YOU WANT.
IT JUST GETS ME EXCITED!
WHAM
!
SLUMP
TM
JERK
DON'T YOU DARE FAINT!
I WANT TO HEAR YOU SCREAM!

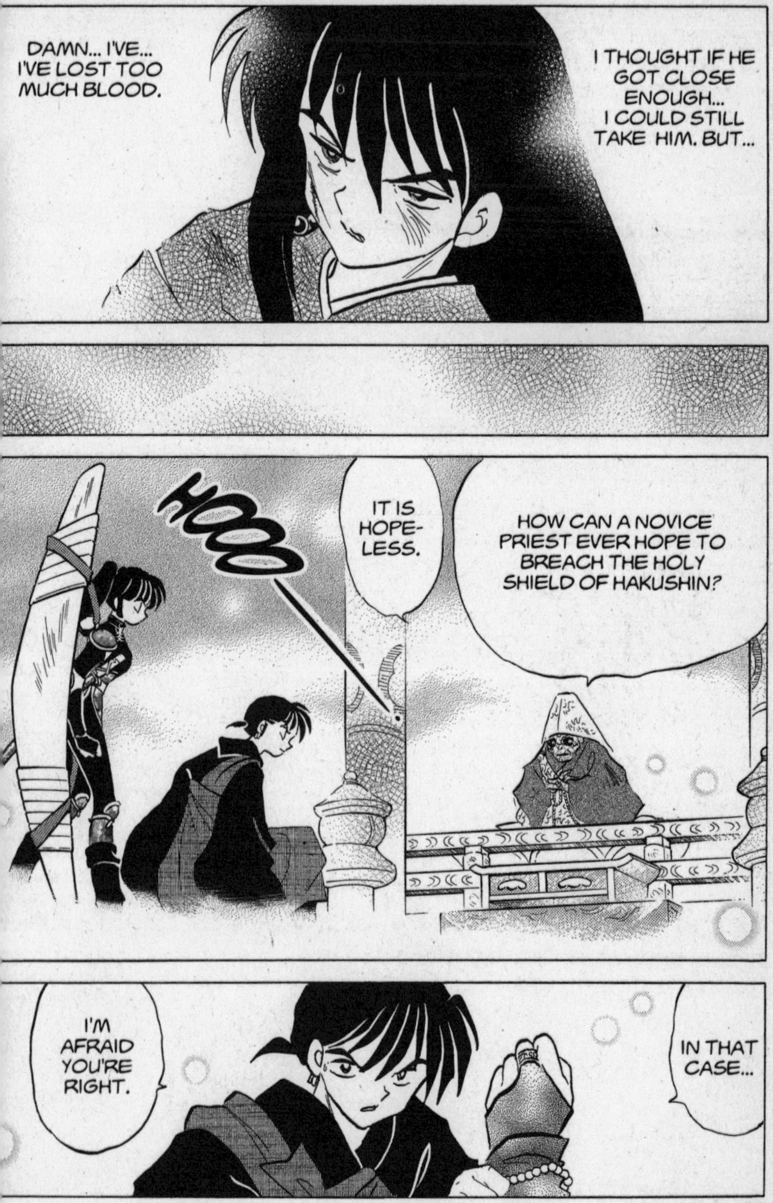
DAMN... I'VE... I'VE LOST TOO MUCH BLOOD.
I THOUGHT IF HE GOT CLOSE ENOUGH... I COULD STILL TAKE HIM. BUT...
HOOO
IT IS HOPE-LESS.
HOW CAN A NOVICE PRIEST EVER HOPE TO BREACH THE HOLY SHIELD OF HAKUSHIN?
I'M AFRAID YOU'RE RIGHT.
IN THAT CASE...

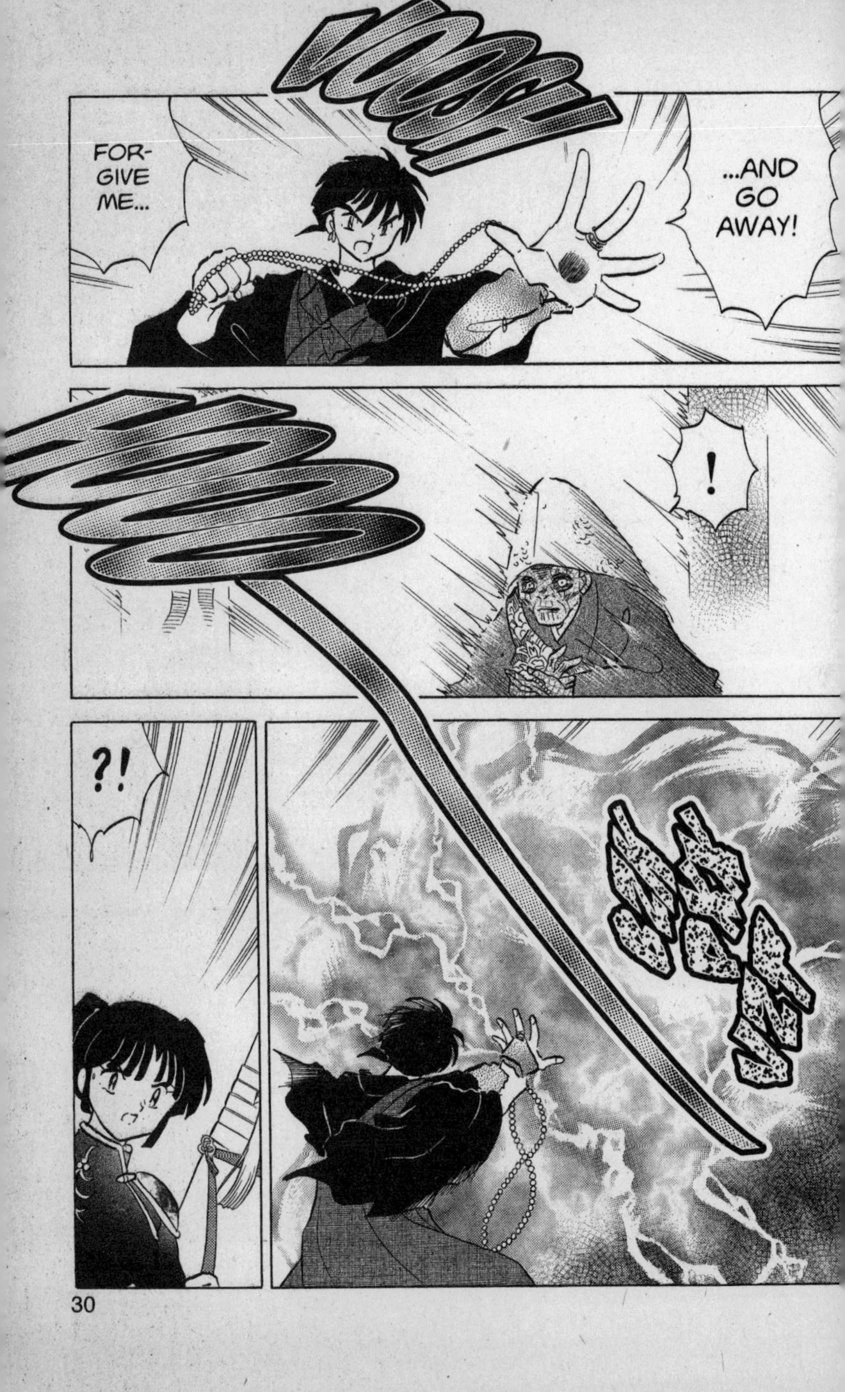
FOR-GIVE ME...
VOOSH!
...AND GO AWAY!
!
?!

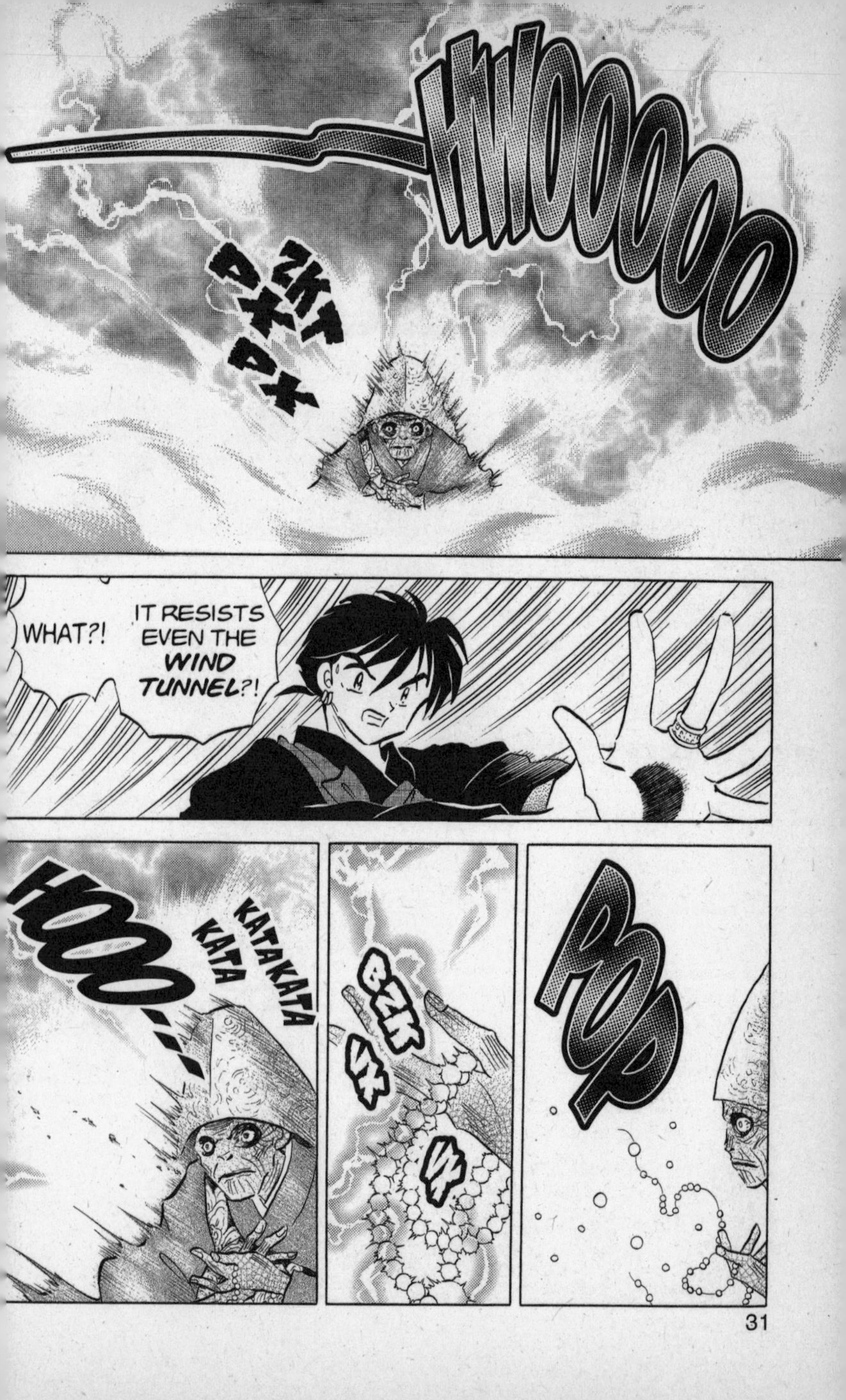
HWOOOOOO
ZKT PX PX
WHAT?!
IT RESISTS EVEN THE *WIND TUNNEL*?!
HOOO...!!
KATAKATA KATA
BZK VK
VK
POP

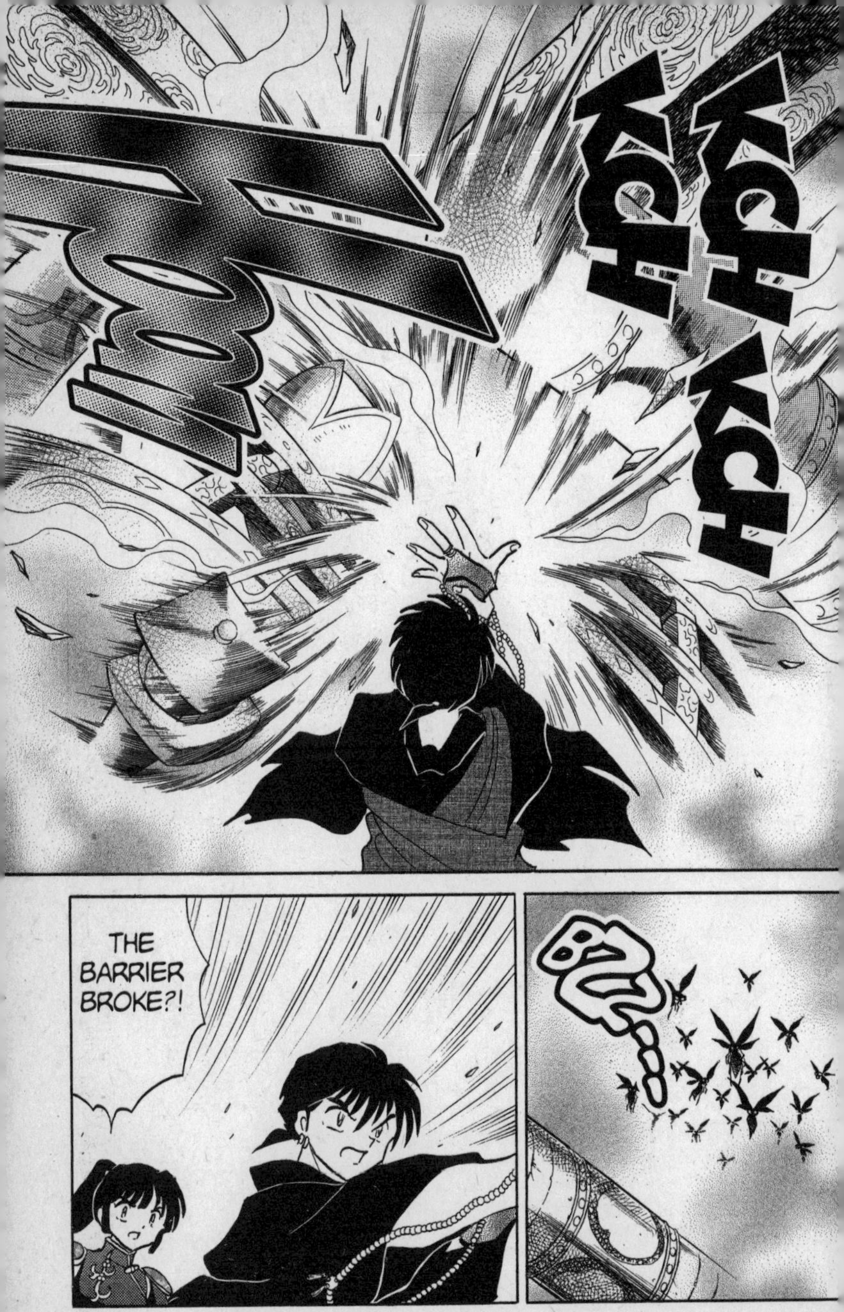
KCH KCH
THE BARRIER BROKE?!

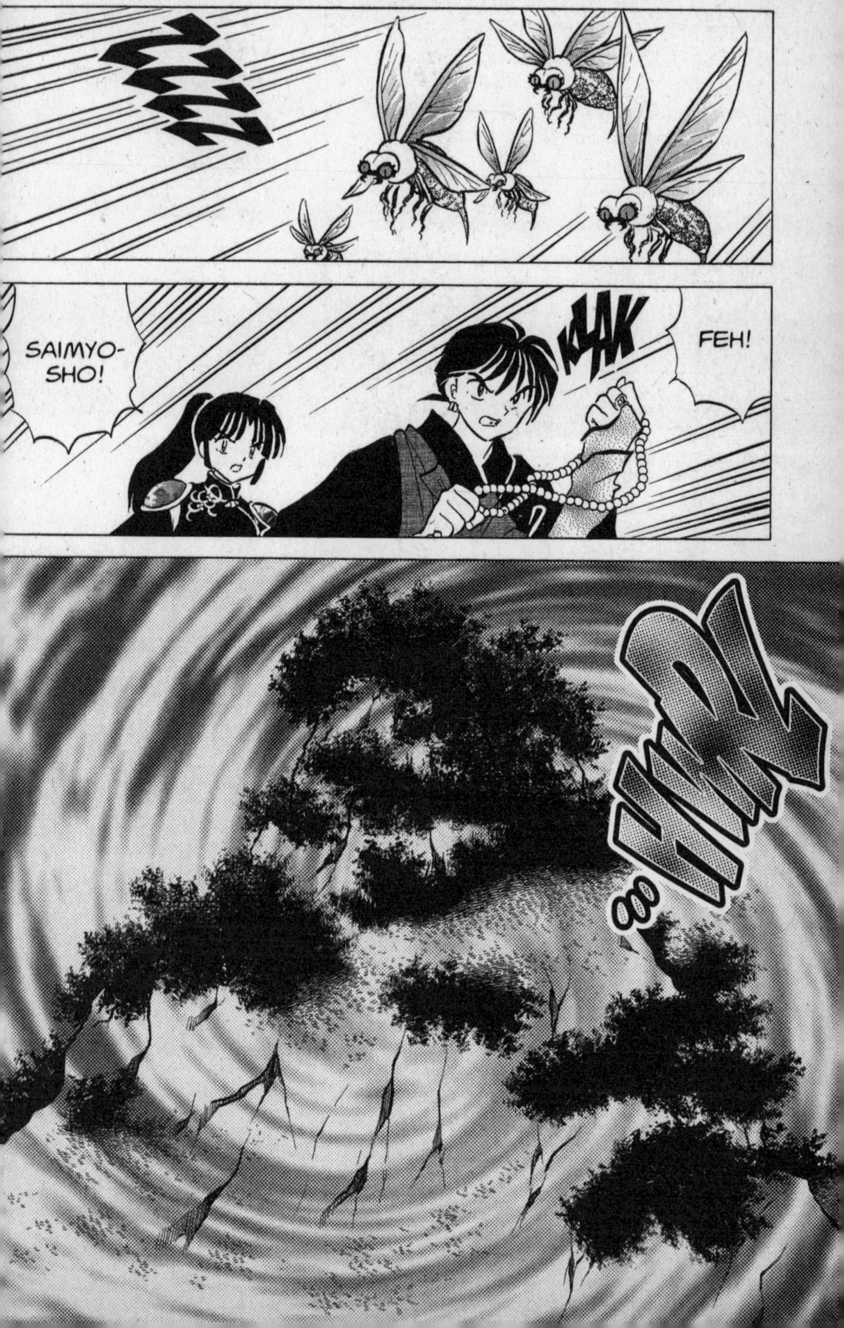
ZZZZ
SAIMYO-
SHO!
KLAK
FEH!
...HMPH

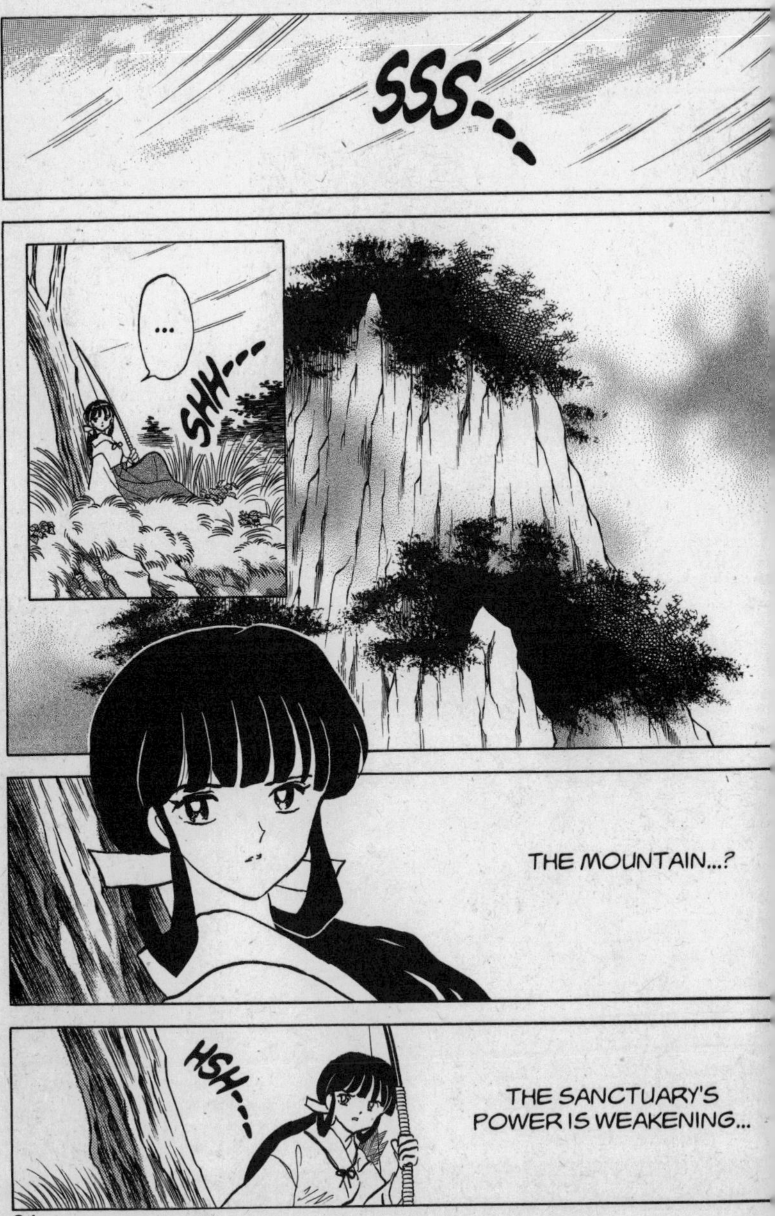
SSS...
...
SHH...
THE MOUNTAIN...?
HSH...
THE SANCTUARY'S POWER IS WEAKENING...

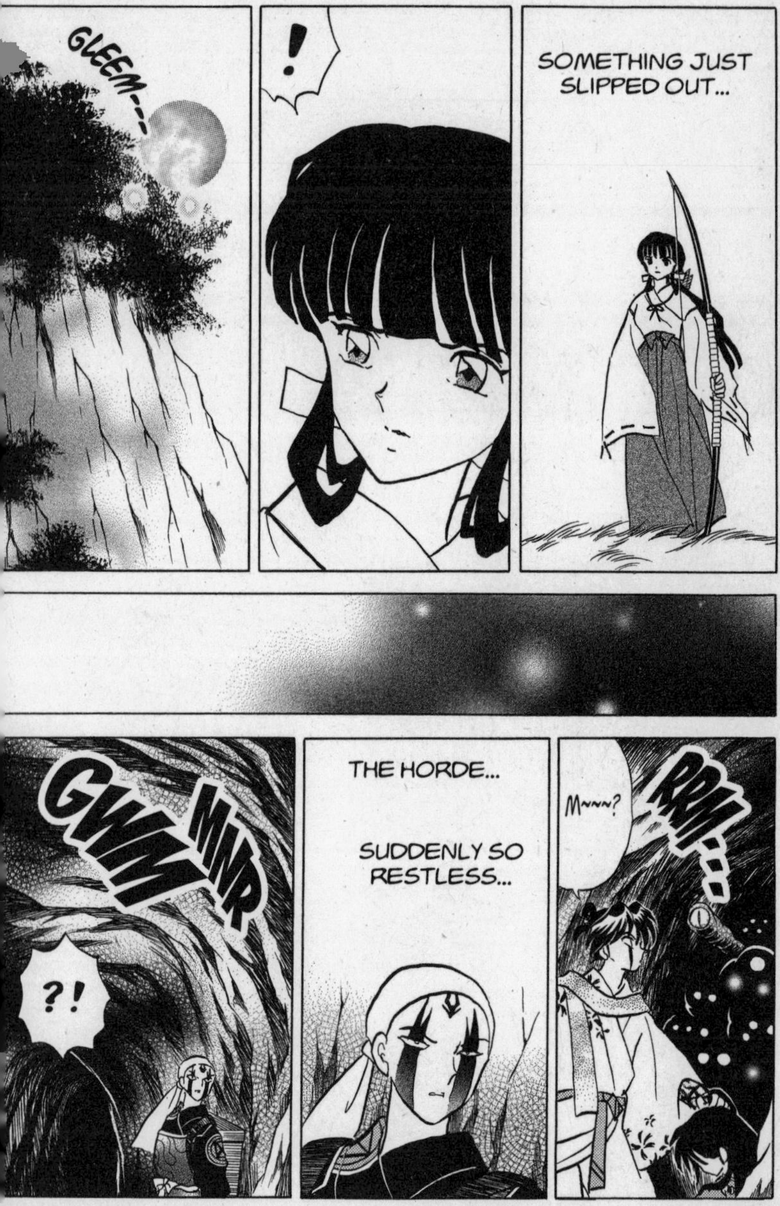
GLEEM...
!
SOMETHING JUST SLIPPED OUT...
GWMMNR
?!
THE HORDE...
SUDDENLY SO RESTLESS...
M~~~?
RRM...

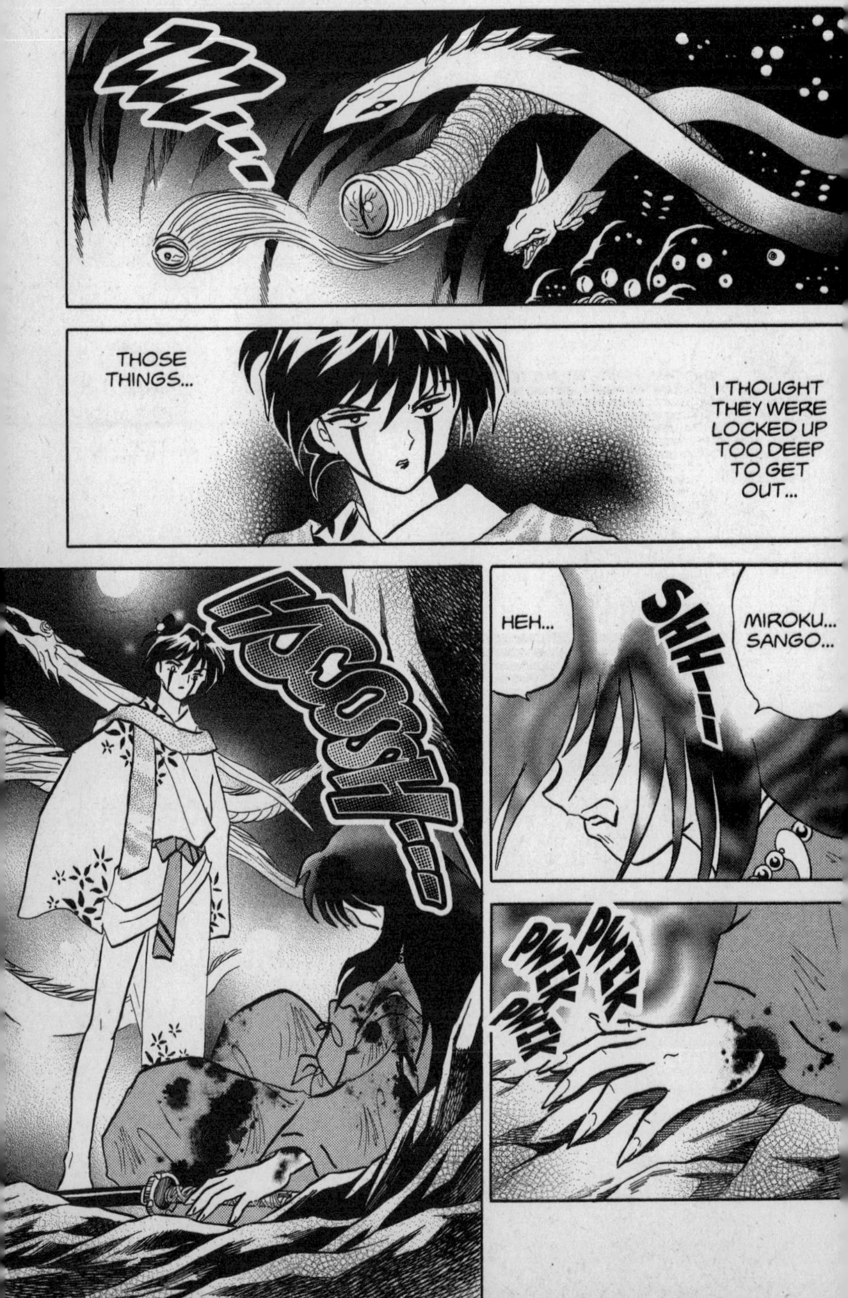
THOSE THINGS...
I THOUGHT THEY WERE LOCKED UP TOO DEEP TO GET OUT...
WHOOSH...
HEH...
SHH...
MIROKU... SANGO...
PWIK PWIK PWIK

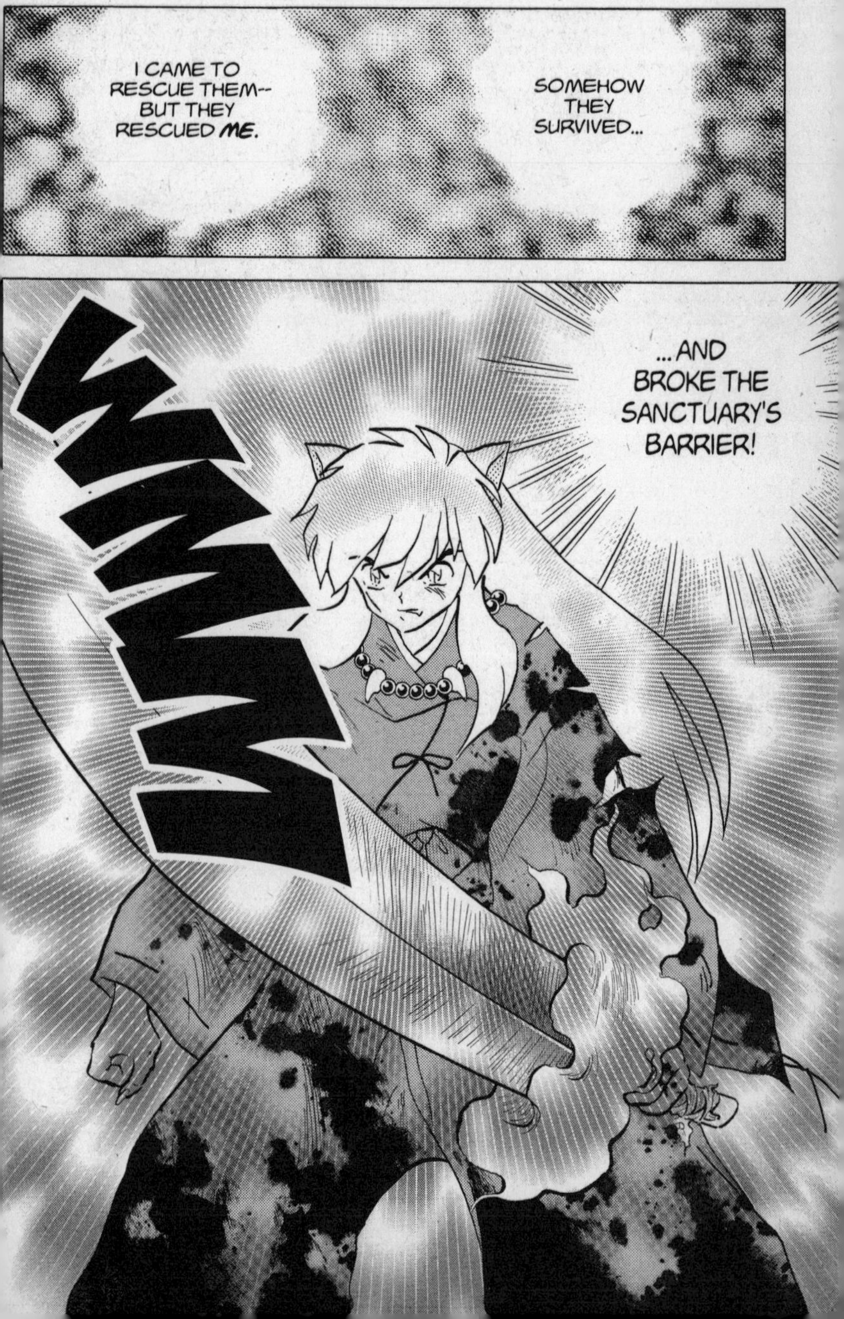
I CAME TO RESCUE THEM-- BUT THEY RESCUED *ME.*
SOMEHOW THEY SURVIVED...
...AND BROKE THE SANCTUARY'S BARRIER!

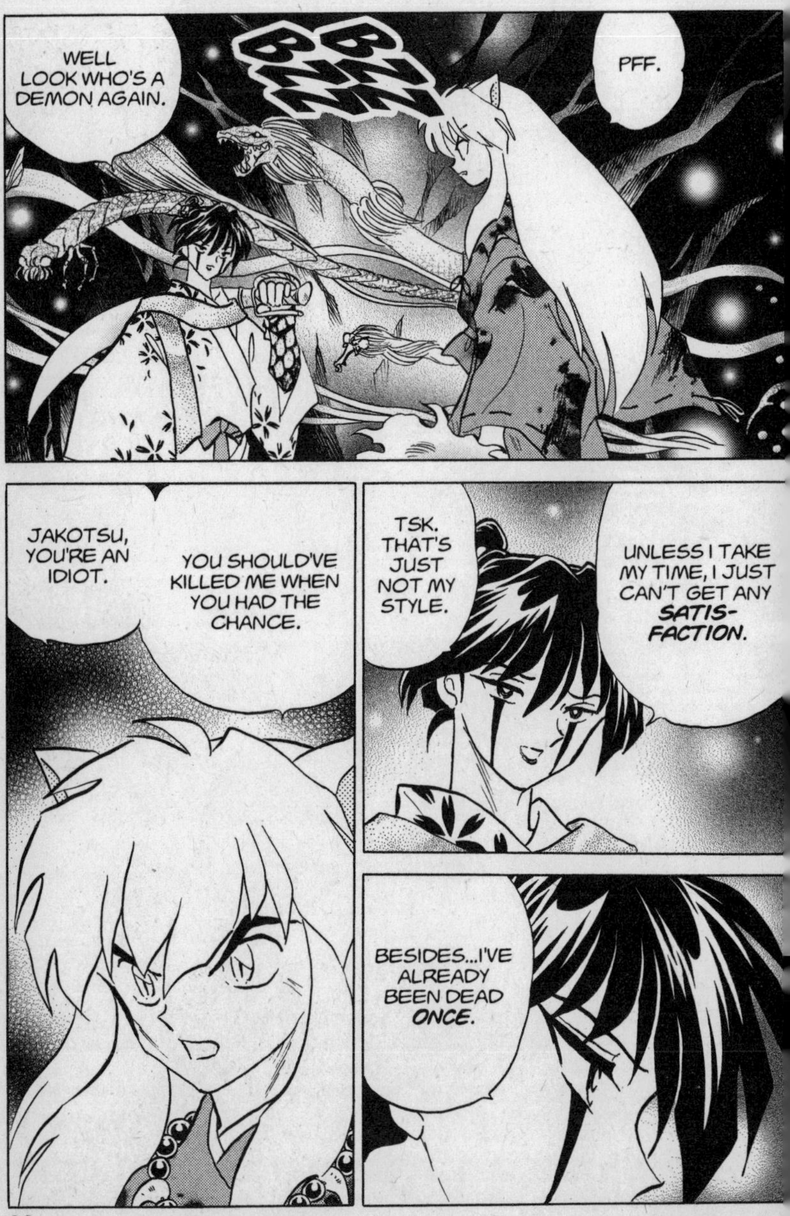
WELL LOOK WHO'S A DEMON AGAIN.
BZZZ
PFF.
JAKOTSU, YOU'RE AN IDIOT.
YOU SHOULD'VE KILLED ME WHEN YOU HAD THE CHANCE.
TSK. THAT'S JUST NOT MY STYLE.
UNLESS I TAKE MY TIME, I JUST CAN'T GET ANY *SATIS-FACTION.*
BESIDES...I'VE ALREADY BEEN DEAD *ONCE.*

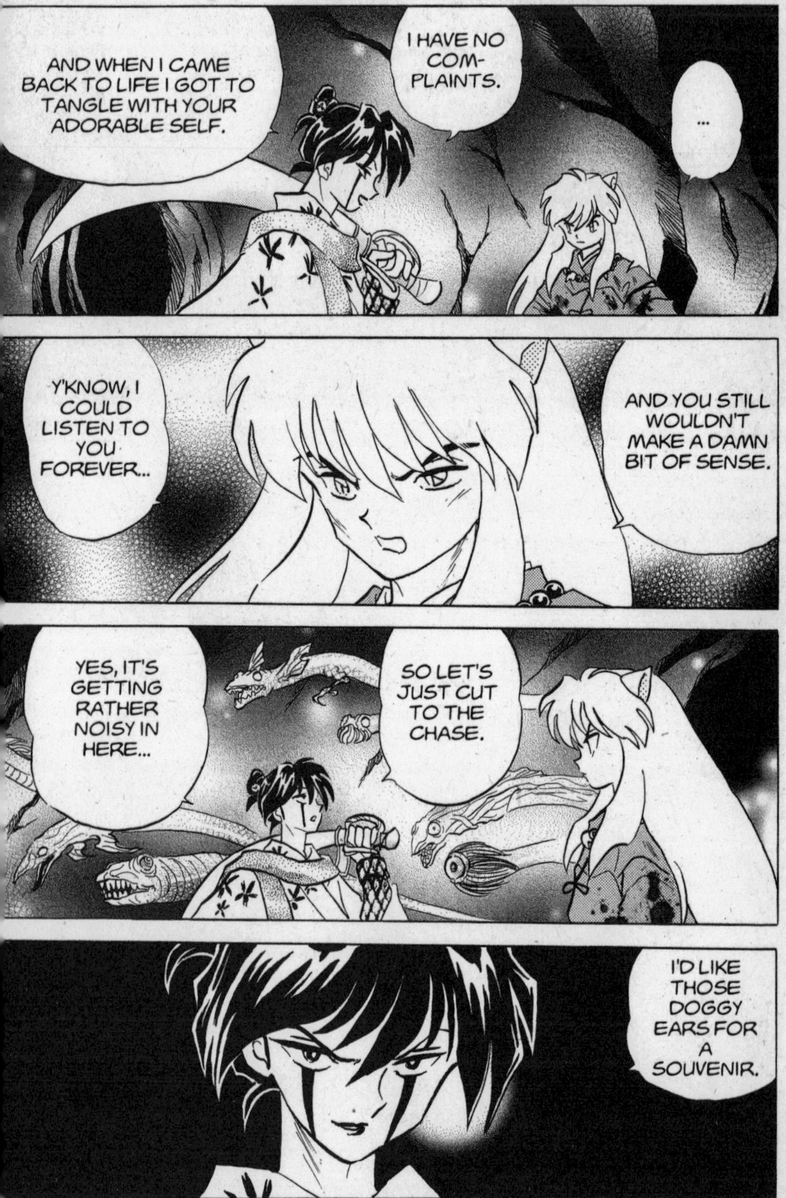
AND WHEN I CAME BACK TO LIFE I GOT TO TANGLE WITH YOUR ADORABLE SELF.
I HAVE NO COM-PLAINTS.
...
Y'KNOW, I COULD LISTEN TO YOU FOREVER...
AND YOU STILL WOULDN'T MAKE A DAMN BIT OF SENSE.
YES, IT'S GETTING RATHER NOISY IN HERE...
SO LET'S JUST CUT TO THE CHASE.
I'D LIKE THOSE DOGGY EARS FOR A SOUVENIR.

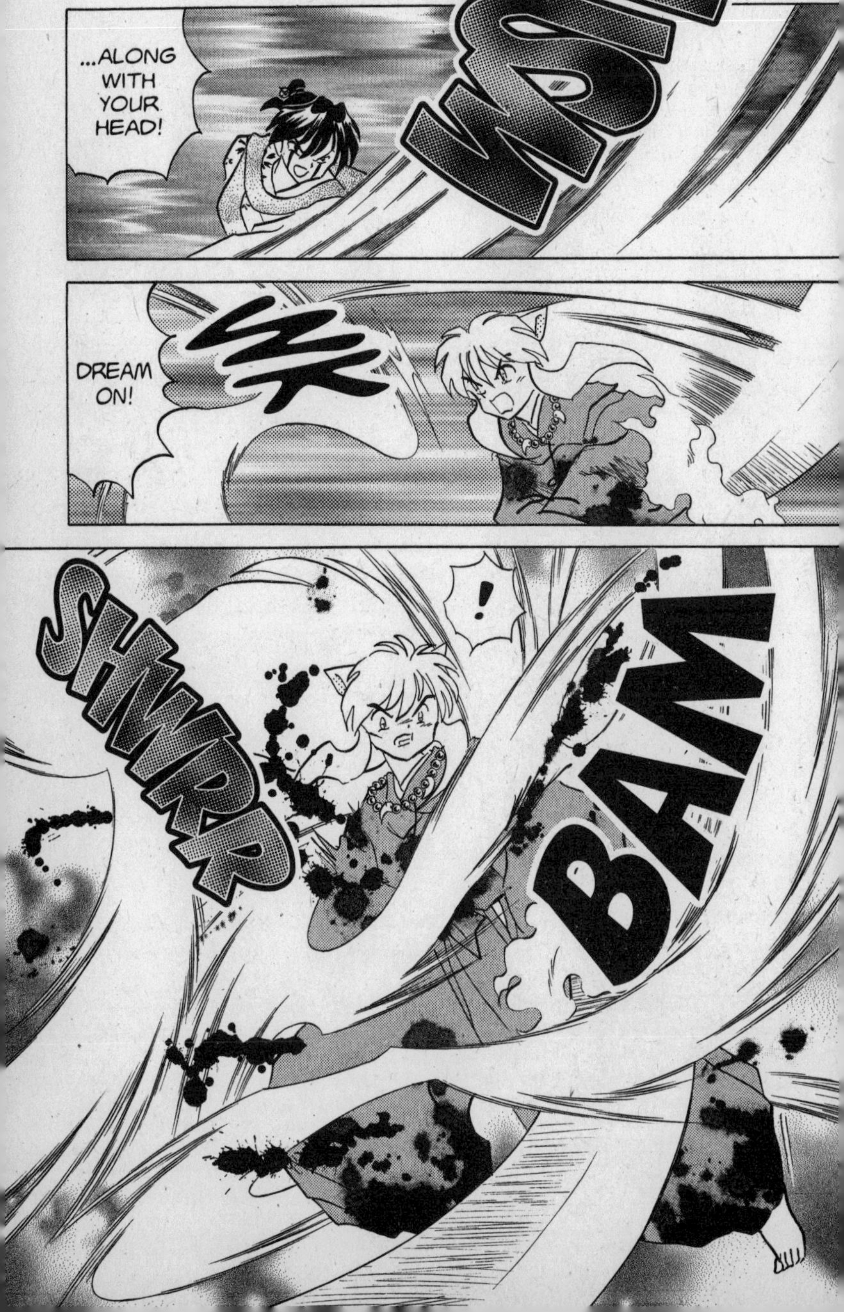
...ALONG WITH YOUR HEAD!
WOSH
WK
DREAM ON!
SHWRR
!
BAM

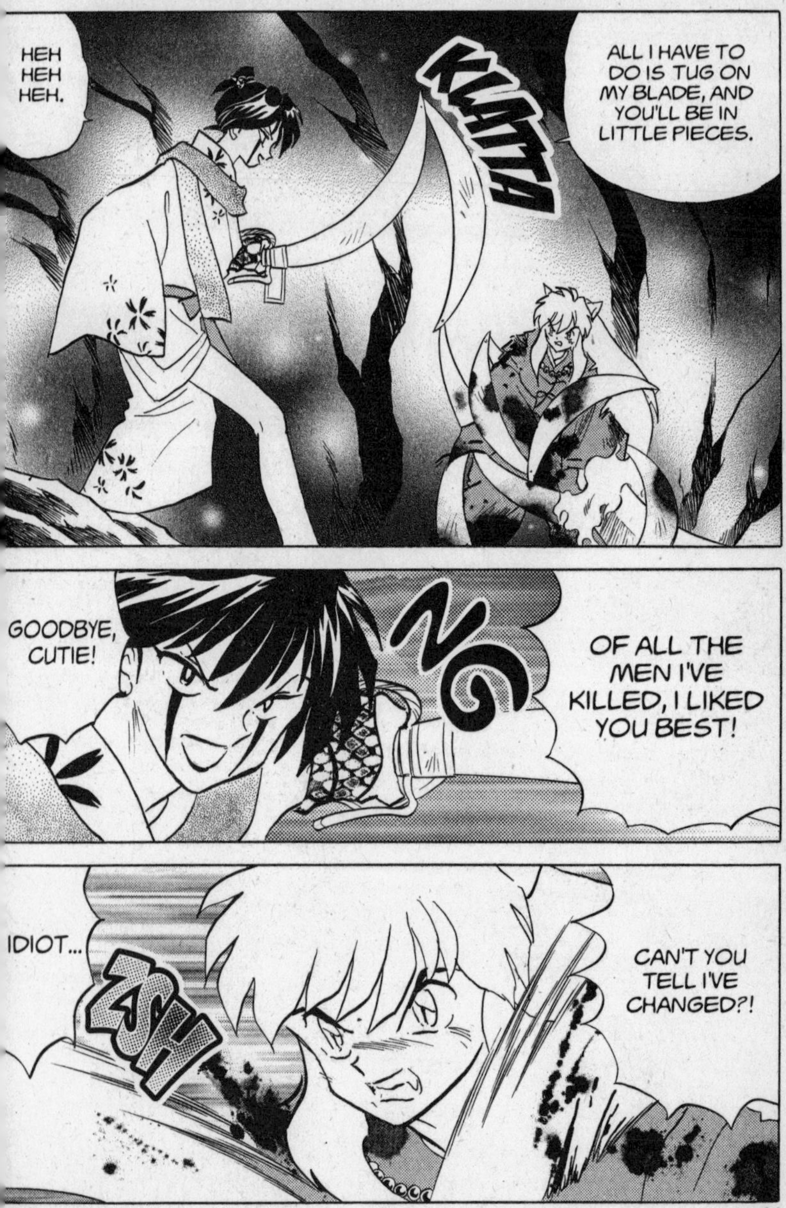
HEH HEH HEH.
KLATTA
ALL I HAVE TO DO IS TUG ON MY BLADE, AND YOU'LL BE IN LITTLE PIECES.
GOODBYE, CUTIE!
NG
OF ALL THE MEN I'VE KILLED, I LIKED YOU BEST!
IDIOT...
ZSH
CAN'T YOU TELL I'VE CHANGED?!

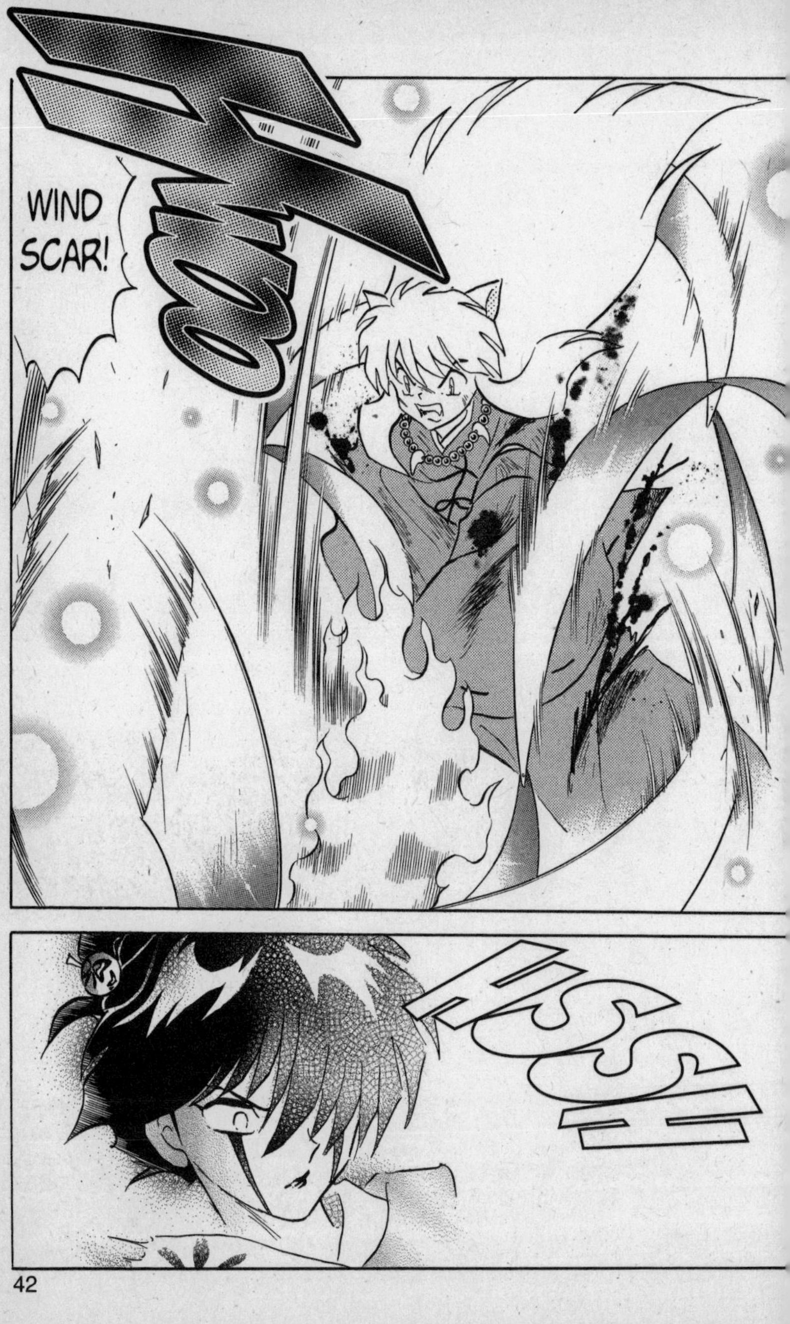
FWOO
WIND SCAR!
HSSH

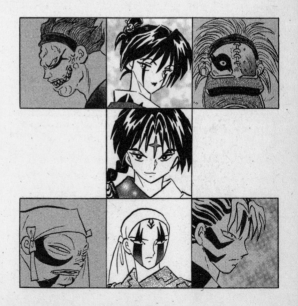

SCROLL 3
THE PULSE

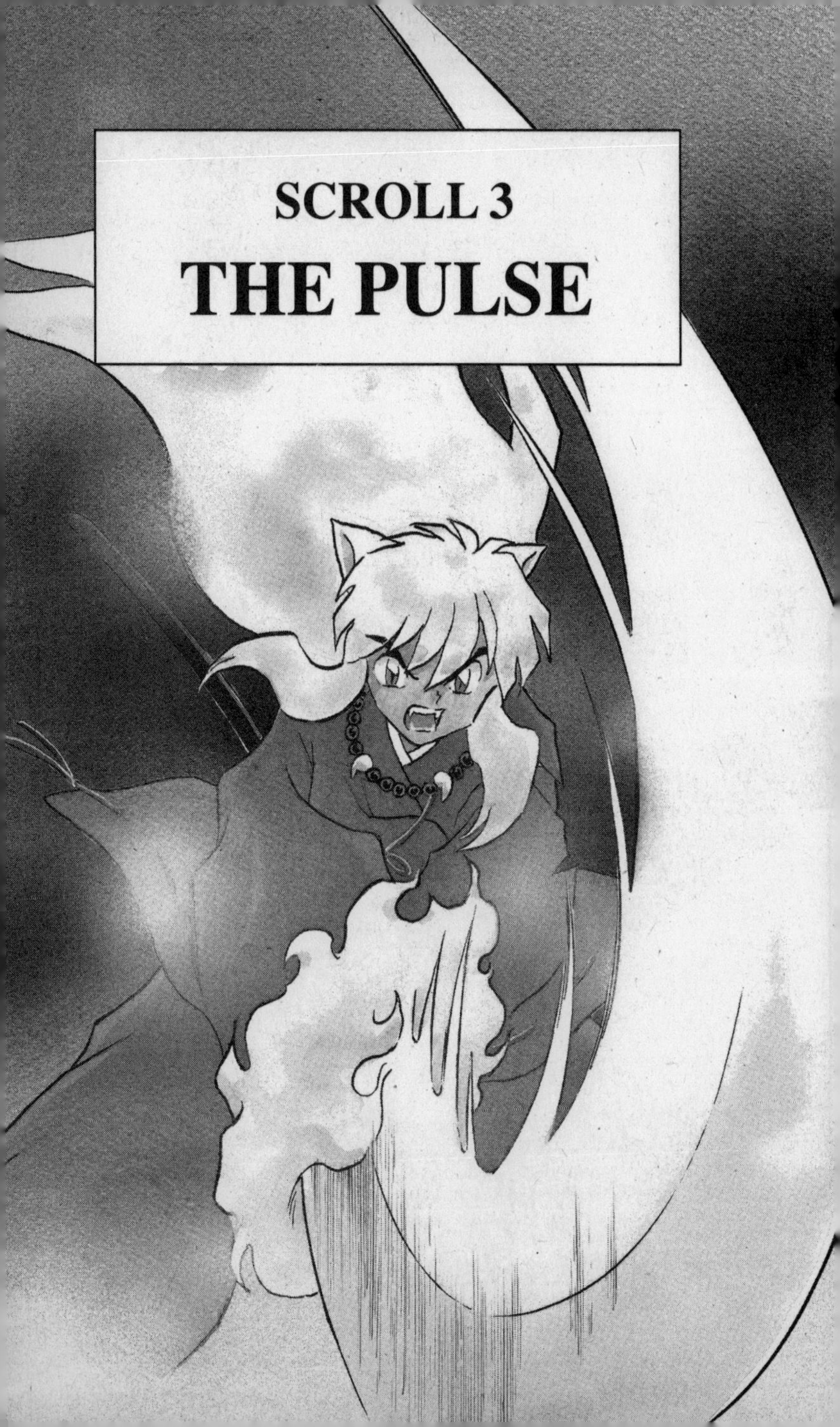

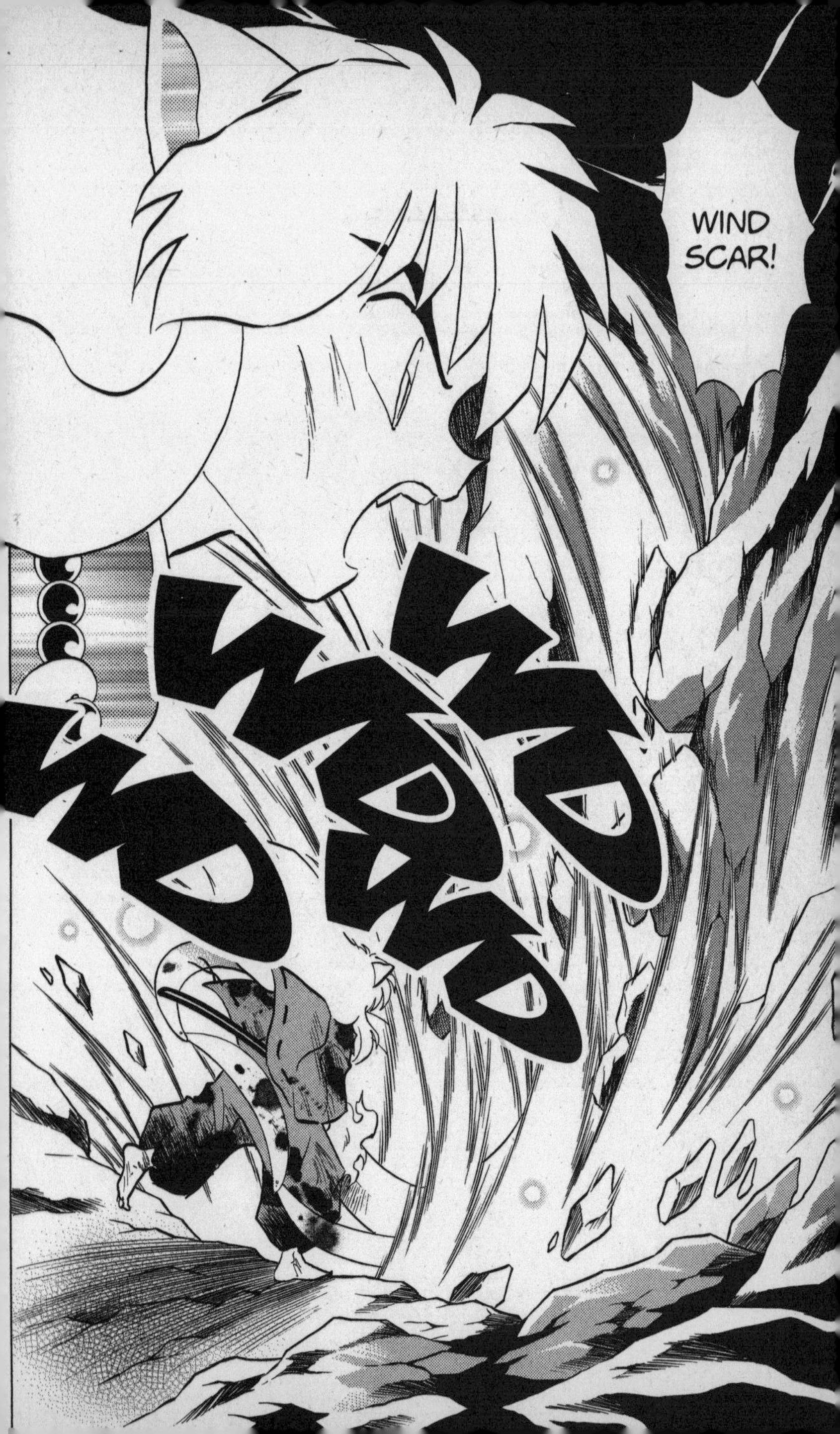
WIND
SCAR!

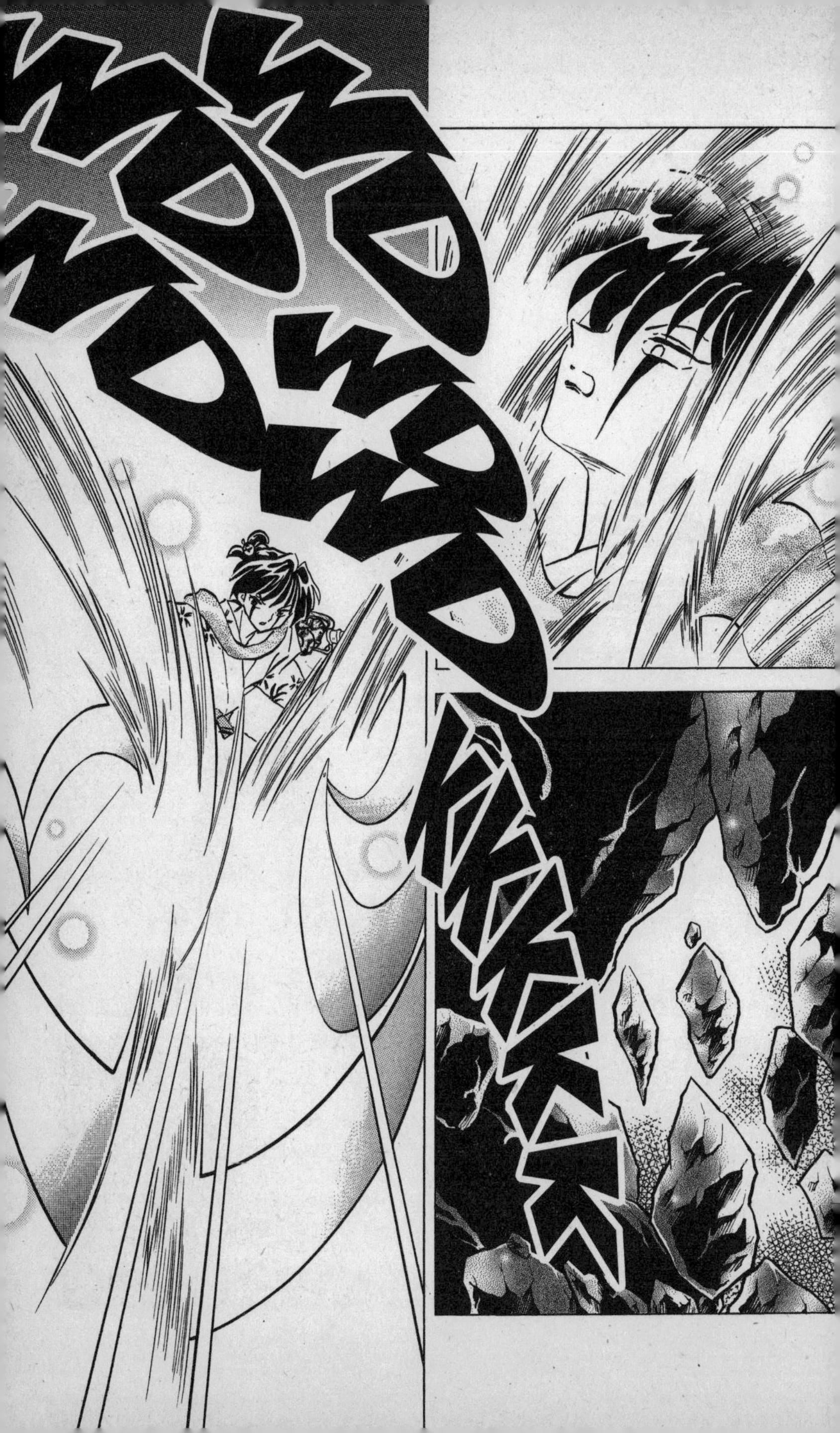

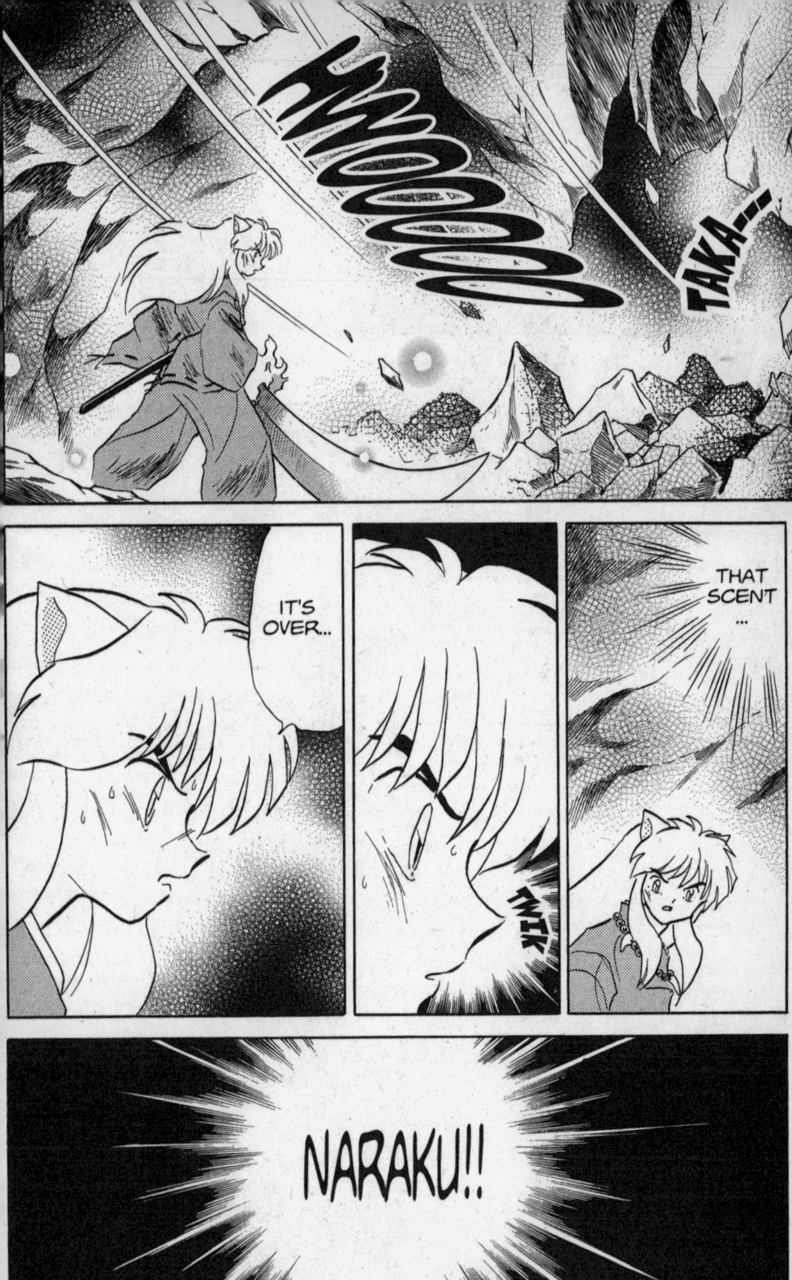
HWOOOOOO
TAKA...
IT'S OVER...
TWIK
THAT SCENT ...
NARAKU!!

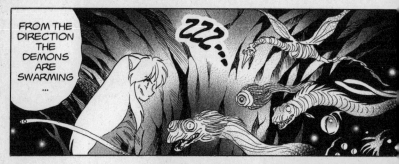

FROM THE DIRECTION THE DEMONS ARE SWARMING...

ZZZ...

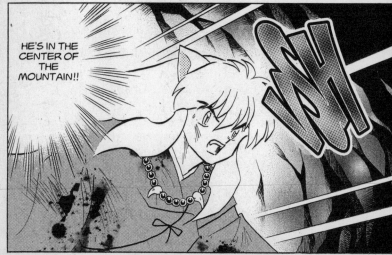

HE'S IN THE CENTER OF THE MOUNTAIN!!

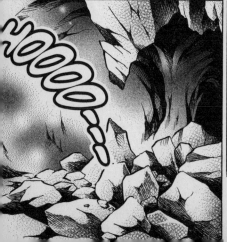

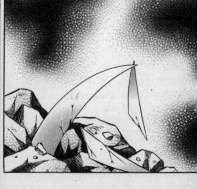

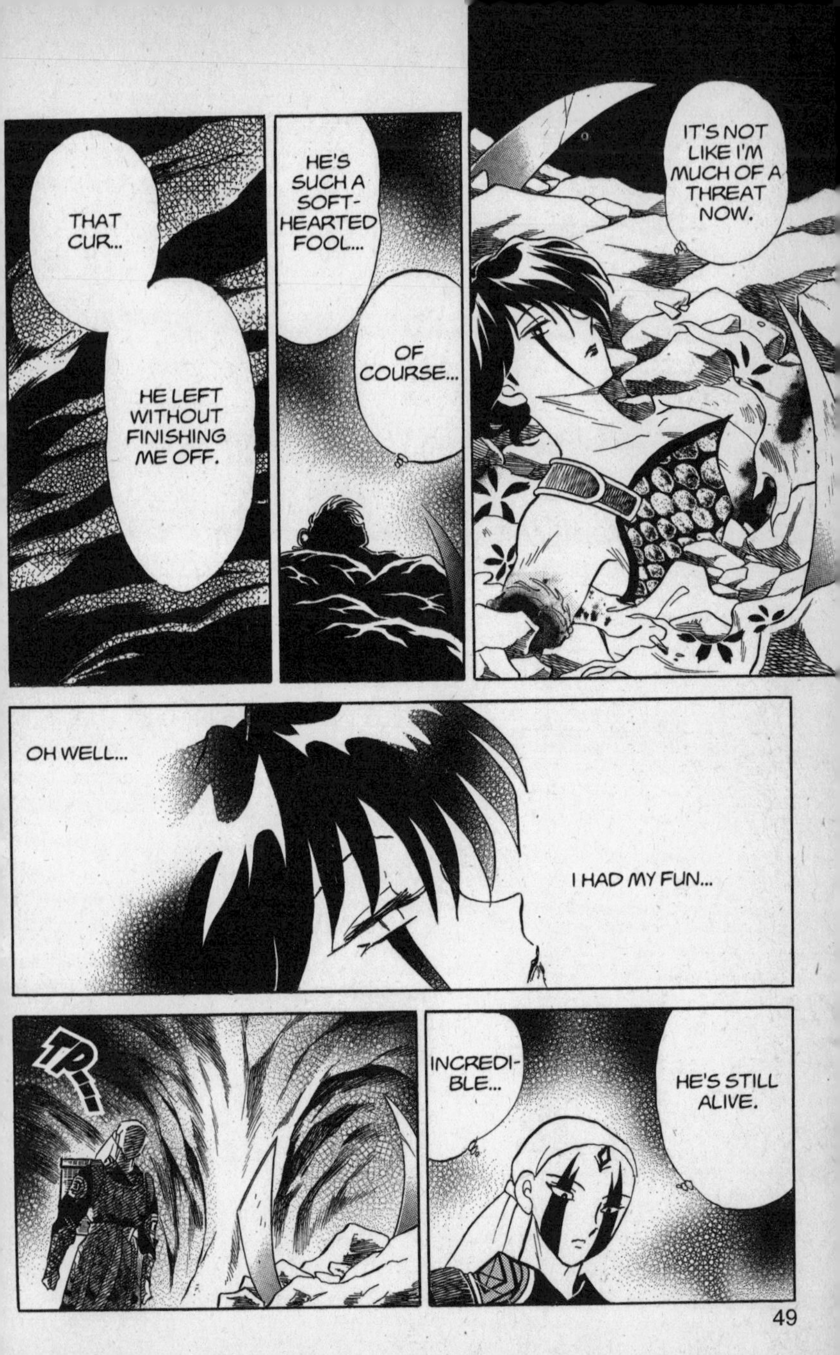
THAT CUR...
HE LEFT WITHOUT FINISHING ME OFF.
HE'S SUCH A SOFT-HEARTED FOOL...
OF COURSE...
IT'S NOT LIKE I'M MUCH OF A THREAT NOW.
OH WELL...
I HAD MY FUN...
TP
INCREDI-BLE...
HE'S STILL ALIVE.

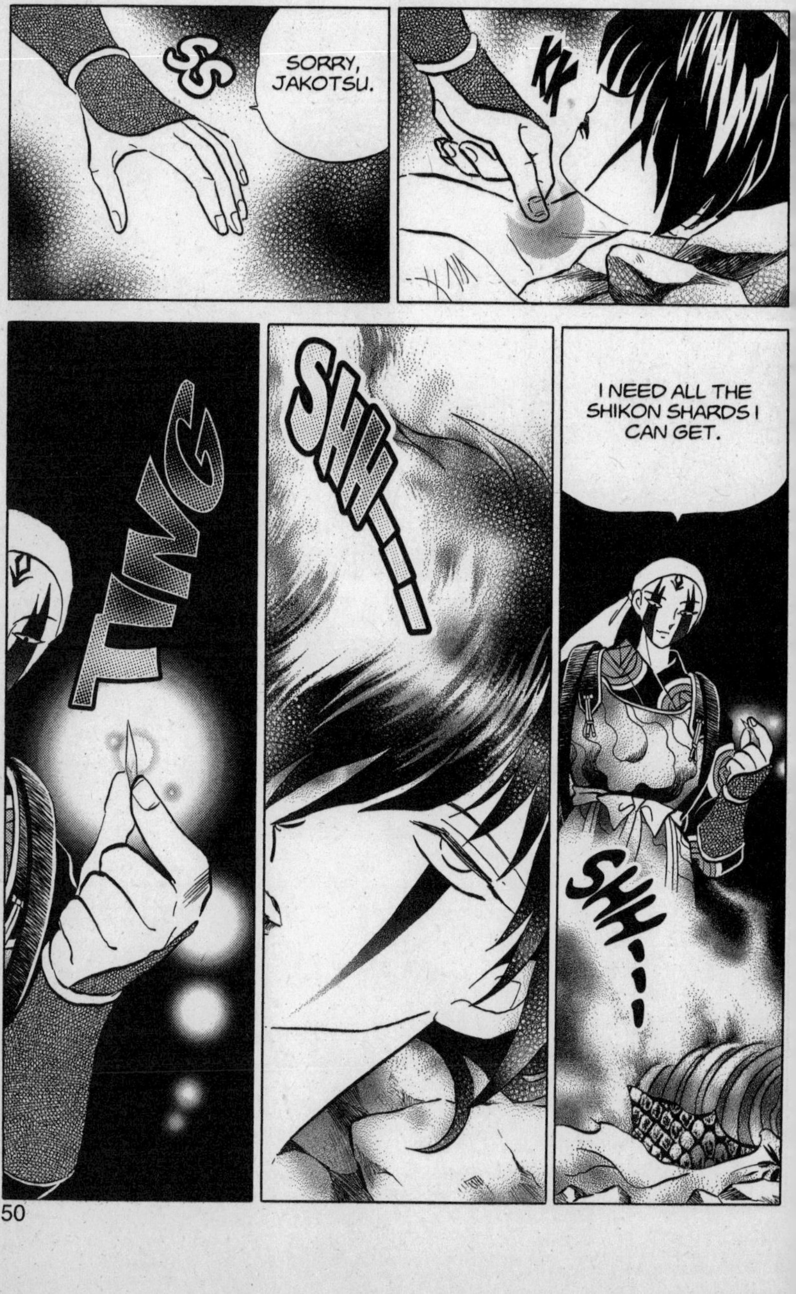
SS
SORRY, JAKOTSU.
KK
TING
SHH...
I NEED ALL THE SHIKON SHARDS I CAN GET.
SHH...

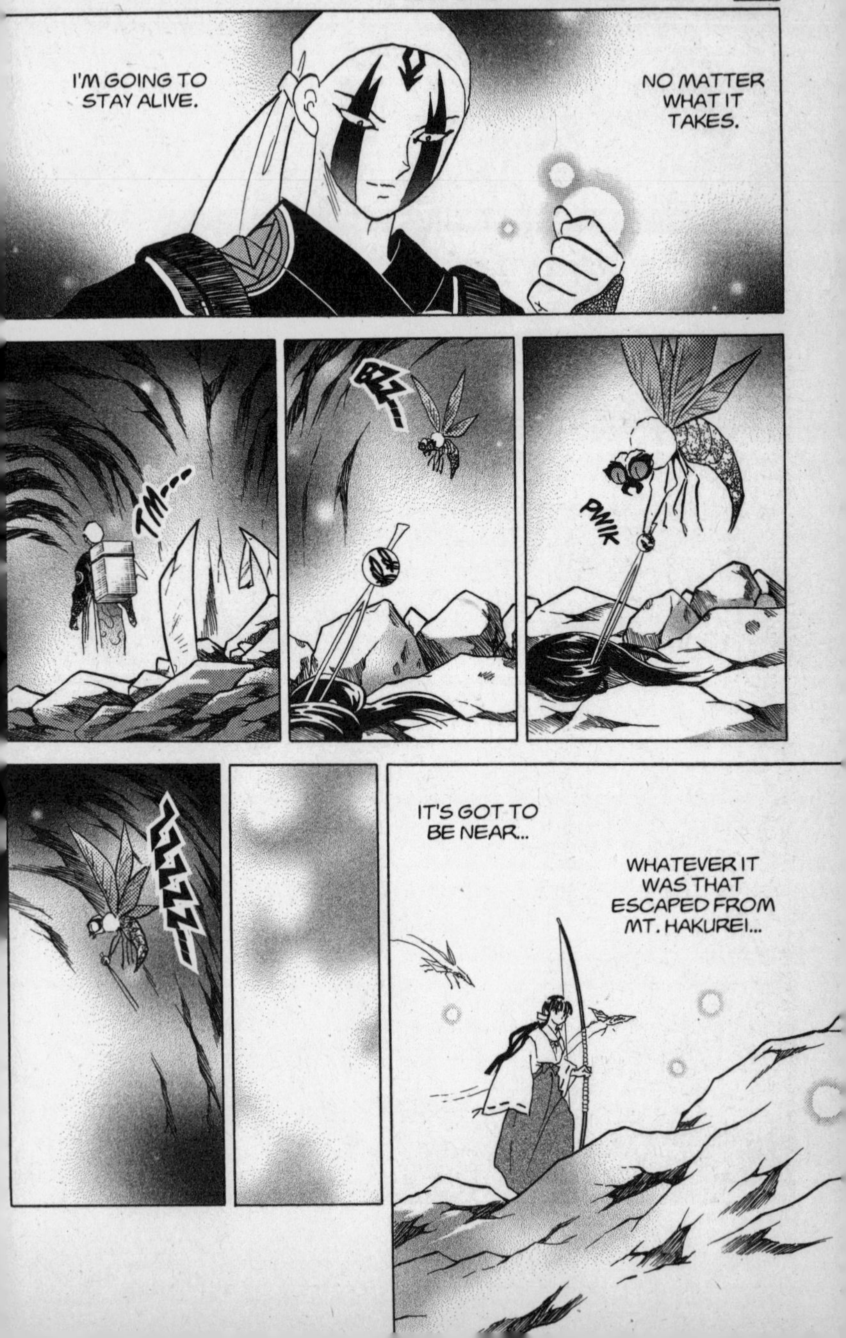
I'M GOING TO STAY ALIVE.
NO MATTER WHAT IT TAKES.
TM...
BZZ...
PWIK
IT'S GOT TO BE NEAR...
WHATEVER IT WAS THAT ESCAPED FROM MT. HAKUREI...

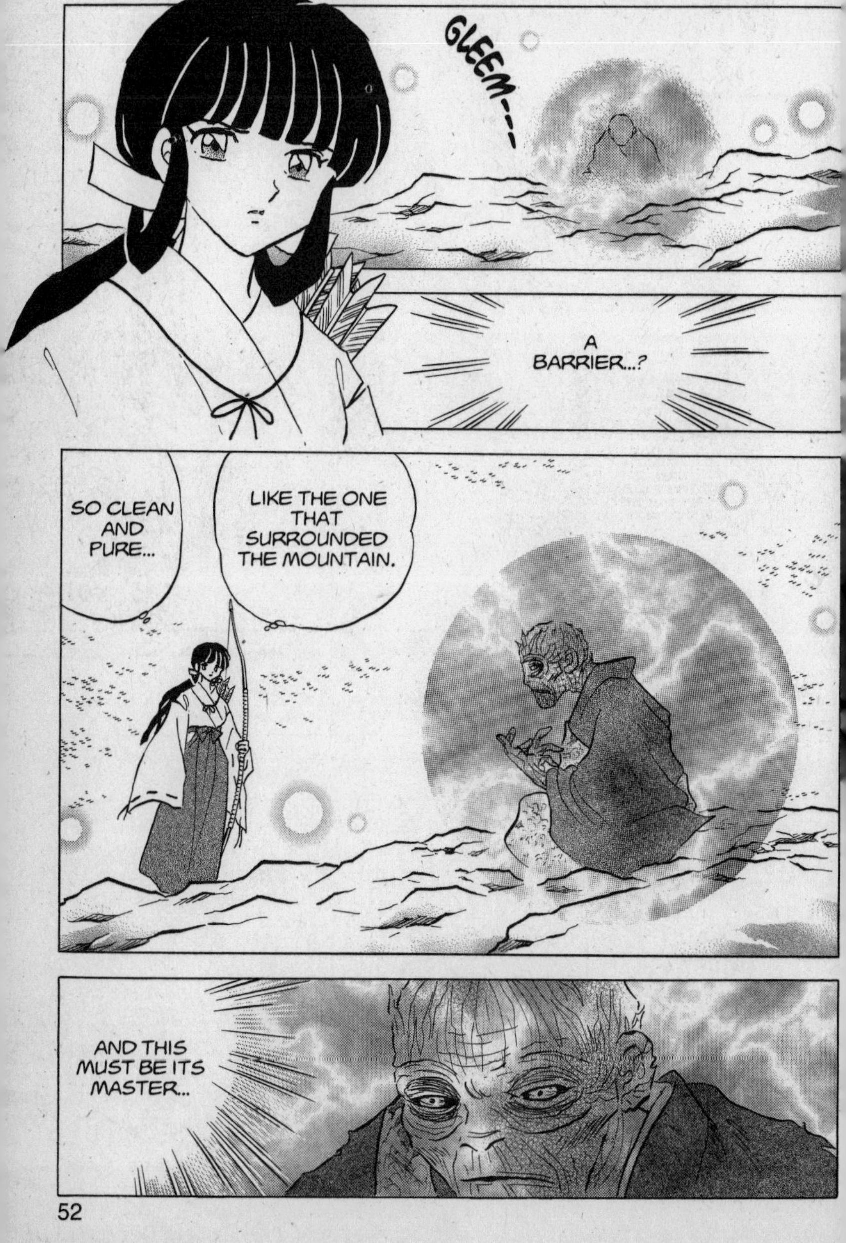
GLEEM---
A BARRIER...?
SO CLEAN AND PURE...
LIKE THE ONE THAT SURROUNDED THE MOUNTAIN.
AND THIS MUST BE ITS MASTER...

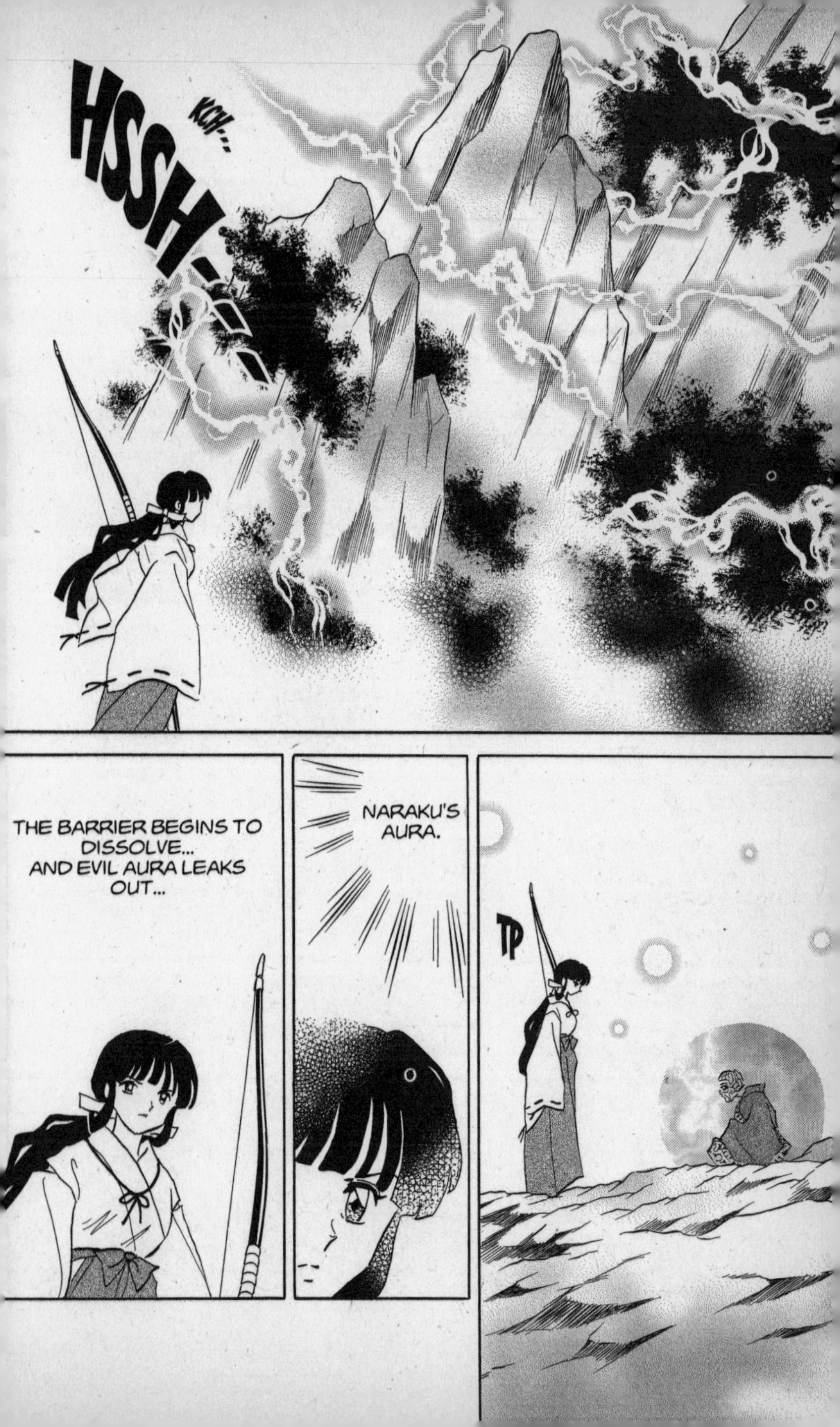
HSSH...
KCH...
THE BARRIER BEGINS TO DISSOLVE... AND EVIL AURA LEAKS OUT...
NARAKU'S AURA.
TP

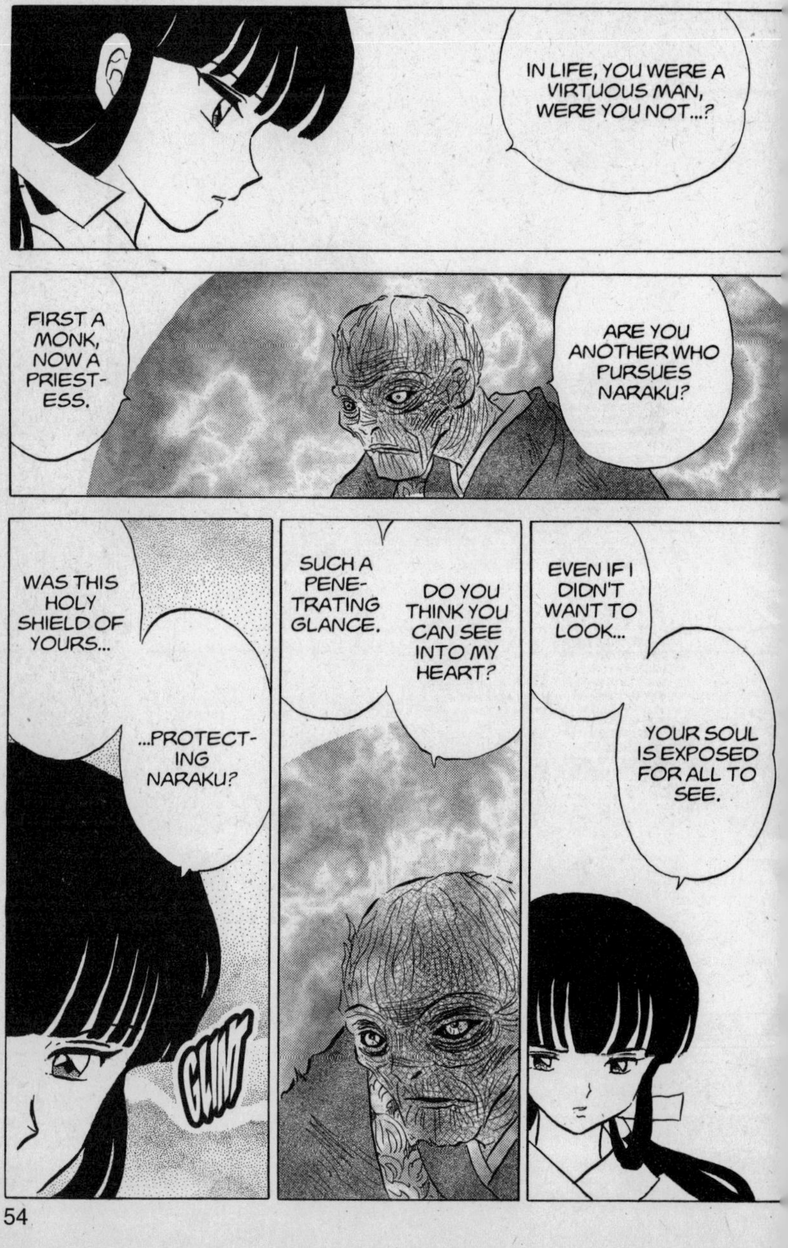
IN LIFE, YOU WERE A VIRTUOUS MAN, WERE YOU NOT...?
FIRST A MONK, NOW A PRIEST- ESS.
ARE YOU ANOTHER WHO PURSUES NARAKU?
WAS THIS HOLY SHIELD OF YOURS...
...PROTECT- ING NARAKU?
GLINT
SUCH A PENE- TRATING GLANCE.
DO YOU THINK YOU CAN SEE INTO MY HEART?
EVEN IF I DIDN'T WANT TO LOOK...
YOUR SOUL IS EXPOSED FOR ALL TO SEE.

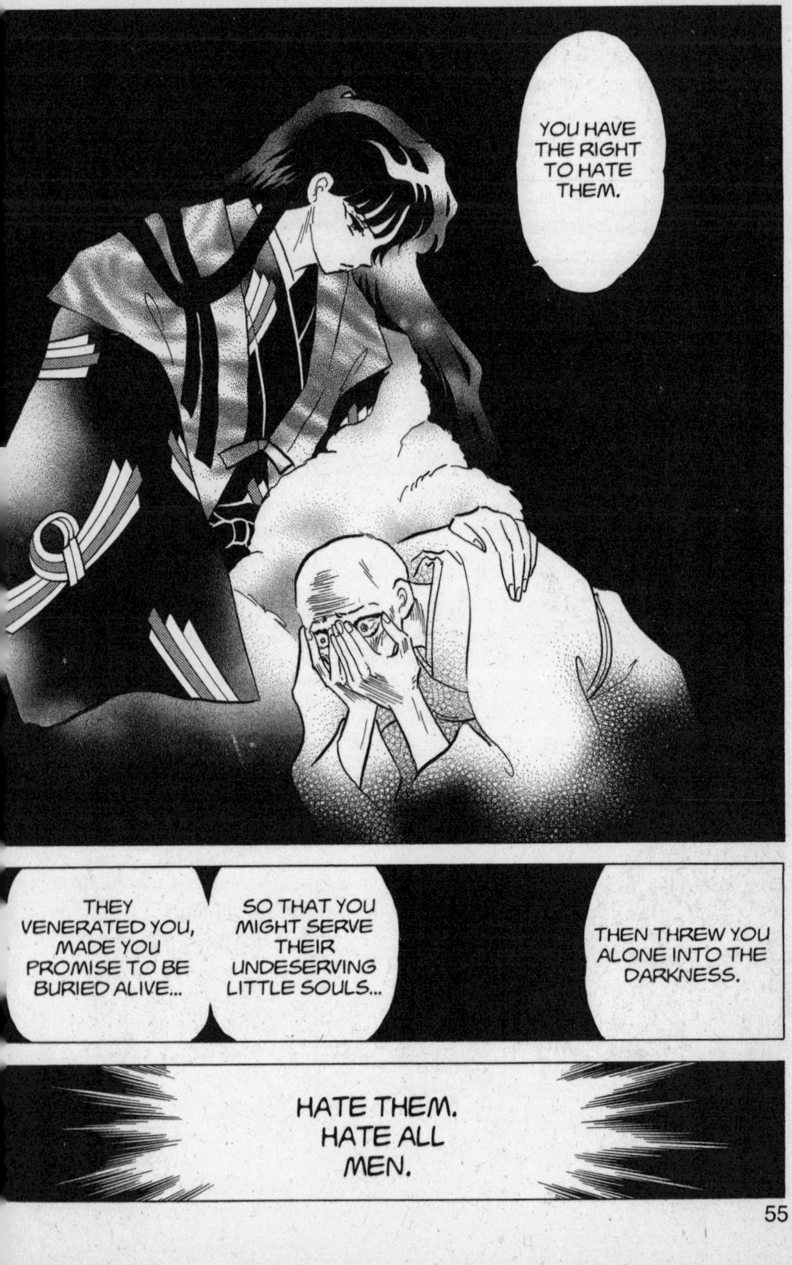
YOU HAVE THE RIGHT TO HATE THEM.
THEY VENERATED YOU, MADE YOU PROMISE TO BE BURIED ALIVE...
SO THAT YOU MIGHT SERVE THEIR UNDESERVING LITTLE SOULS...
THEN THREW YOU ALONE INTO THE DARKNESS.
HATE THEM. HATE ALL MEN.

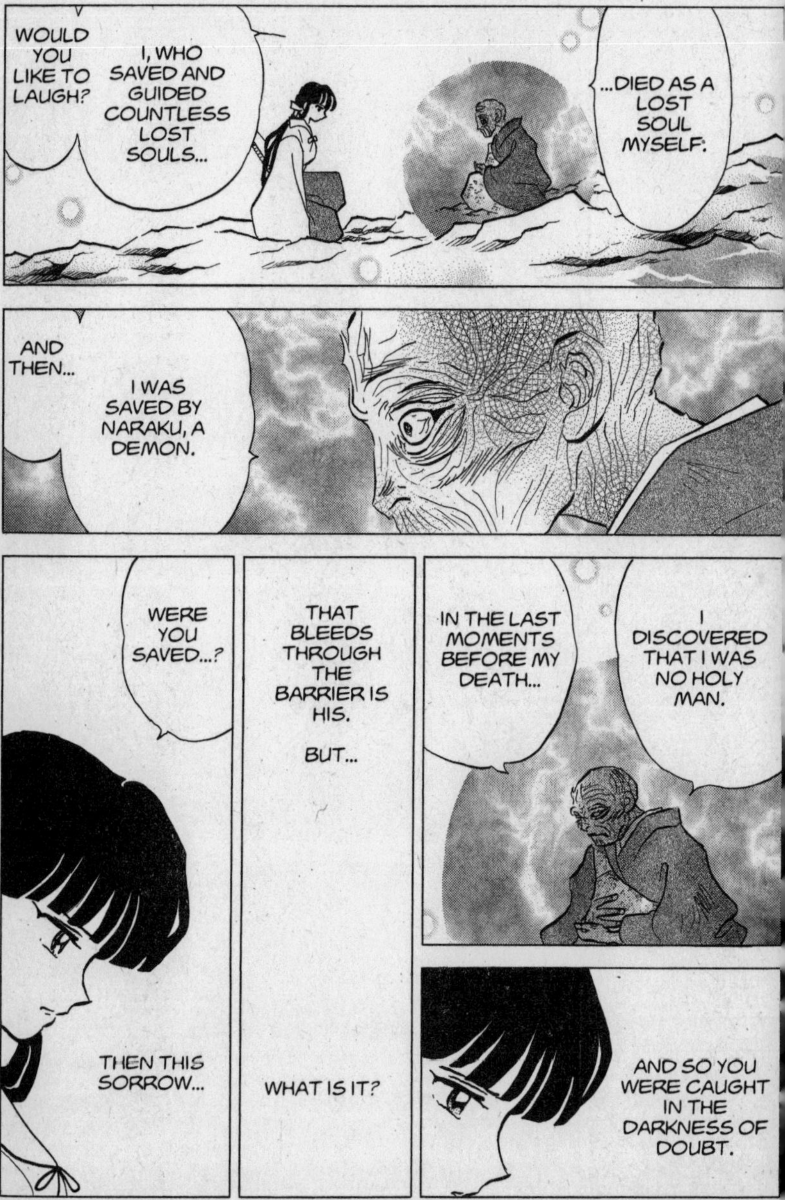
WOULD YOU LIKE TO LAUGH?
I, WHO SAVED AND GUIDED COUNTLESS LOST SOULS...
...DIED AS A LOST SOUL MYSELF.
AND THEN...
I WAS SAVED BY NARAKU, A DEMON.
WERE YOU SAVED...?
THEN THIS SORROW...
THAT BLEEDS THROUGH THE BARRIER IS HIS.
BUT...
WHAT IS IT?
IN THE LAST MOMENTS BEFORE MY DEATH...
I DISCOVERED THAT I WAS NO HOLY MAN.
AND SO YOU WERE CAUGHT IN THE DARKNESS OF DOUBT.

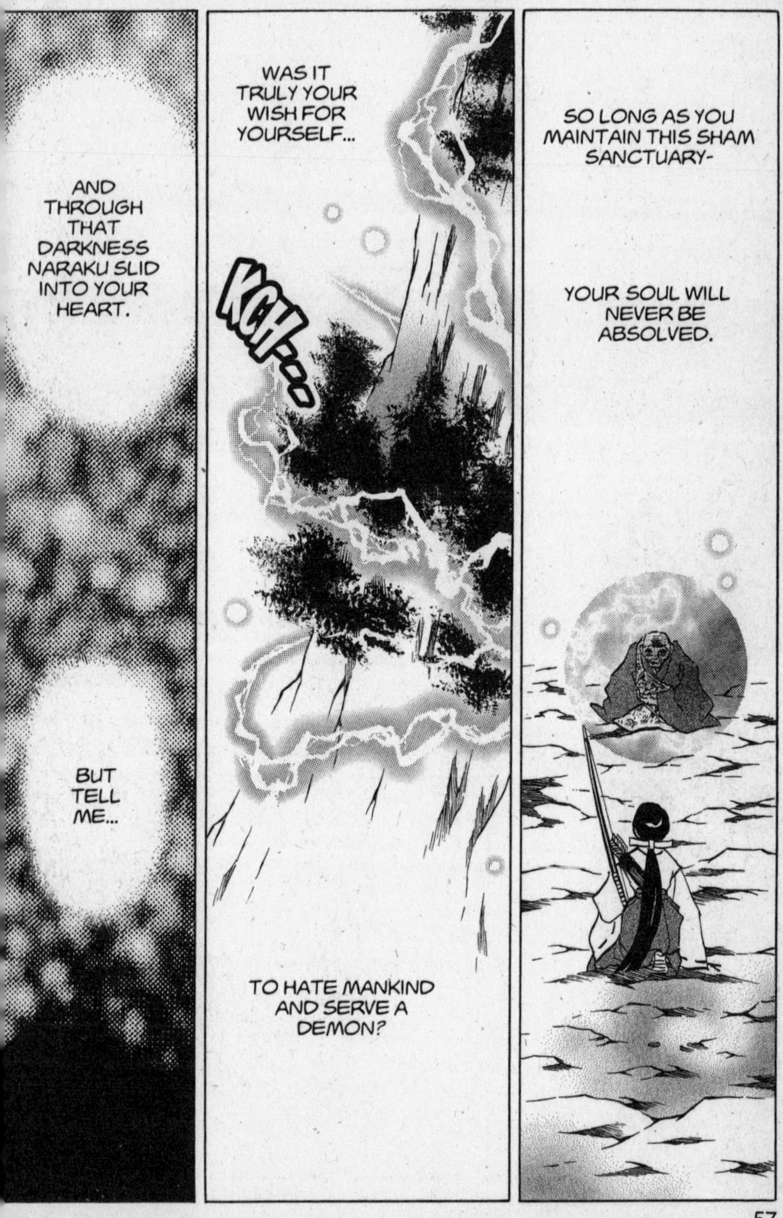
AND THROUGH THAT DARKNESS NARAKU SLID INTO YOUR HEART.
BUT TELL ME...
WAS IT TRULY YOUR WISH FOR YOURSELF...
KCH-OO
TO HATE MANKIND AND SERVE A DEMON?
SO LONG AS YOU MAINTAIN THIS SHAM SANCTUARY-
YOUR SOUL WILL NEVER BE ABSOLVED.

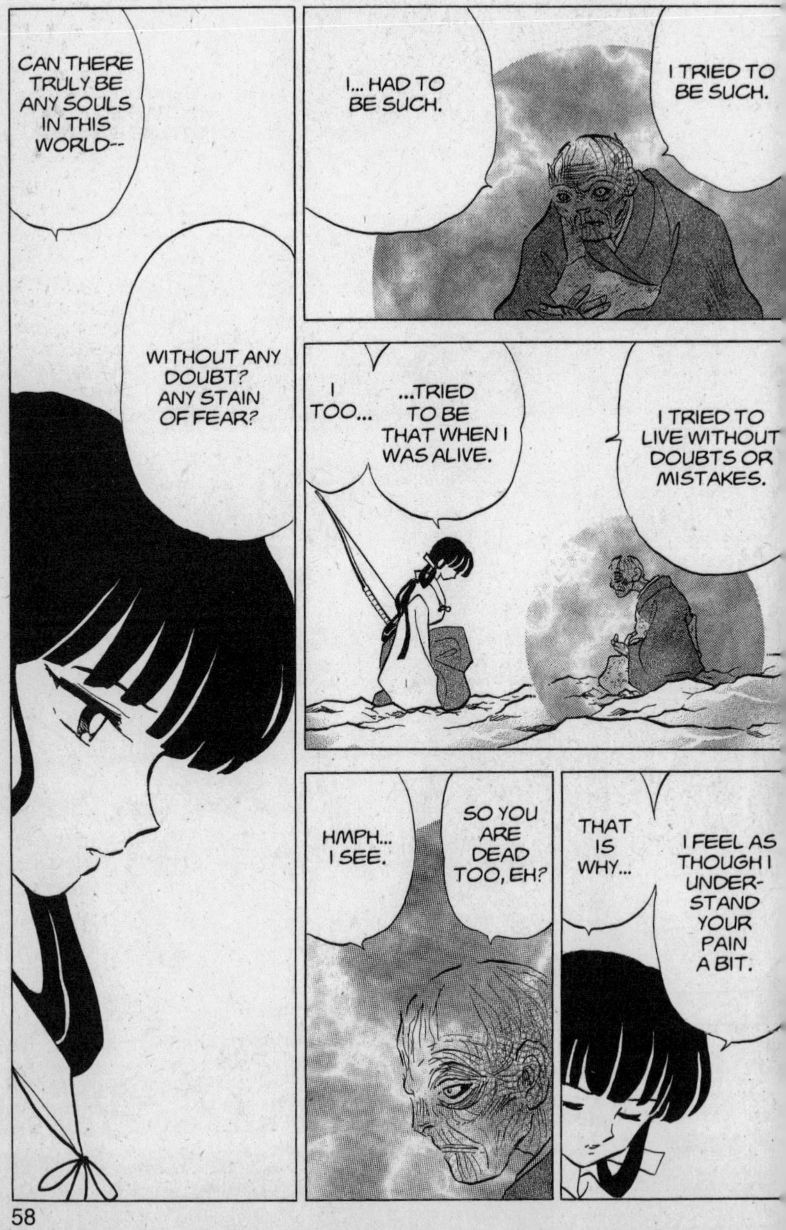
CAN THERE TRULY BE ANY SOULS IN THIS WORLD--
WITHOUT ANY DOUBT? ANY STAIN OF FEAR?
I... HAD TO BE SUCH.
I TRIED TO BE SUCH.
I TOO...
...TRIED TO BE THAT WHEN I WAS ALIVE.
I TRIED TO LIVE WITHOUT DOUBTS OR MISTAKES.
HMPH... I SEE.
SO YOU ARE DEAD TOO, EH?
THAT IS WHY...
I FEEL AS THOUGH I UNDERSTAND YOUR PAIN A BIT.

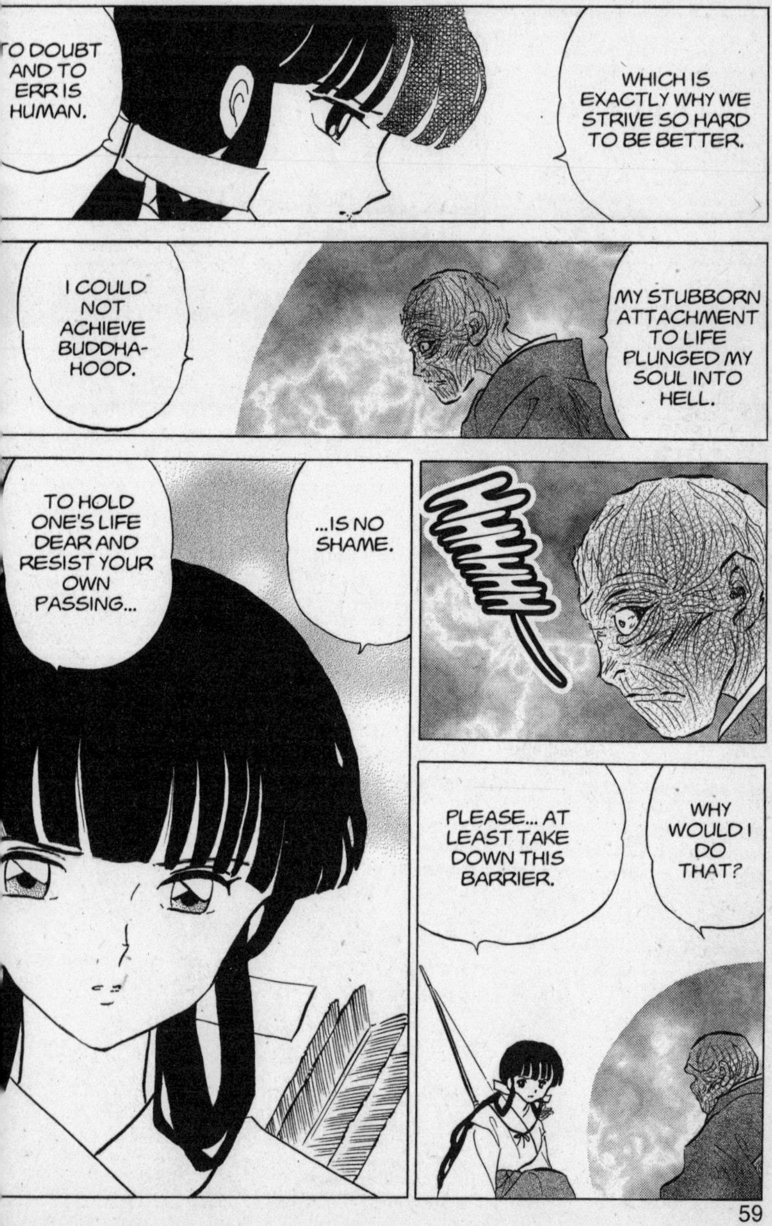
TO DOUBT AND TO ERR IS HUMAN.
WHICH IS EXACTLY WHY WE STRIVE SO HARD TO BE BETTER.
I COULD NOT ACHIEVE BUDDHA-HOOD.
MY STUBBORN ATTACHMENT TO LIFE PLUNGED MY SOUL INTO HELL.
TO HOLD ONE'S LIFE DEAR AND RESIST YOUR OWN PASSING...
...IS NO SHAME.
PLEASE... AT LEAST TAKE DOWN THIS BARRIER.
WHY WOULD I DO THAT?

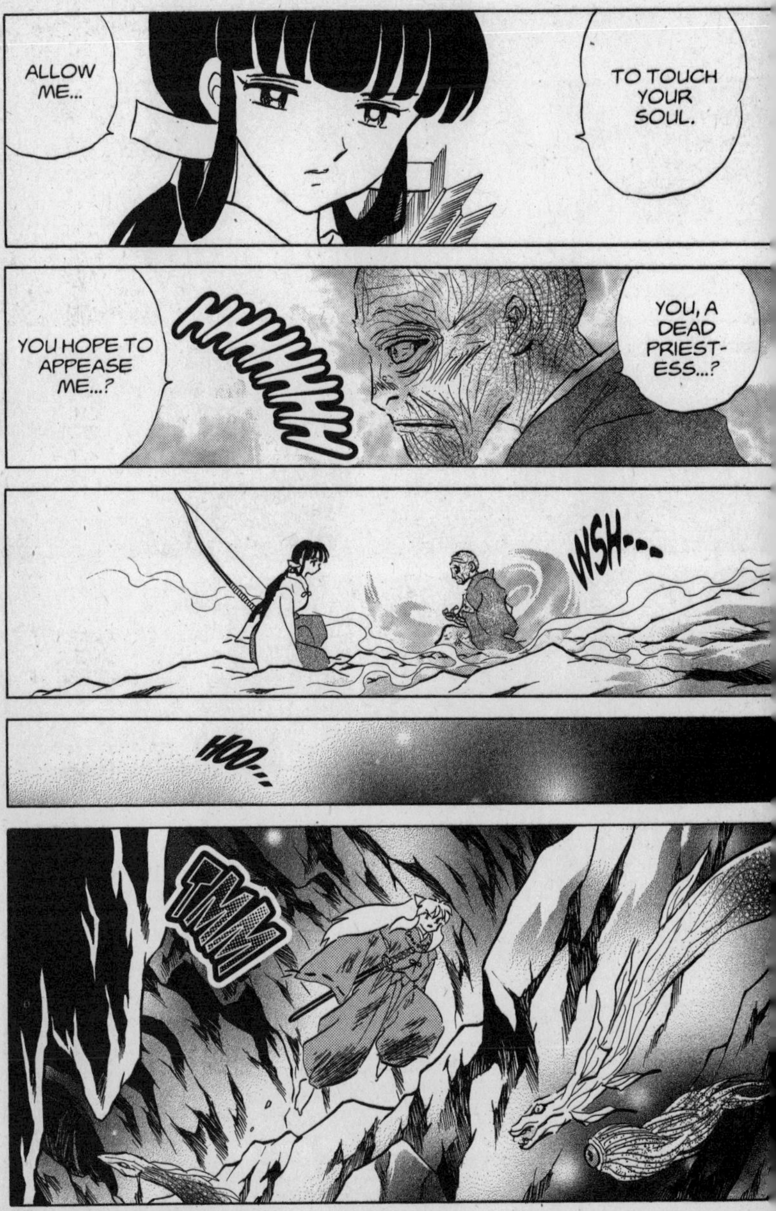

ALLOW ME...
TO TOUCH YOUR SOUL.
YOU HOPE TO APPEASE ME...?
CHHHHH
YOU, A DEAD PRIEST-ESS...?
WSH...
HOO...
TMM

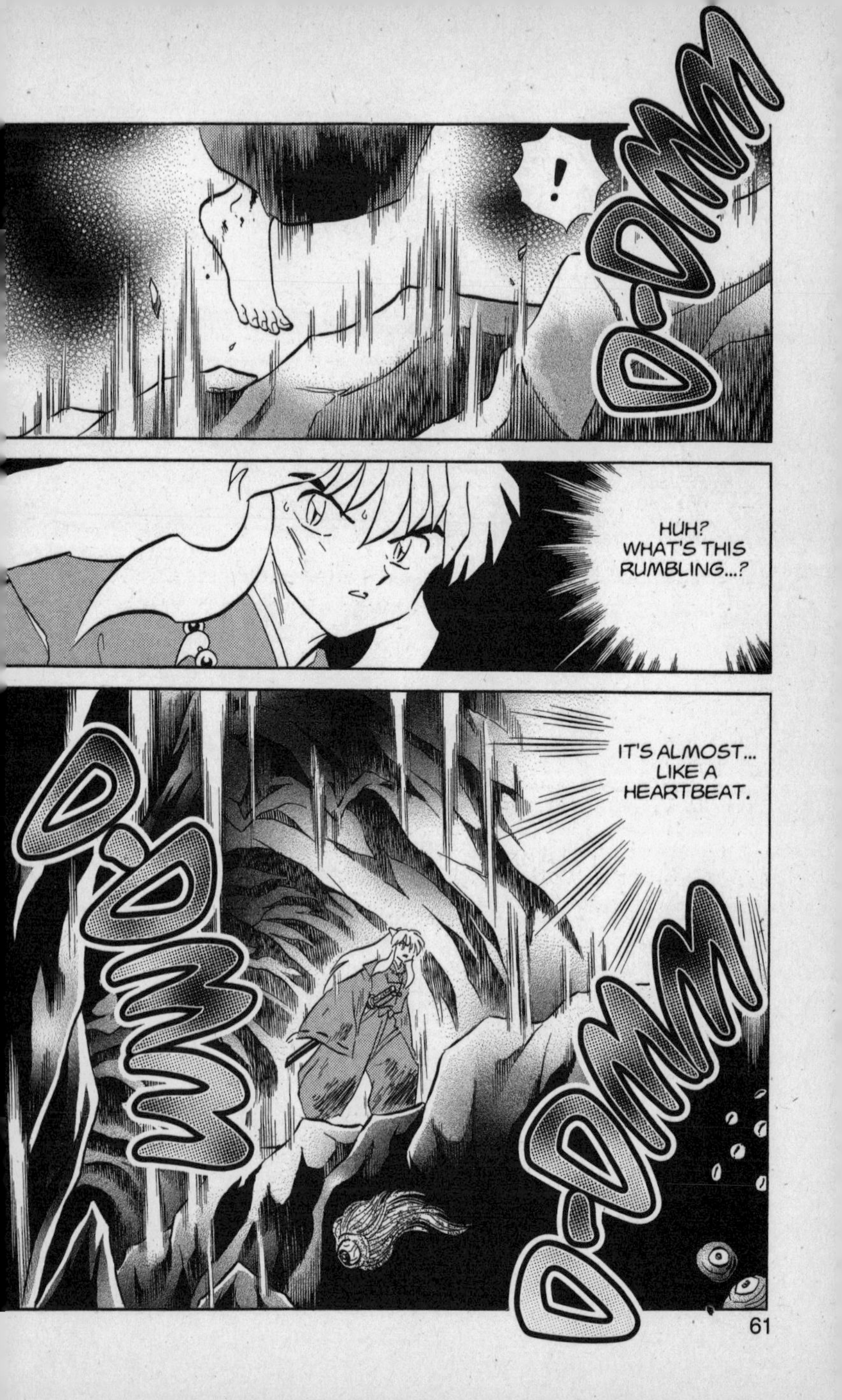
!
D-DMM
HUH? WHAT'S THIS RUMBLING...?
D-DMMM
IT'S ALMOST... LIKE A HEARTBEAT.
D-DMMM

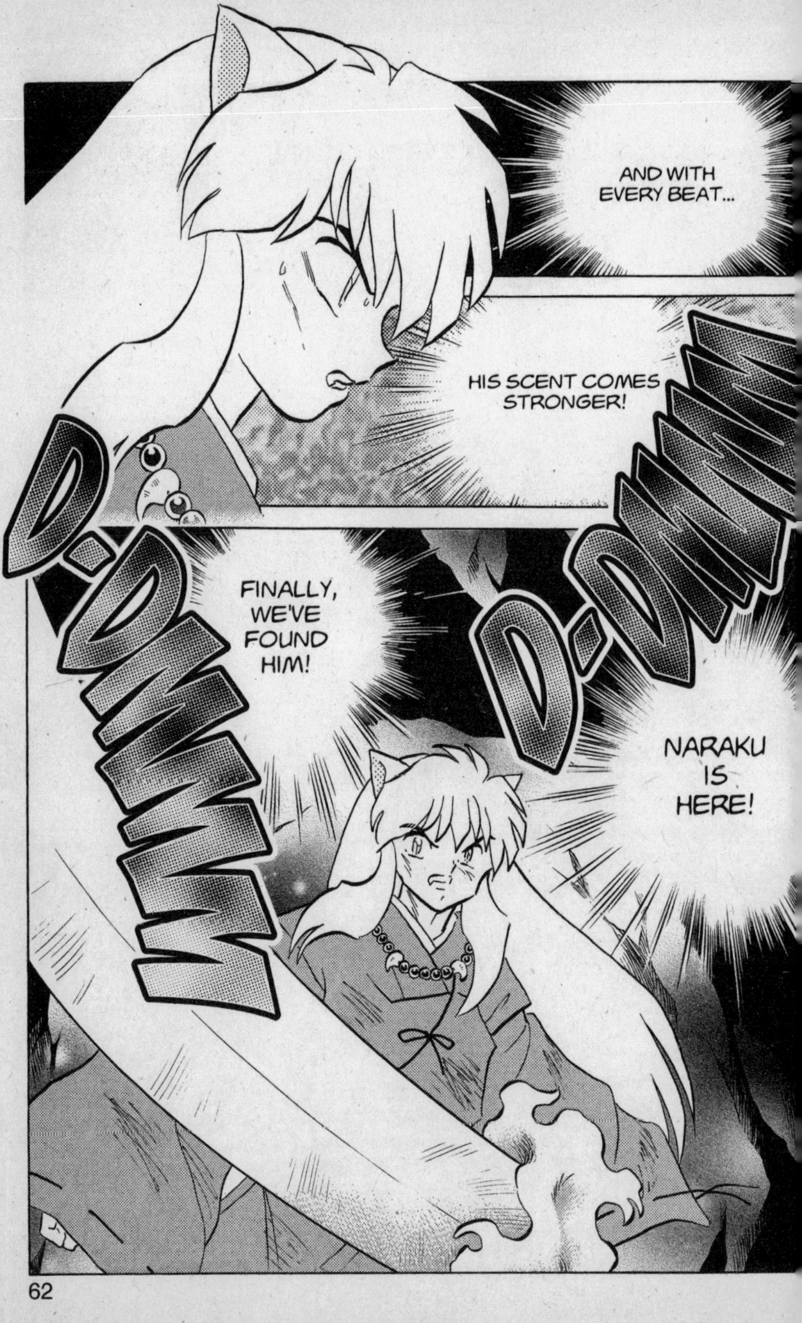

AND WITH EVERY BEAT...
HIS SCENT COMES STRONGER!
D-DMMMM!
FINALLY, WE'VE FOUND HIM!
D-DMMMM
NARAKU IS HERE!

SCROLL 4
THE SANCTUARY DESTROYED

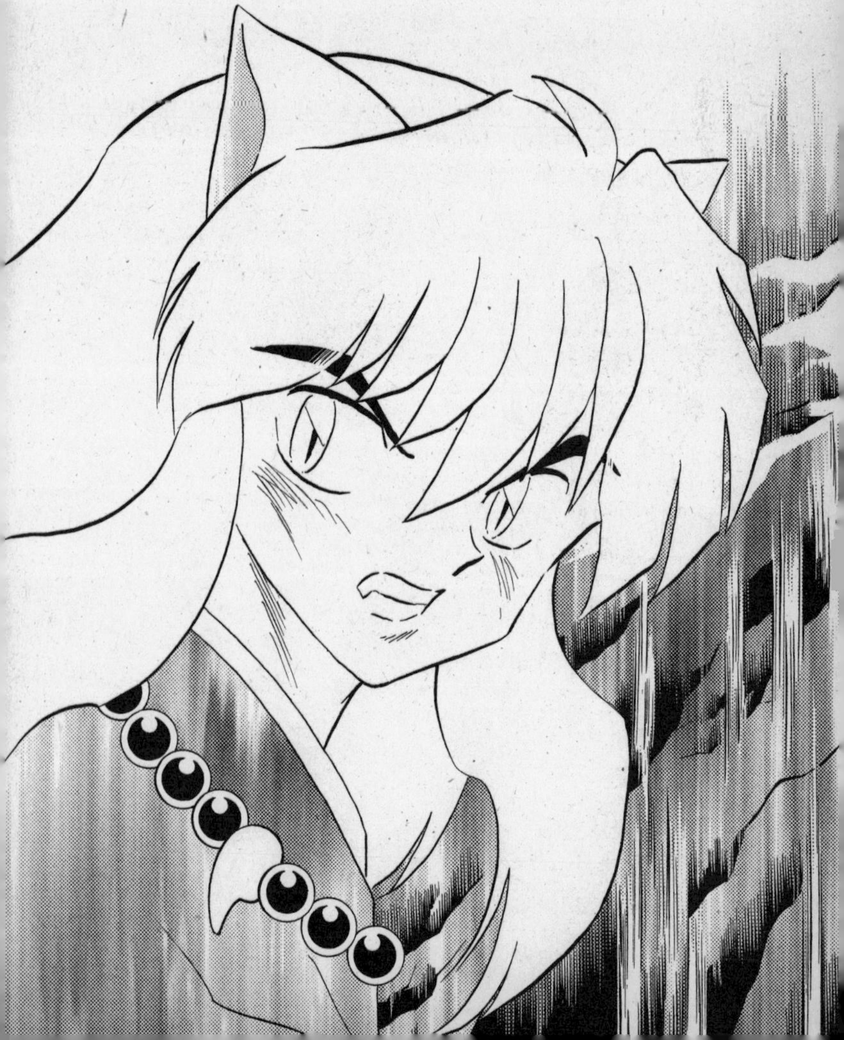

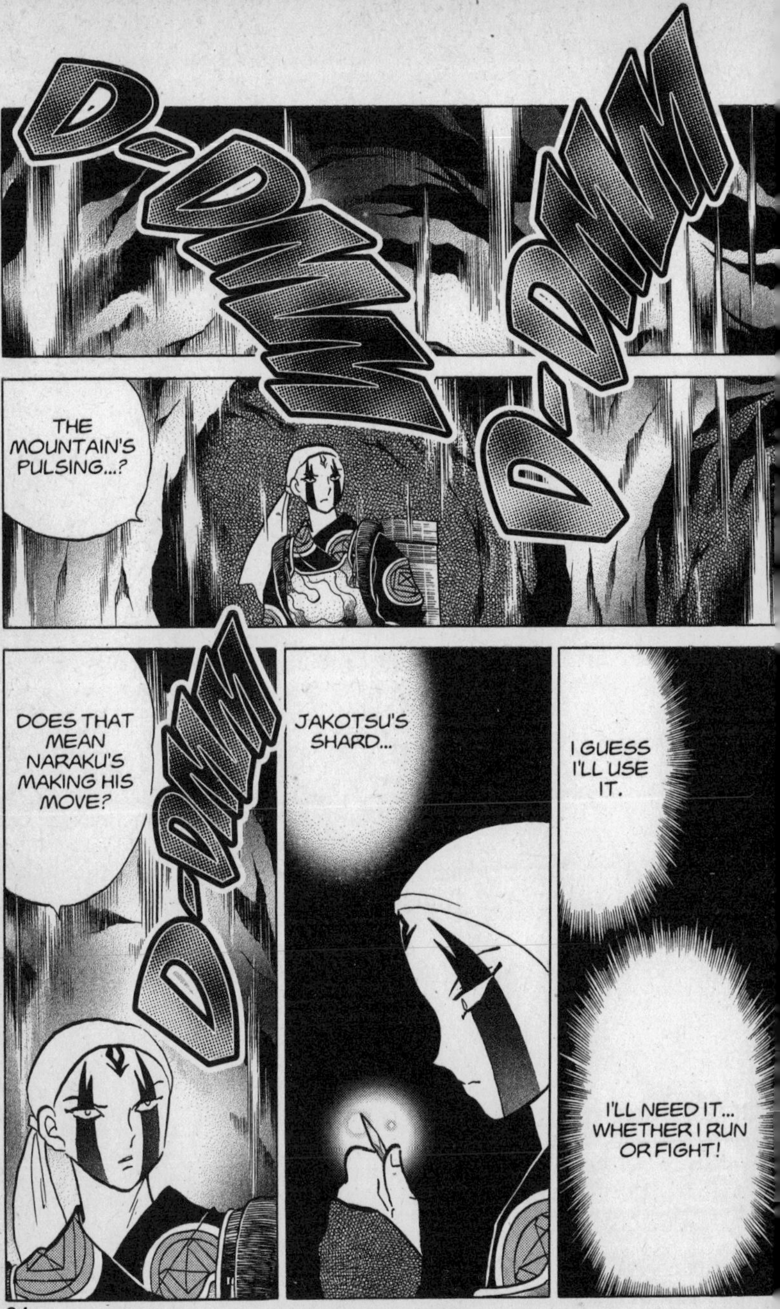
D-DMM
D-DMM
THE MOUNTAIN'S PULSING...?
DOES THAT MEAN NARAKU'S MAKING HIS MOVE?
D-DMM
JAKOTSU'S SHARD...
I GUESS I'LL USE IT.
I'LL NEED IT... WHETHER I RUN OR FIGHT!

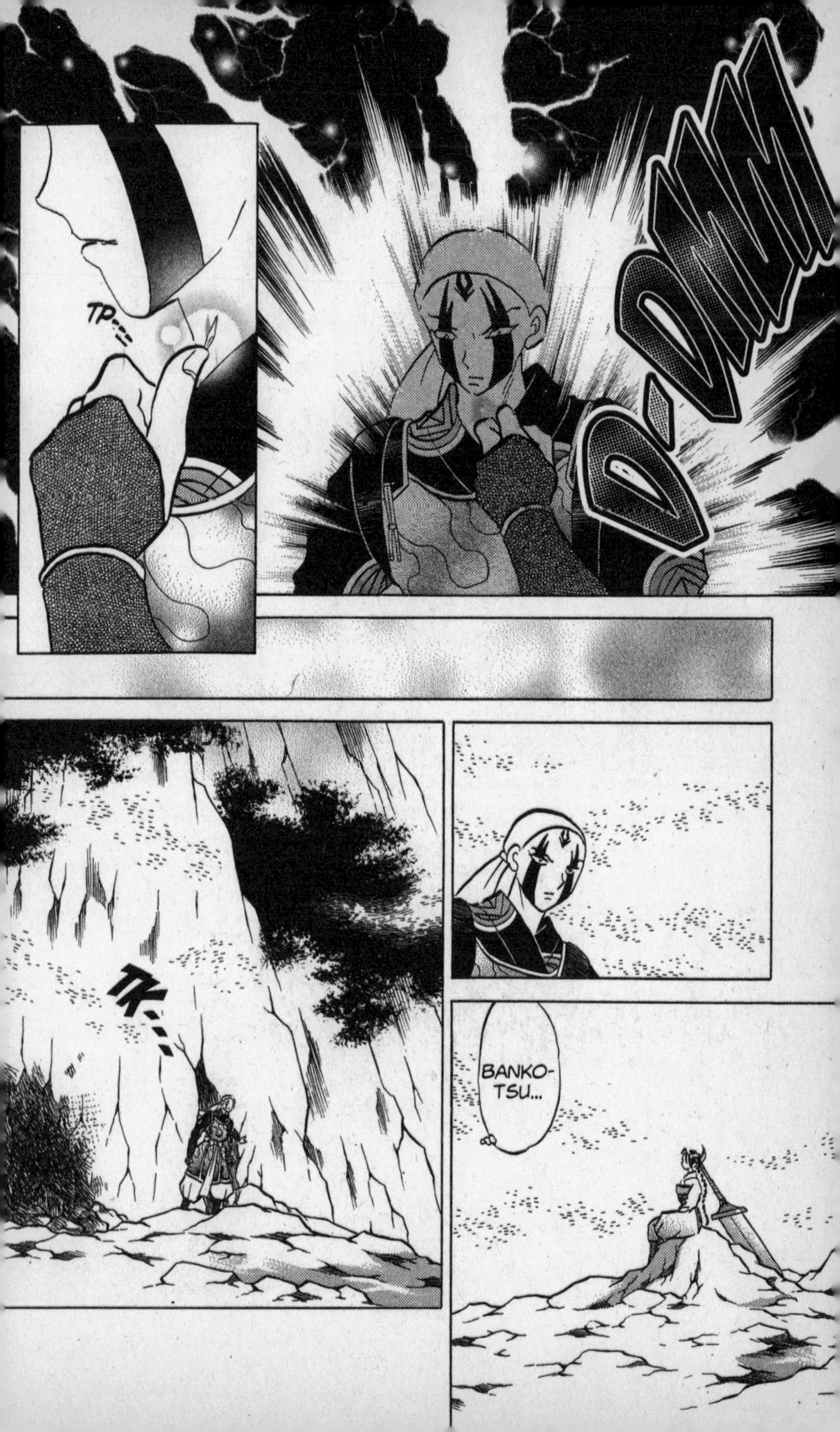
TP...
D-DMM
TK...
BANKO-
TSU...

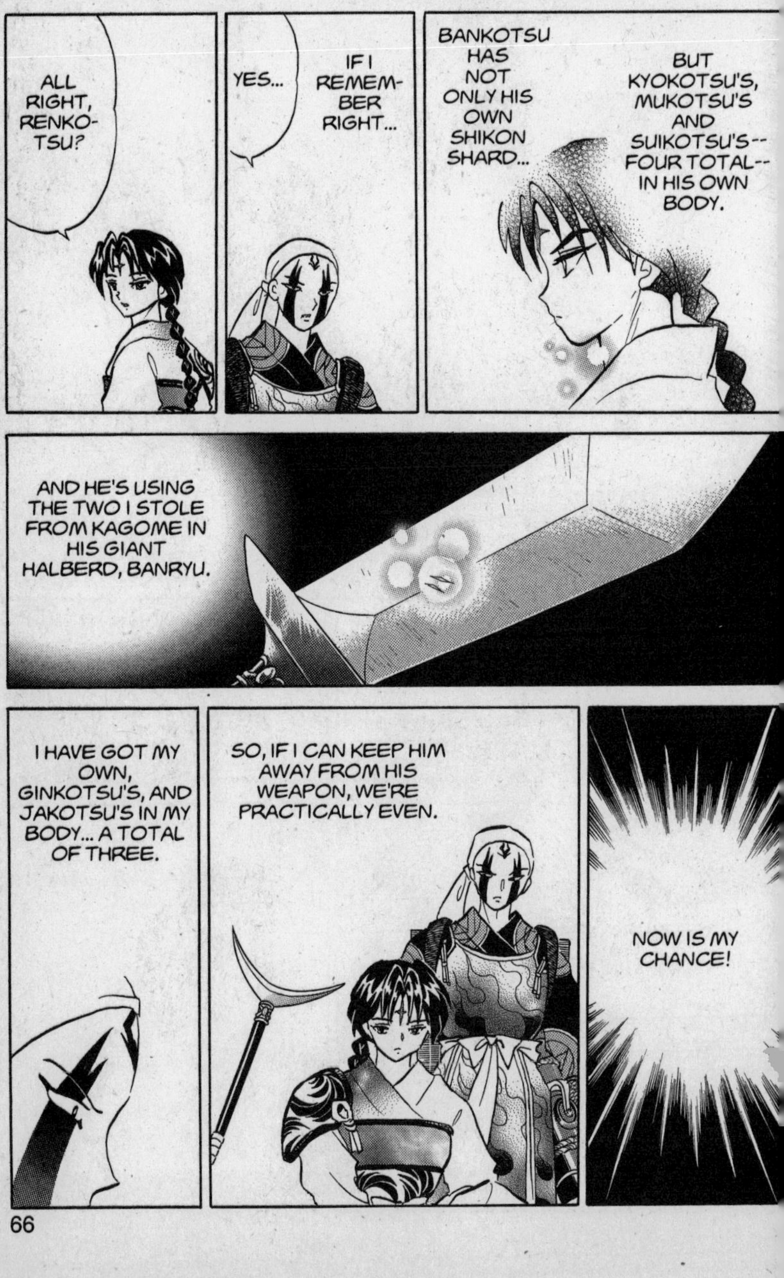
ALL RIGHT, RENKOTSU?
YES...
IF I REMEMBER RIGHT...
BANKOTSU HAS NOT ONLY HIS OWN SHIKON SHARD...
BUT KYOKOTSU'S, MUKOTSU'S AND SUIKOTSU'S-- FOUR TOTAL-- IN HIS OWN BODY.
AND HE'S USING THE TWO I STOLE FROM KAGOME IN HIS GIANT HALBERD, BANRYU.
I HAVE GOT MY OWN, GINKOTSU'S, AND JAKOTSU'S IN MY BODY... A TOTAL OF THREE.
SO, IF I CAN KEEP HIM AWAY FROM HIS WEAPON, WE'RE PRACTICALLY EVEN.
NOW IS MY CHANCE!

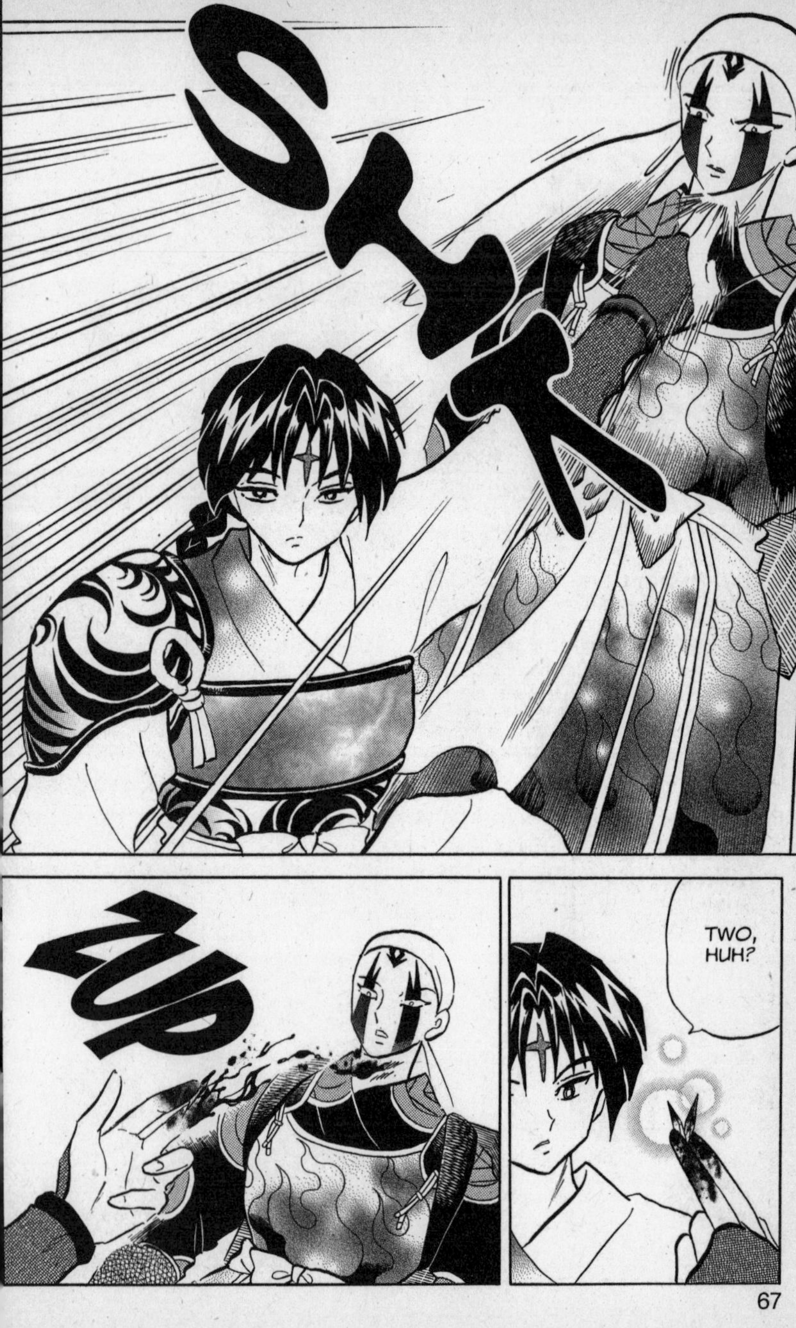
SIT
ZUP
TWO, HUH?

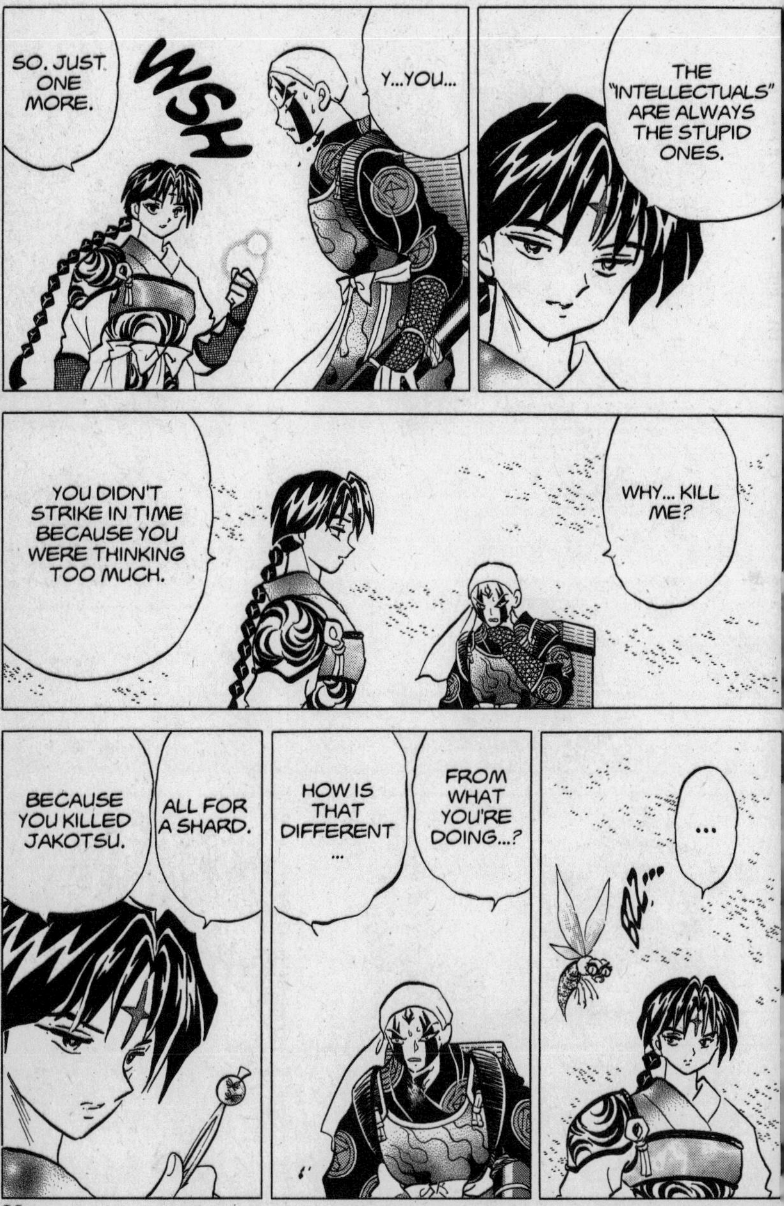
SO. JUST ONE MORE.
WSH
Y...YOU...
THE "INTELLECTUALS" ARE ALWAYS THE STUPID ONES.
YOU DIDN'T STRIKE IN TIME BECAUSE YOU WERE THINKING TOO MUCH.
WHY... KILL ME?
BECAUSE YOU KILLED JAKOTSU.
ALL FOR A SHARD.
HOW IS THAT DIFFERENT ...
FROM WHAT YOU'RE DOING...?
BZZ...
...

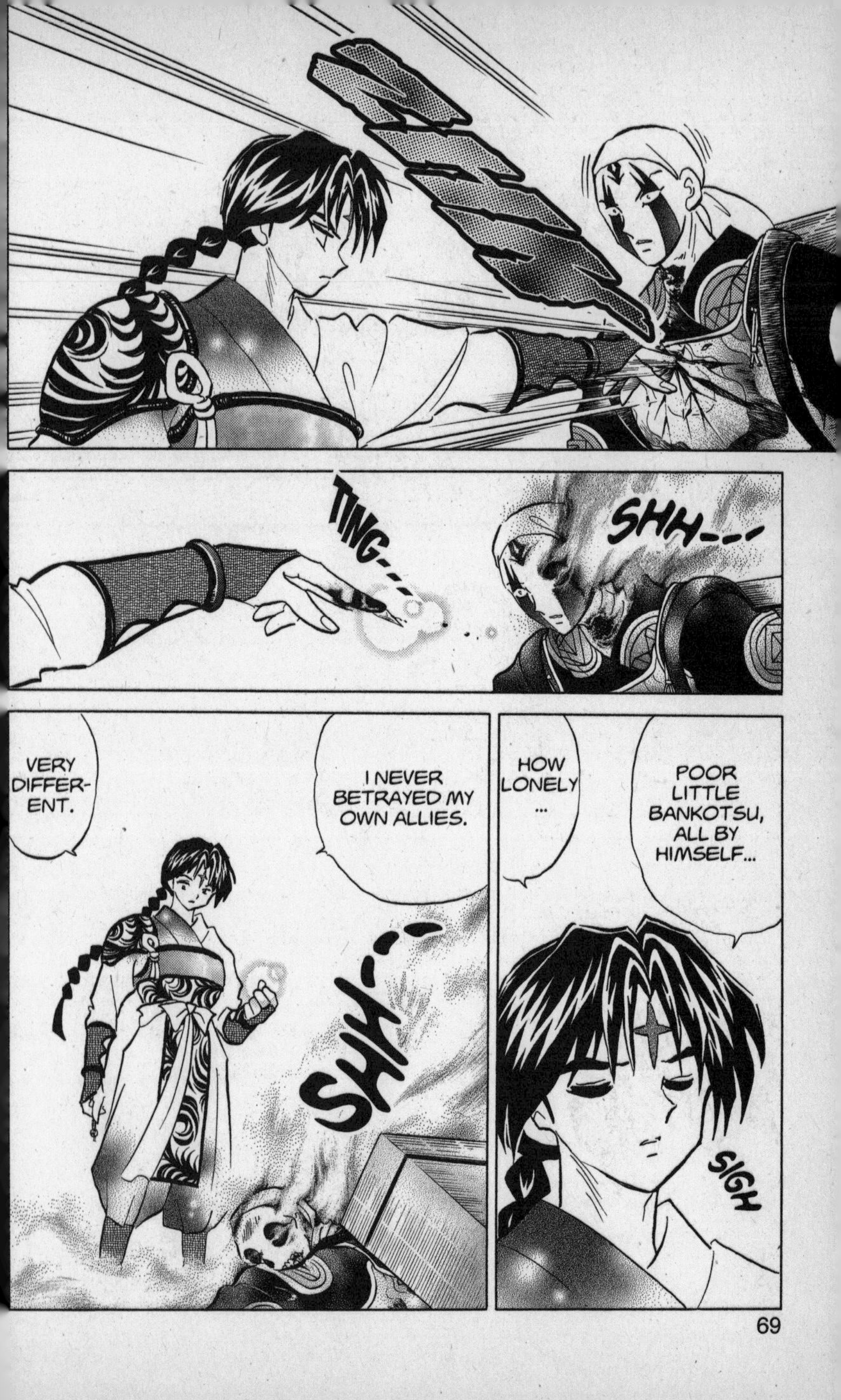
TING...
SHH...
VERY DIFFER-ENT.
I NEVER BETRAYED MY OWN ALLIES.
SHH...
HOW LONELY ...
POOR LITTLE BANKOTSU, ALL BY HIMSELF...
SIGH

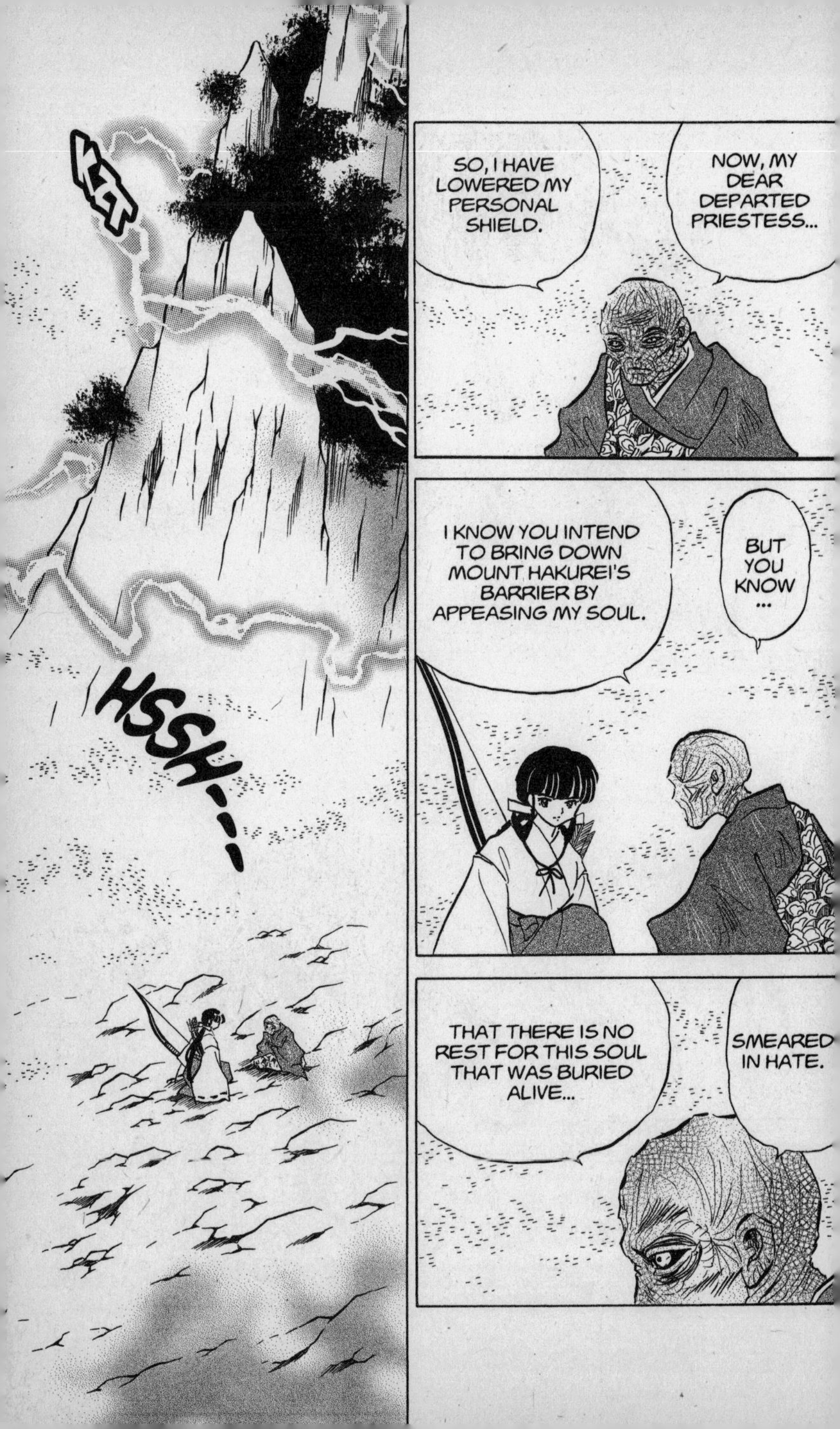
NOW, MY DEAR DEPARTED PRIESTESS...
SO, I HAVE LOWERED MY PERSONAL SHIELD.
I KNOW YOU INTEND TO BRING DOWN MOUNT HAKUREI'S BARRIER BY APPEASING MY SOUL.
BUT YOU KNOW ...
THAT THERE IS NO REST FOR THIS SOUL THAT WAS BURIED ALIVE...
SMEARED IN HATE.
KZZT
HSSH...

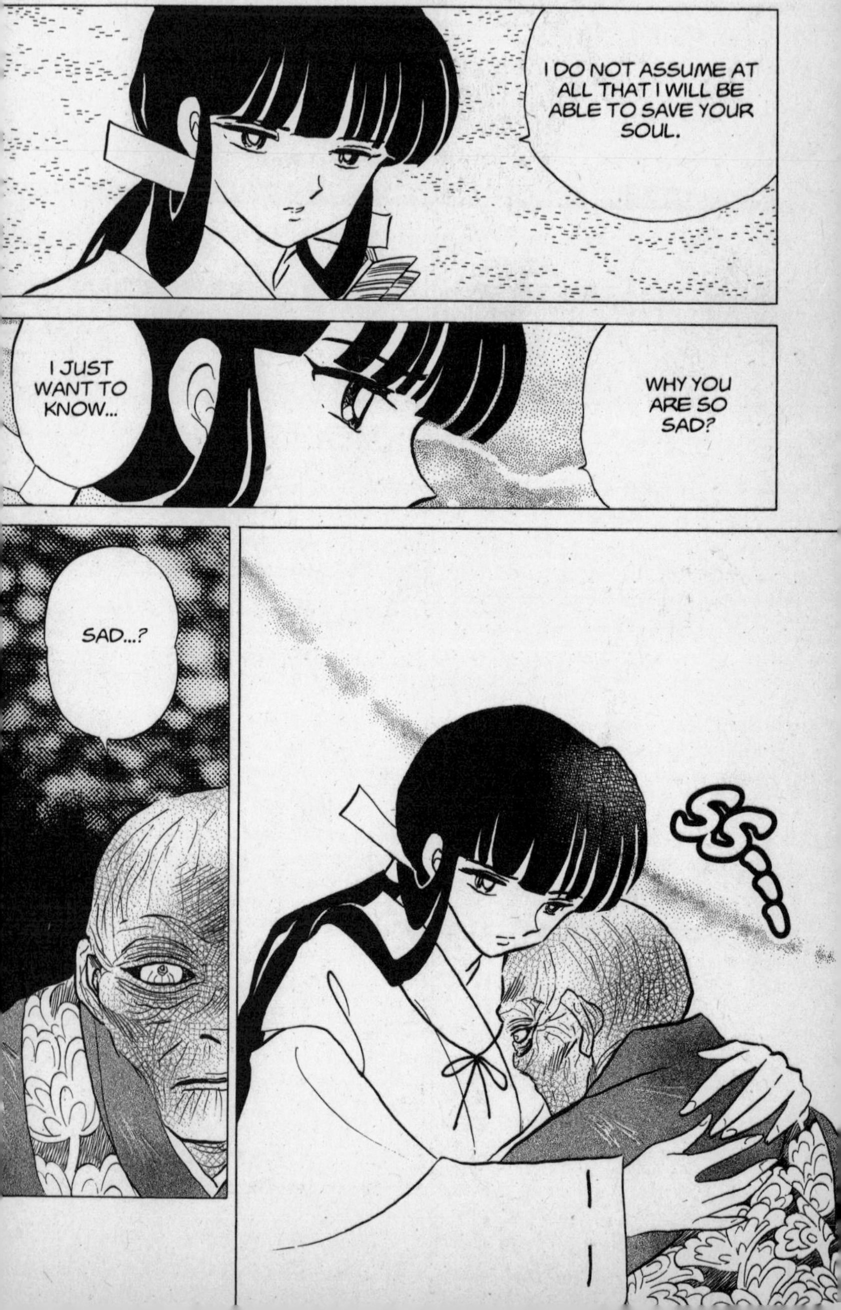
I DO NOT ASSUME AT ALL THAT I WILL BE ABLE TO SAVE YOUR SOUL.
I JUST WANT TO KNOW...
WHY YOU ARE SO SAD?
SAD...?
SSSSSS

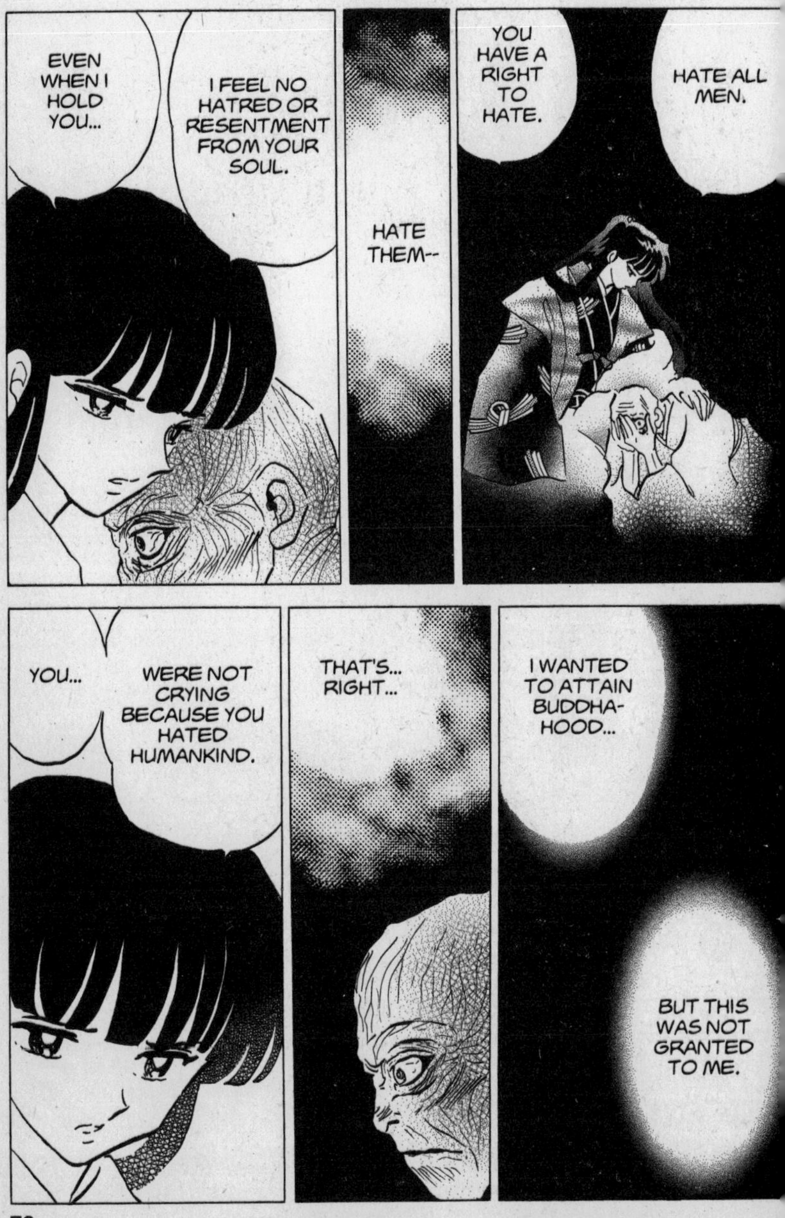
EVEN WHEN I HOLD YOU...
I FEEL NO HATRED OR RESENTMENT FROM YOUR SOUL.
HATE THEM--
YOU HAVE A RIGHT TO HATE.
HATE ALL MEN.
YOU...
WERE NOT CRYING BECAUSE YOU HATED HUMANKIND.
THAT'S... RIGHT...
I WANTED TO ATTAIN BUDDHA-HOOD...
BUT THIS WAS NOT GRANTED TO ME.

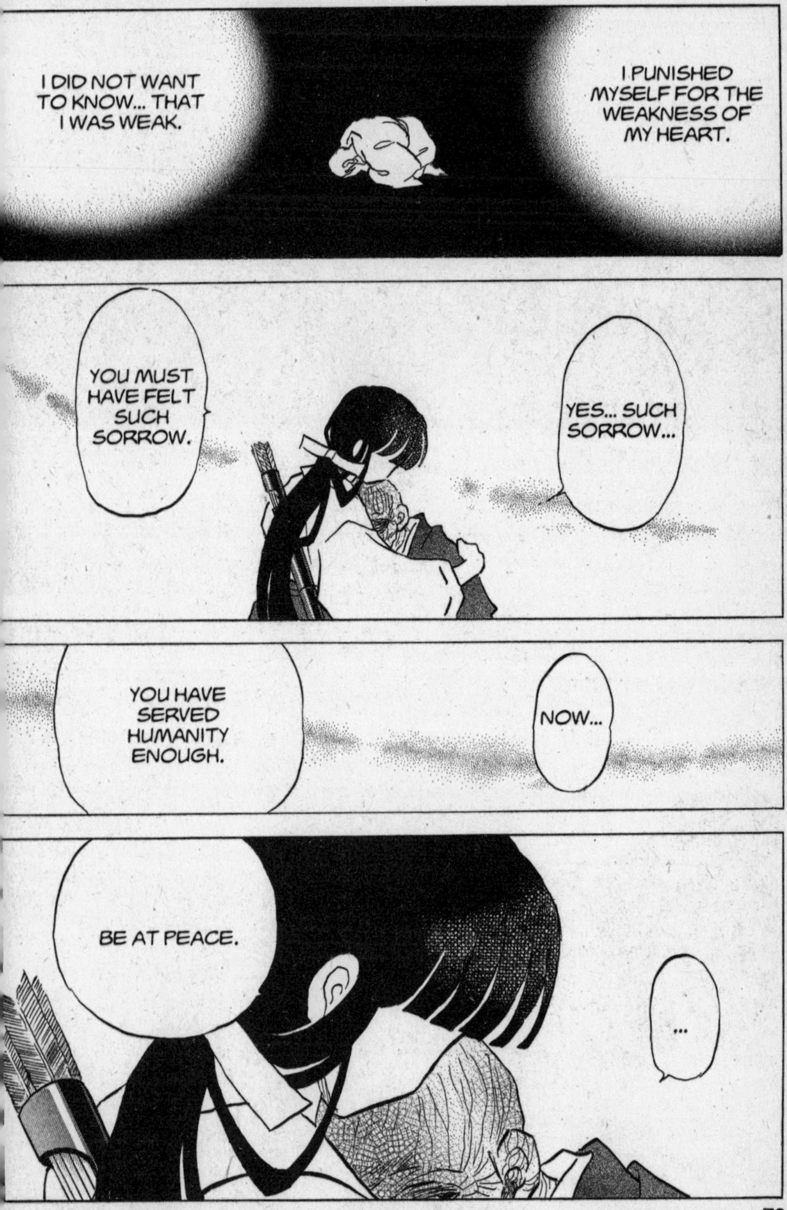
I DID NOT WANT TO KNOW... THAT I WAS WEAK.
I PUNISHED MYSELF FOR THE WEAKNESS OF MY HEART.
YOU MUST HAVE FELT SUCH SORROW.
YES... SUCH SORROW...
YOU HAVE SERVED HUMANITY ENOUGH.
NOW...
BE AT PEACE.
...

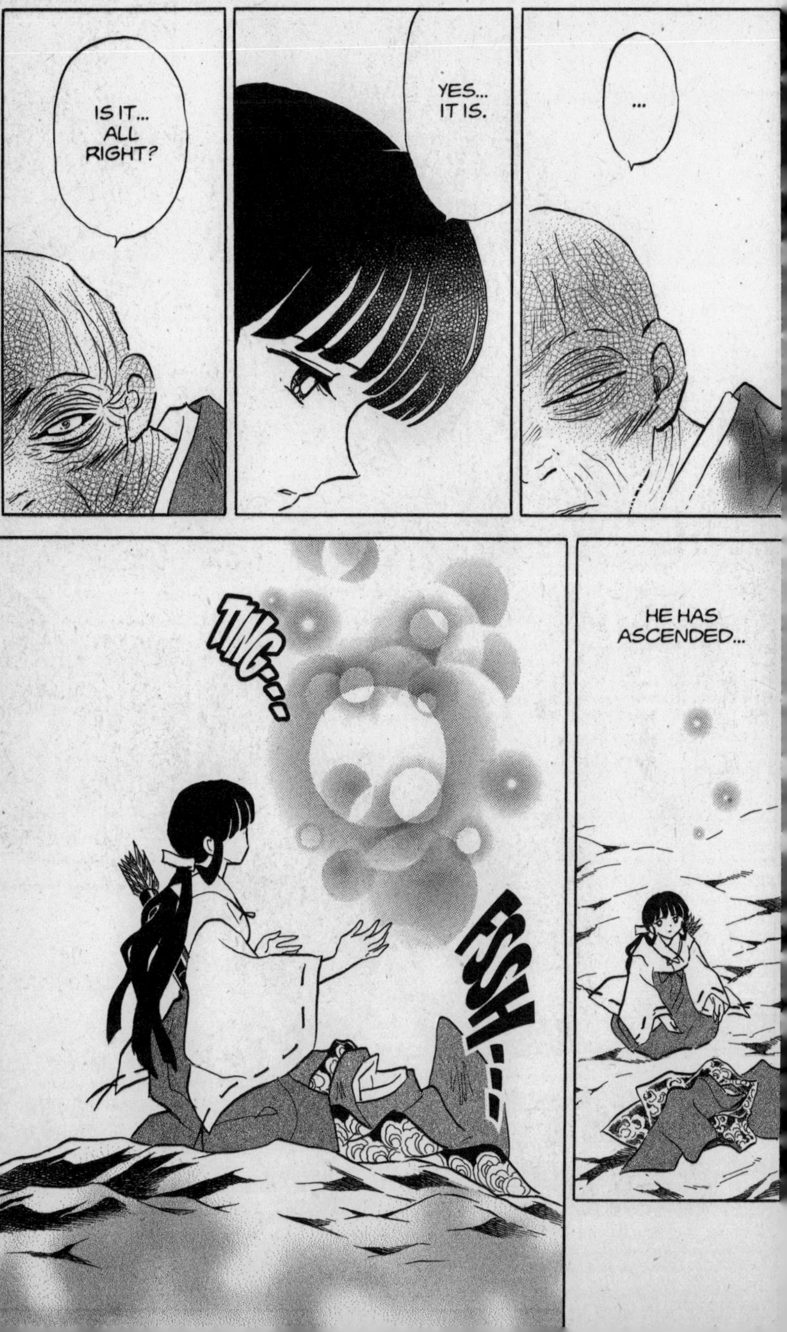
IS IT... ALL RIGHT?
YES... IT IS.
...
TING...
FSSH...
HE HAS ASCENDED...

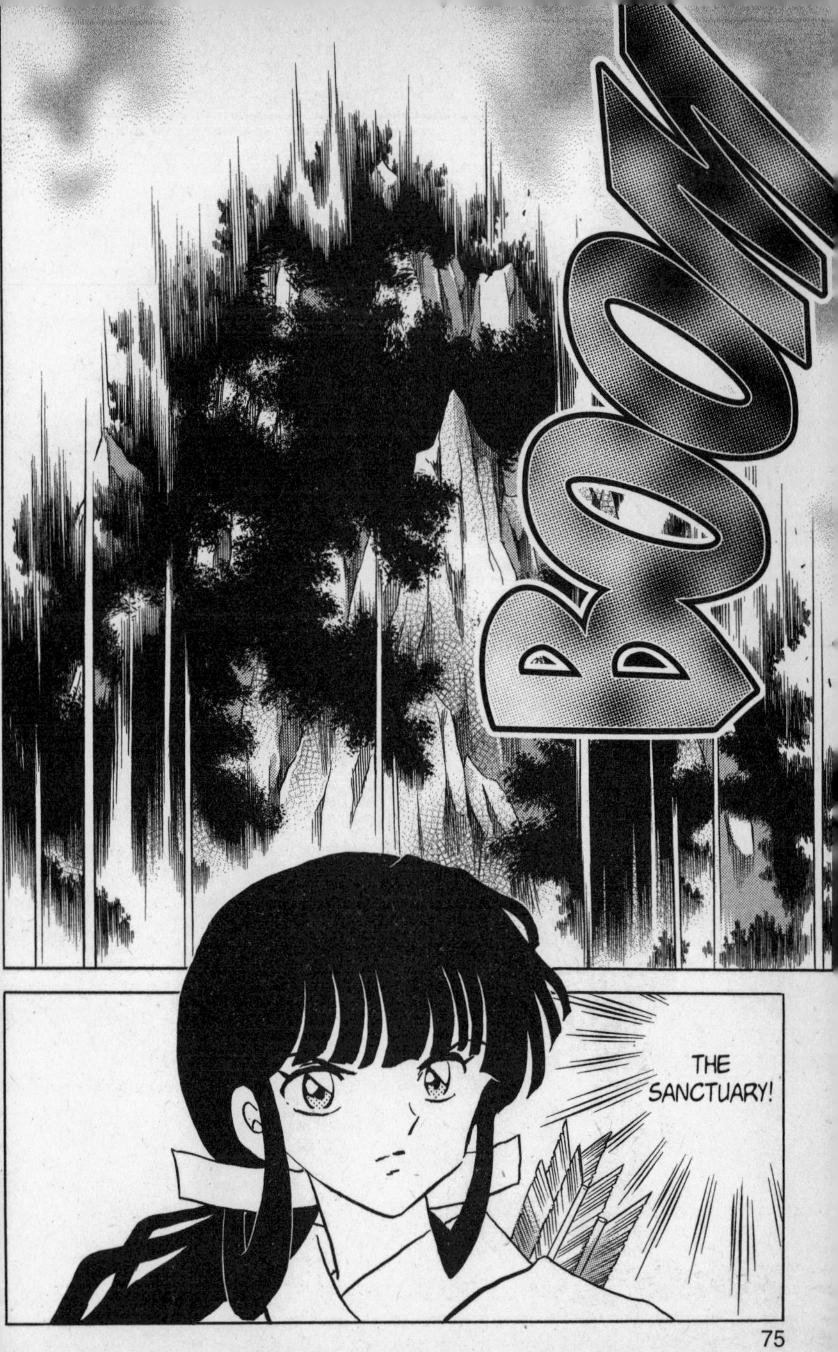
BOOM
THE SANCTUARY!

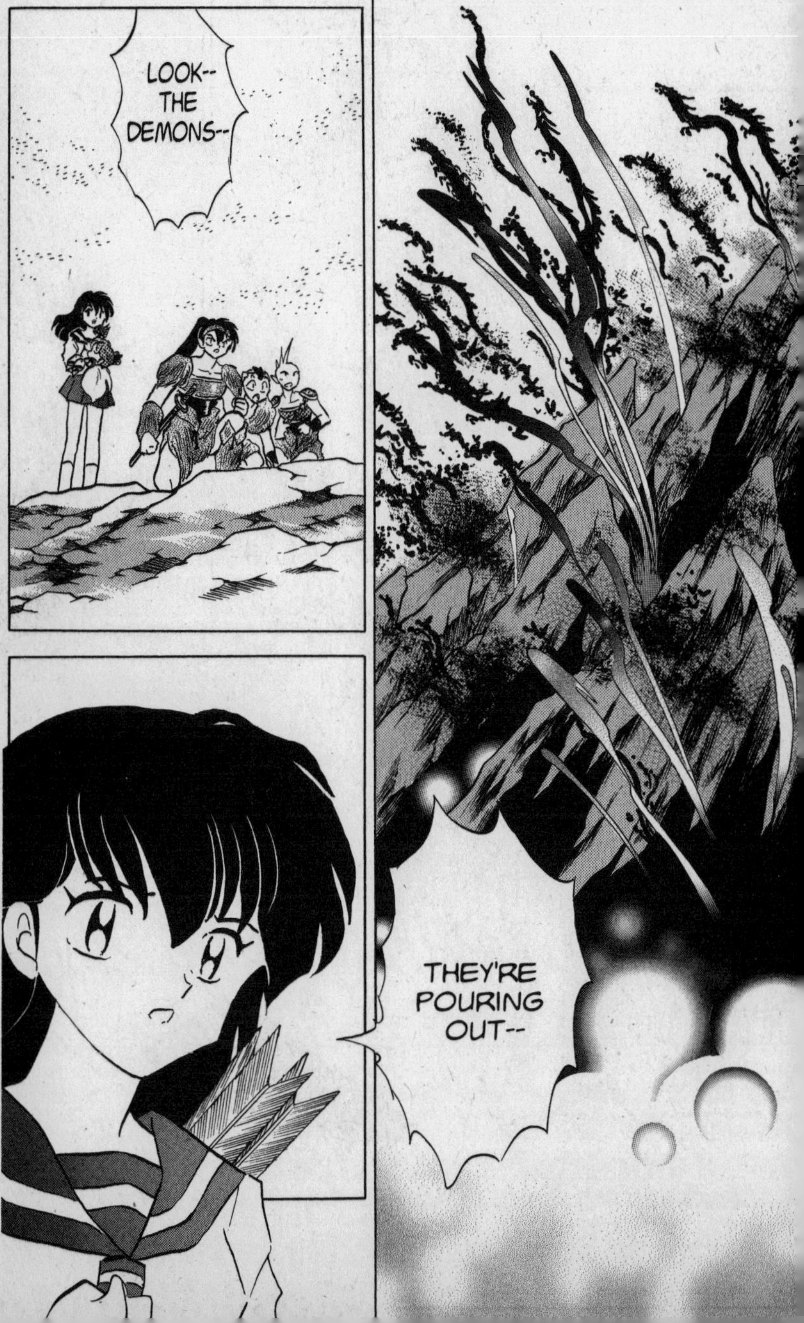
LOOK--
THE
DEMONS--
THEY'RE
POURING
OUT--

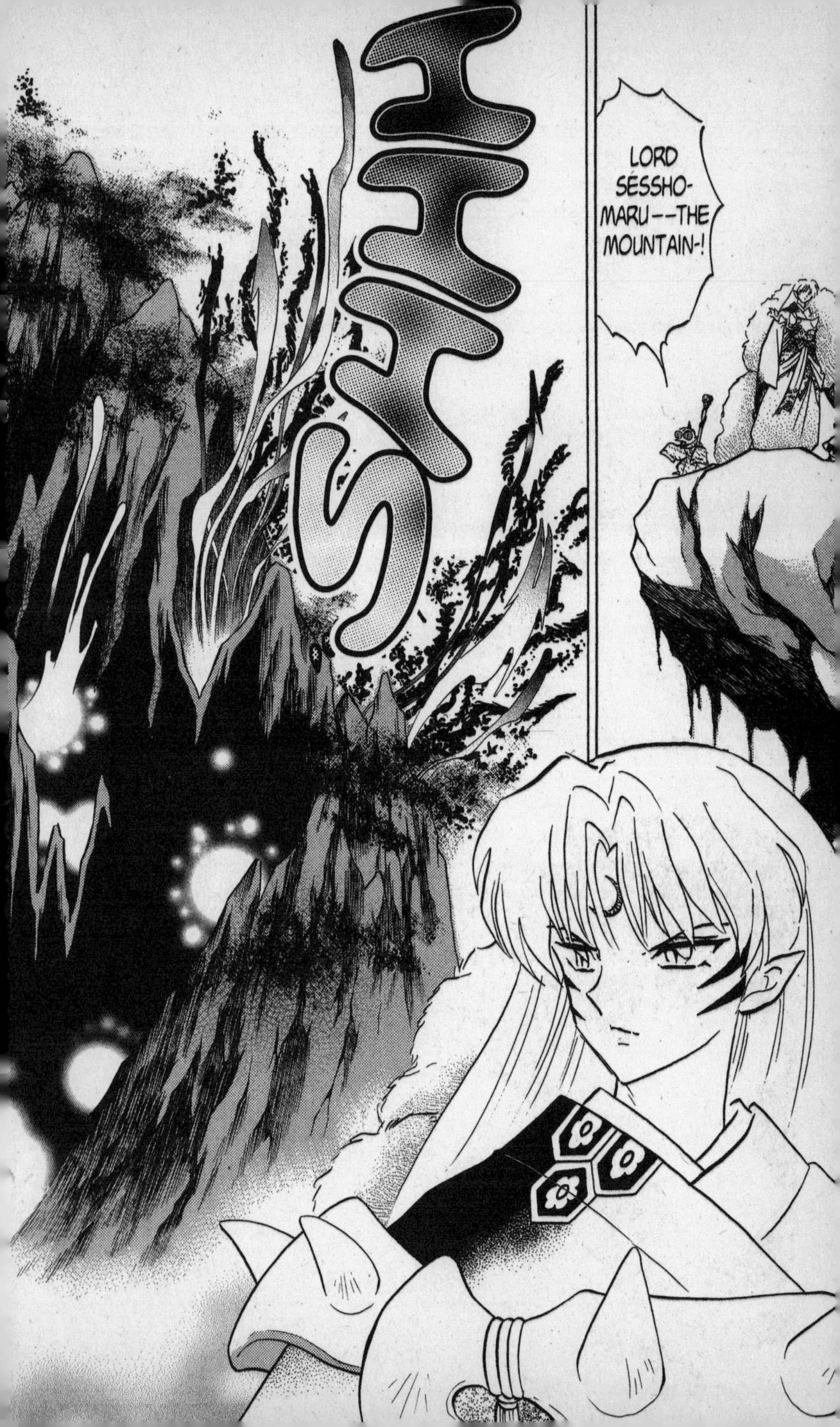
LORD SESSHO-MARU--THE MOUNTAIN-!

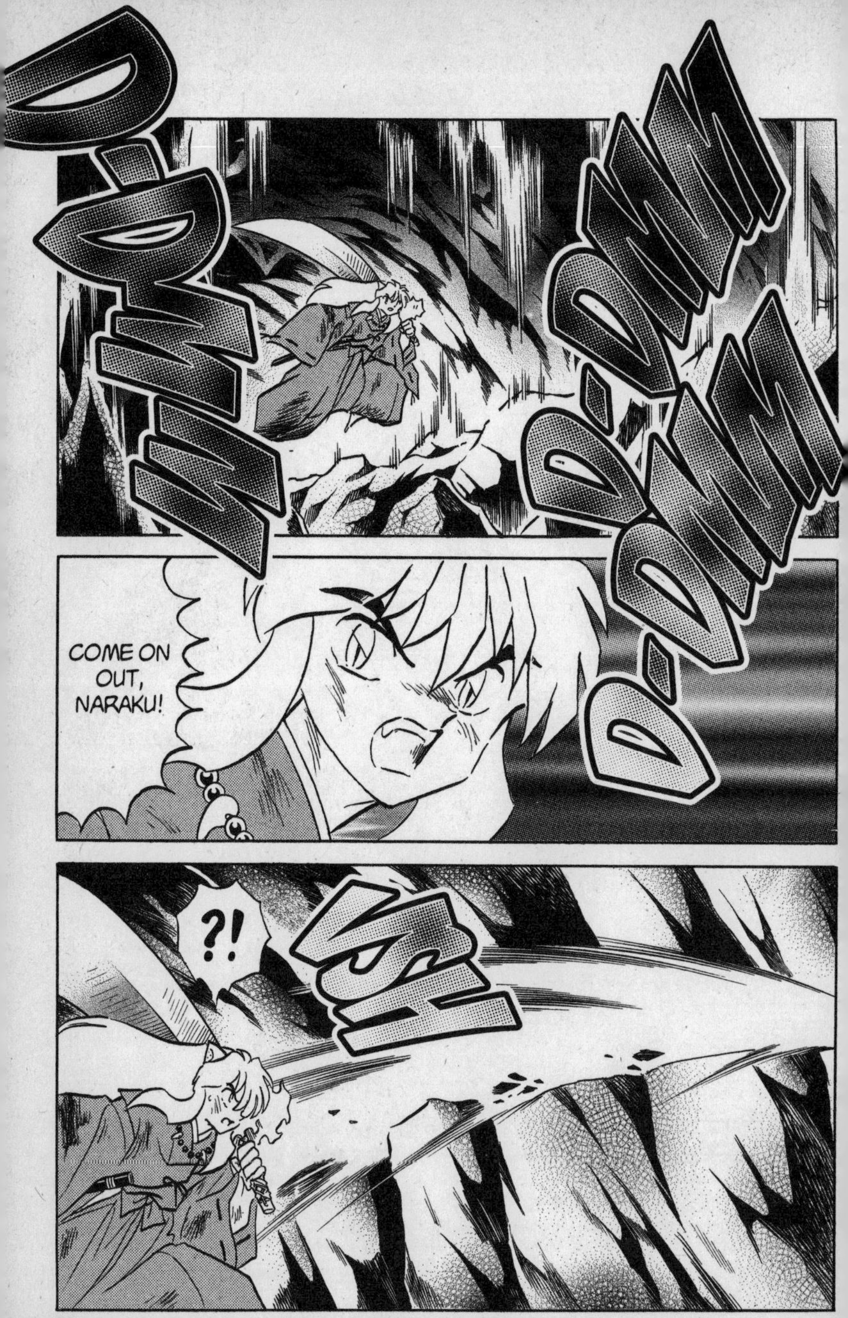
COME ON OUT, NARAKU!
?!

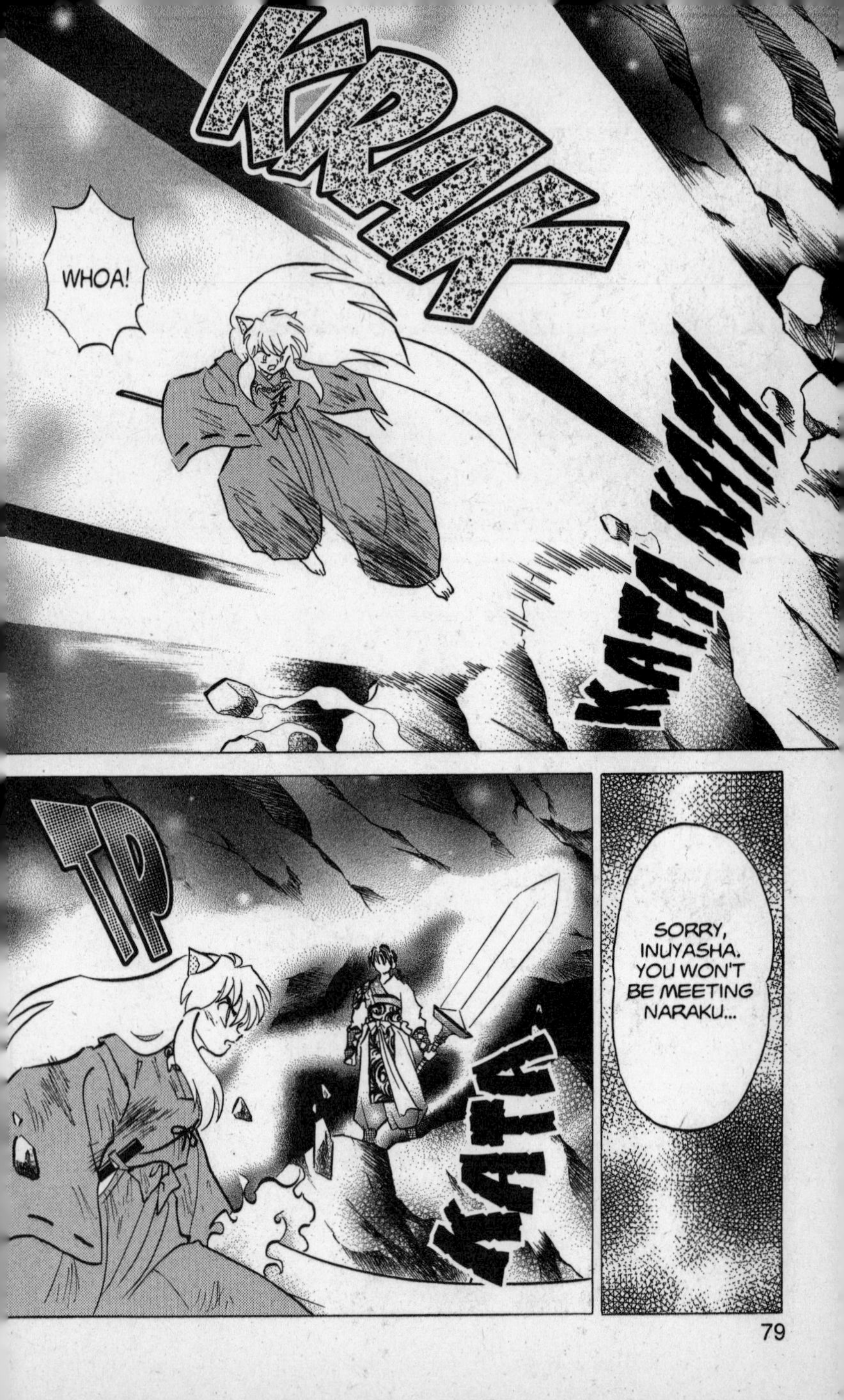
KRAK
WHOA!
KATA KATA
TP
KATA
SORRY, INUYASHA. YOU WON'T BE MEETING NARAKU...

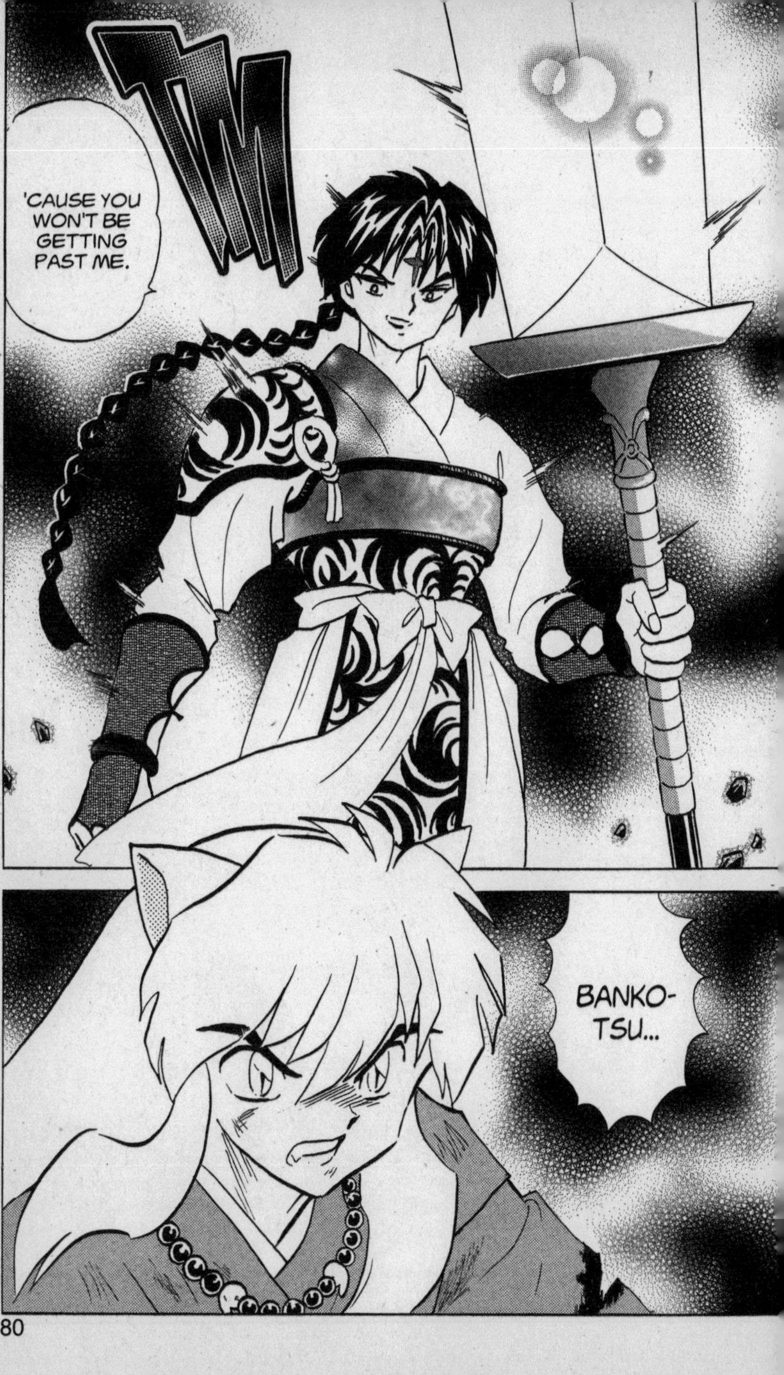
TM
'CAUSE YOU WON'T BE GETTING PAST ME.
BANKO-TSU...

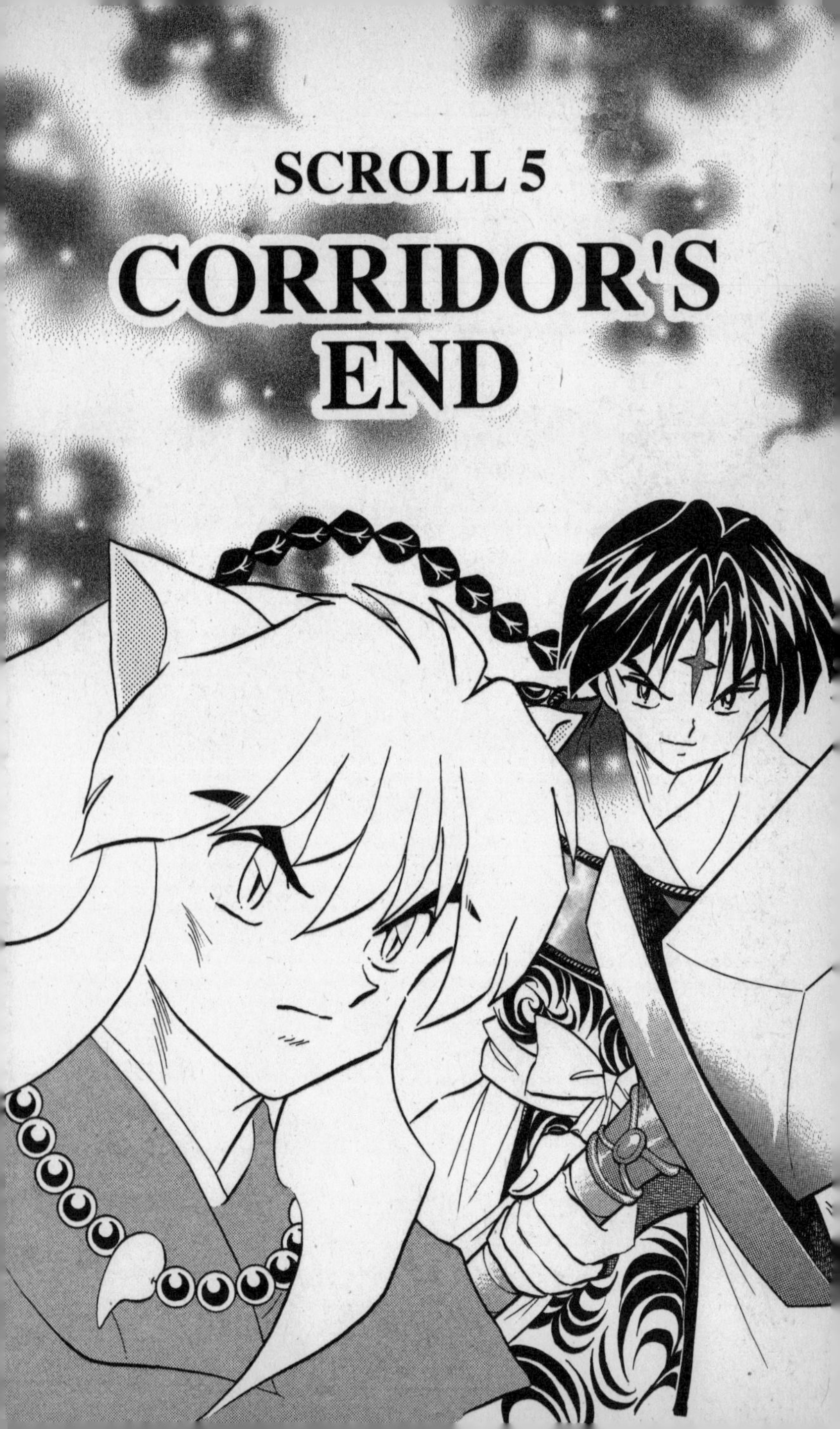
SCROLL 5
CORRIDOR'S END

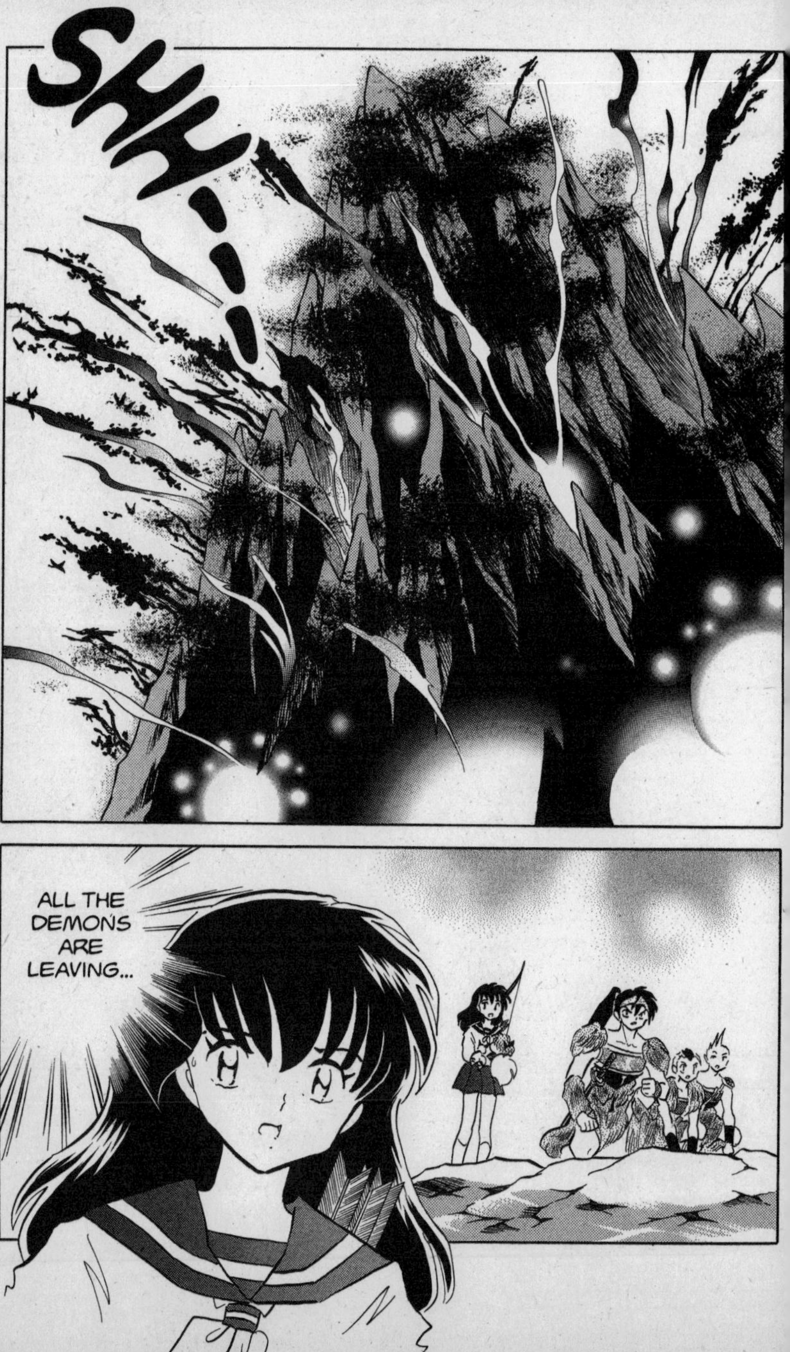
SHH...
ALL THE DEMONS ARE LEAVING...

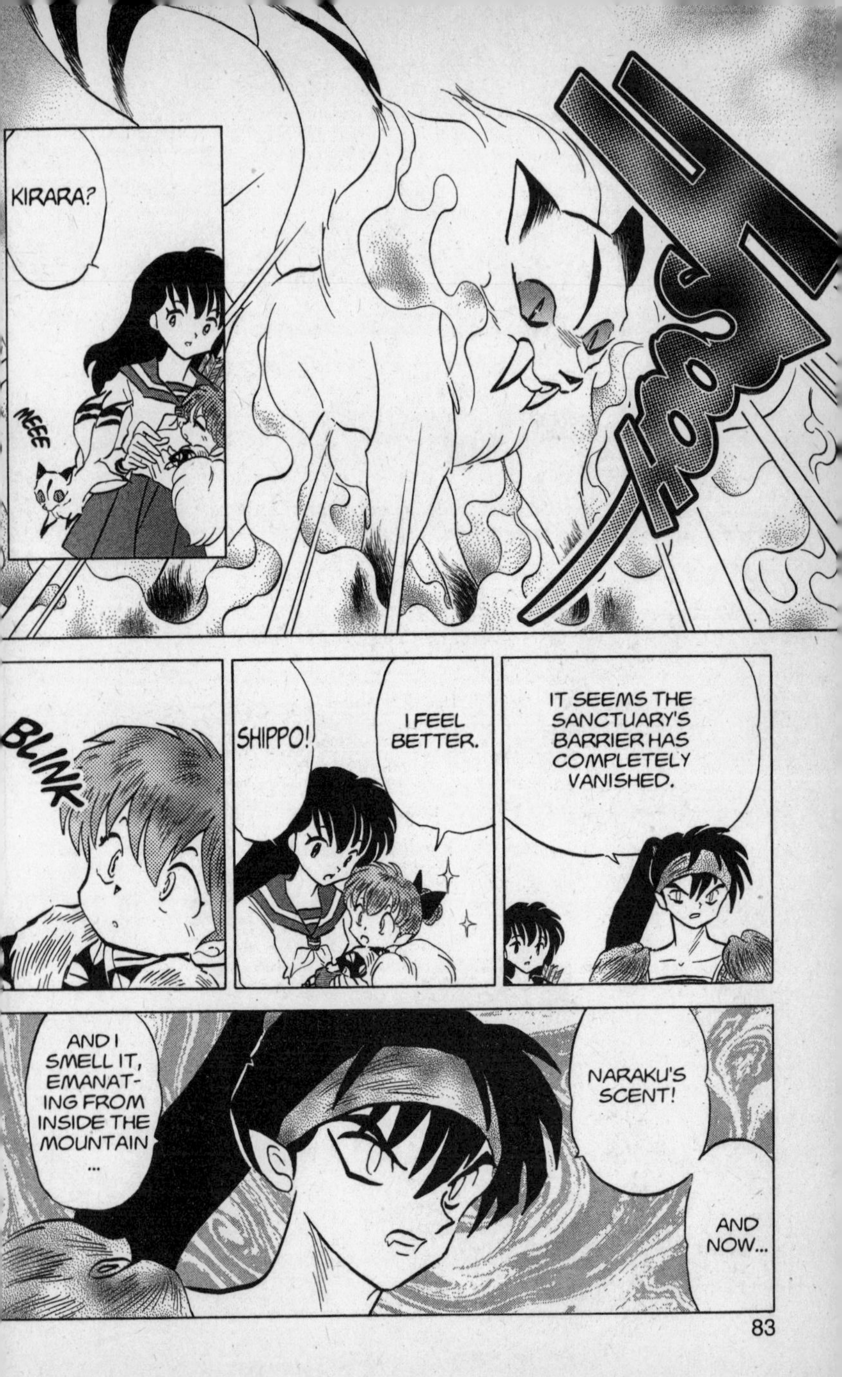
KIRARA?
MEEE
WHOOSH
BLINK
SHIPPO!
I FEEL BETTER.
IT SEEMS THE SANCTUARY'S BARRIER HAS COMPLETELY VANISHED.
AND I SMELL IT, EMANATING FROM INSIDE THE MOUNTAIN...
NARAKU'S SCENT!
AND NOW...

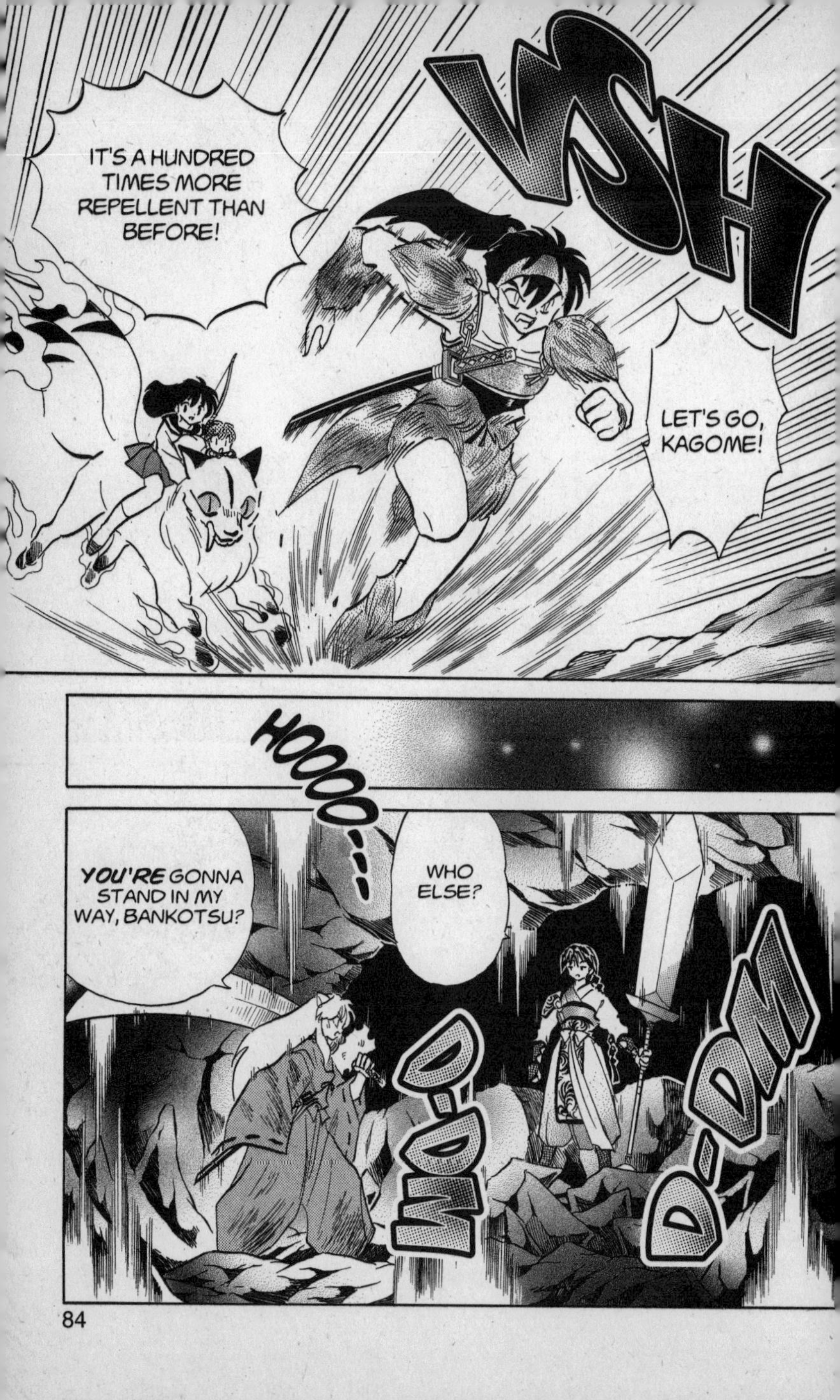

IT'S A HUNDRED TIMES MORE REPELLENT THAN BEFORE!
VSSH
LET'S GO, KAGOME!
HOOOO...
YOU'RE GONNA STAND IN MY WAY, BANKOTSU?
WHO ELSE?
D-DMM
D-DMM

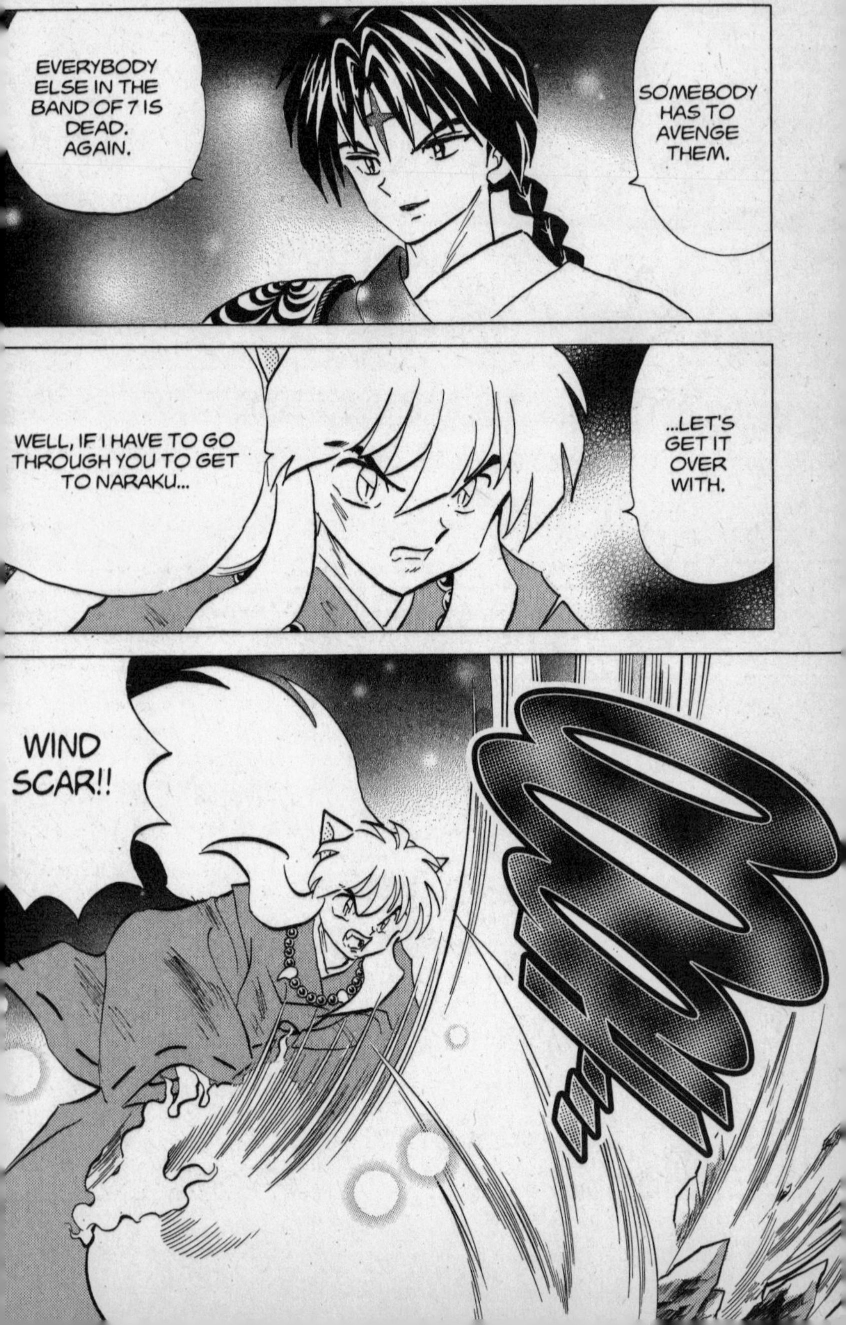
EVERYBODY ELSE IN THE BAND OF 7 IS DEAD. AGAIN.
SOMEBODY HAS TO AVENGE THEM.
WELL, IF I HAVE TO GO THROUGH YOU TO GET TO NARAKU...
...LET'S GET IT OVER WITH.
WIND SCAR!!

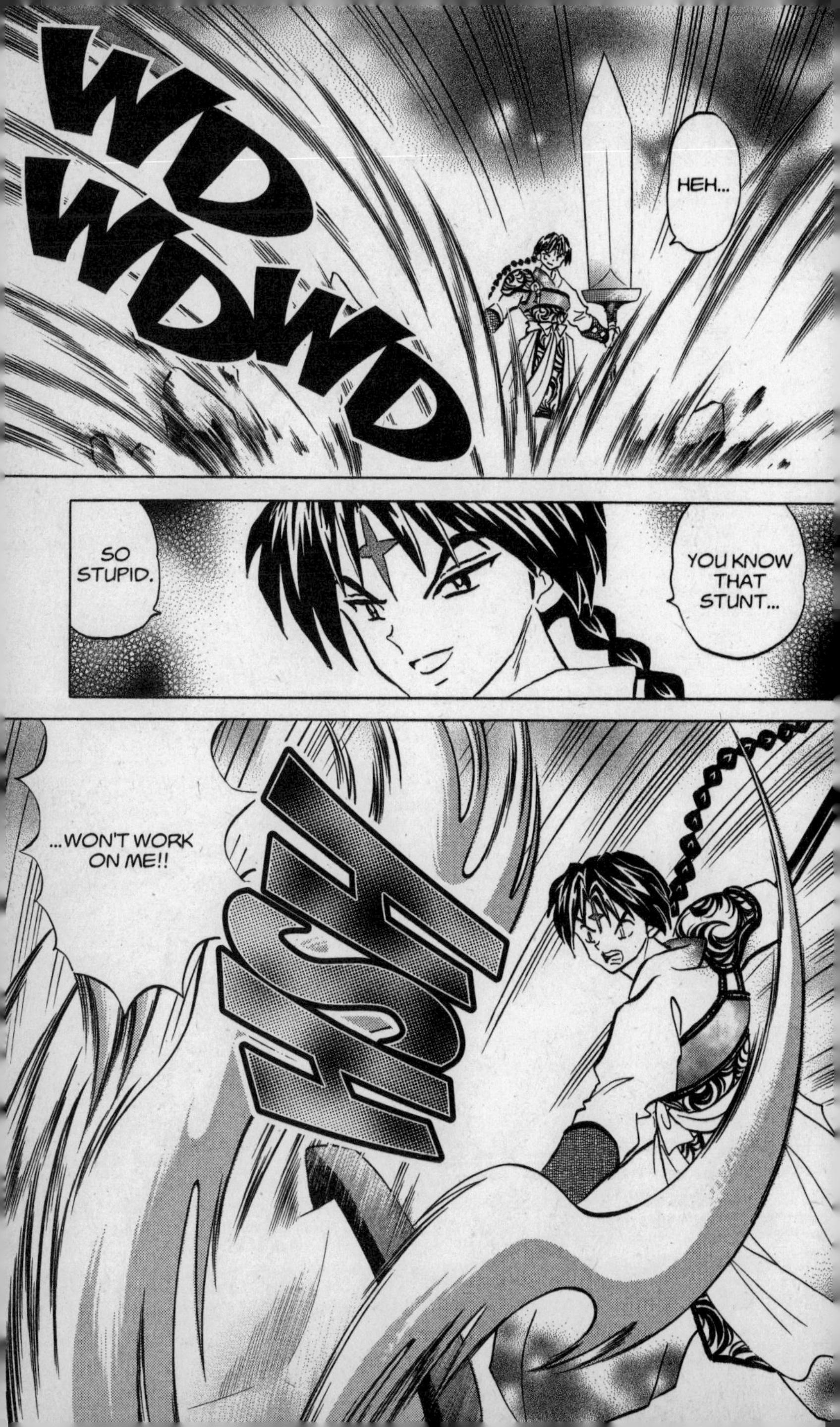
WD
WWDWD
HEH...
SO STUPID.
YOU KNOW THAT STUNT...
...WON'T WORK ON ME!!

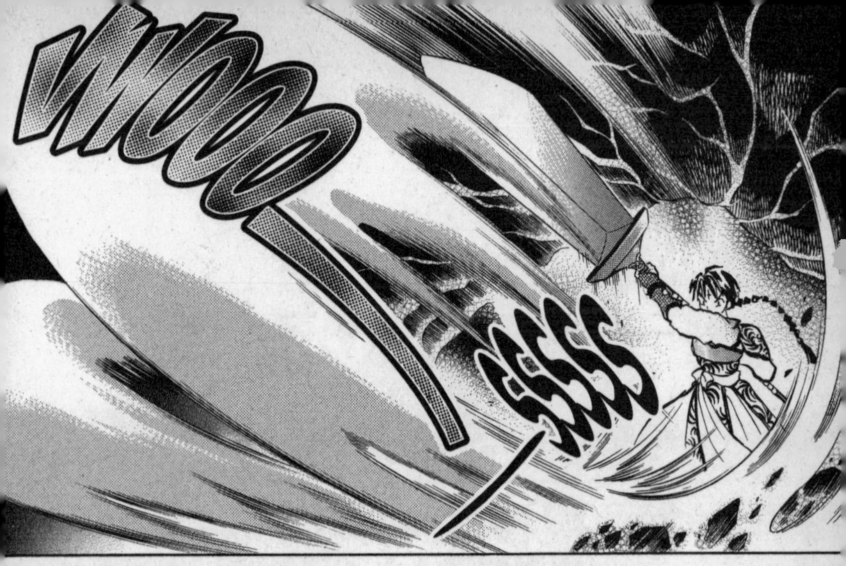

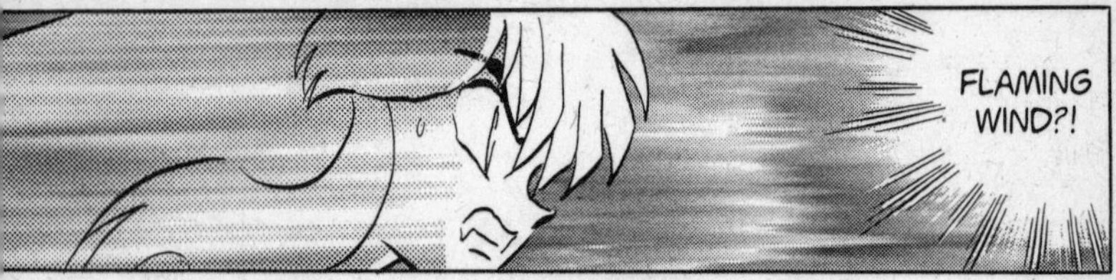

FLAMING WIND?!

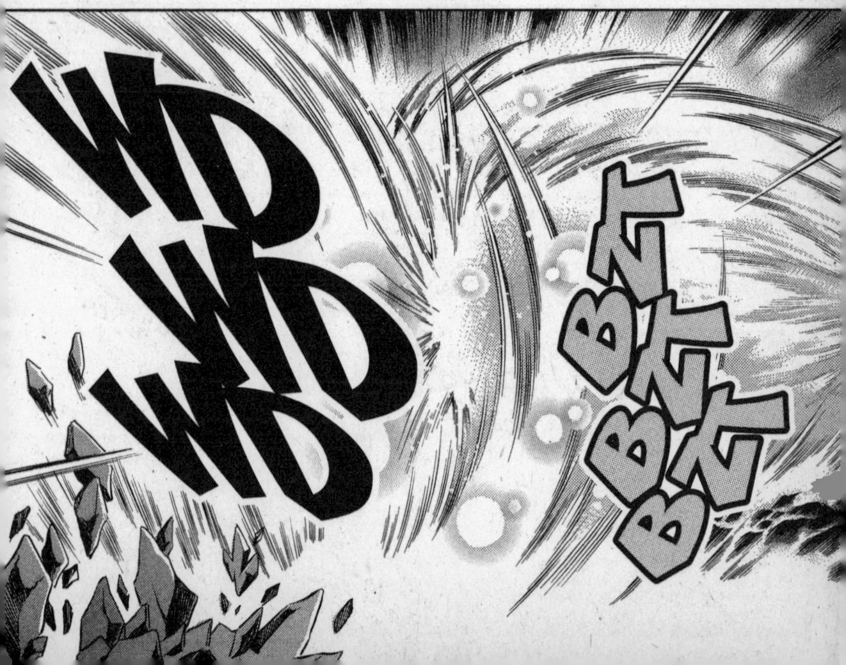

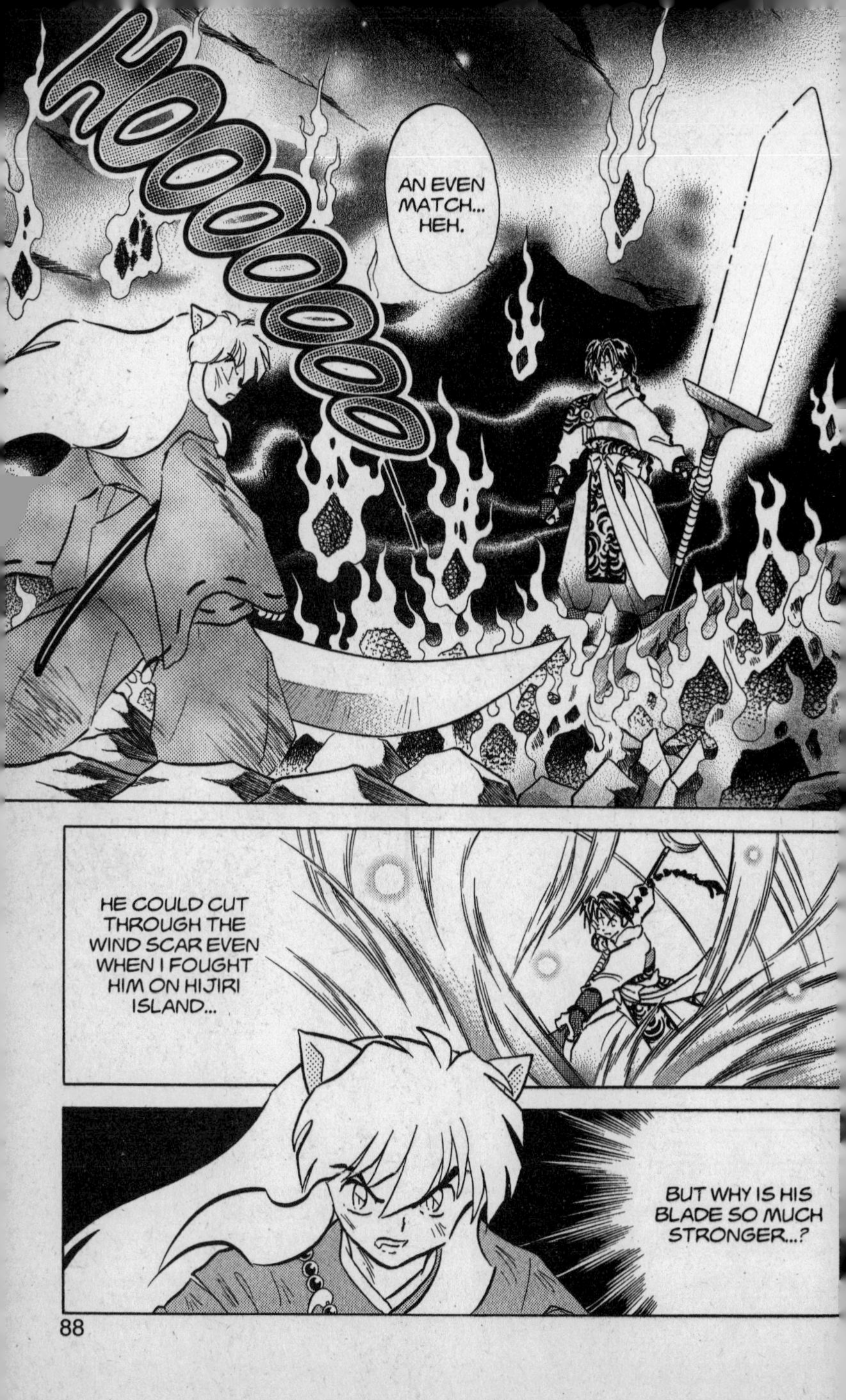
HOOOOOOOO
AN EVEN MATCH... HEH.
HE COULD CUT THROUGH THE WIND SCAR EVEN WHEN I FOUGHT HIM ON HIJIRI ISLAND...
BUT WHY IS HIS BLADE SO MUCH STRONGER...?

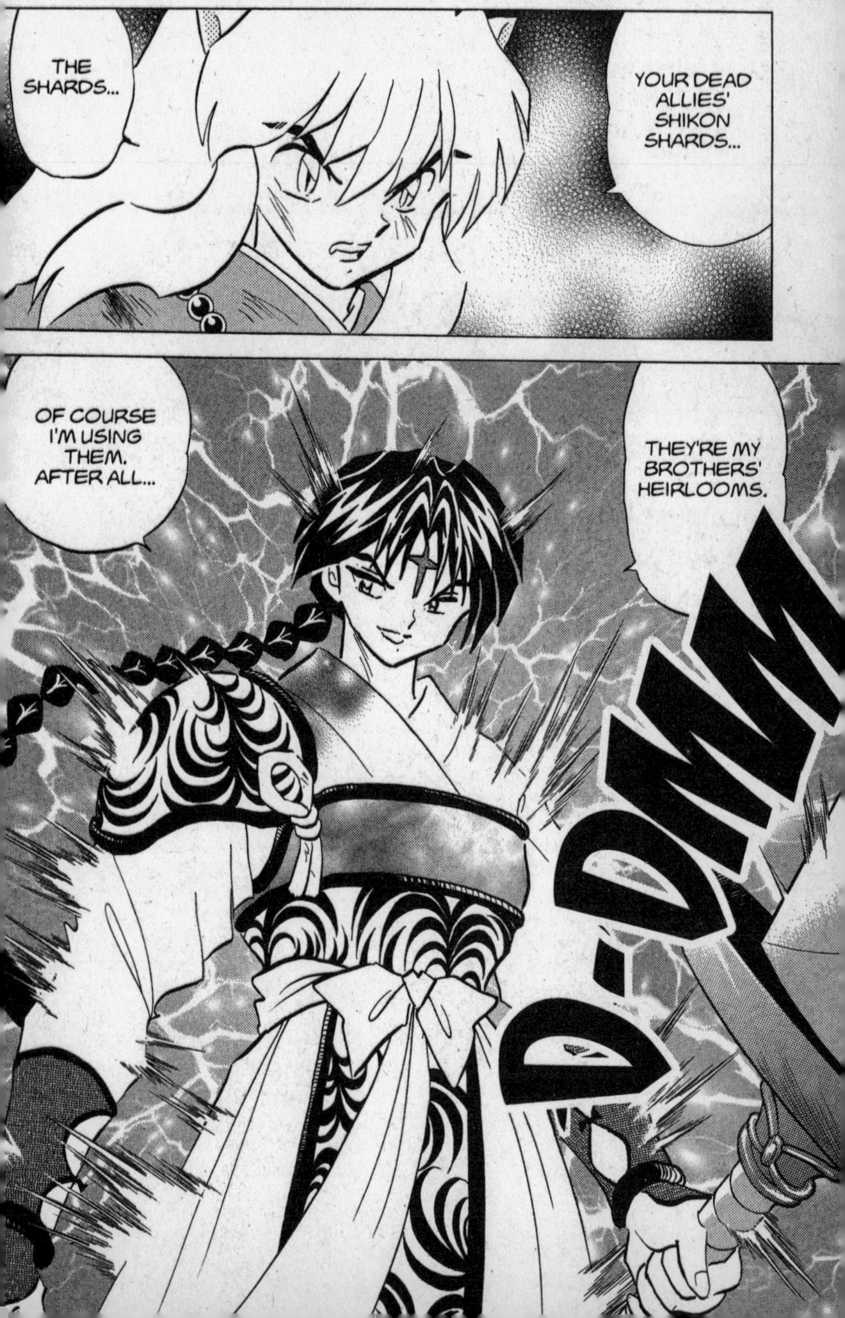
THE SHARDS...
YOUR DEAD ALLIES' SHIKON SHARDS...
OF COURSE I'M USING THEM. AFTER ALL...
THEY'RE MY BROTHERS' HEIRLOOMS.
D-DMM

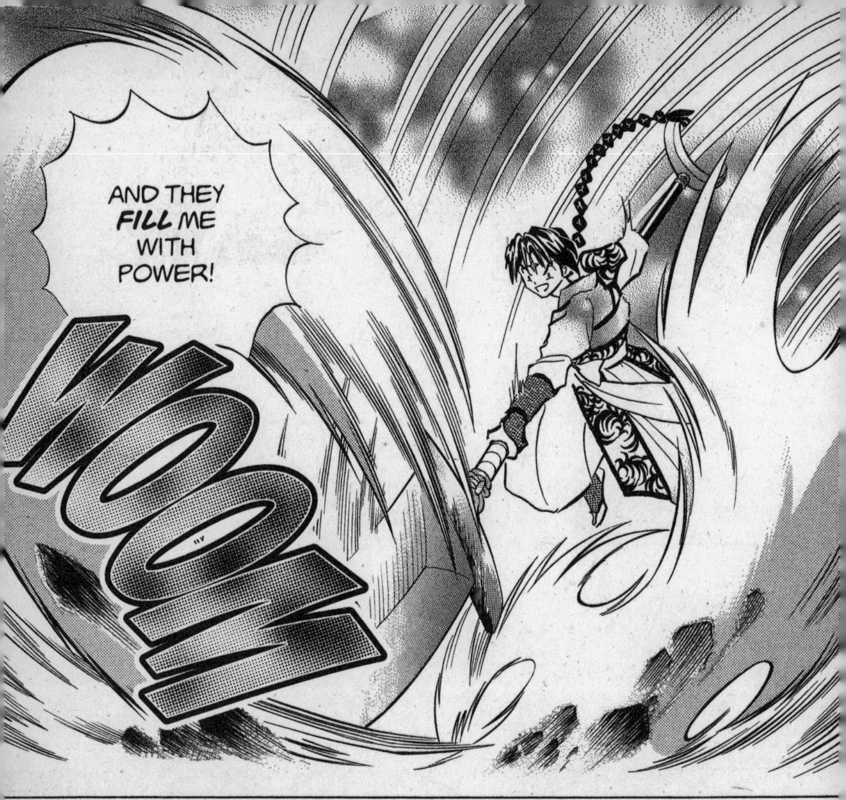
AND THEY FILL ME WITH POWER!

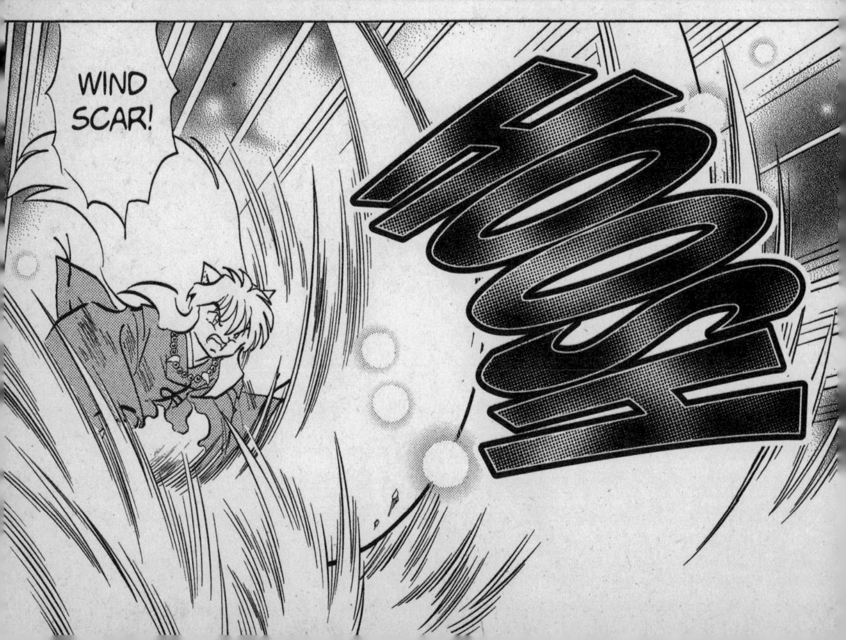
WIND SCAR!

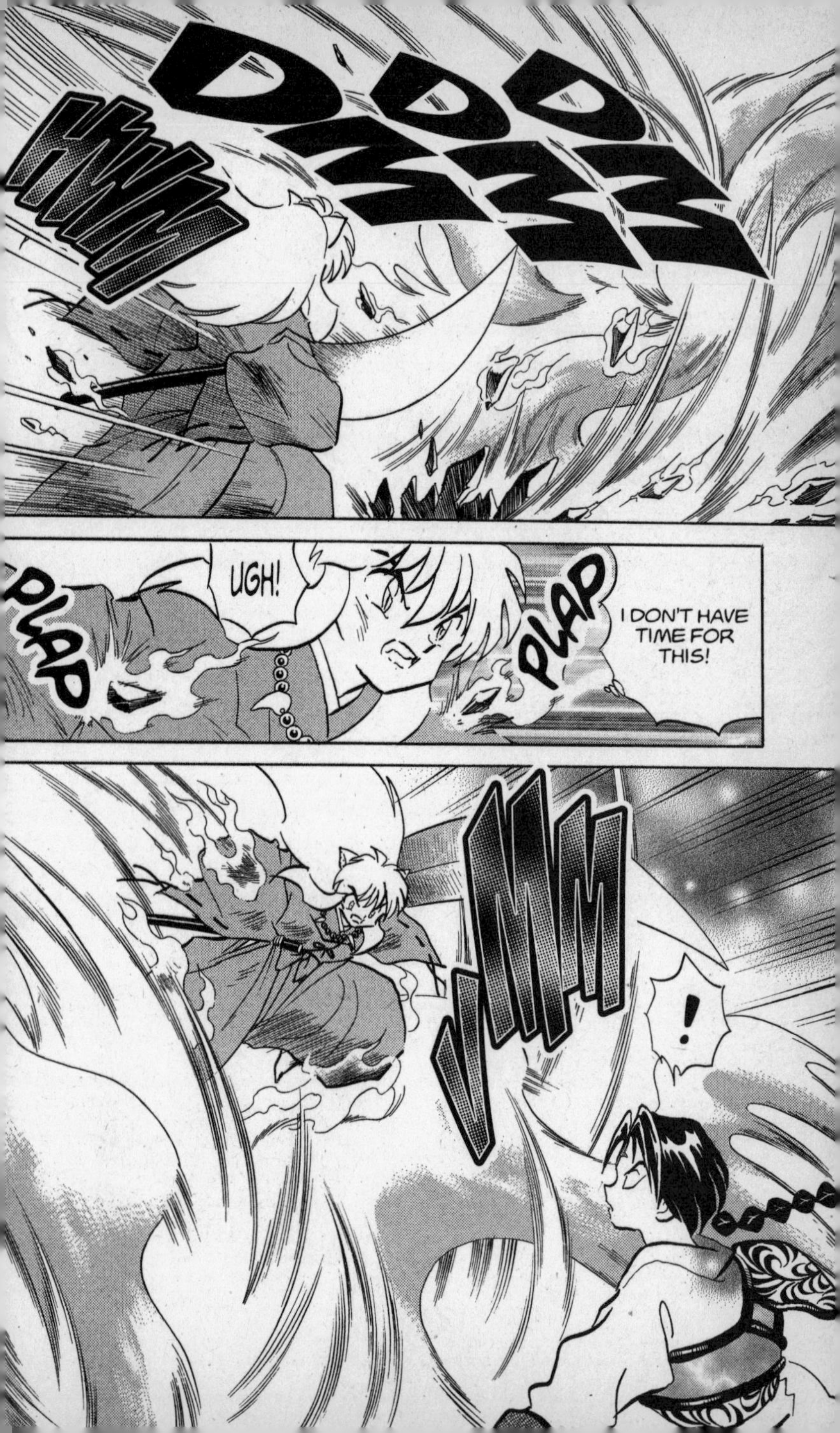
HWMM
PLAP
UGH!
PLAP
I DON'T HAVE TIME FOR THIS!
!

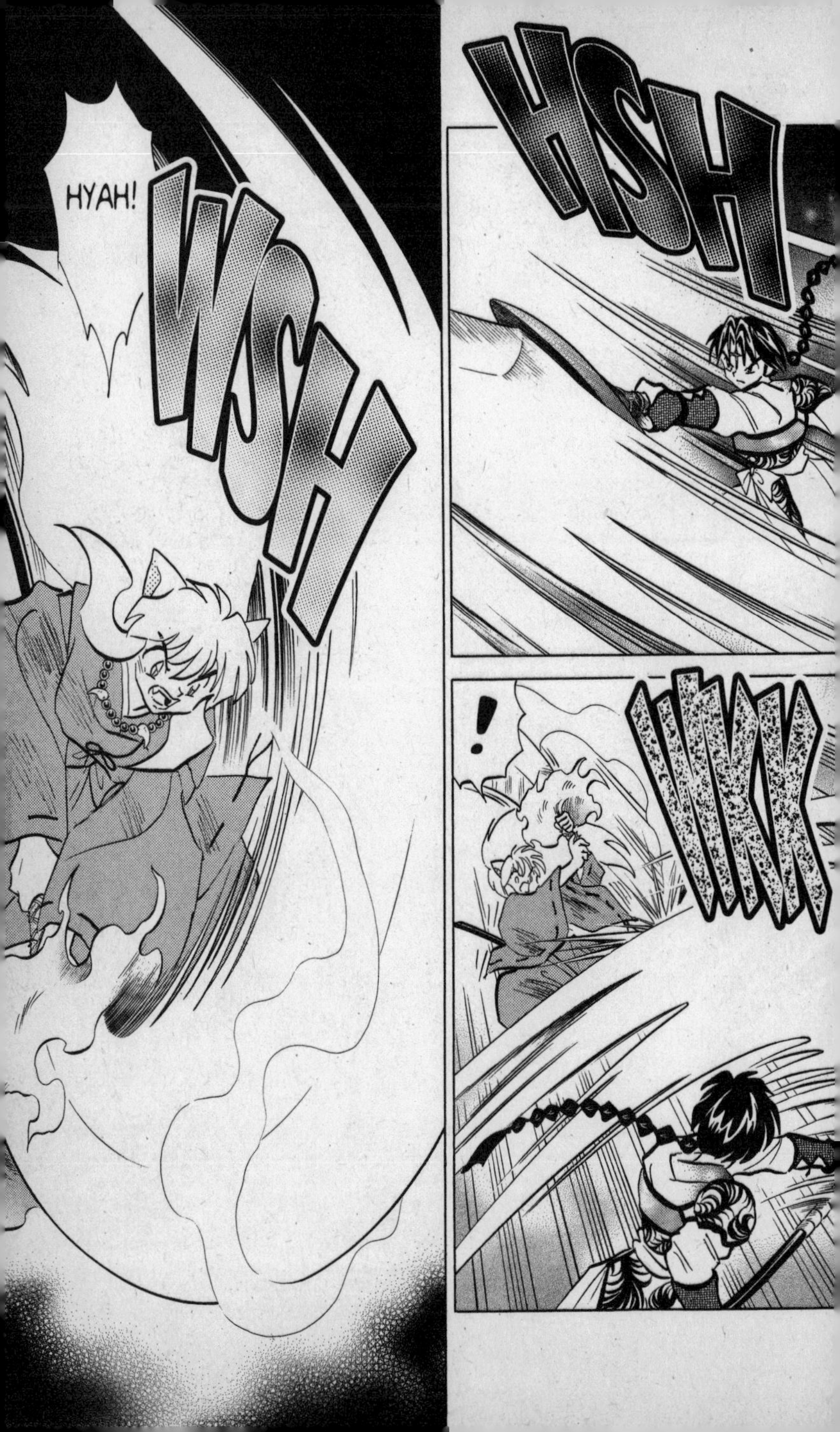
HYAH!
WSH
HSH
!
WKK

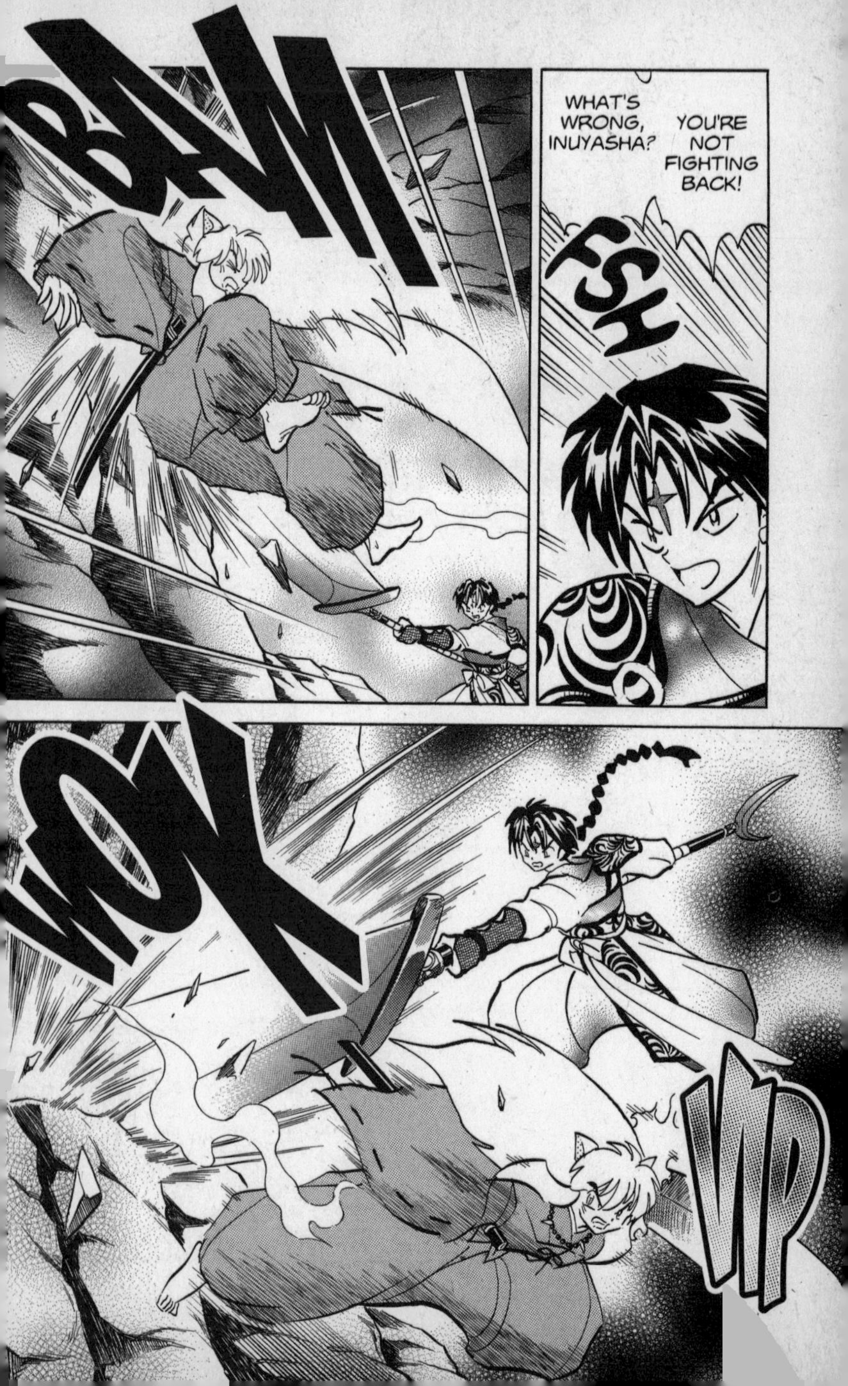
BAM
WHAT'S WRONG, INUYASHA?
YOU'RE NOT FIGHTING BACK!
FSH

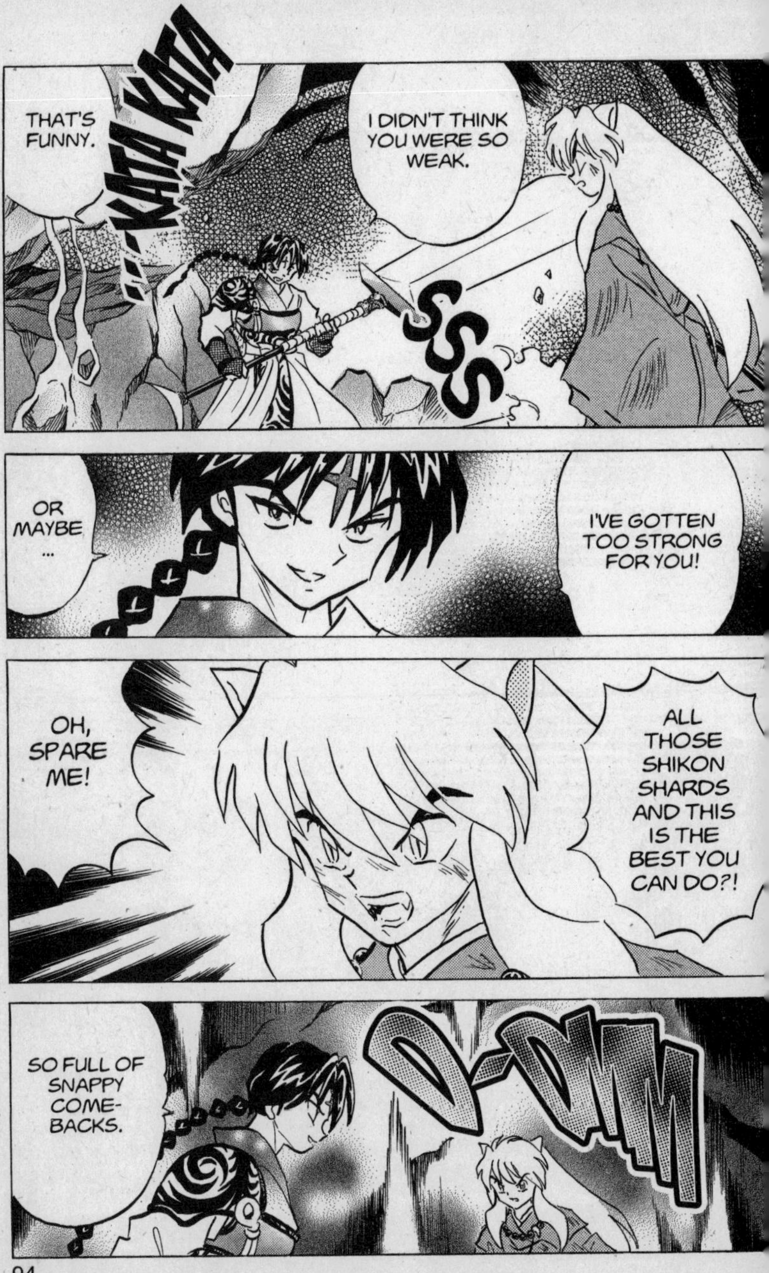
THAT'S FUNNY.
...KATA KATA
I DIDN'T THINK YOU WERE SO WEAK.
SSS
OR MAYBE ...
I'VE GOTTEN TOO STRONG FOR YOU!
OH, SPARE ME!
ALL THOSE SHIKON SHARDS AND THIS IS THE BEST YOU CAN DO?!
SO FULL OF SNAPPY COME-BACKS.
D-DMM

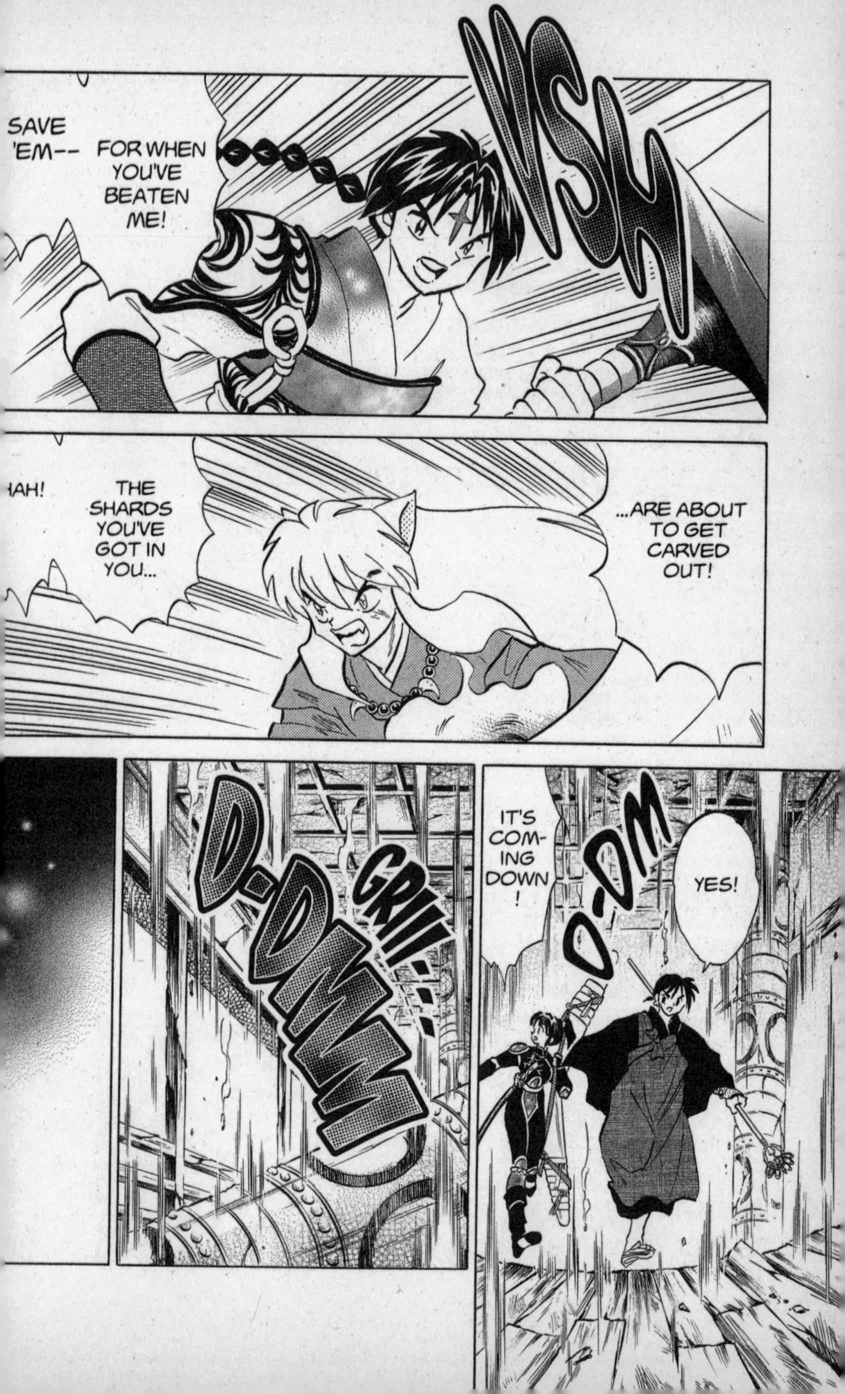
SAVE 'EM--
FOR WHEN YOU'VE BEATEN ME!
VSH
AH!
THE SHARDS YOU'VE GOT IN YOU...
...ARE ABOUT TO GET CARVED OUT!
D-DMMM!
GRII...
IT'S COM-ING DOWN!
D-DM
YES!

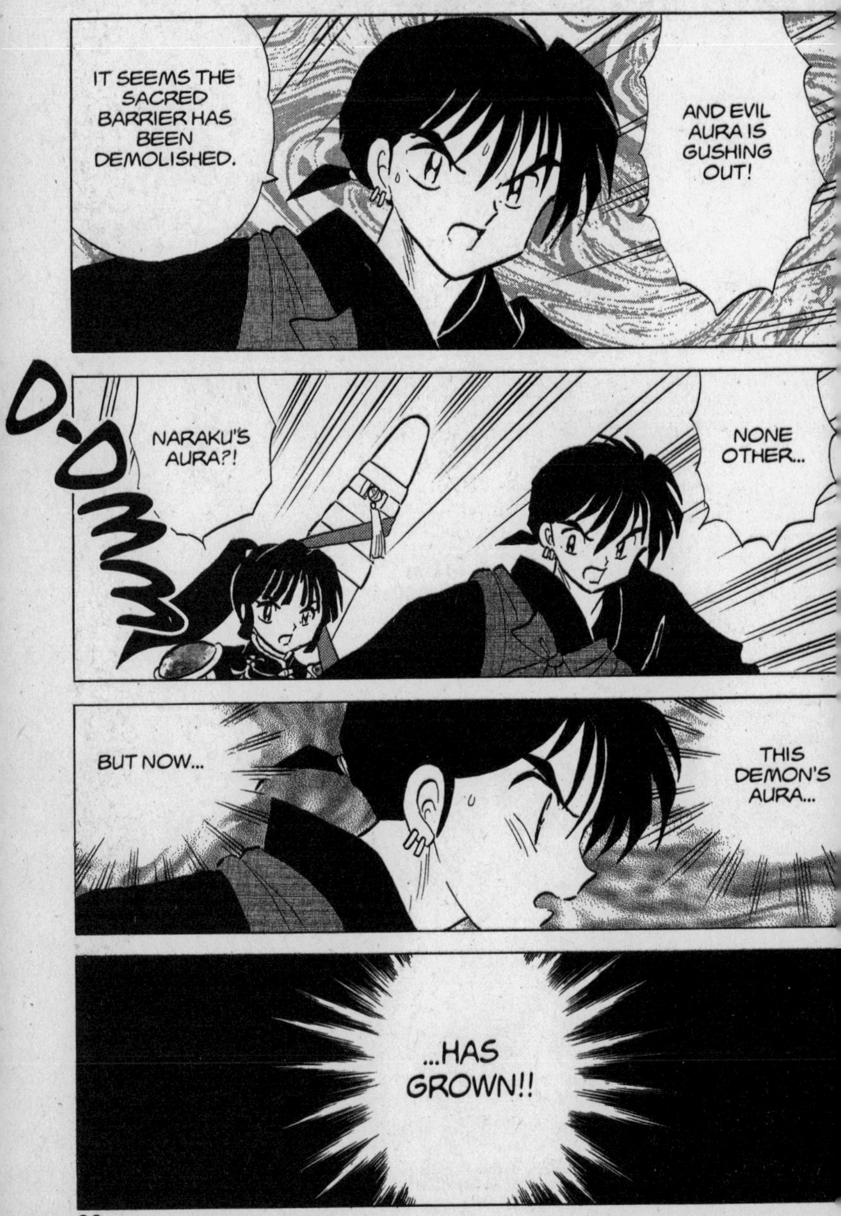

IT SEEMS THE SACRED BARRIER HAS BEEN DEMOLISHED.
AND EVIL AURA IS GUSHING OUT!
D-DMM
NARAKU'S AURA?!
NONE OTHER...
BUT NOW...
THIS DEMON'S AURA...
...HAS GROWN!!

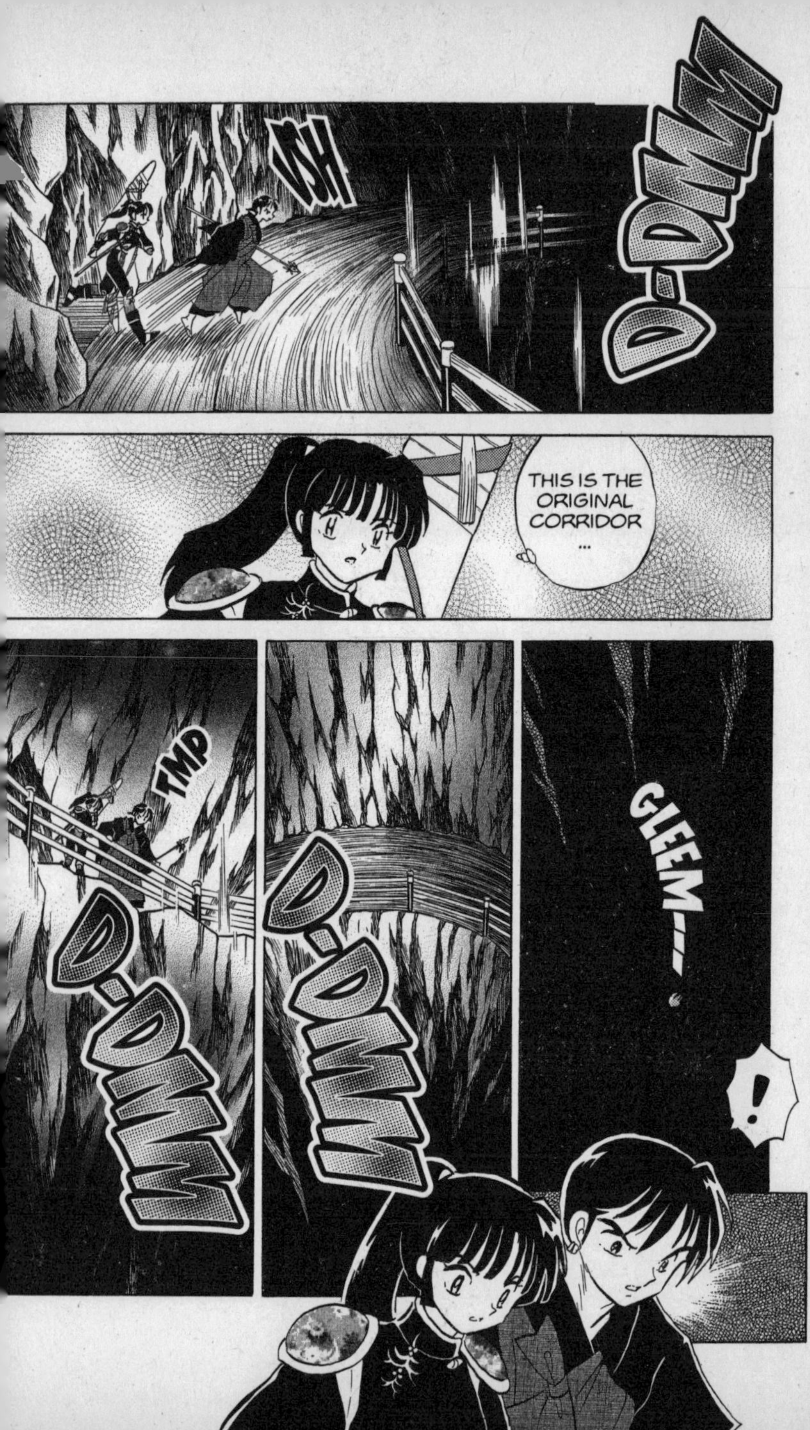
VSH
D-DWMM
THIS IS THE ORIGINAL CORRIDOR ...
TMP
D-DWMM
D-DWMM
GLEEM...
!

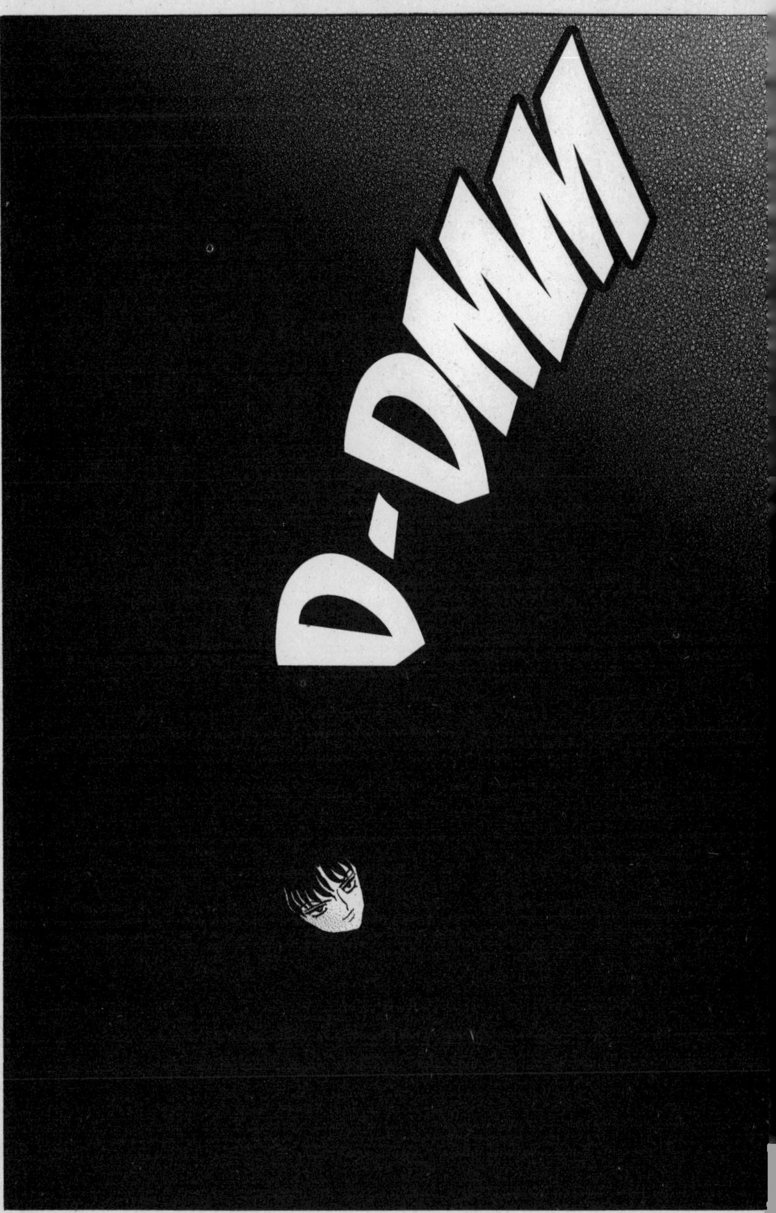
D-DMM

SCROLL 6
THE TWO AURAS

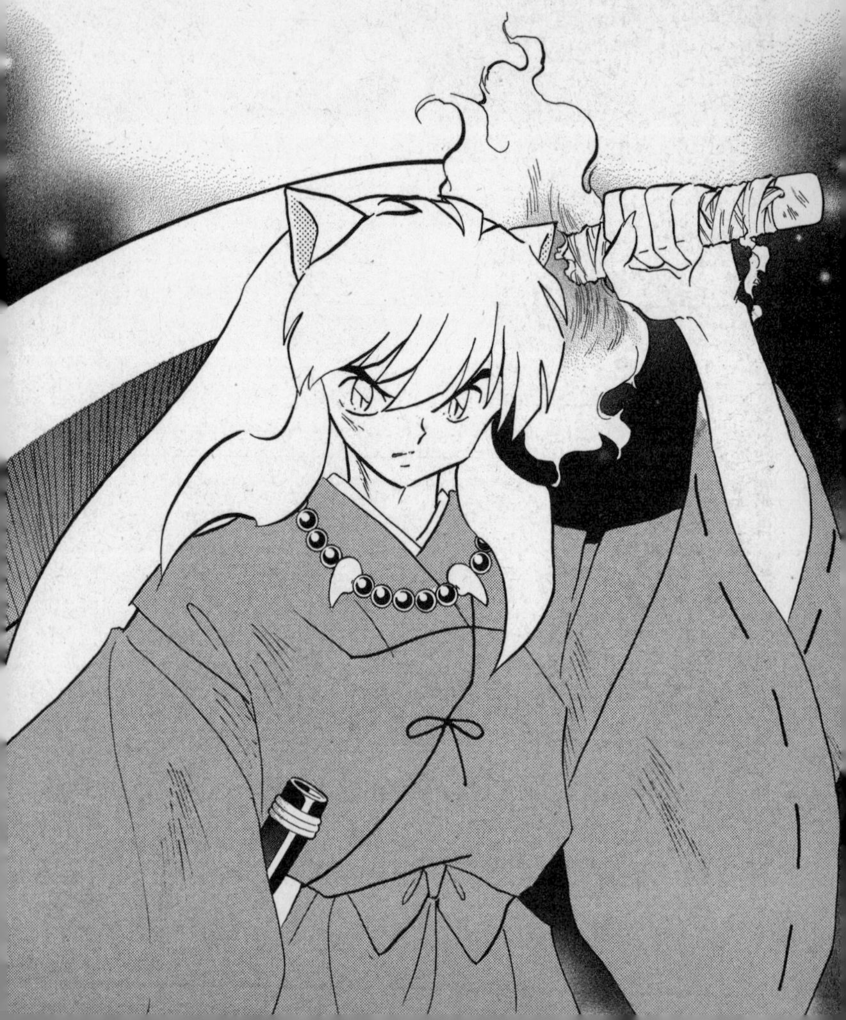

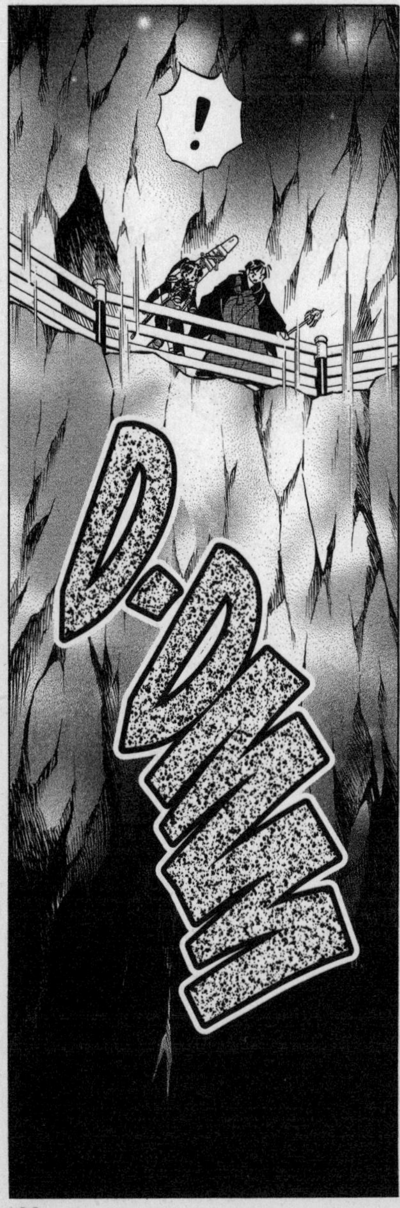
!
D-DMM
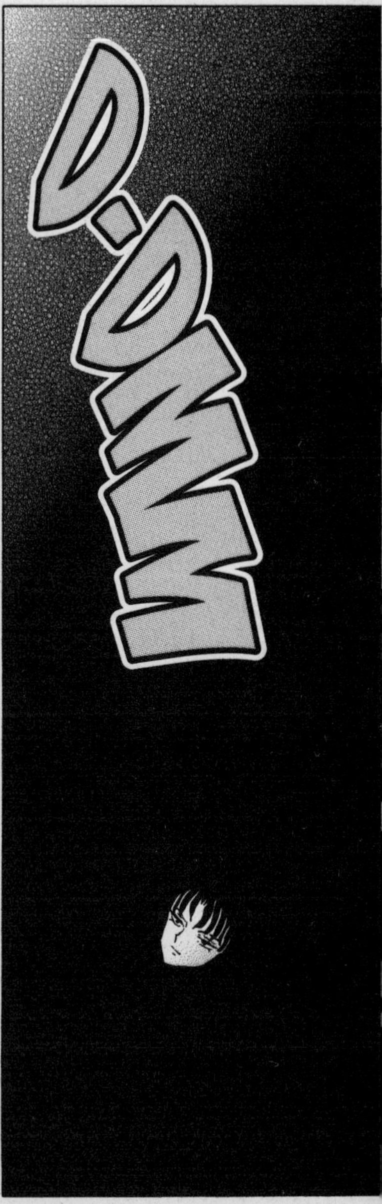
D-DMM

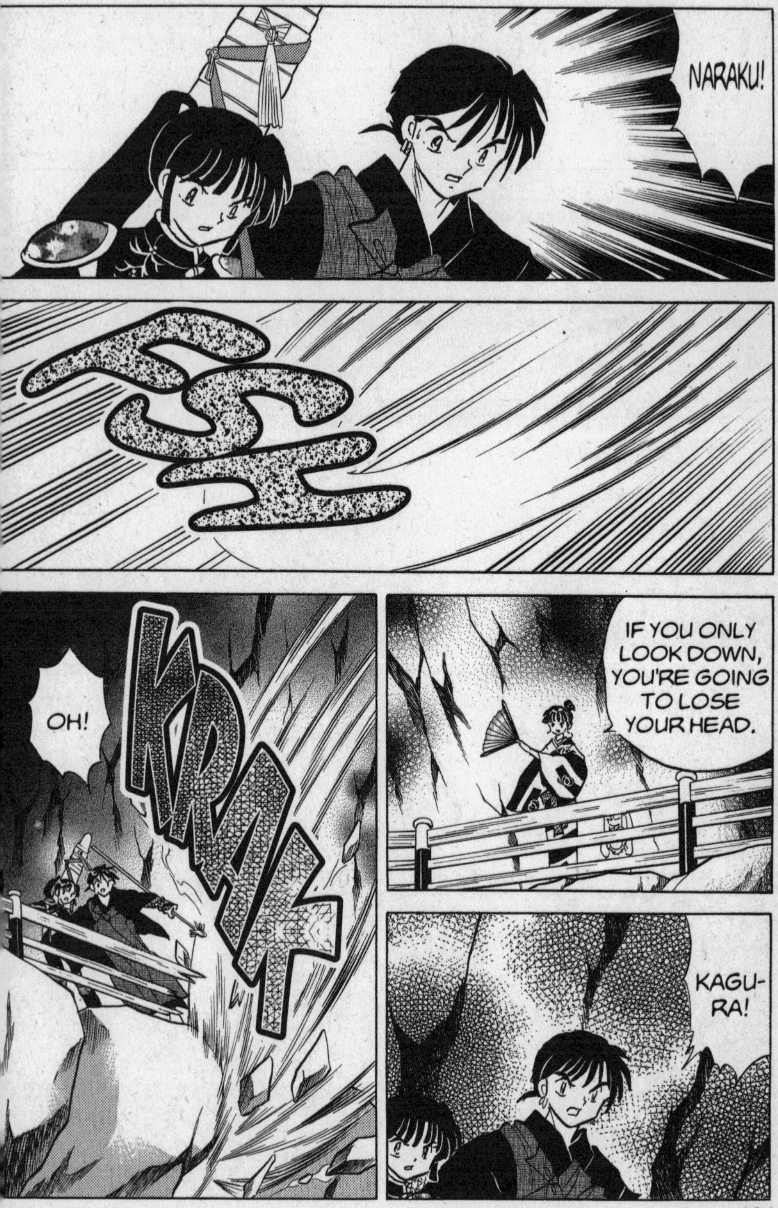
NARAKU!
FSSH
OH!
KRAK
IF YOU ONLY LOOK DOWN, YOU'RE GOING TO LOSE YOUR HEAD.
KAGU-RA!

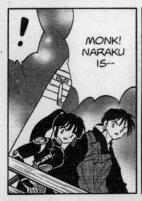

MONK! NARAKU IS--

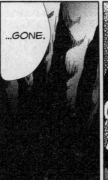

...GONE.

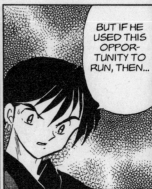

BUT IF HE USED THIS OPPORTUNITY TO RUN, THEN...

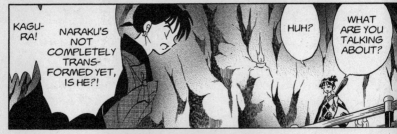

KAGURA! NARAKU'S NOT COMPLETELY TRANSFORMED YET, IS HE?!

HUH?

WHAT ARE YOU TALKING ABOUT?

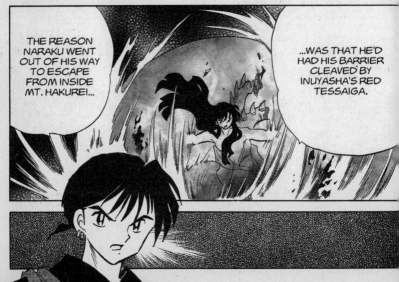

THE REASON NARAKU WENT OUT OF HIS WAY TO ESCAPE FROM INSIDE MT. HAKUREI...

...WAS THAT HE'D HAD HIS BARRIER CLEAVED BY INUYASHA'S RED TESSAIGA.

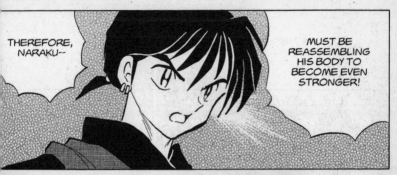

MUST BE REASSEMBLING HIS BODY TO BECOME EVEN STRONGER!

THEREFORE, NARAKU--

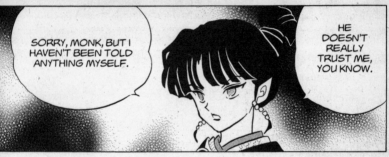

HE DOESN'T REALLY TRUST ME, YOU KNOW.

SORRY, MONK, BUT I HAVEN'T BEEN TOLD ANYTHING MYSELF.

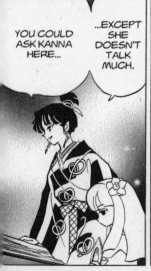

YOU COULD ASK KANNA HERE...

...EXCEPT SHE DOESN'T TALK MUCH.

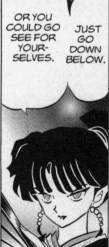

OR YOU COULD GO SEE FOR YOUR-SELVES.

JUST GO DOWN BELOW.

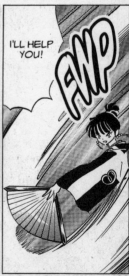

I'LL HELP YOU!

FWP

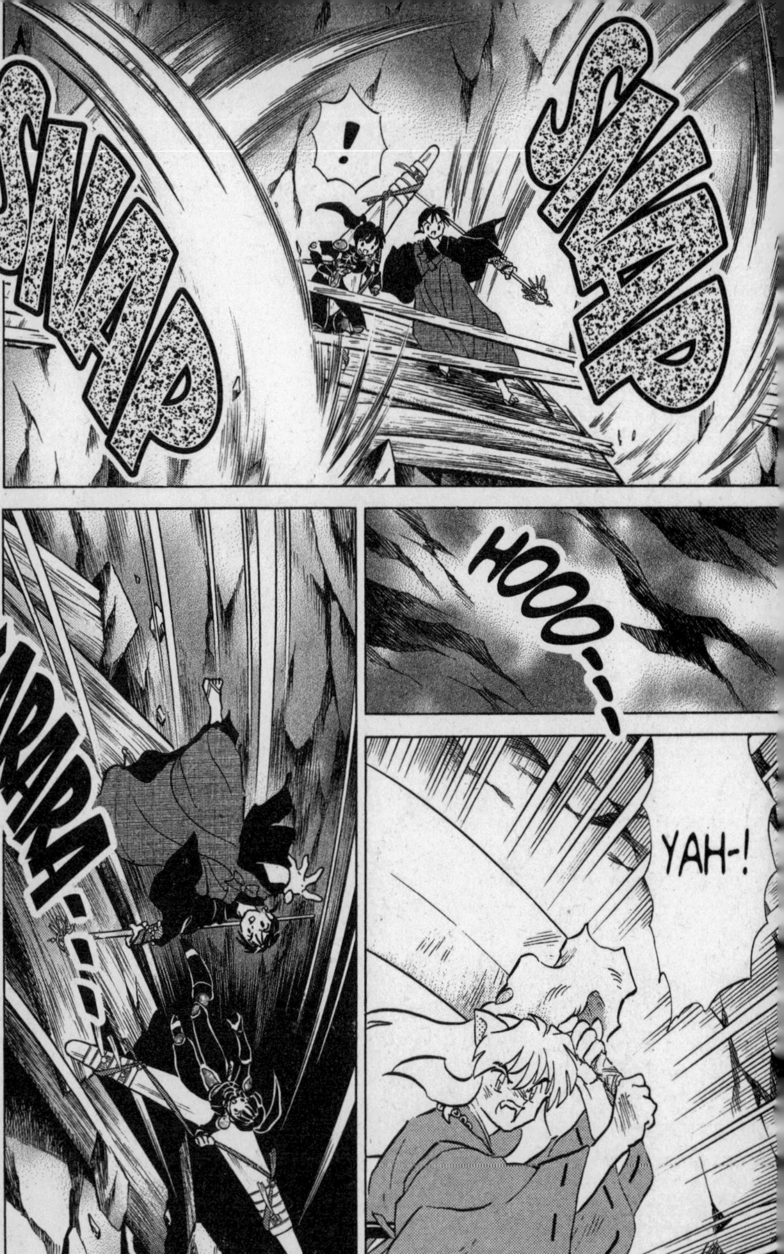
SNAP
!
SNAP
KARARA...
HOOO...
YAH-!

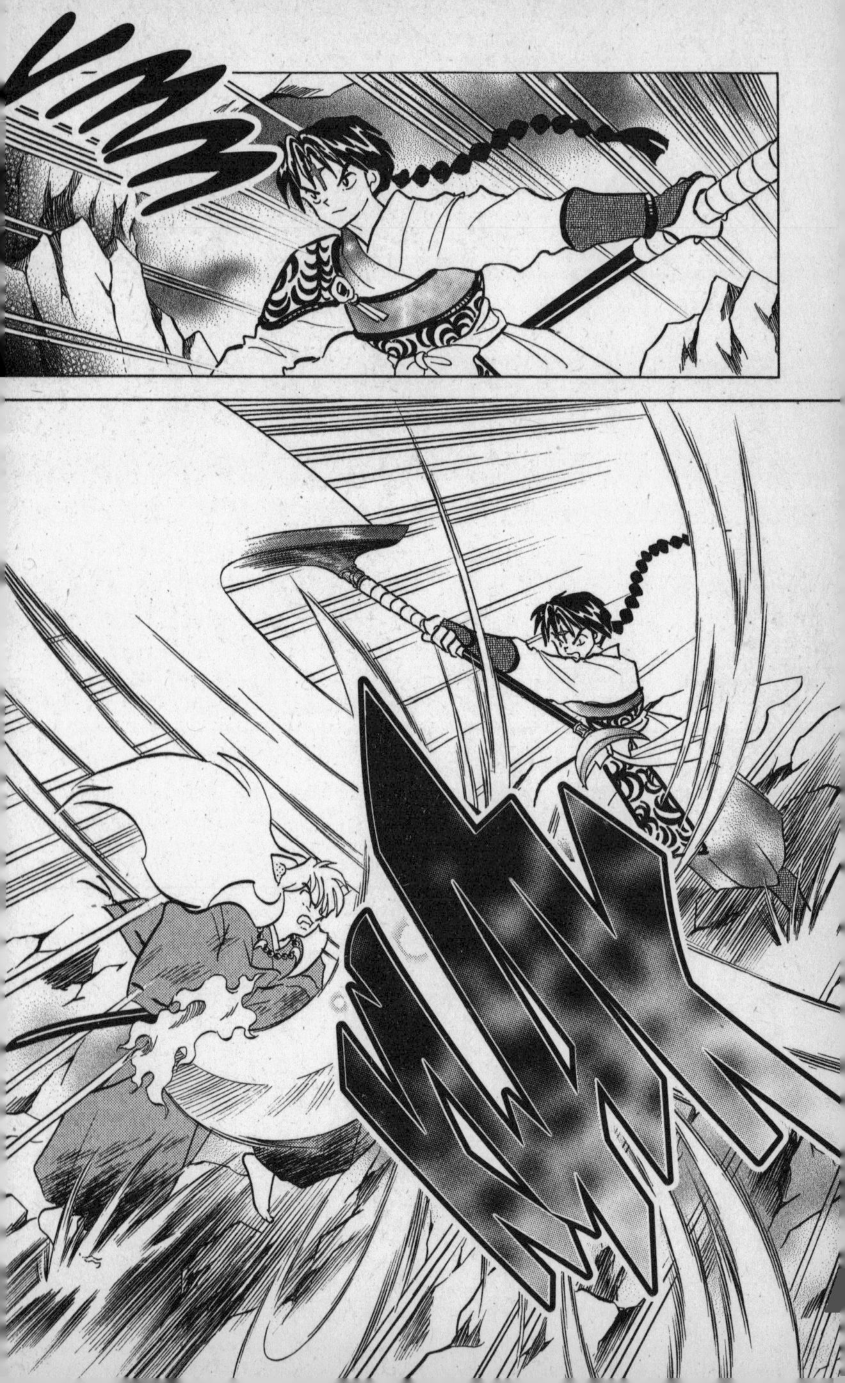
VMM

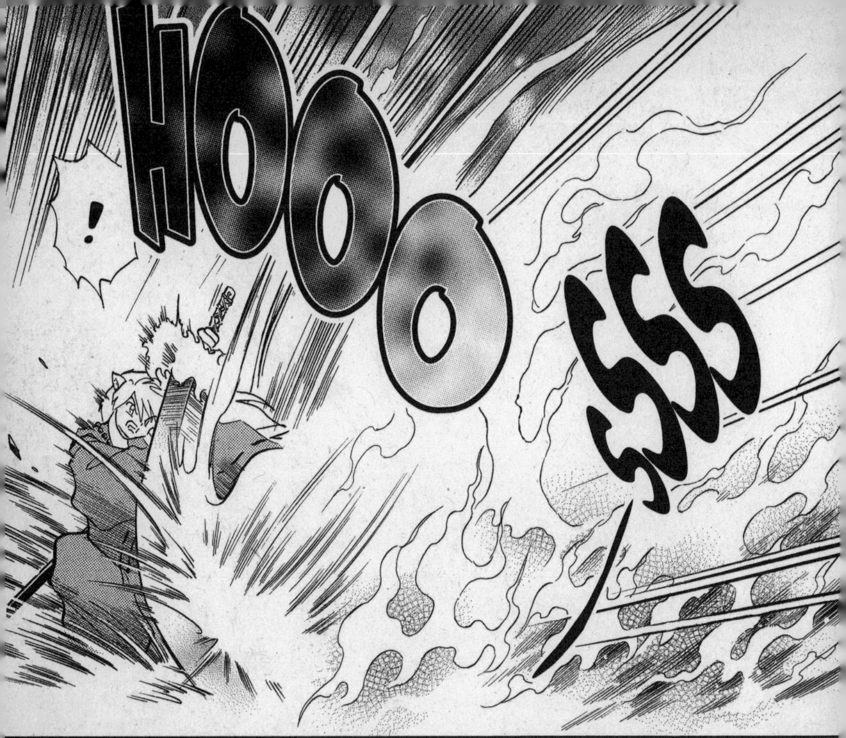
!
HOOOOSSS

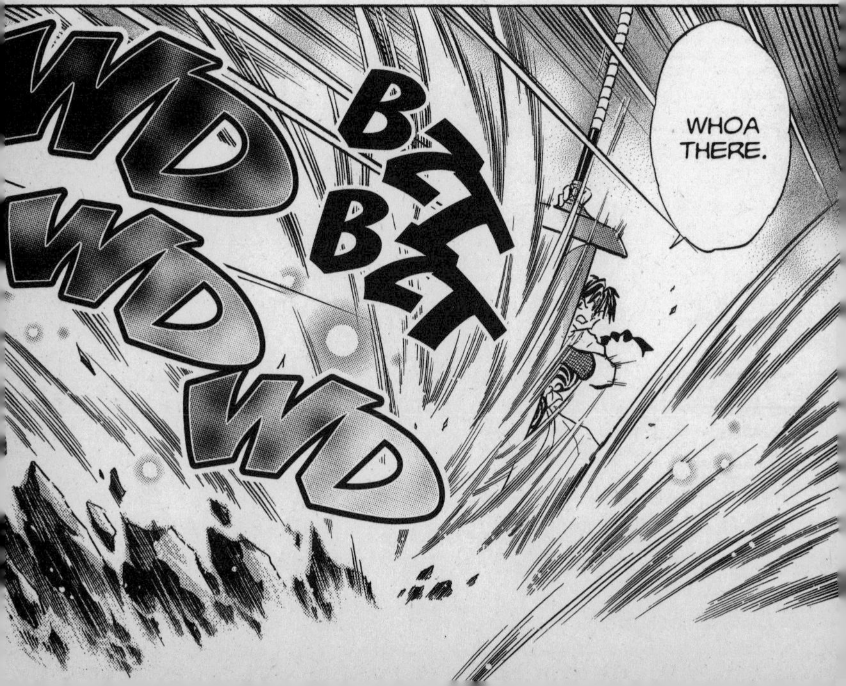
BZT
BZT
WHOA THERE.

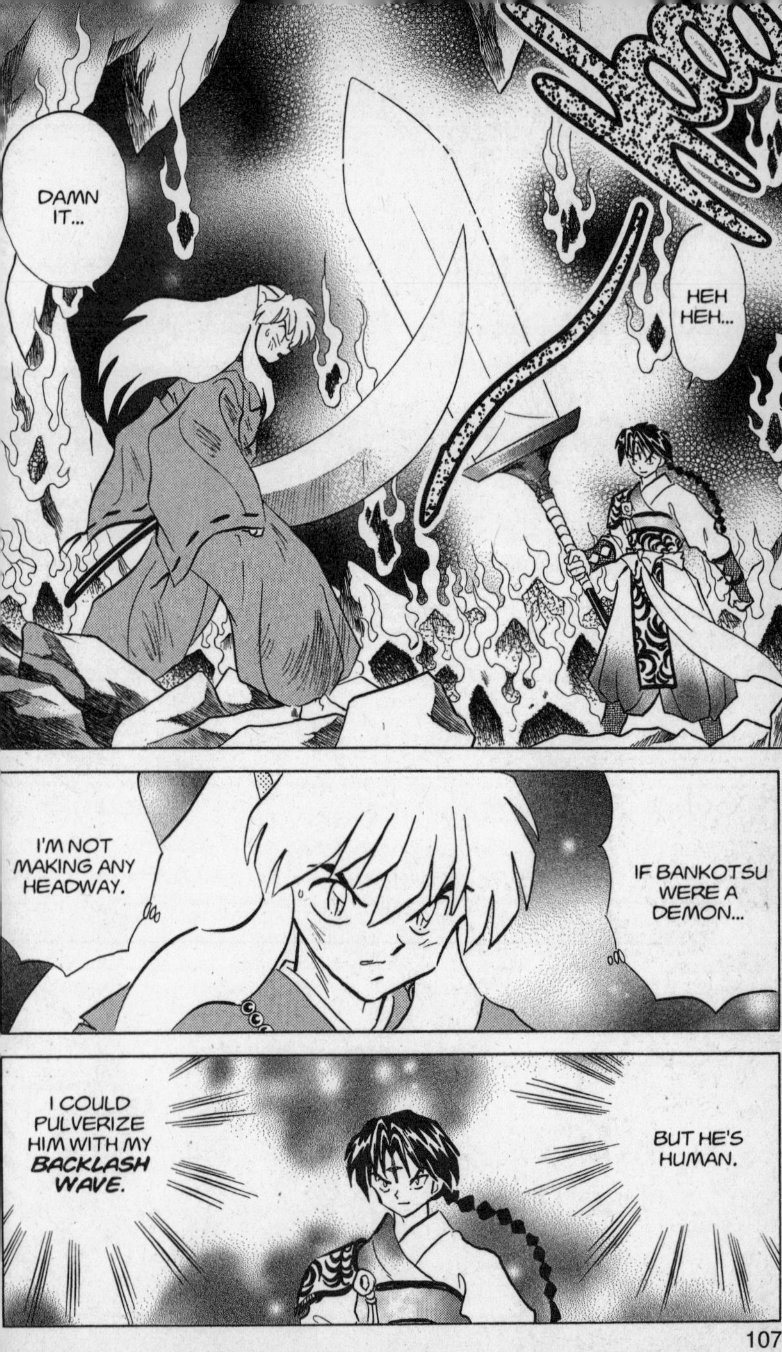
DAMN IT...
HEH HEH...
I'M NOT MAKING ANY HEADWAY.
IF BANKOTSU WERE A DEMON...
I COULD PULVERIZE HIM WITH MY ***BACKLASH WAVE.***
BUT HE'S HUMAN.

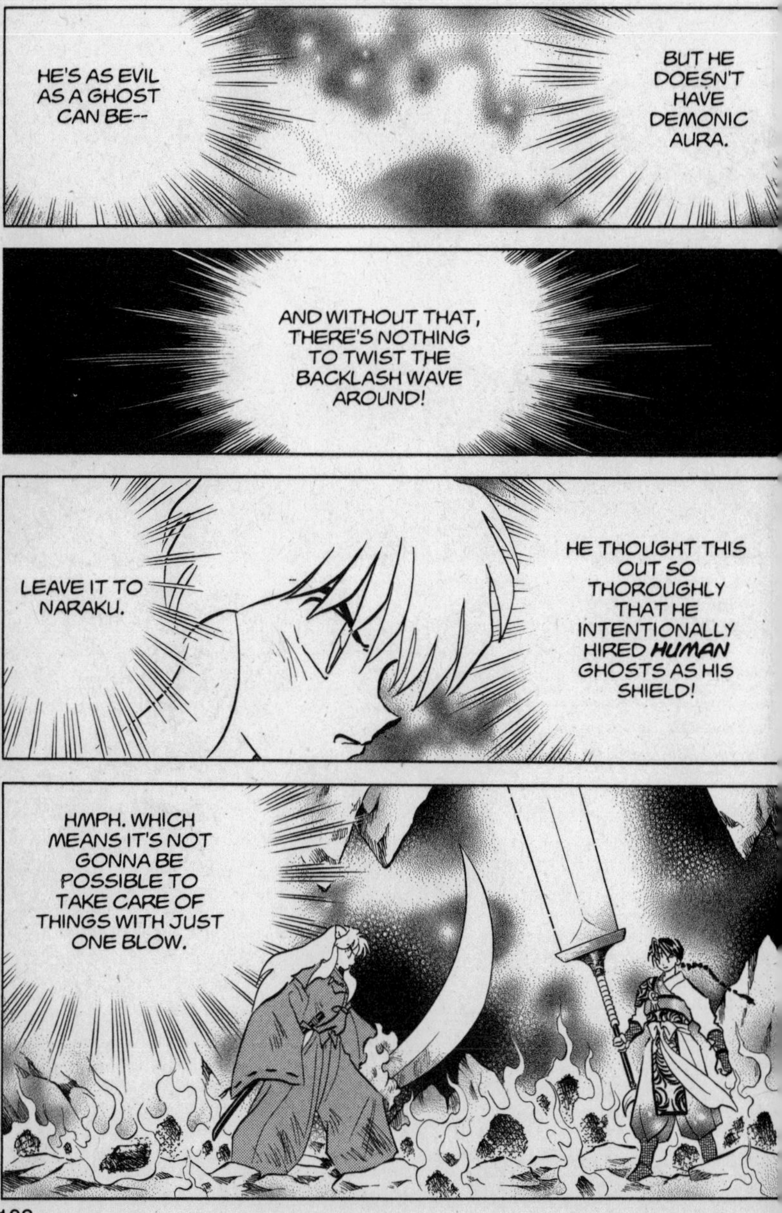
HE'S AS EVIL AS A GHOST CAN BE--
BUT HE DOESN'T HAVE DEMONIC AURA.
AND WITHOUT THAT, THERE'S NOTHING TO TWIST THE BACKLASH WAVE AROUND!
LEAVE IT TO NARAKU.
HE THOUGHT THIS OUT SO THOROUGHLY THAT HE INTENTIONALLY HIRED *HUMAN* GHOSTS AS HIS SHIELD!
HMPH. WHICH MEANS IT'S NOT GONNA BE POSSIBLE TO TAKE CARE OF THINGS WITH JUST ONE BLOW.

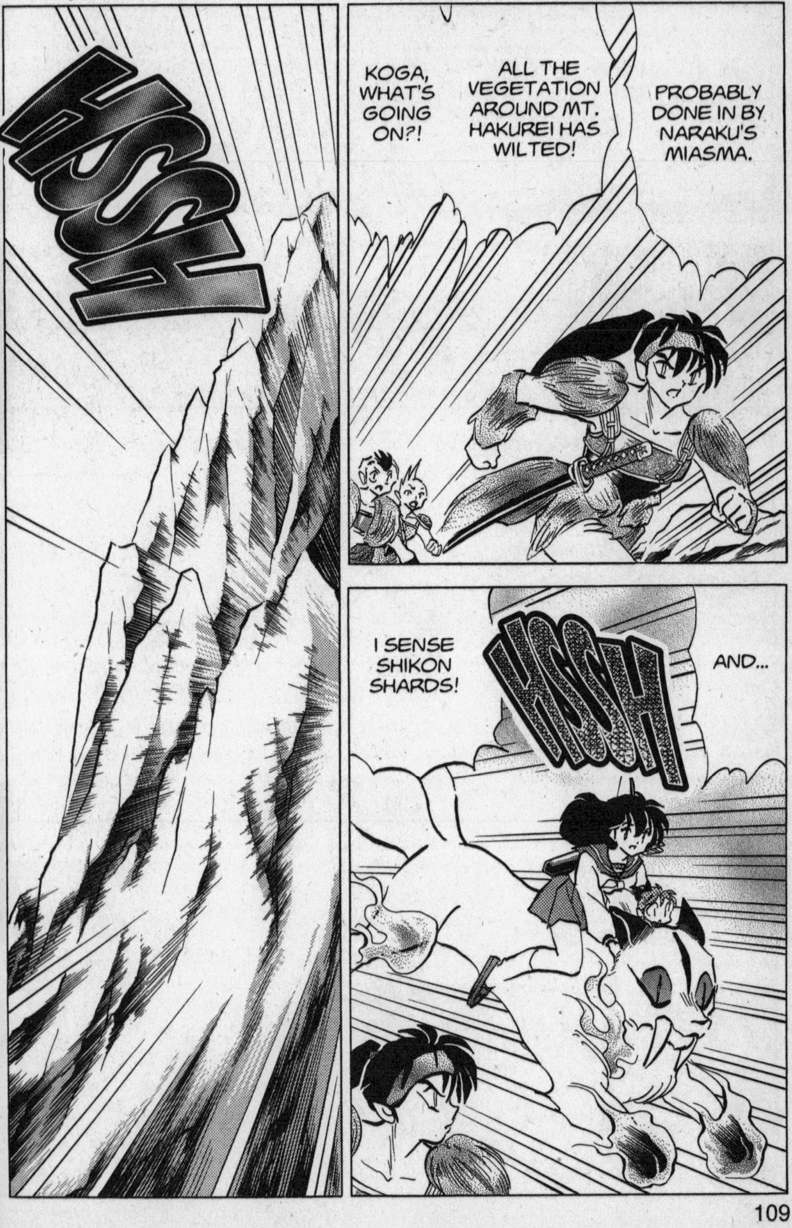
HSSH
KOGA, WHAT'S GOING ON?!
ALL THE VEGETATION AROUND MT. HAKUREI HAS WILTED!
PROBABLY DONE IN BY NARAKU'S MIASMA.
I SENSE SHIKON SHARDS!
HSSH
AND...

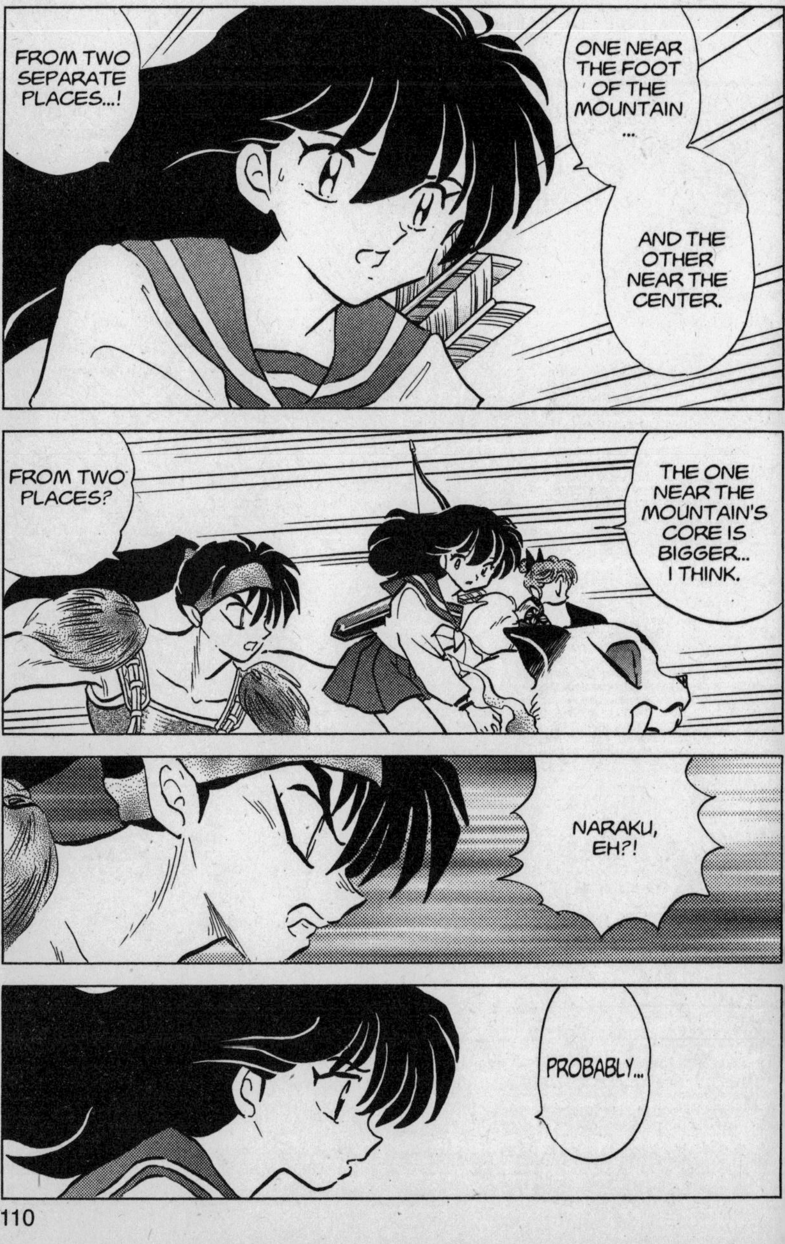
FROM TWO SEPARATE PLACES...!
ONE NEAR THE FOOT OF THE MOUNTAIN ...
AND THE OTHER NEAR THE CENTER.
FROM TWO PLACES?
THE ONE NEAR THE MOUNTAIN'S CORE IS BIGGER... I THINK.
NARAKU, EH?!
PROBABLY...

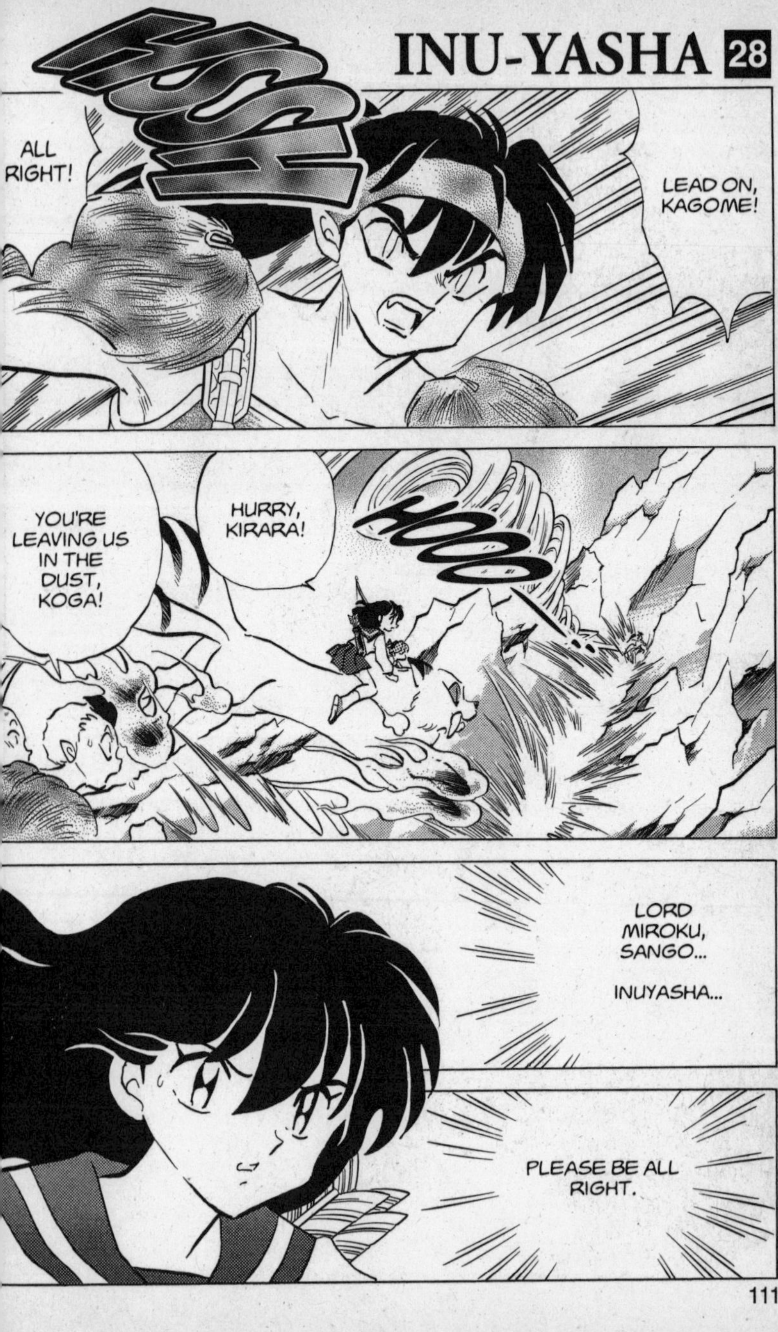
ALL RIGHT!
HSSH
LEAD ON, KAGOME!
YOU'RE LEAVING US IN THE DUST, KOGA!
HURRY, KIRARA!
HOOO
LORD MIROKU, SANGO...
INUYASHA...
PLEASE BE ALL RIGHT.

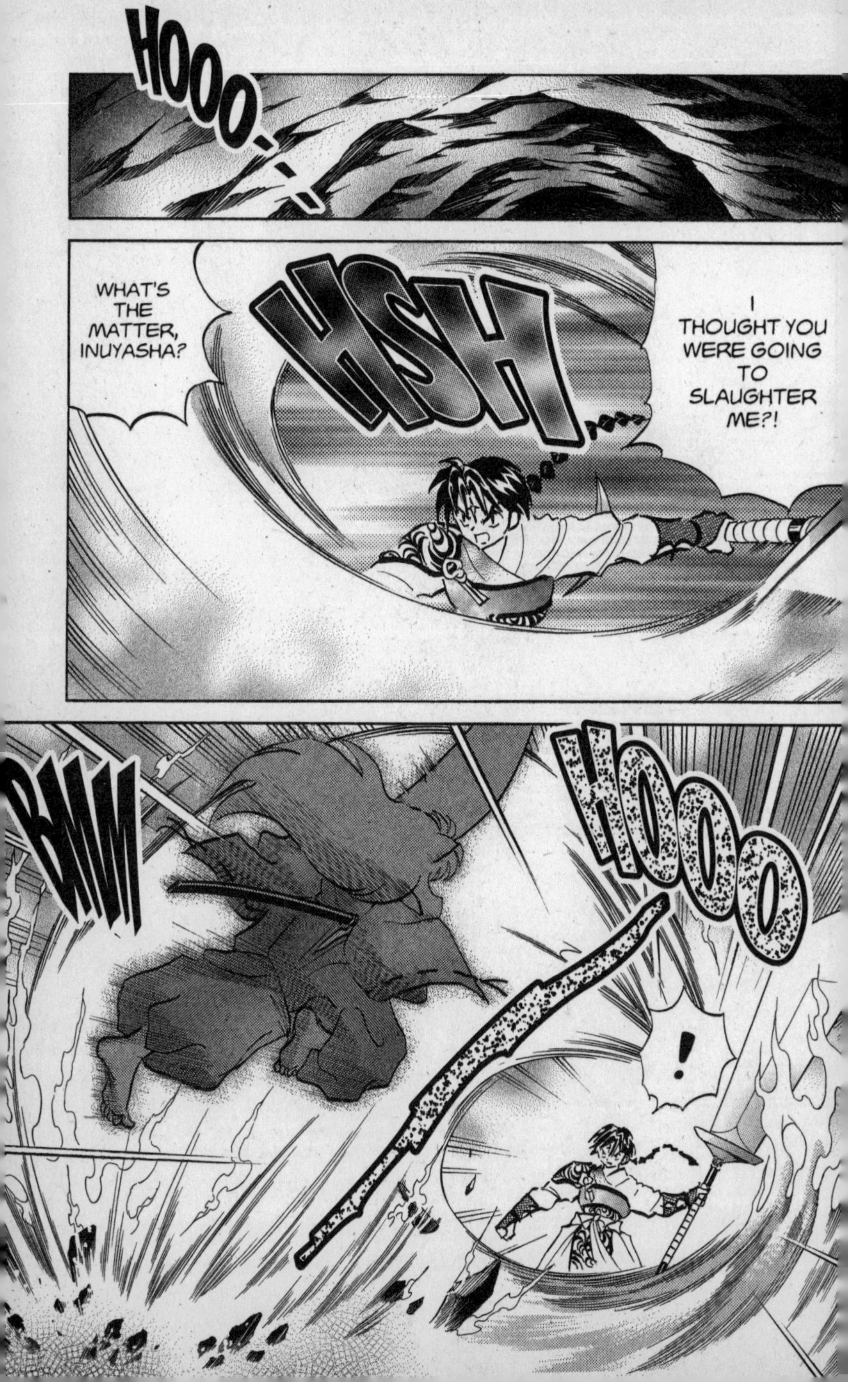
HOOO...
WHAT'S THE MATTER, INUYASHA?
HSH...
I THOUGHT YOU WERE GOING TO SLAUGHTER ME?!
BMM
HOOOO
!

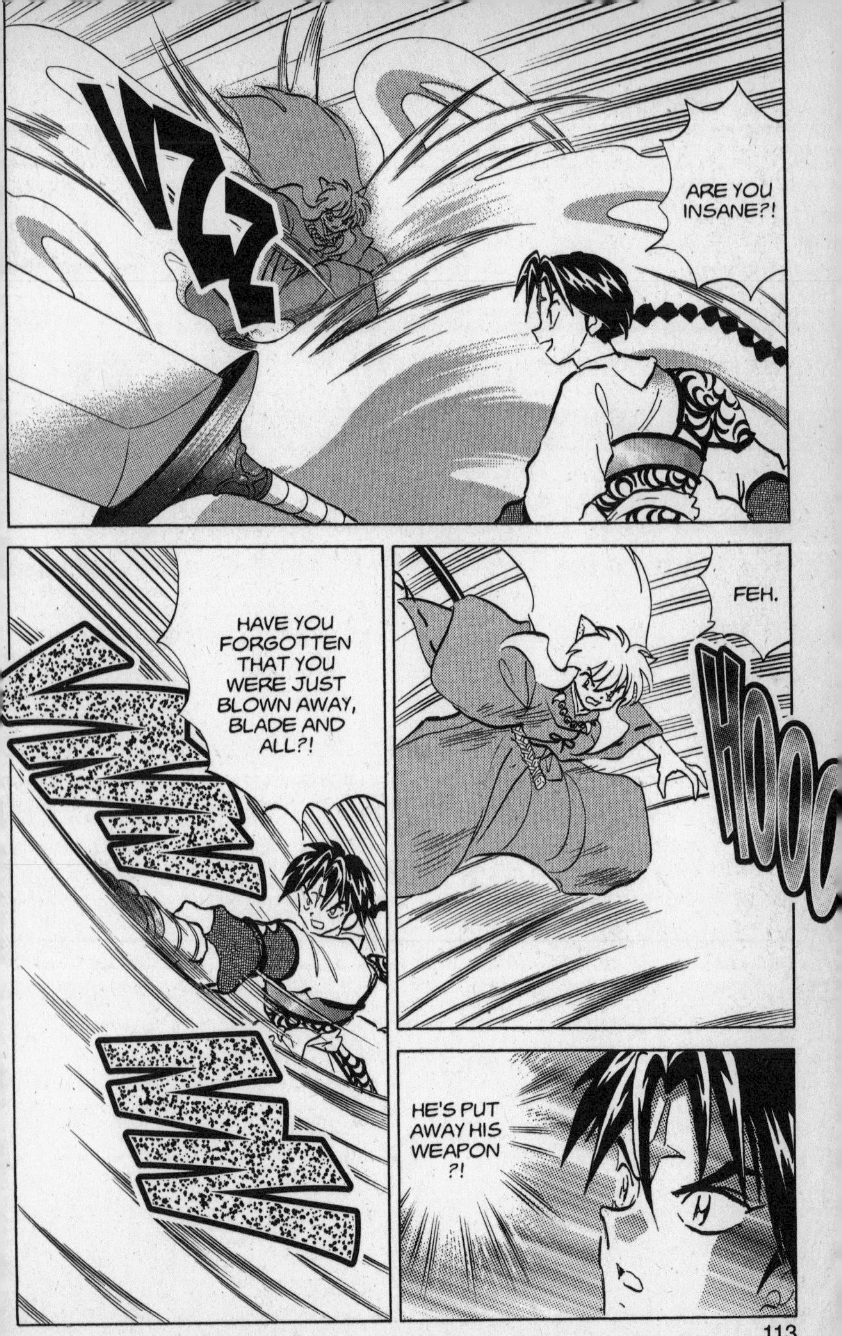
VZZ
ARE YOU INSANE?!
HAVE YOU FORGOTTEN THAT YOU WERE JUST BLOWN AWAY, BLADE AND ALL?!
FEH.
HOOO
HE'S PUT AWAY HIS WEAPON ?!

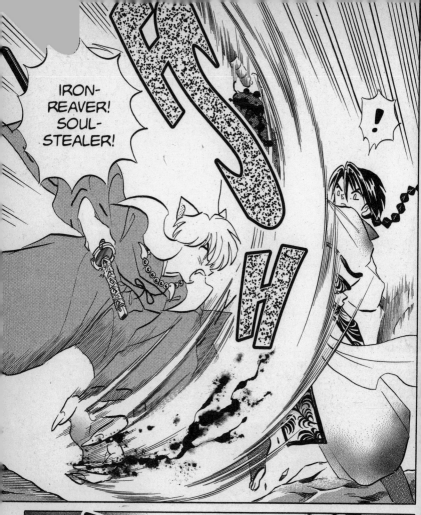

IRON-
REAVER!
SOUL-
STEALER!

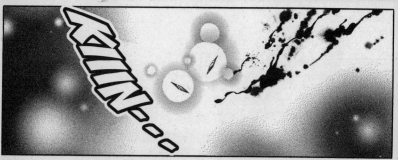

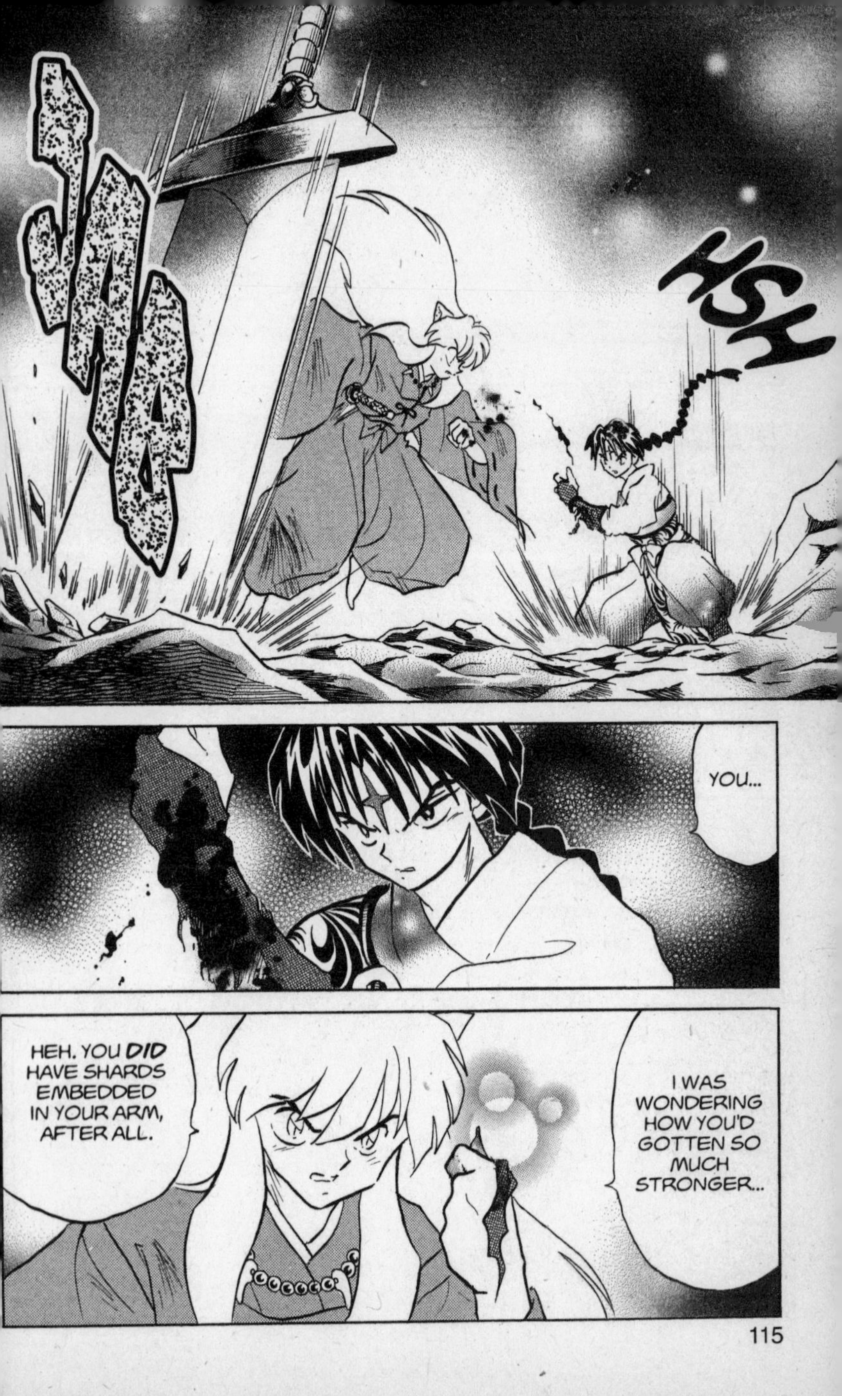
JAB
HSH
YOU...
HEH. YOU DID HAVE SHARDS EMBEDDED IN YOUR ARM, AFTER ALL.
I WAS WONDERING HOW YOU'D GOTTEN SO MUCH STRONGER...

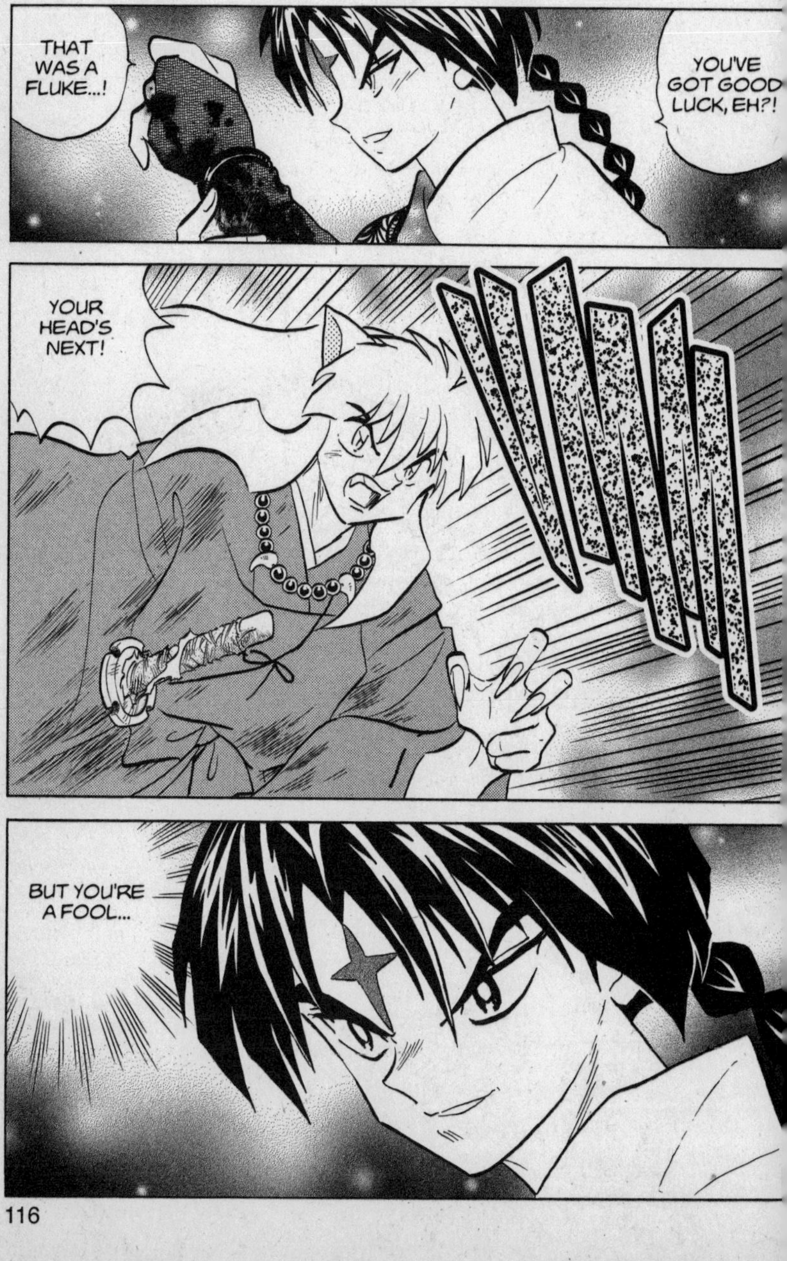
THAT WAS A FLUKE...!
YOU'VE GOT GOOD LUCK, EH?!
YOUR HEAD'S NEXT!
BUT YOU'RE A FOOL...

SCROLL 7
BANKOTSU'S STRENGTH

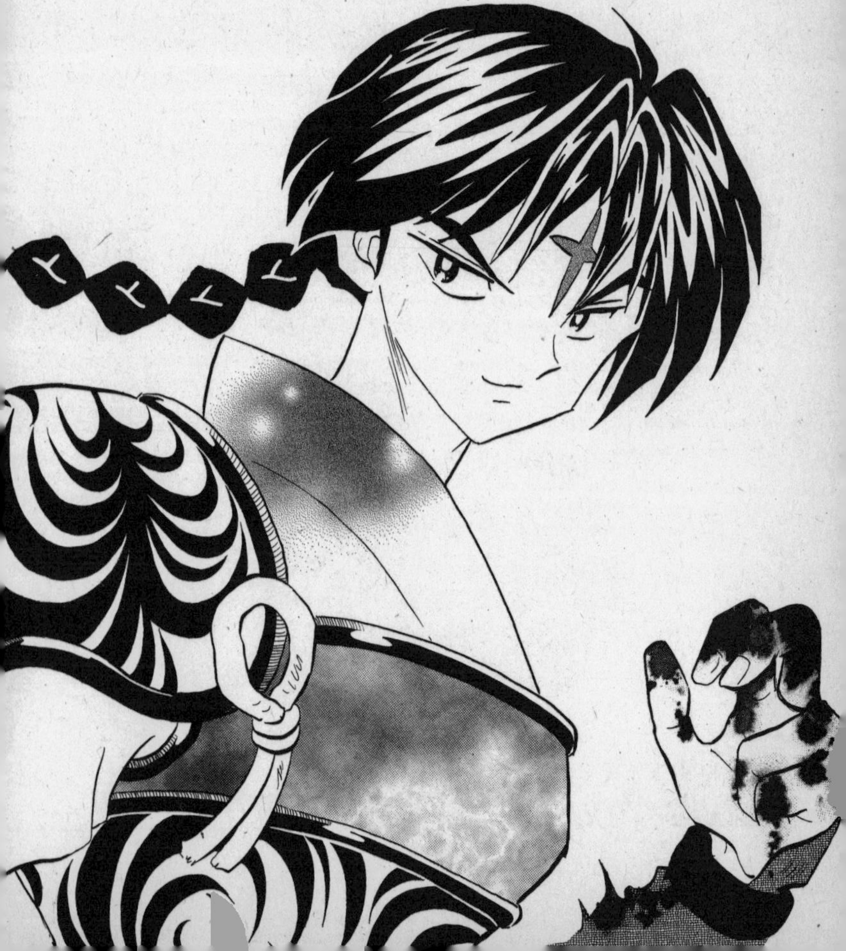

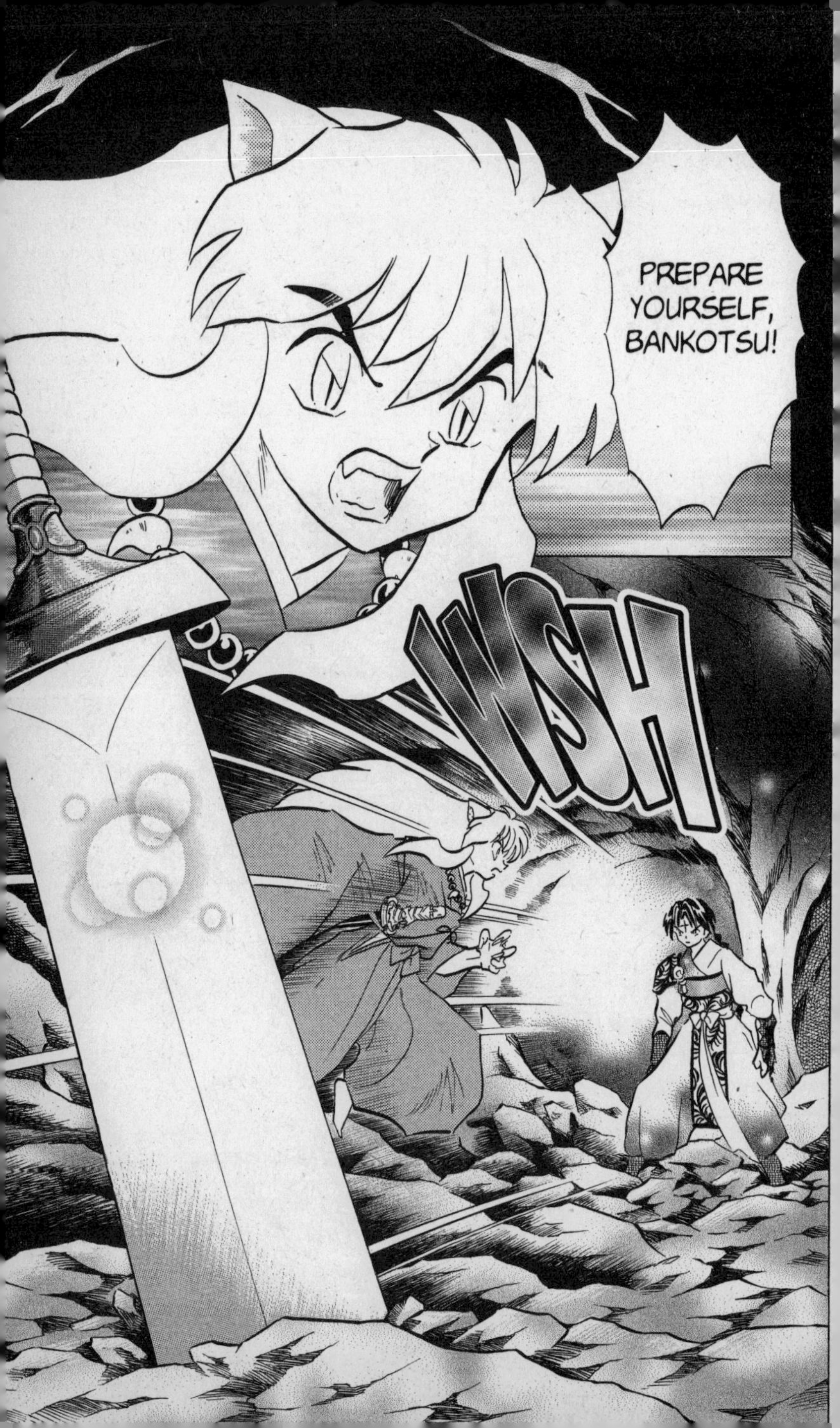
PREPARE YOURSELF, BANKOTSU!
WSSH

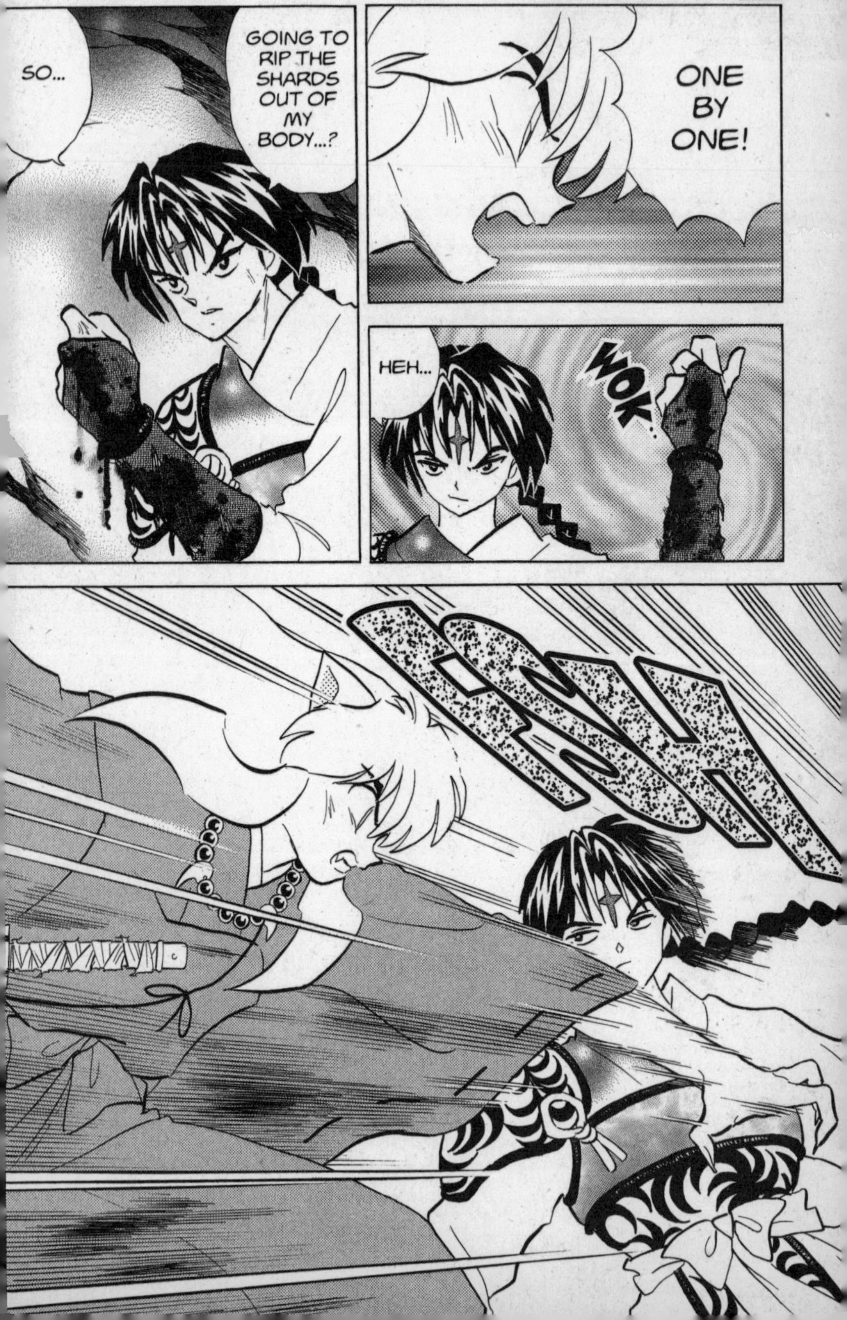
SO...
GOING TO RIP THE SHARDS OUT OF MY BODY...?
ONE BY ONE!
HEH...
WOK...

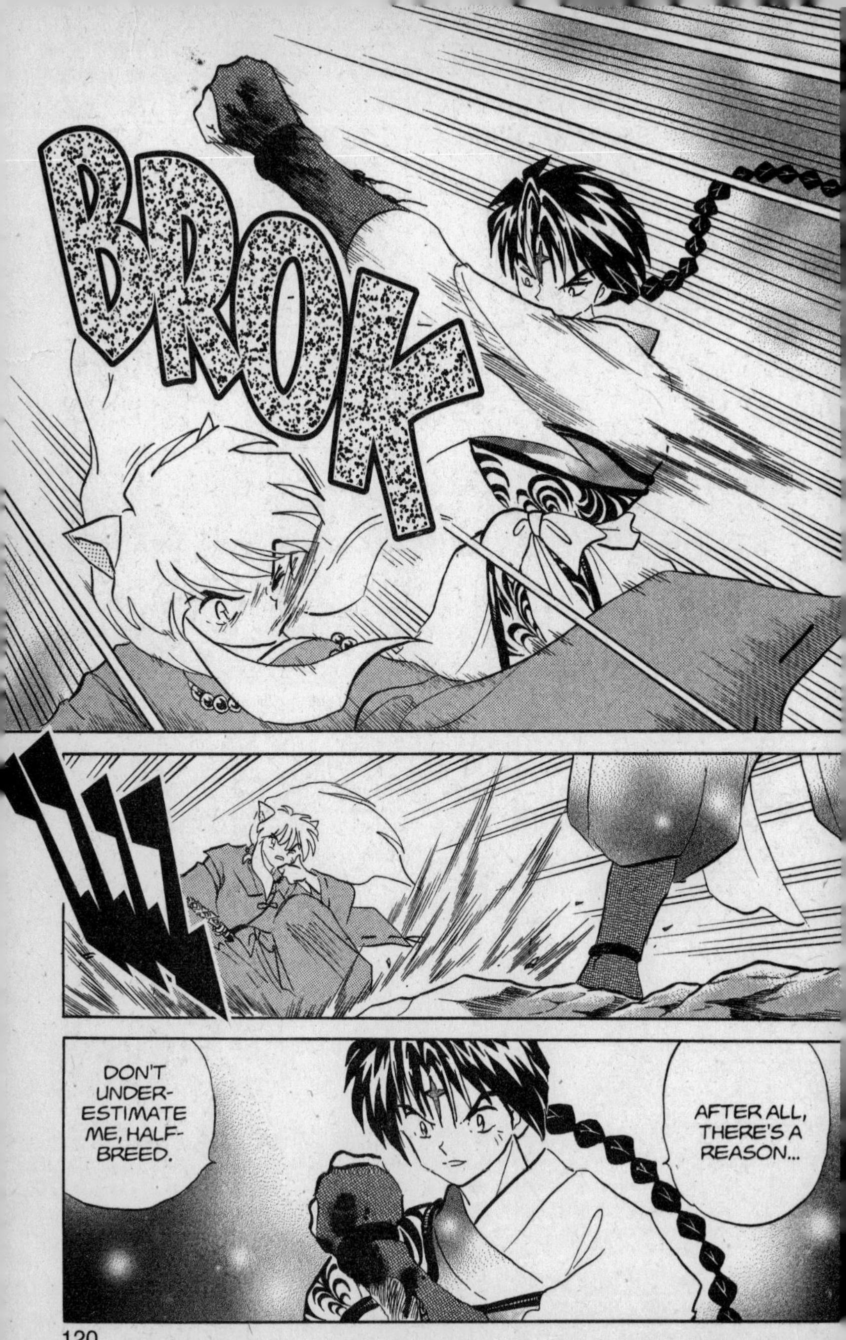
BROK
DON'T UNDER-ESTIMATE ME, HALF-BREED.
AFTER ALL, THERE'S A REASON...

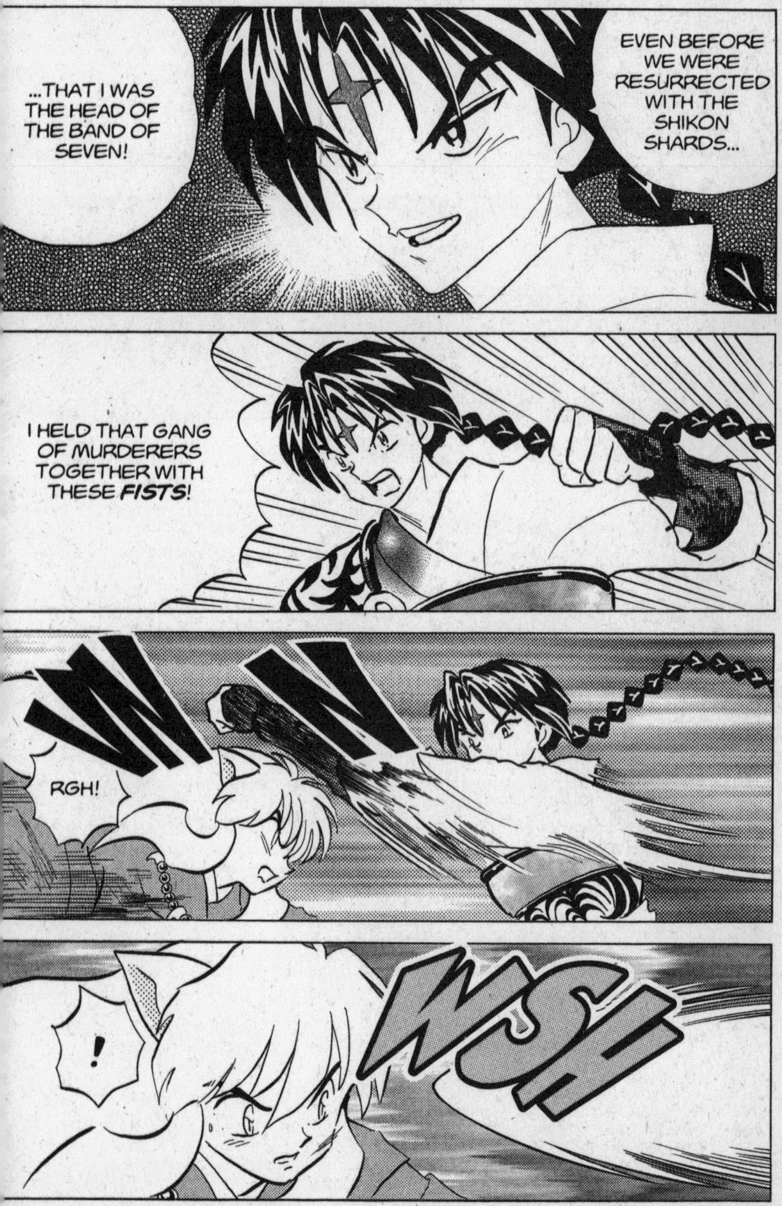
...THAT I WAS THE HEAD OF THE BAND OF SEVEN!
EVEN BEFORE WE WERE RESURRECTED WITH THE SHIKON SHARDS...
I HELD THAT GANG OF MURDERERS TOGETHER WITH THESE ***FISTS***!
RGH!
!
WSH!

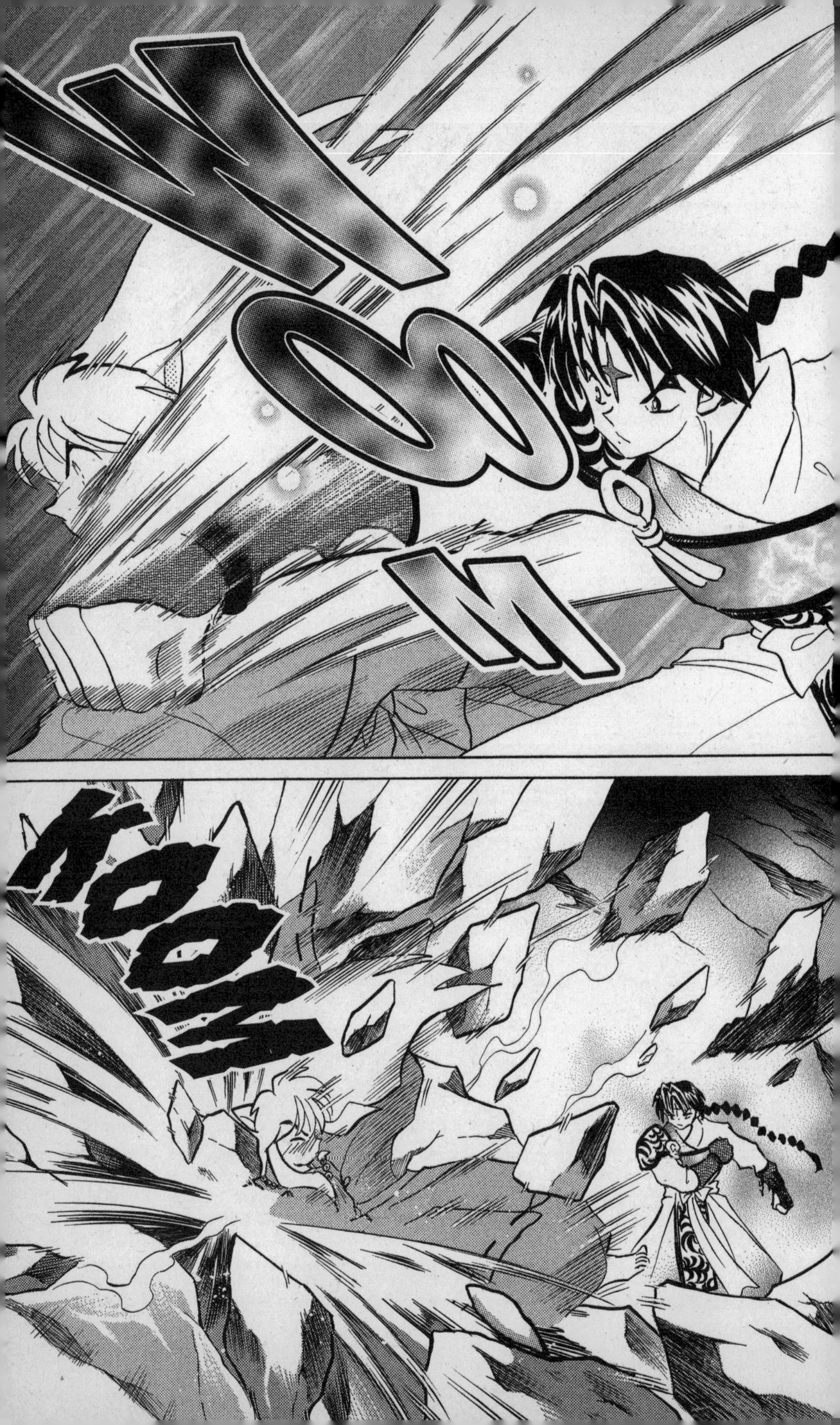
WOOM
KOOM

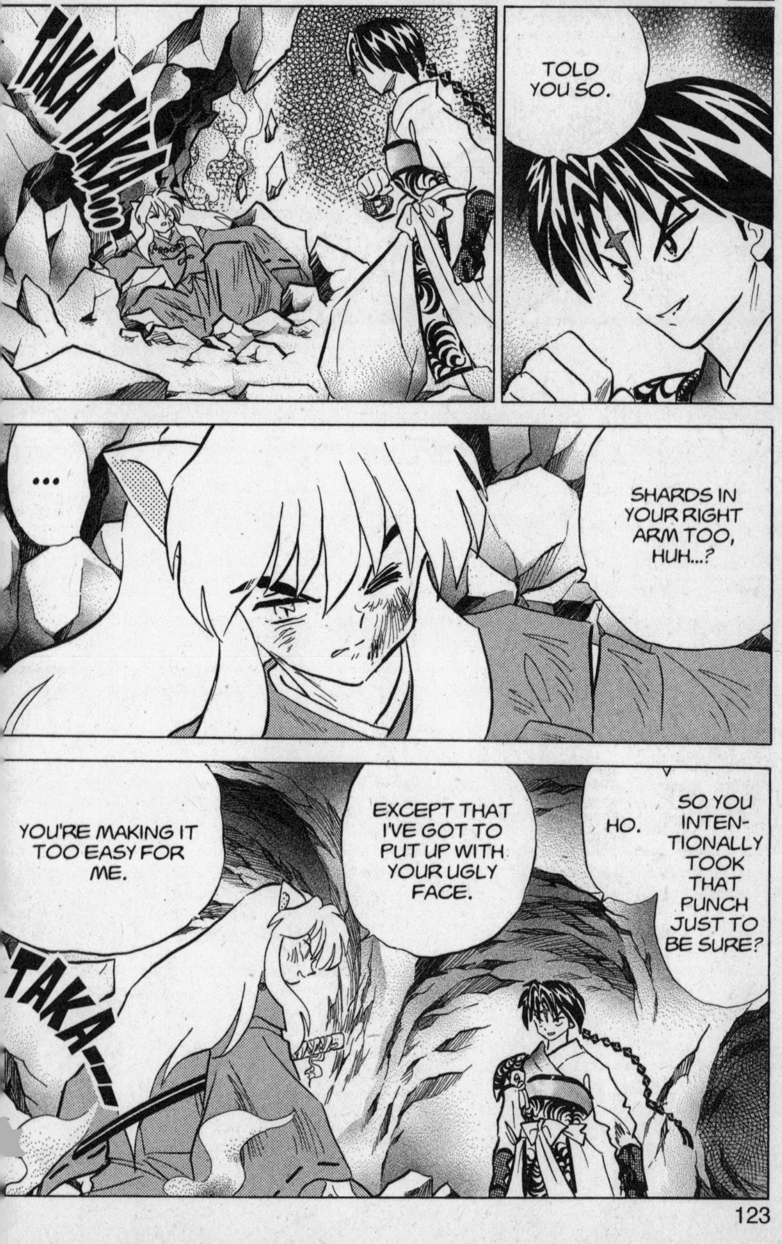
TAKA TAKA...
TOLD YOU SO.
...
SHARDS IN YOUR RIGHT ARM TOO, HUH...?
YOU'RE MAKING IT TOO EASY FOR ME.
EXCEPT THAT I'VE GOT TO PUT UP WITH YOUR UGLY FACE.
HO.
SO YOU INTENTIONALLY TOOK THAT PUNCH JUST TO BE SURE?
TAKA--

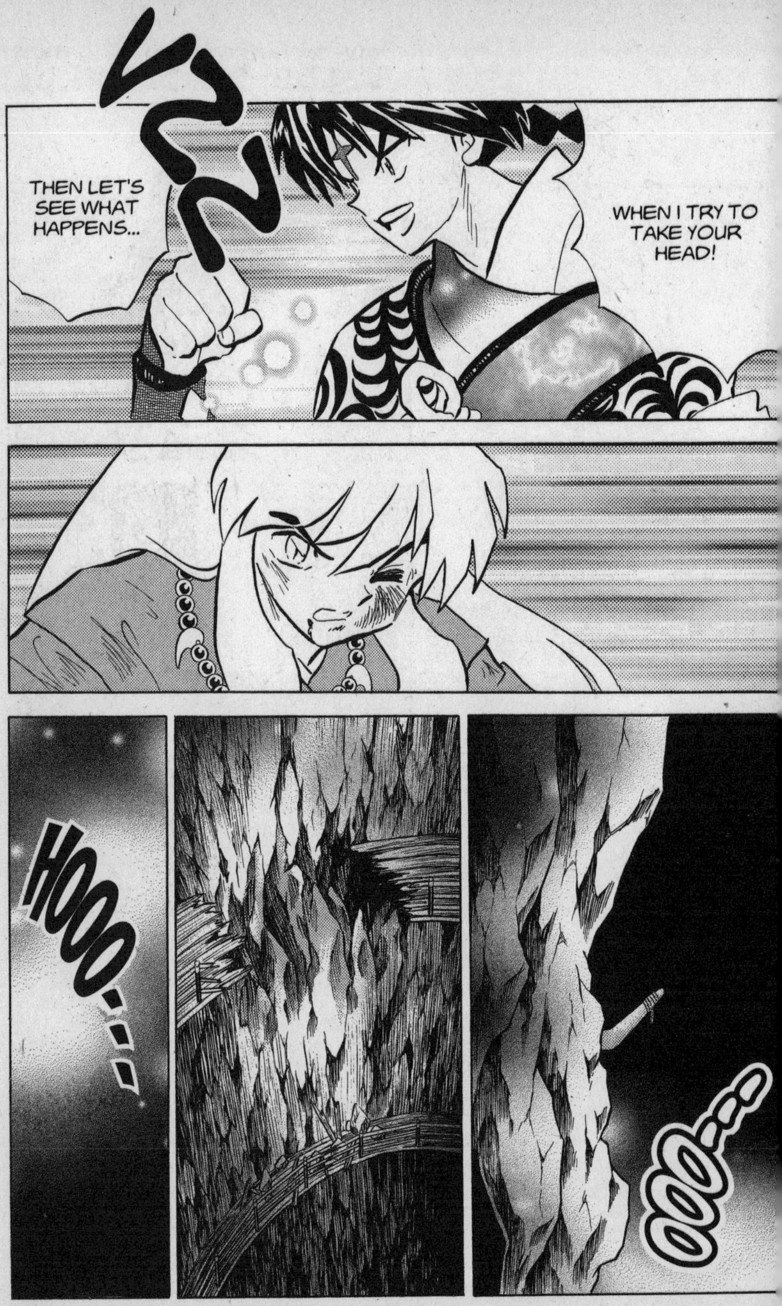
THEN LET'S SEE WHAT HAPPENS...
WHEN I TRY TO TAKE YOUR HEAD!
HOOO...
OOOO...

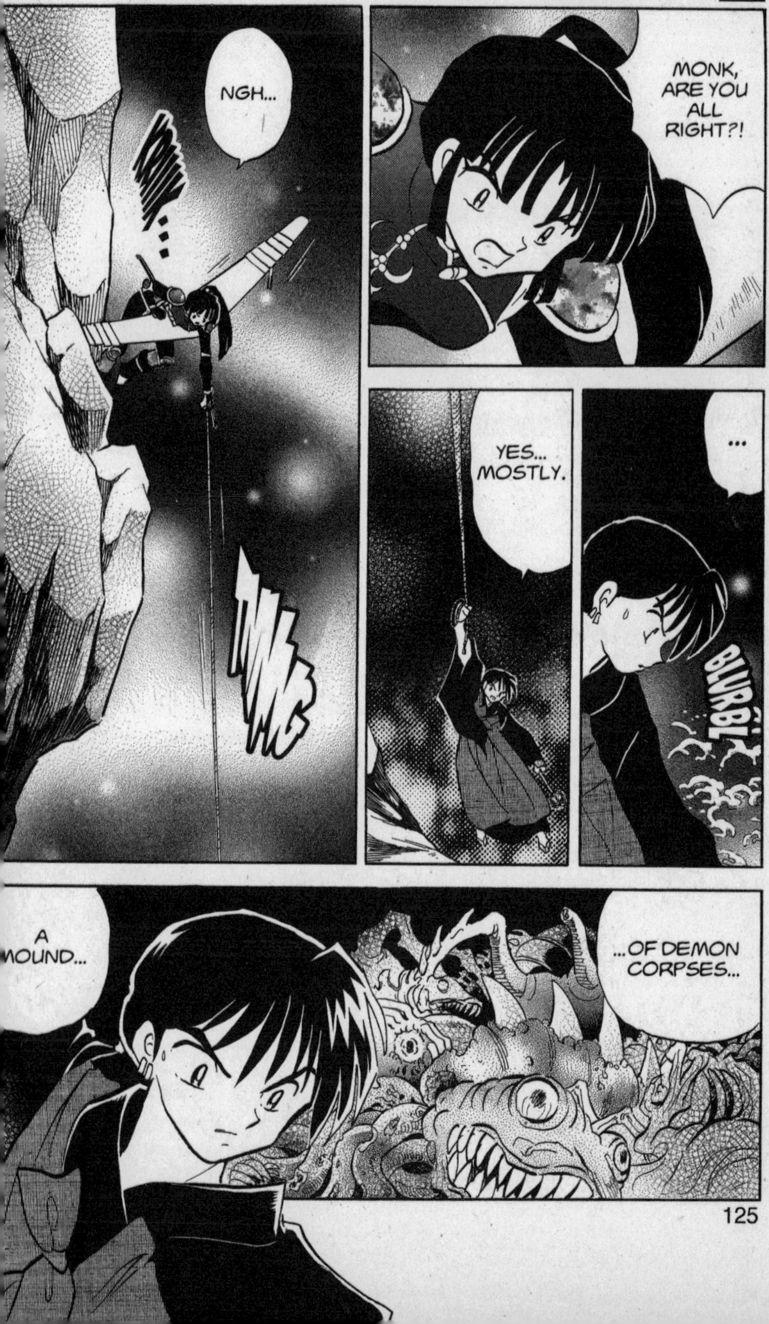
NGH...
MONK, ARE YOU ALL RIGHT?!
YES... MOSTLY.
...
BLURBL
A MOUND...
...OF DEMON CORPSES...

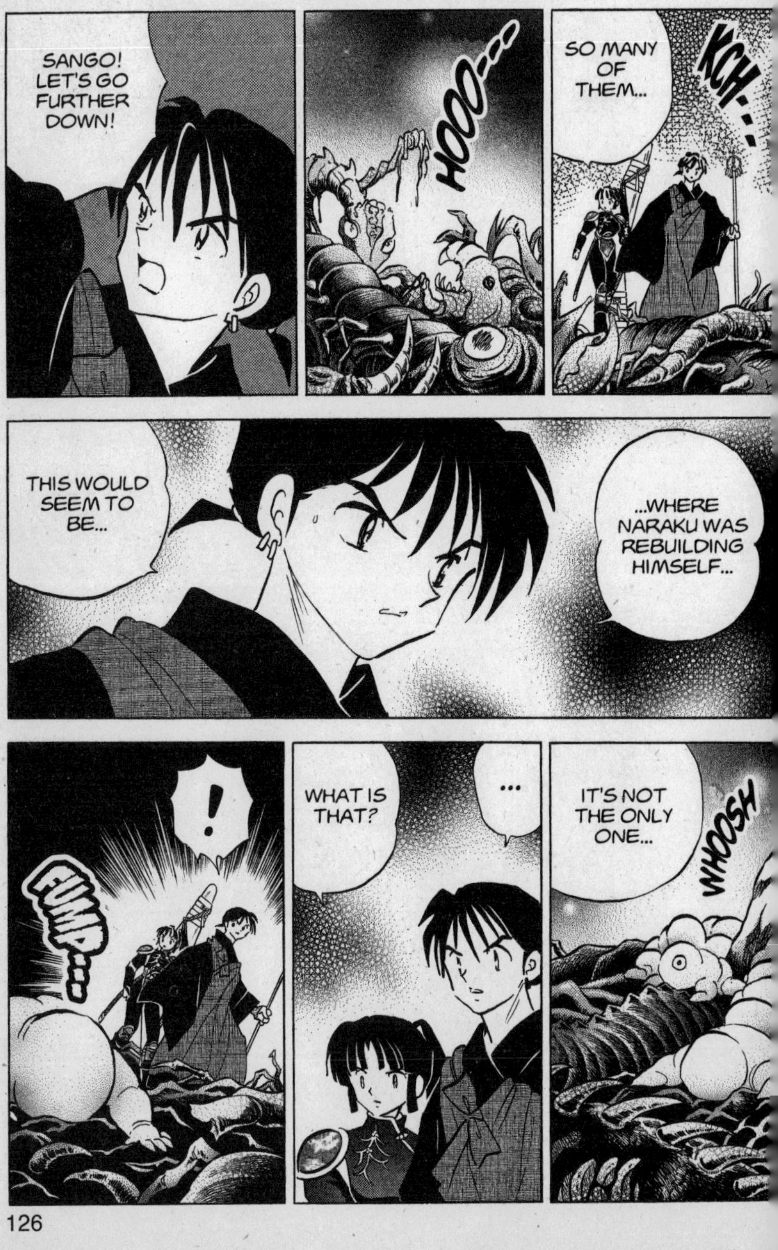
SANGO! LET'S GO FURTHER DOWN!
HOOO...
SO MANY OF THEM...
KCH...
THIS WOULD SEEM TO BE...
...WHERE NARAKU WAS REBUILDING HIMSELF...
!
FUMP...
WHAT IS THAT?
...
IT'S NOT THE ONLY ONE...
WHOOSH

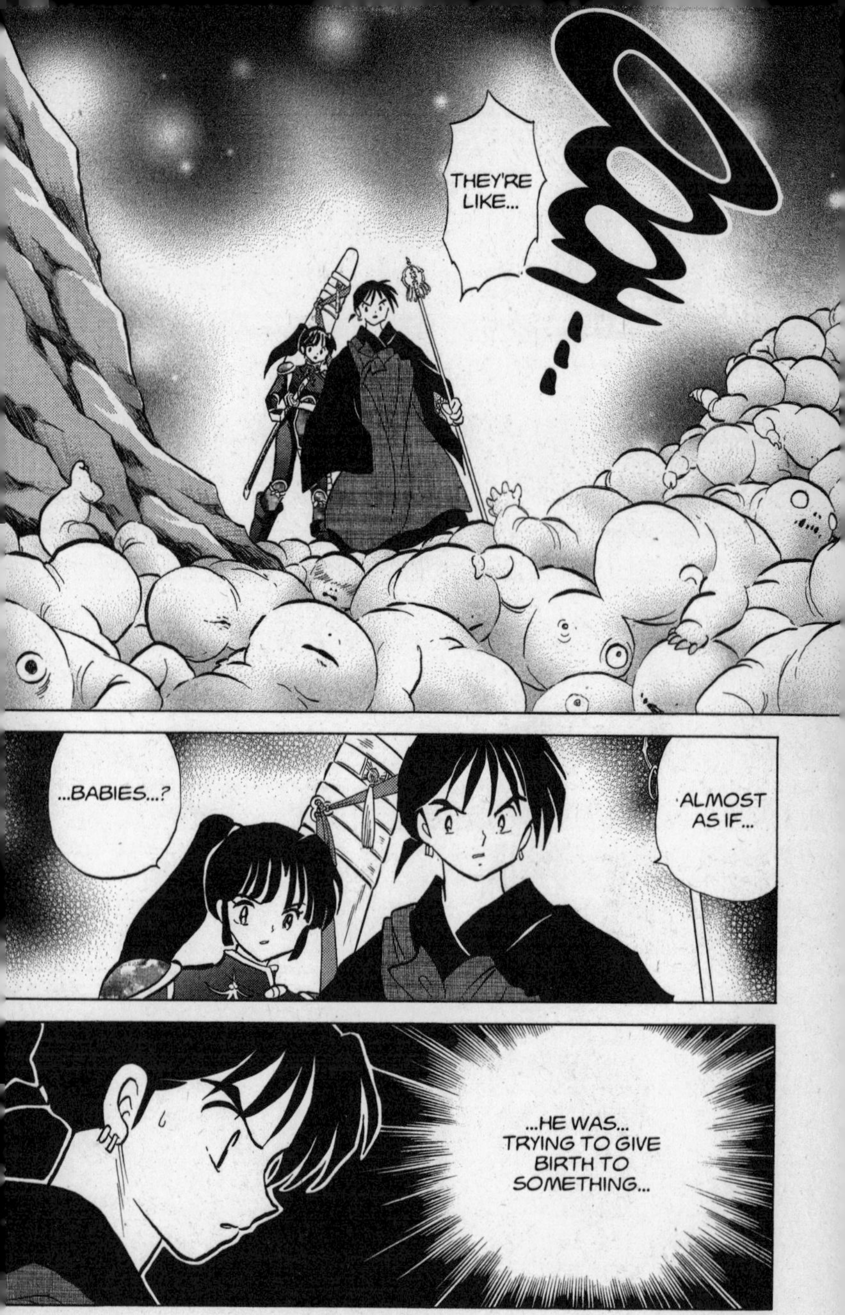
THEY'RE LIKE...
...BABIES...?
ALMOST AS IF...
...HE WAS... TRYING TO GIVE BIRTH TO SOMETHING...

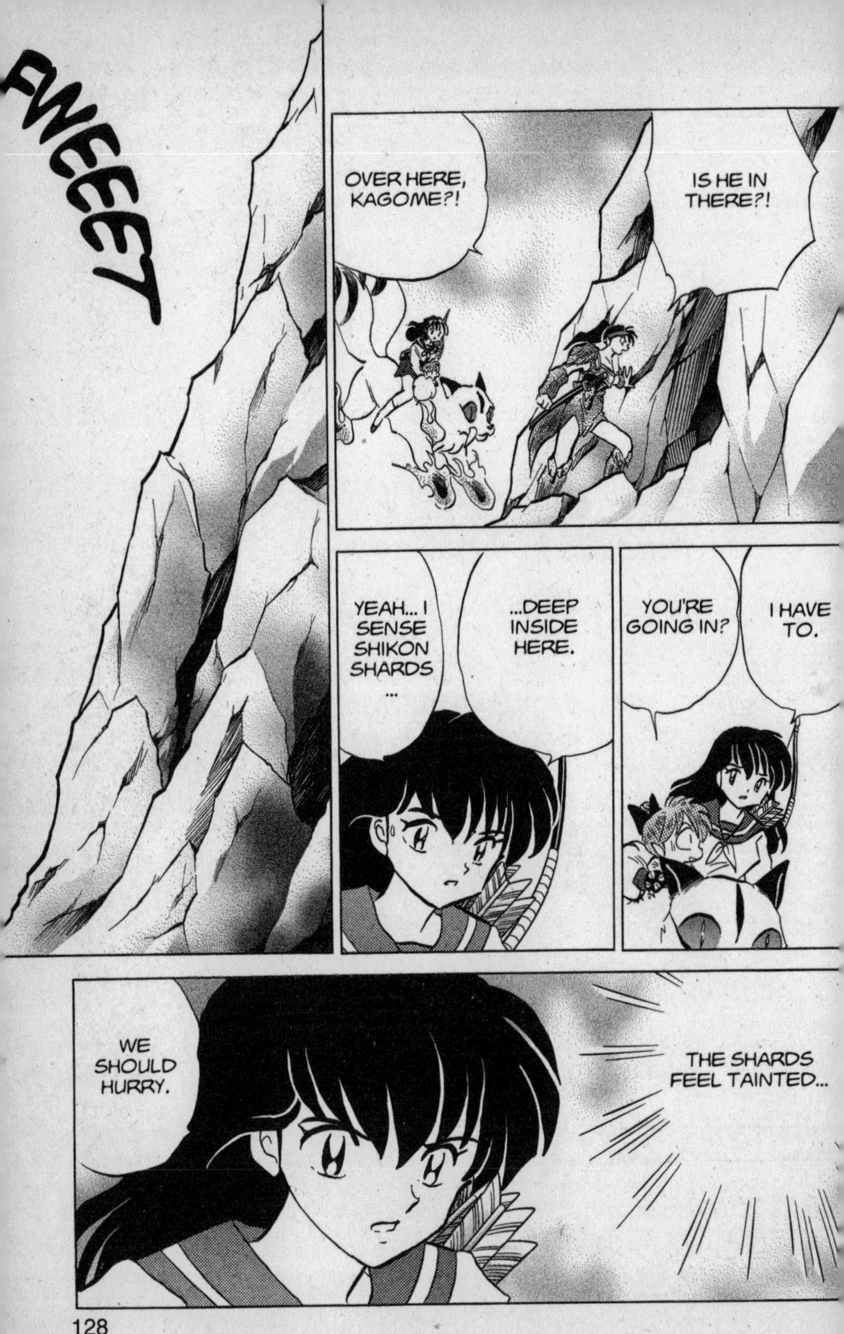
FWEEET
OVER HERE, KAGOME?!
IS HE IN THERE?!
YEAH... I SENSE SHIKON SHARDS ...
...DEEP INSIDE HERE.
YOU'RE GOING IN?
I HAVE TO.
WE SHOULD HURRY.
THE SHARDS FEEL TAINTED...

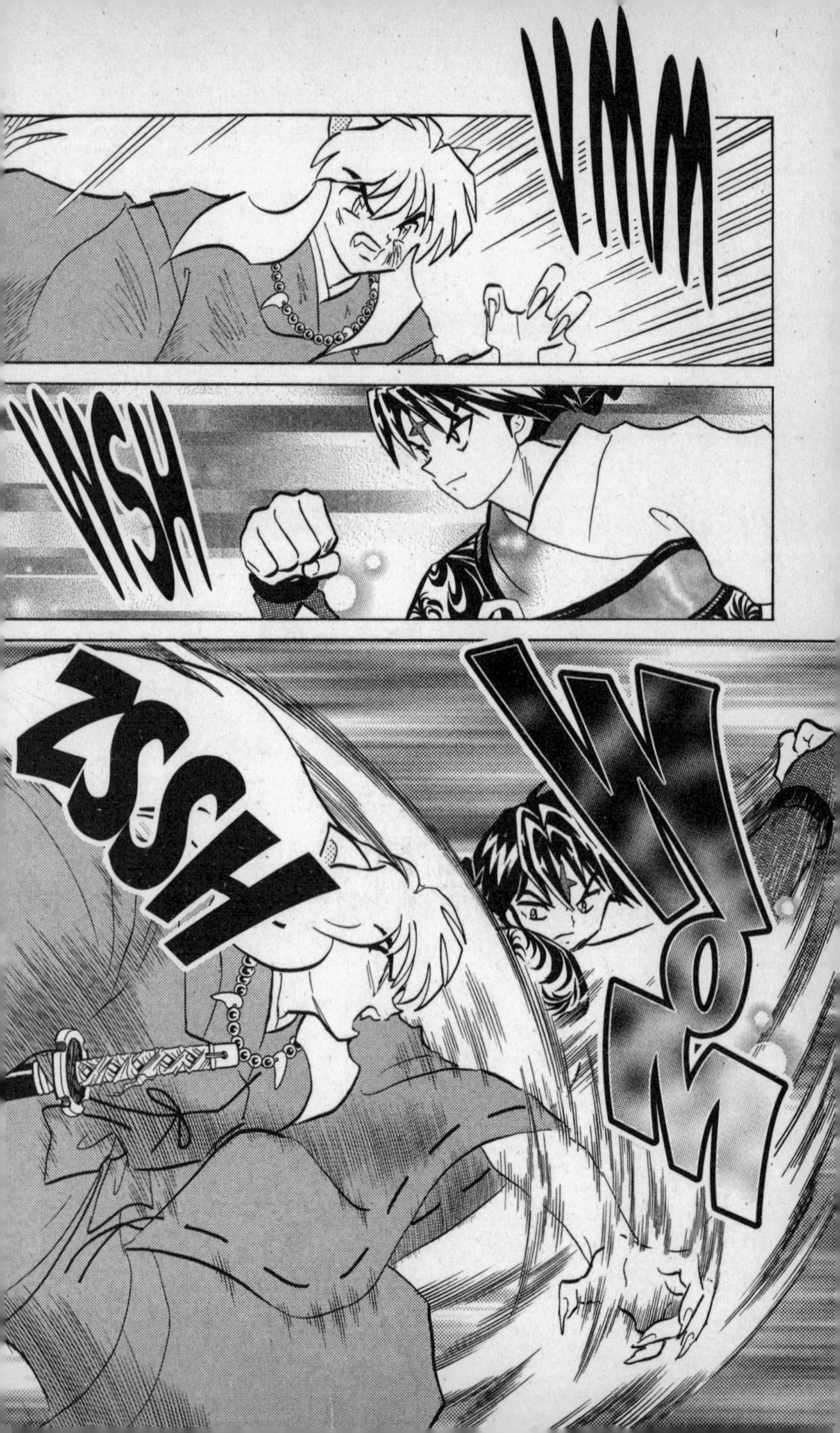
VMM
WSH
ZSH
WOM

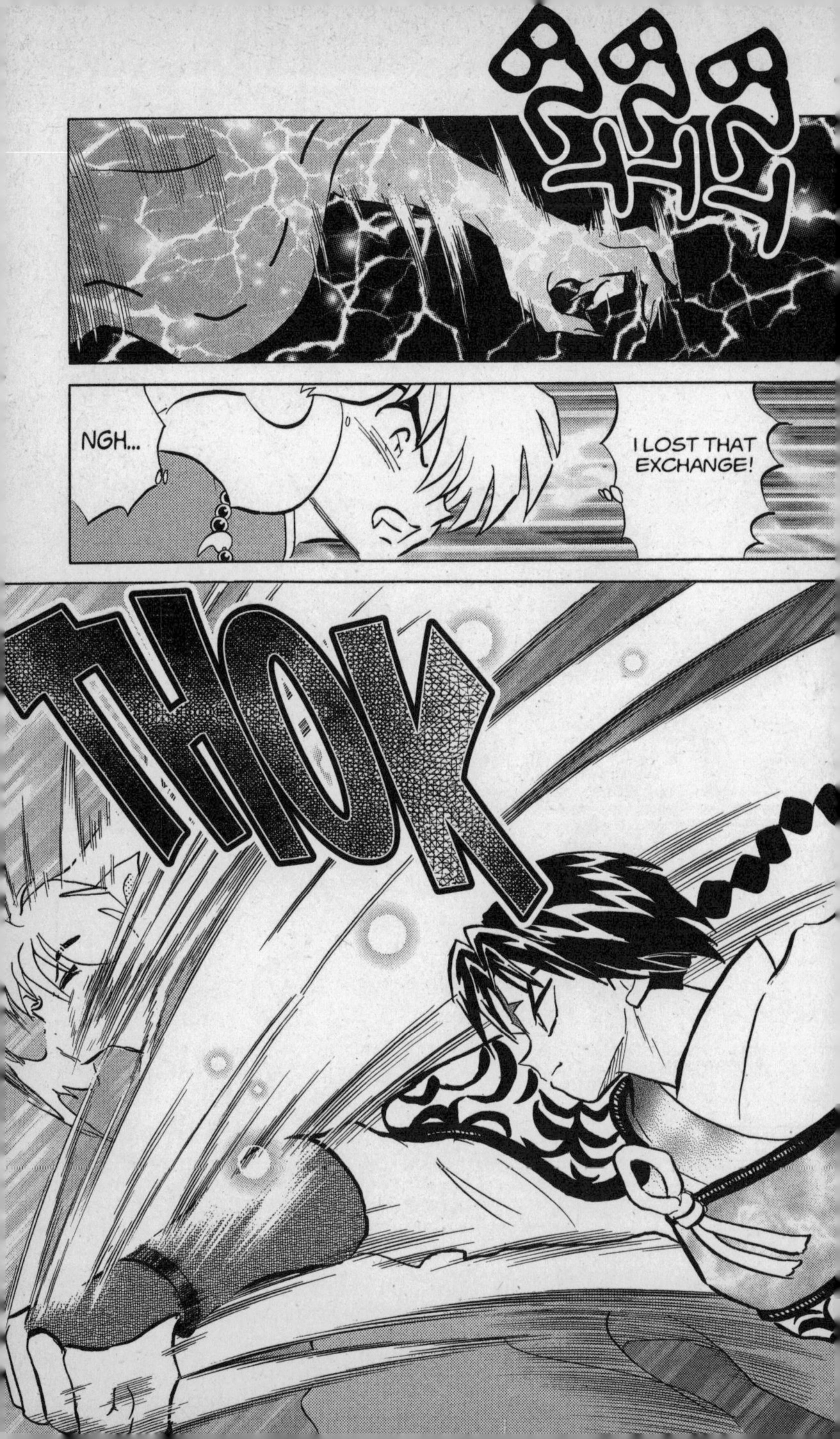
BZZZT
NGH...
I LOST THAT EXCHANGE!
THOK

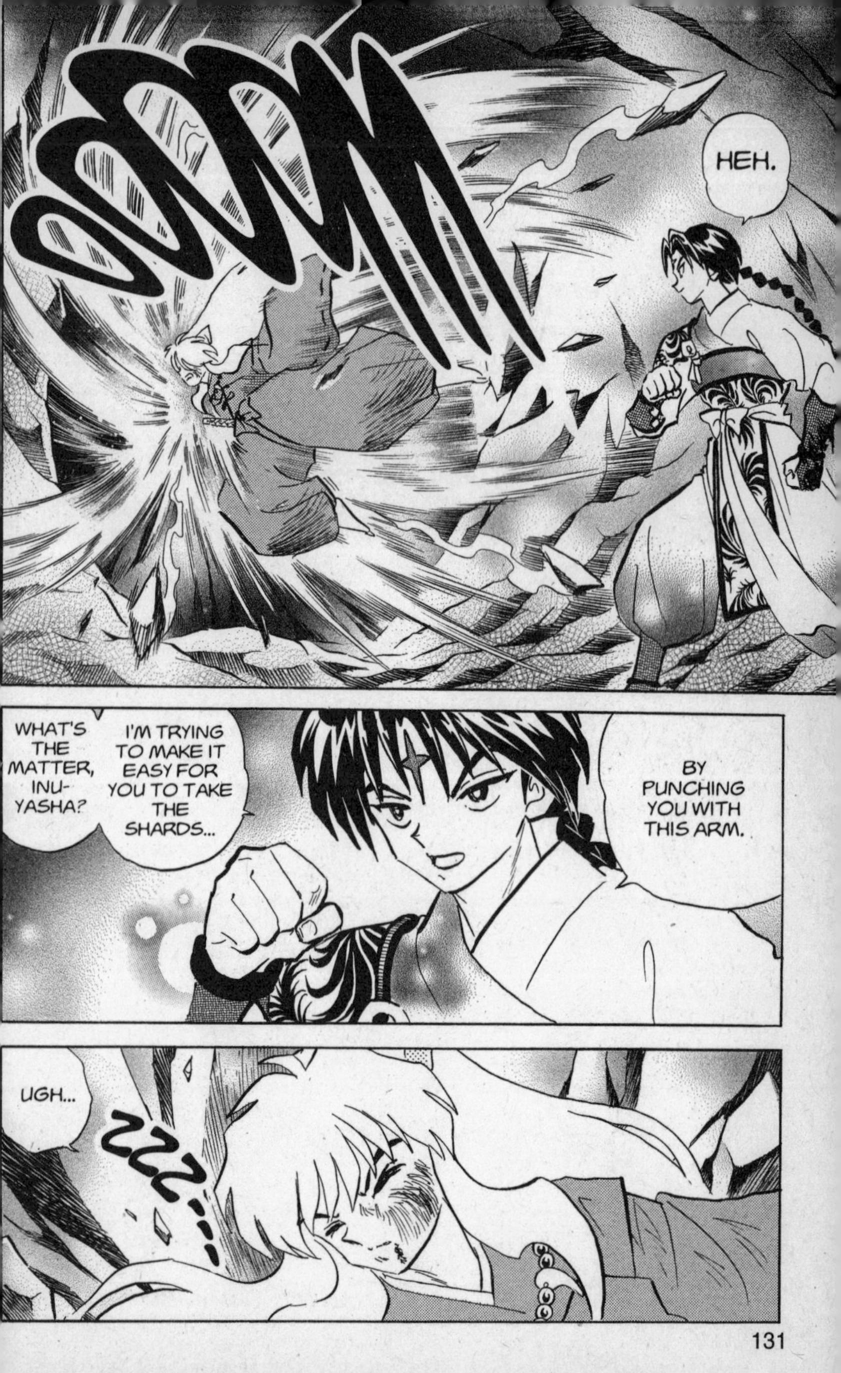
HEH.
WHAT'S THE MATTER, INU-YASHA?
I'M TRYING TO MAKE IT EASY FOR YOU TO TAKE THE SHARDS...
BY PUNCHING YOU WITH THIS ARM.
UGH...

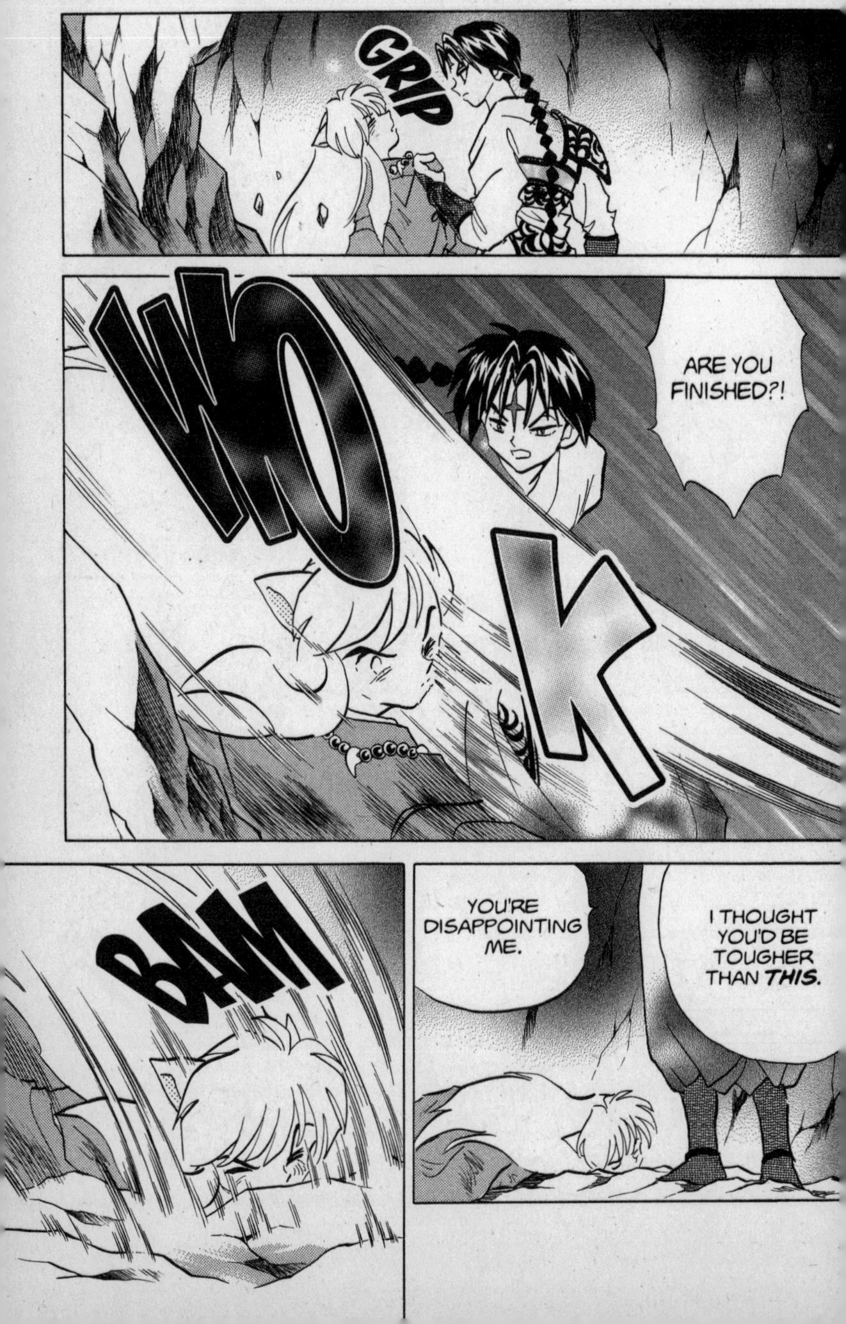
GRIP
WHOK
ARE YOU FINISHED?!
BAM
YOU'RE DISAPPOINTING ME.
I THOUGHT YOU'D BE TOUGHER THAN ***THIS.***

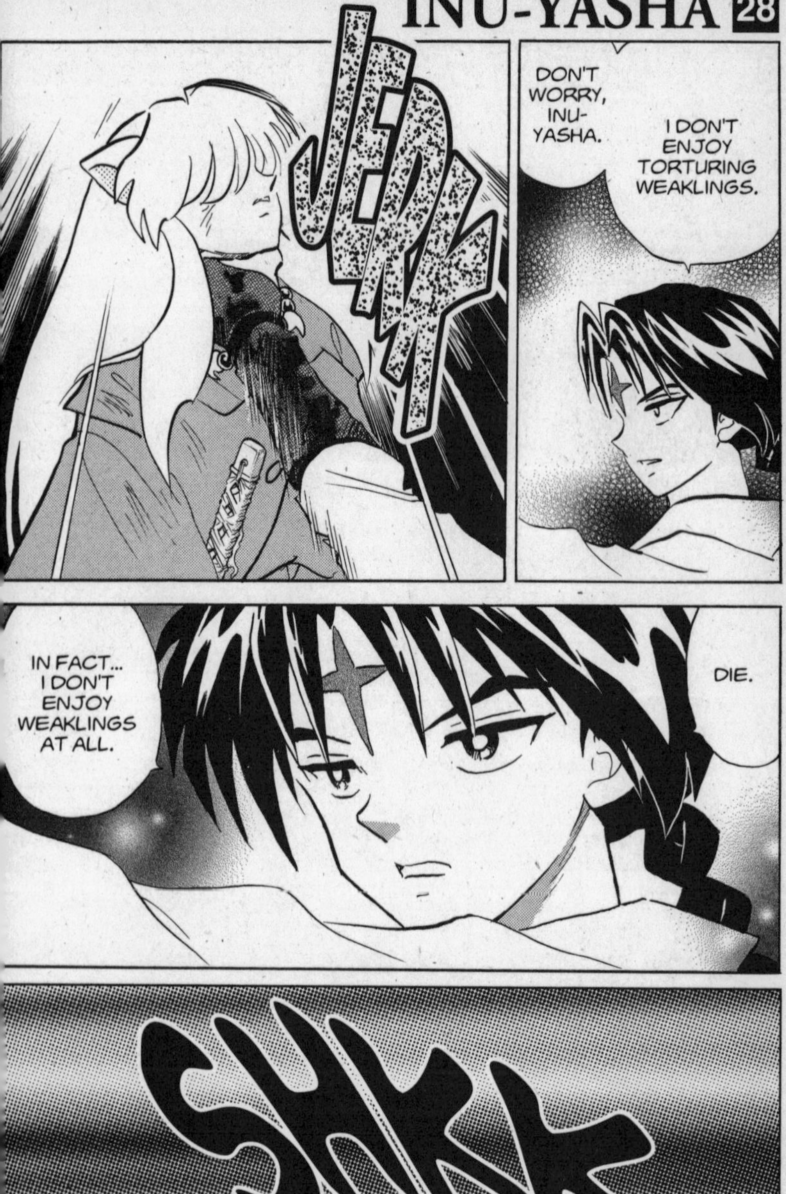
JERK
DON'T WORRY, INU-YASHA.
I DON'T ENJOY TORTURING WEAKLINGS.
IN FACT... I DON'T ENJOY WEAKLINGS AT ALL.
DIE.
SHK

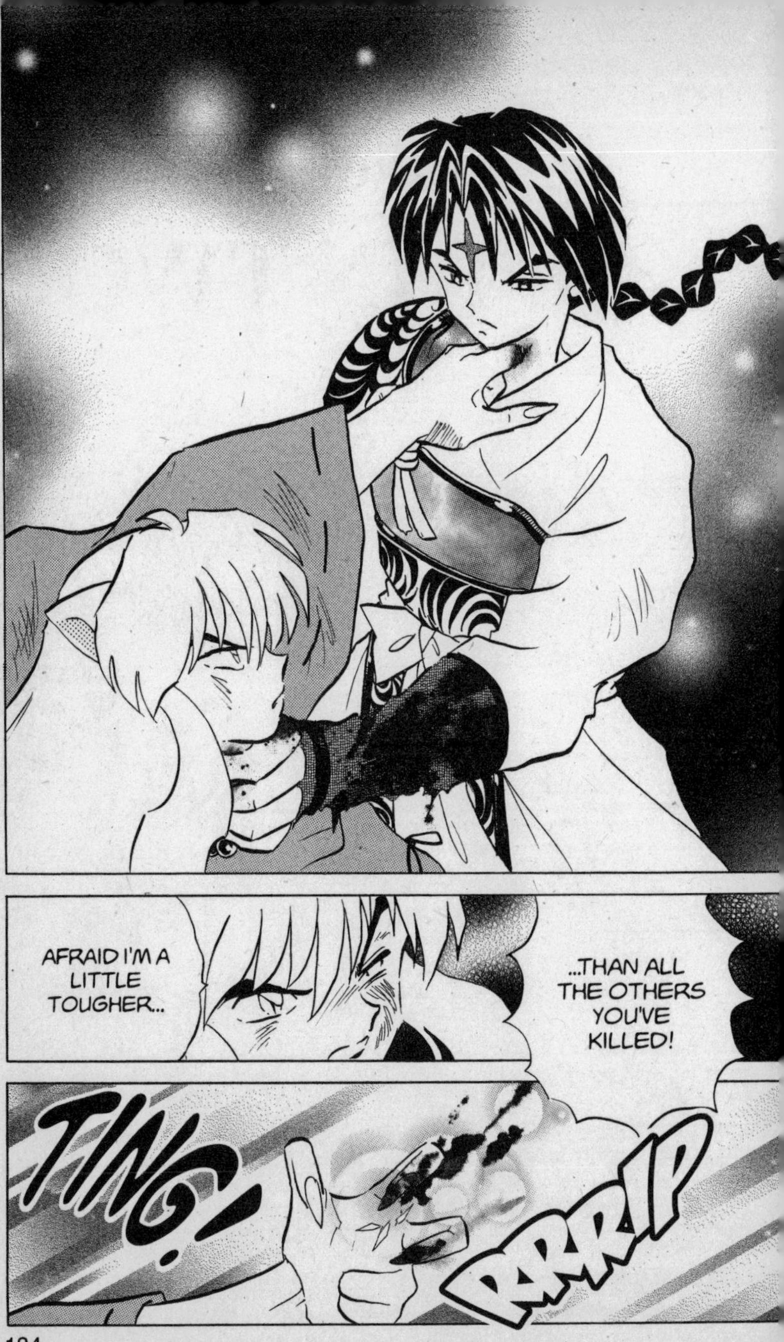

AFRAID I'M A LITTLE TOUGHER...
...THAN ALL THE OTHERS YOU'VE KILLED!
TING!
RRRIP

SCROLL 8

CUT IN TWO

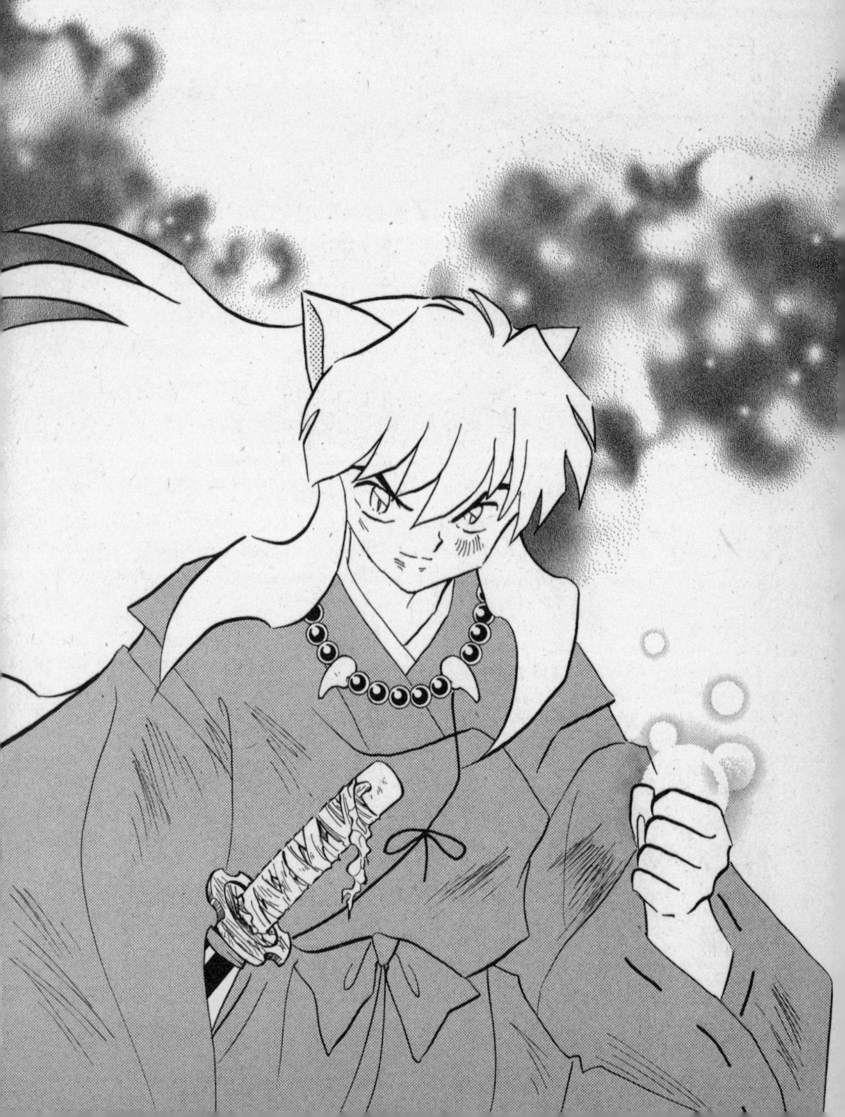

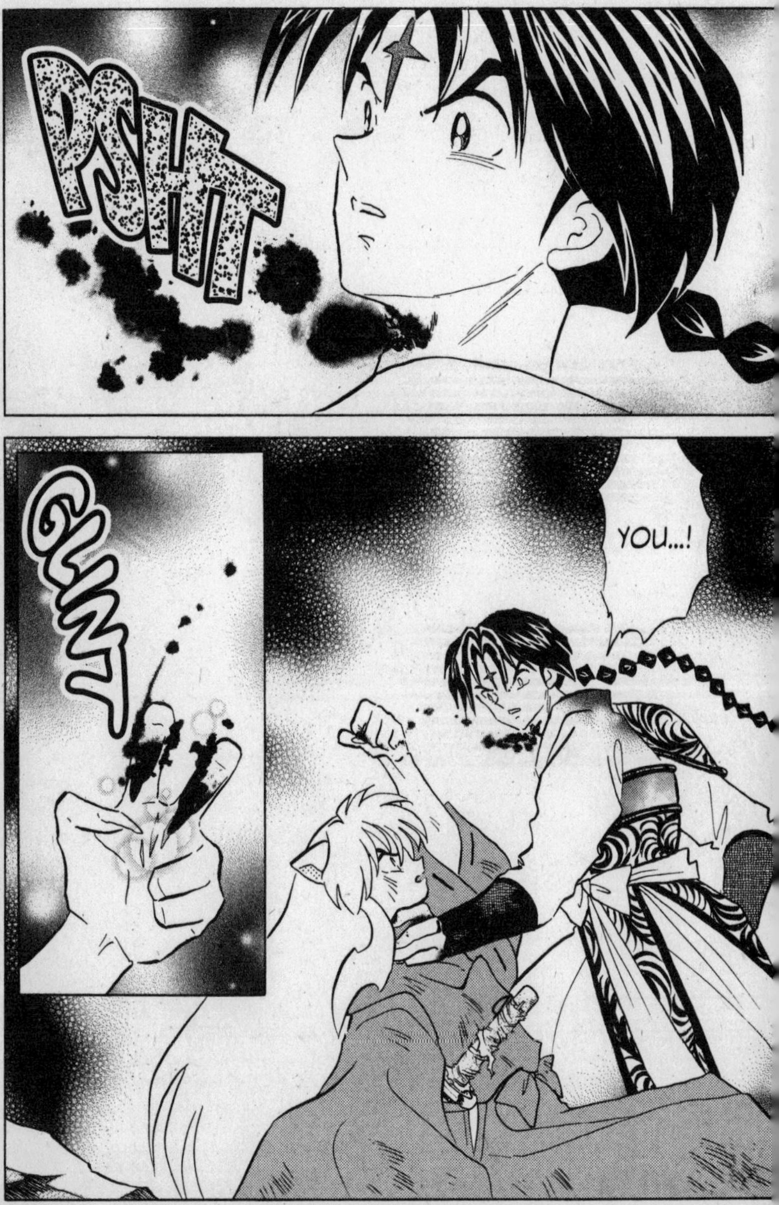
PSHT
GLINT
YOU...!

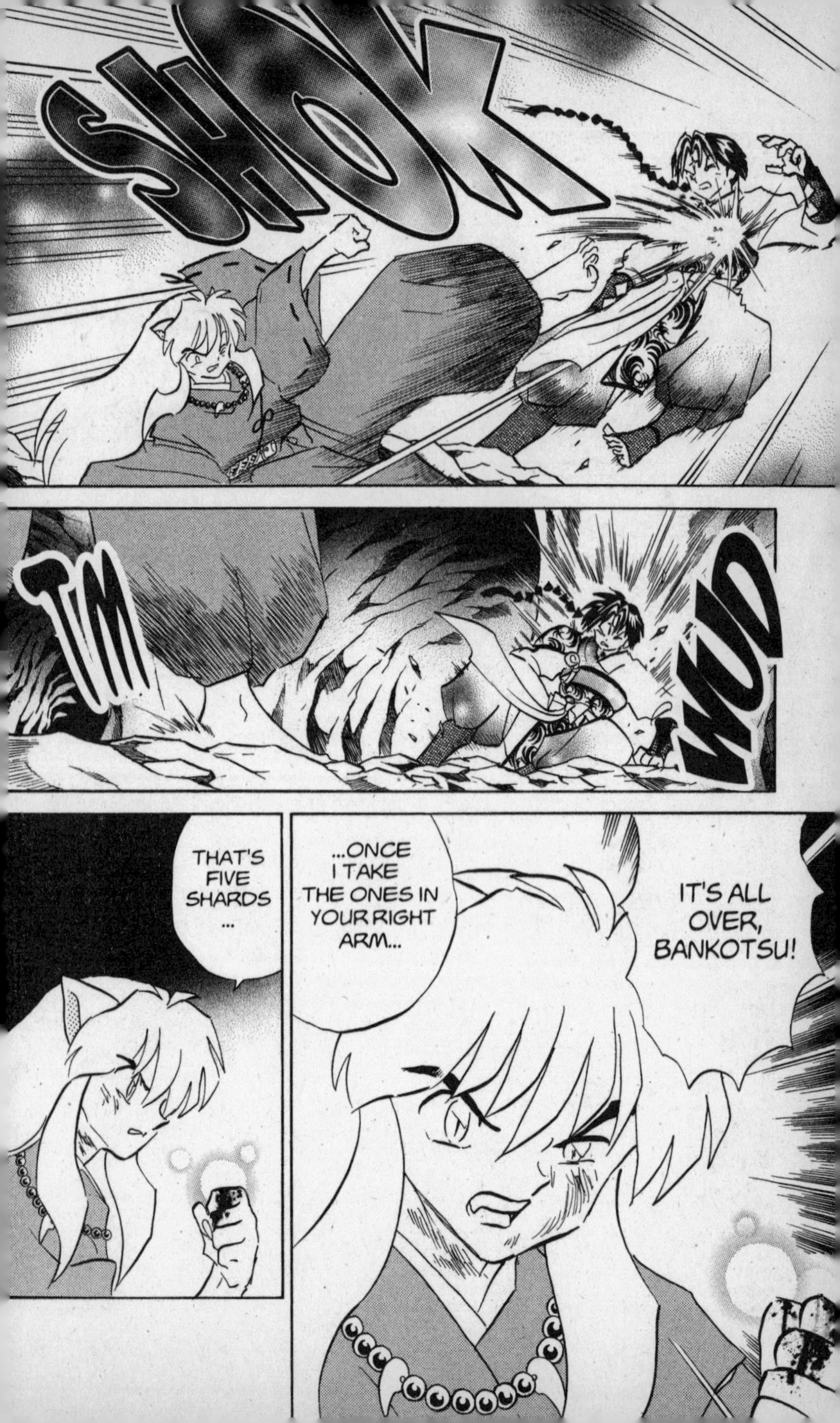
THAT'S FIVE SHARDS ...
...ONCE I TAKE THE ONES IN YOUR RIGHT ARM...
IT'S ALL OVER, BANKOTSU!

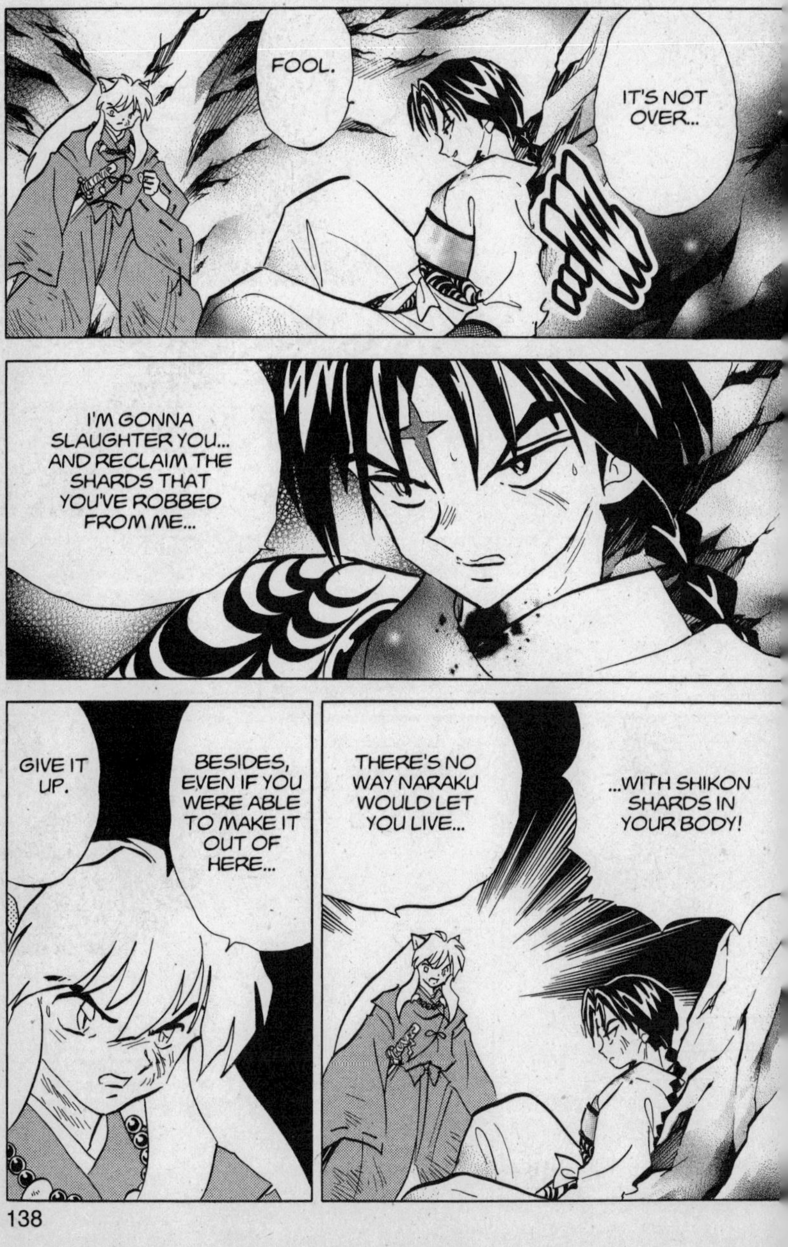
FOOL.
IT'S NOT OVER...
I'M GONNA SLAUGHTER YOU... AND RECLAIM THE SHARDS THAT YOU'VE ROBBED FROM ME...
GIVE IT UP.
BESIDES, EVEN IF YOU WERE ABLE TO MAKE IT OUT OF HERE...
THERE'S NO WAY NARAKU WOULD LET YOU LIVE...
...WITH SHIKON SHARDS IN YOUR BODY!

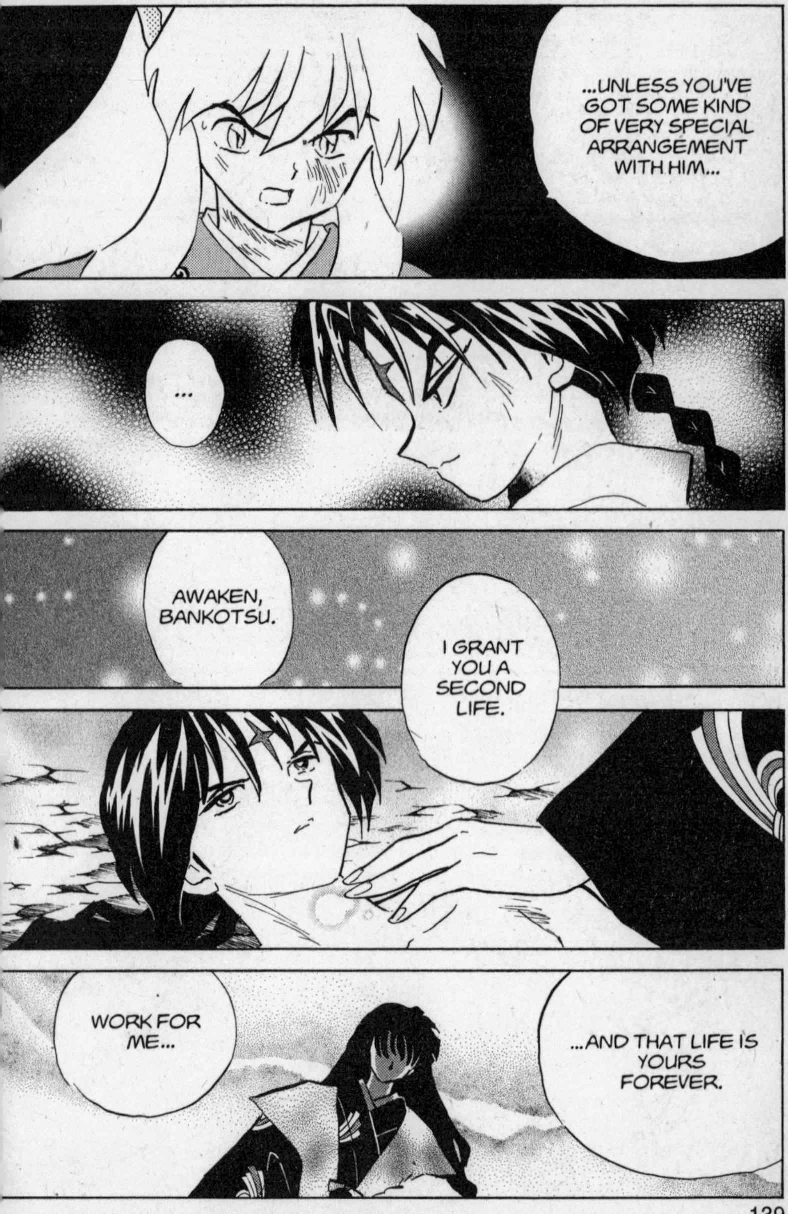
...UNLESS YOU'VE GOT SOME KIND OF VERY SPECIAL ARRANGEMENT WITH HIM...
...
AWAKEN, BANKOTSU.
I GRANT YOU A SECOND LIFE.
WORK FOR ME...
...AND THAT LIFE IS YOURS FOREVER.

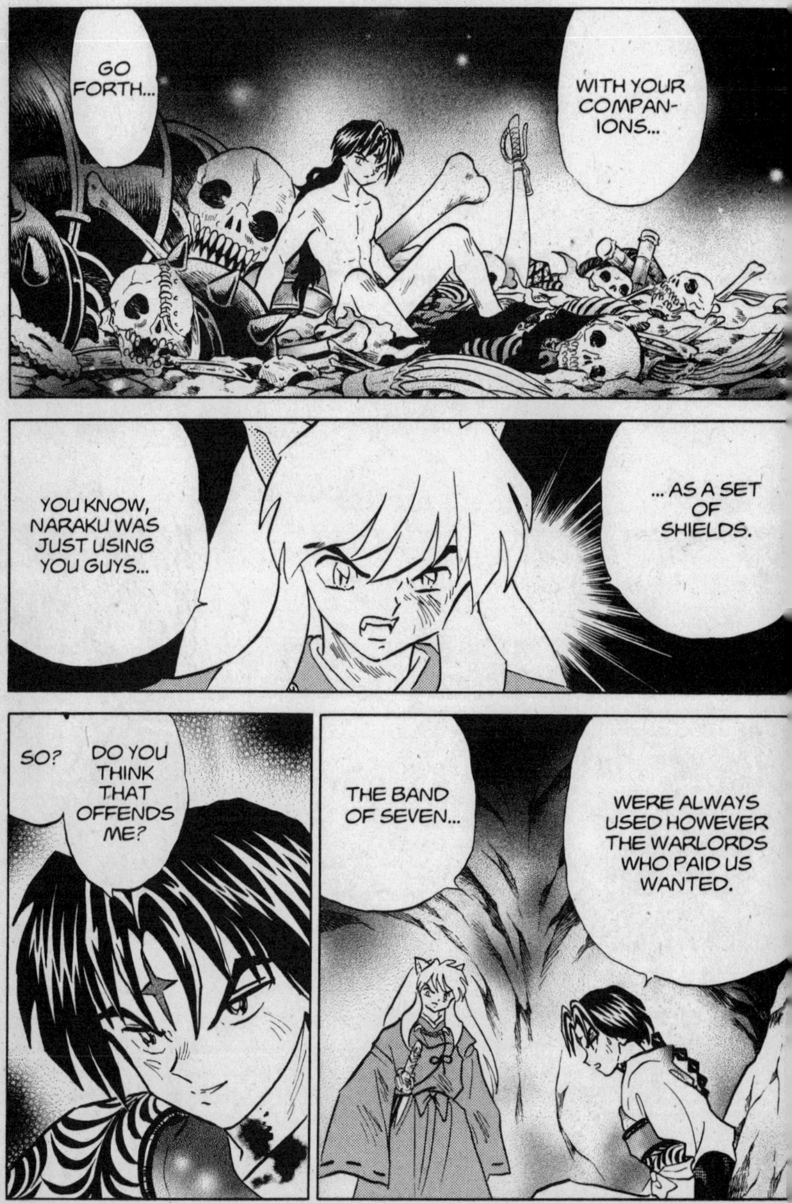
GO FORTH...
WITH YOUR COMPAN-IONS...
YOU KNOW, NARAKU WAS JUST USING YOU GUYS...
...AS A SET OF SHIELDS.
SO?
DO YOU THINK THAT OFFENDS ME?
THE BAND OF SEVEN...
WERE ALWAYS USED HOWEVER THE WARLORDS WHO PAID US WANTED.

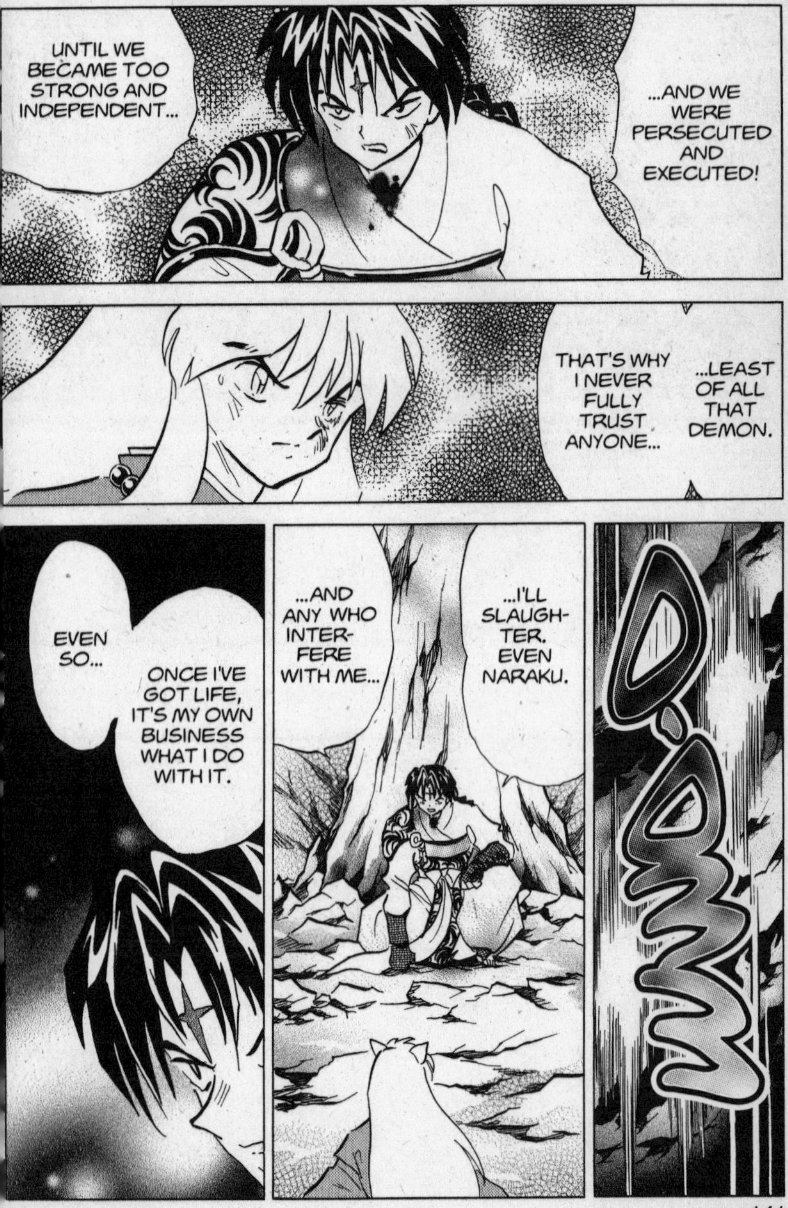
UNTIL WE BECAME TOO STRONG AND INDEPENDENT...
...AND WE WERE PERSECUTED AND EXECUTED!
THAT'S WHY I NEVER FULLY TRUST ANYONE...
...LEAST OF ALL THAT DEMON.
EVEN SO...
ONCE I'VE GOT LIFE, IT'S MY OWN BUSINESS WHAT I DO WITH IT.
...AND ANY WHO INTERFERE WITH ME...
...I'LL SLAUGHTER. EVEN NARAKU.
D-DMM

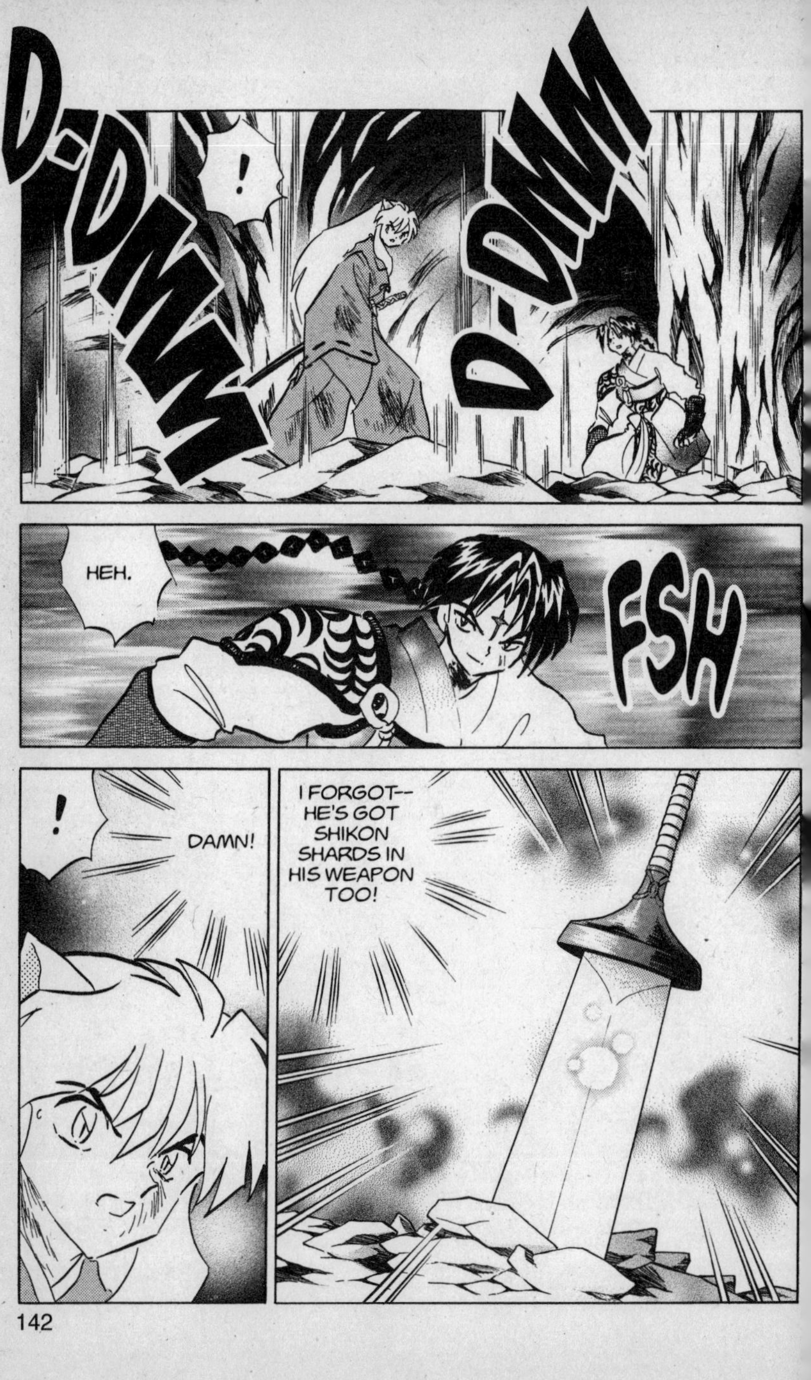
D-DMM
!
D-DMM!
HEH.
FSH
!
DAMN!
I FORGOT-- HE'S GOT SHIKON SHARDS IN HIS WEAPON TOO!

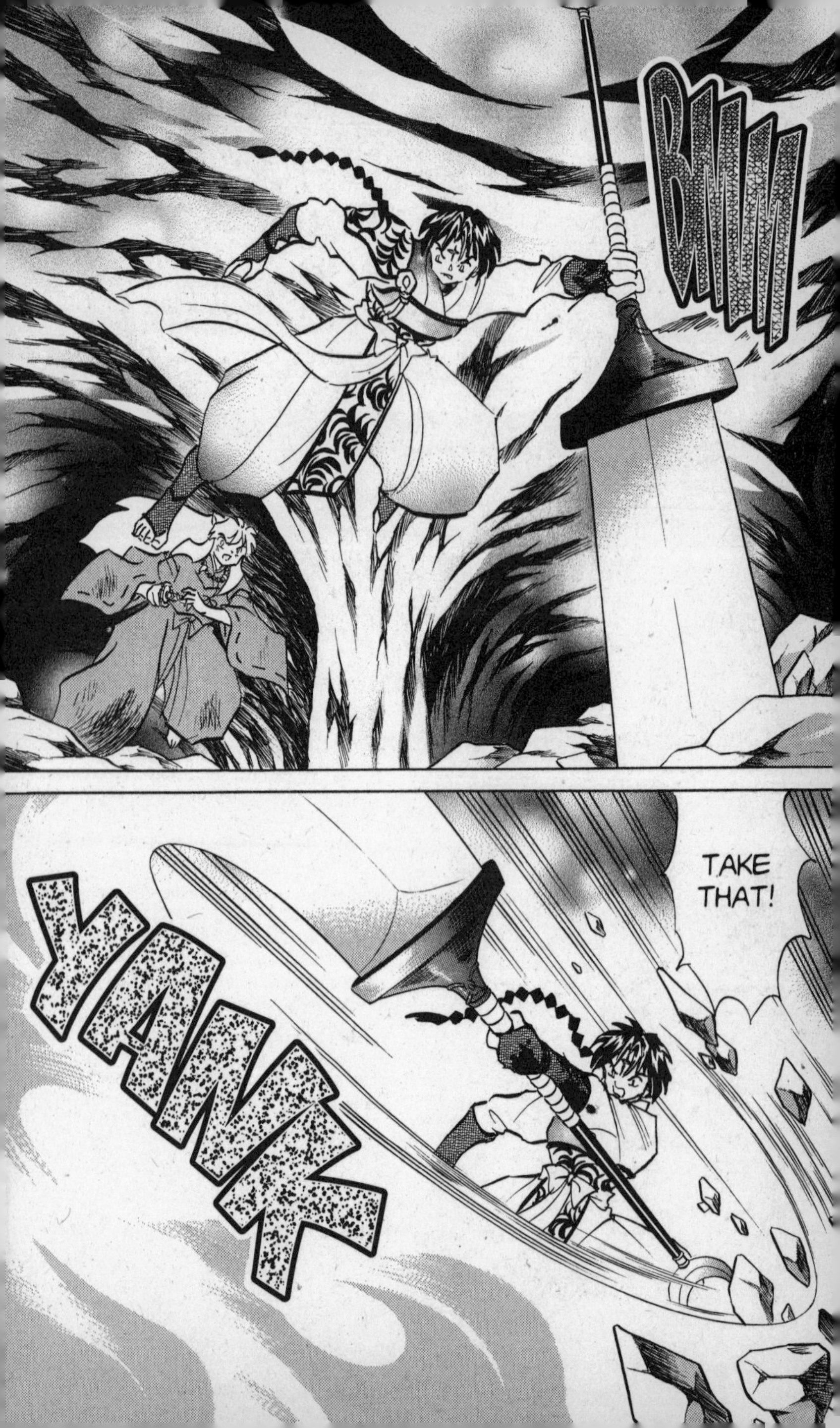
TAKE THAT!
YANK

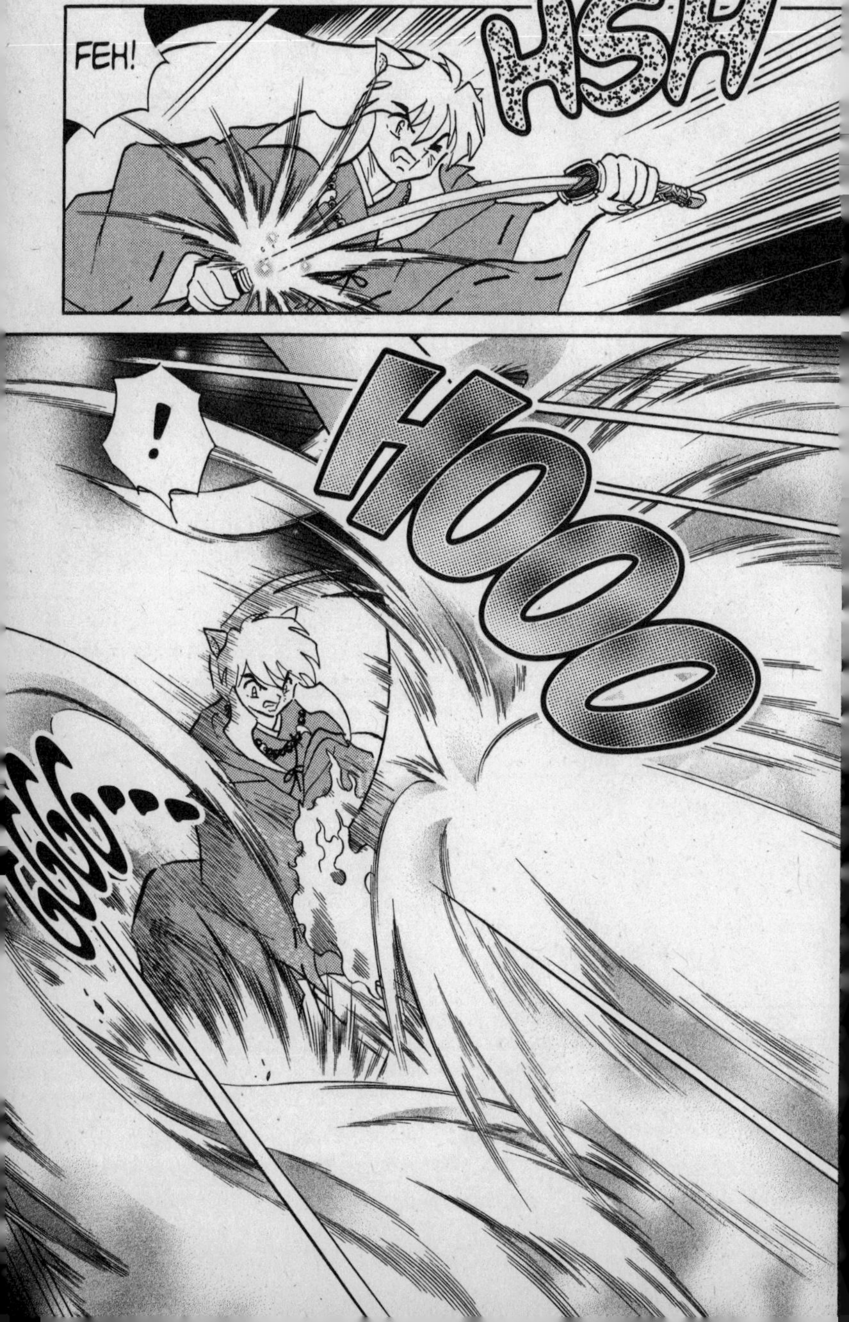
FEH!
HSH
!
HOOOO
GGGG...

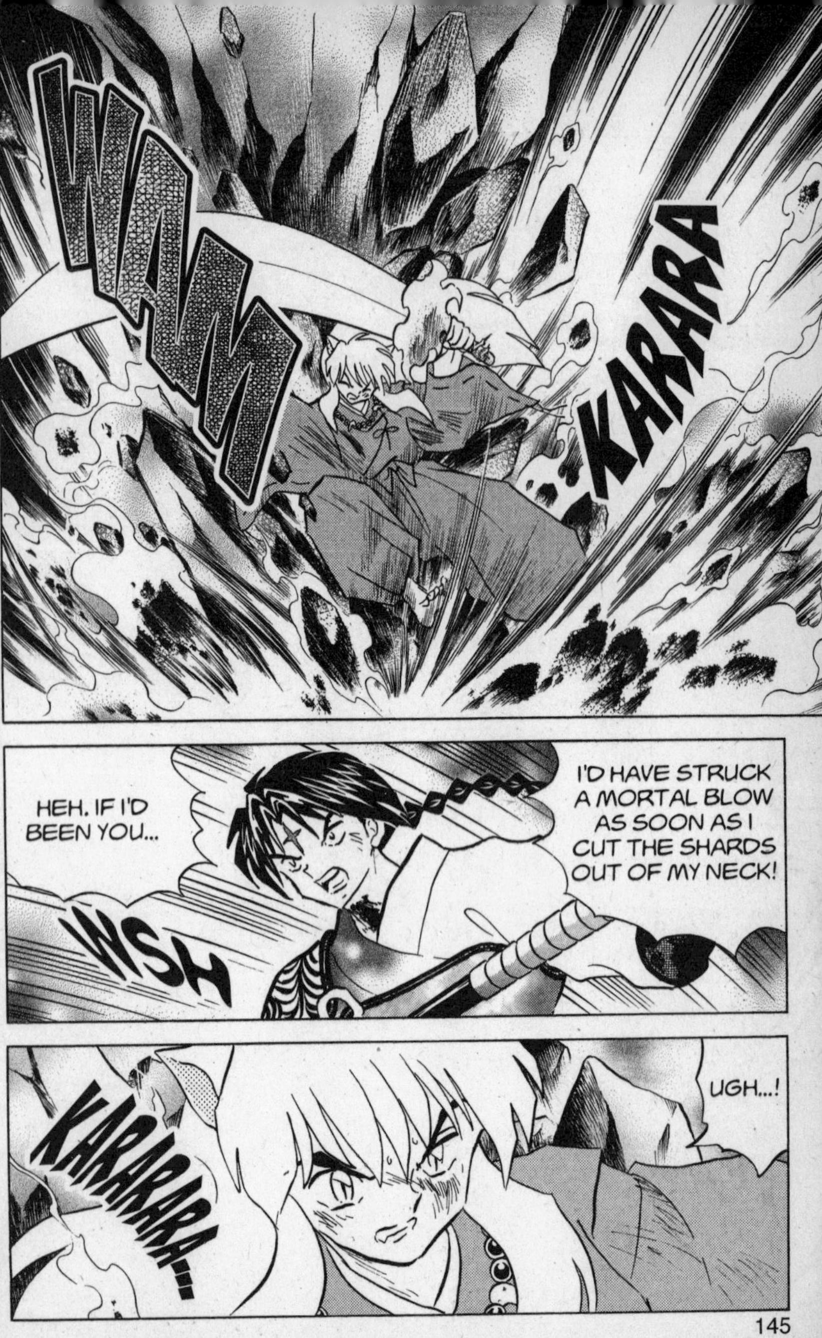
WAAM
KARARA
HEH. IF I'D BEEN YOU...
I'D HAVE STRUCK A MORTAL BLOW AS SOON AS I CUT THE SHARDS OUT OF MY NECK!
WSH
KARARARA...
UGH...!

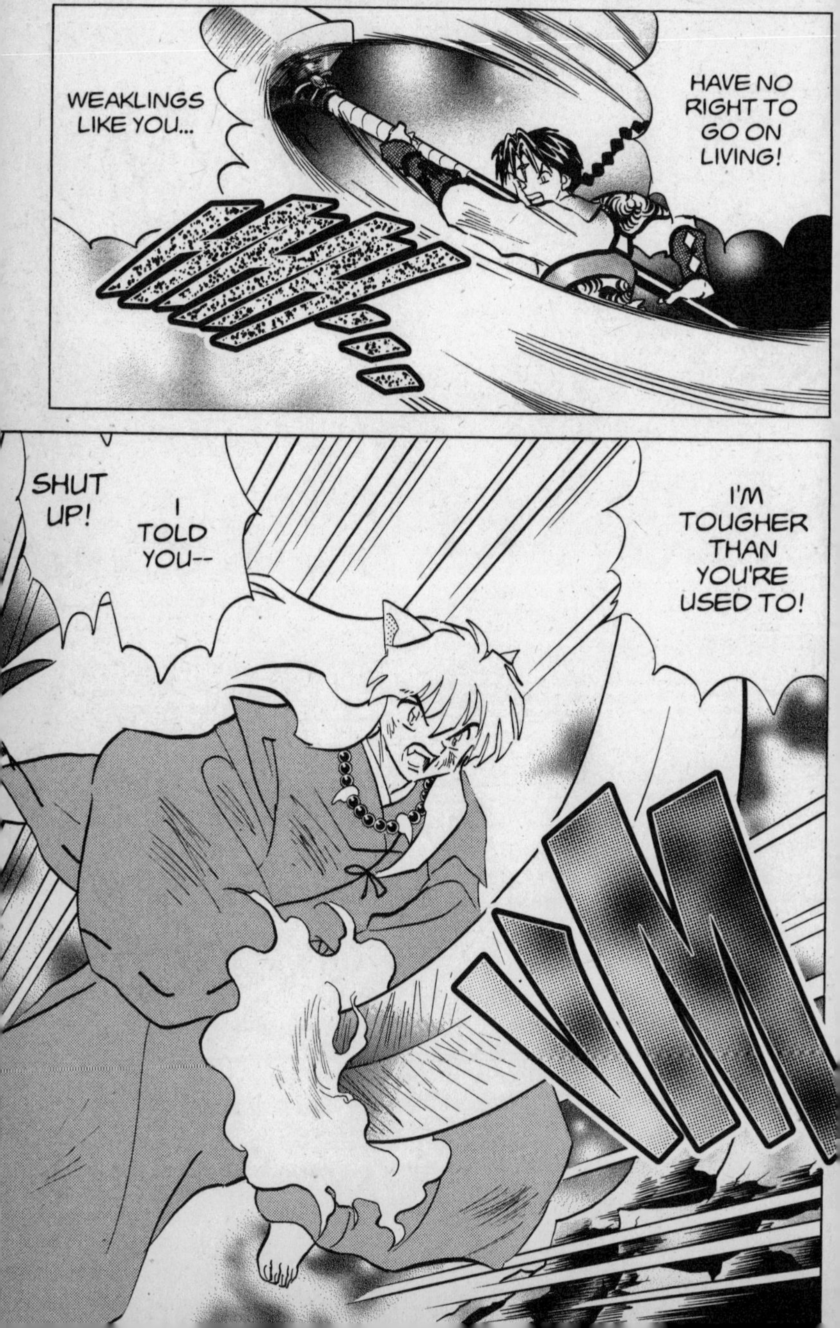
WEAKLINGS LIKE YOU...
HAVE NO RIGHT TO GO ON LIVING!
SHUT UP!
I TOLD YOU--
I'M TOUGHER THAN YOU'RE USED TO!

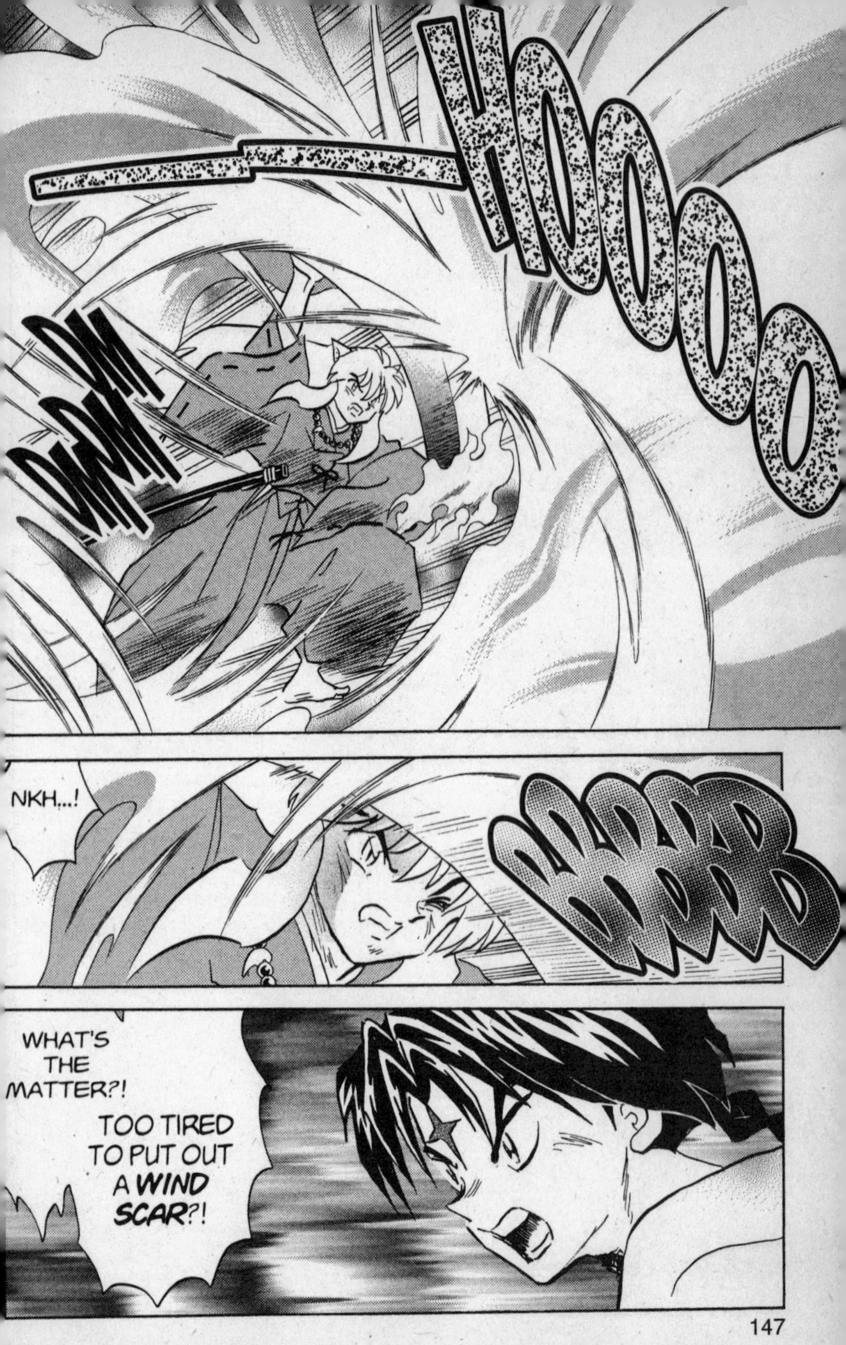
HOOOOOO
DWOW
NKH...!
BBBB
WHAT'S THE MATTER?!
TOO TIRED TO PUT OUT A **WIND SCAR**?!

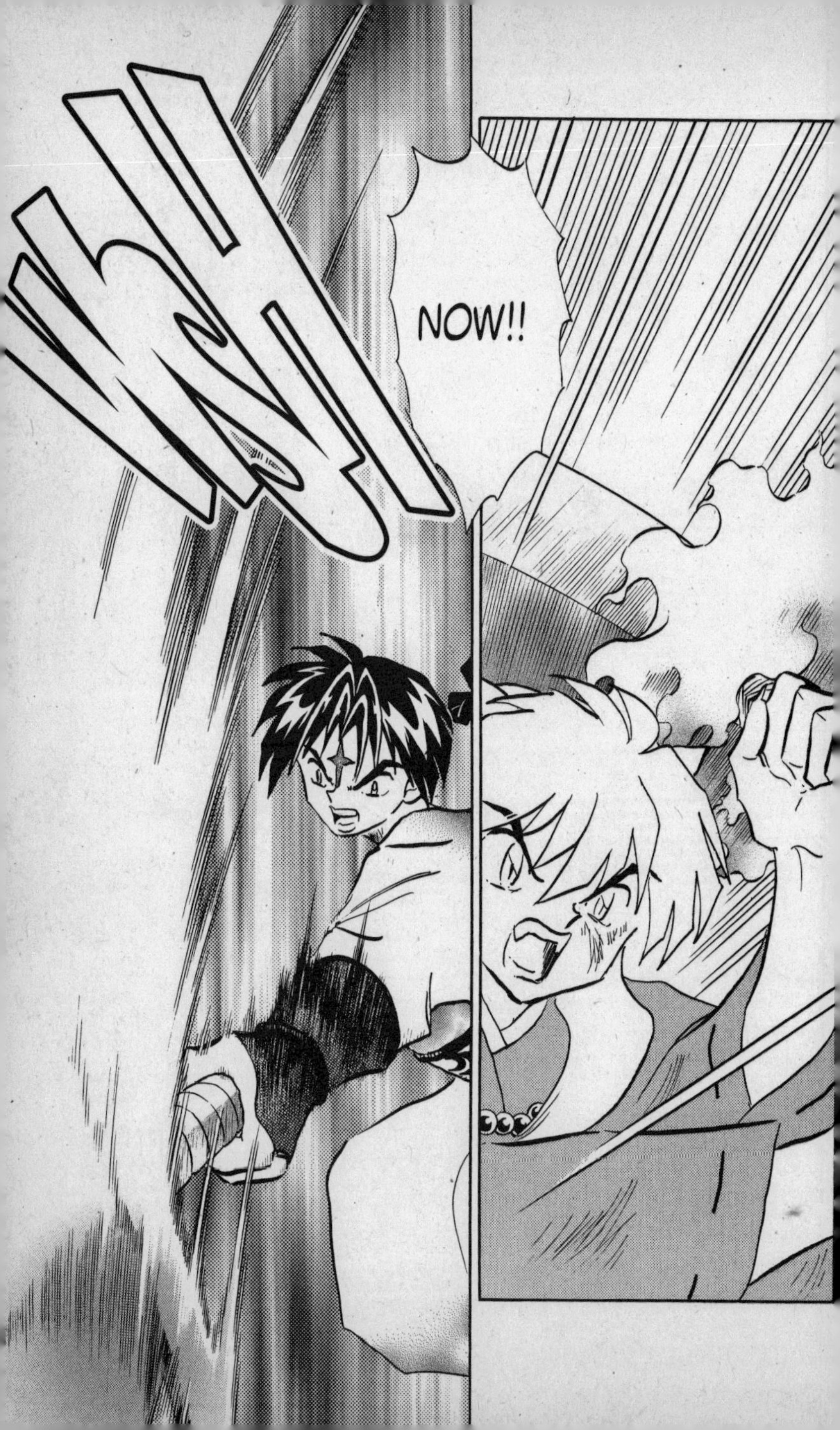
NOW!!

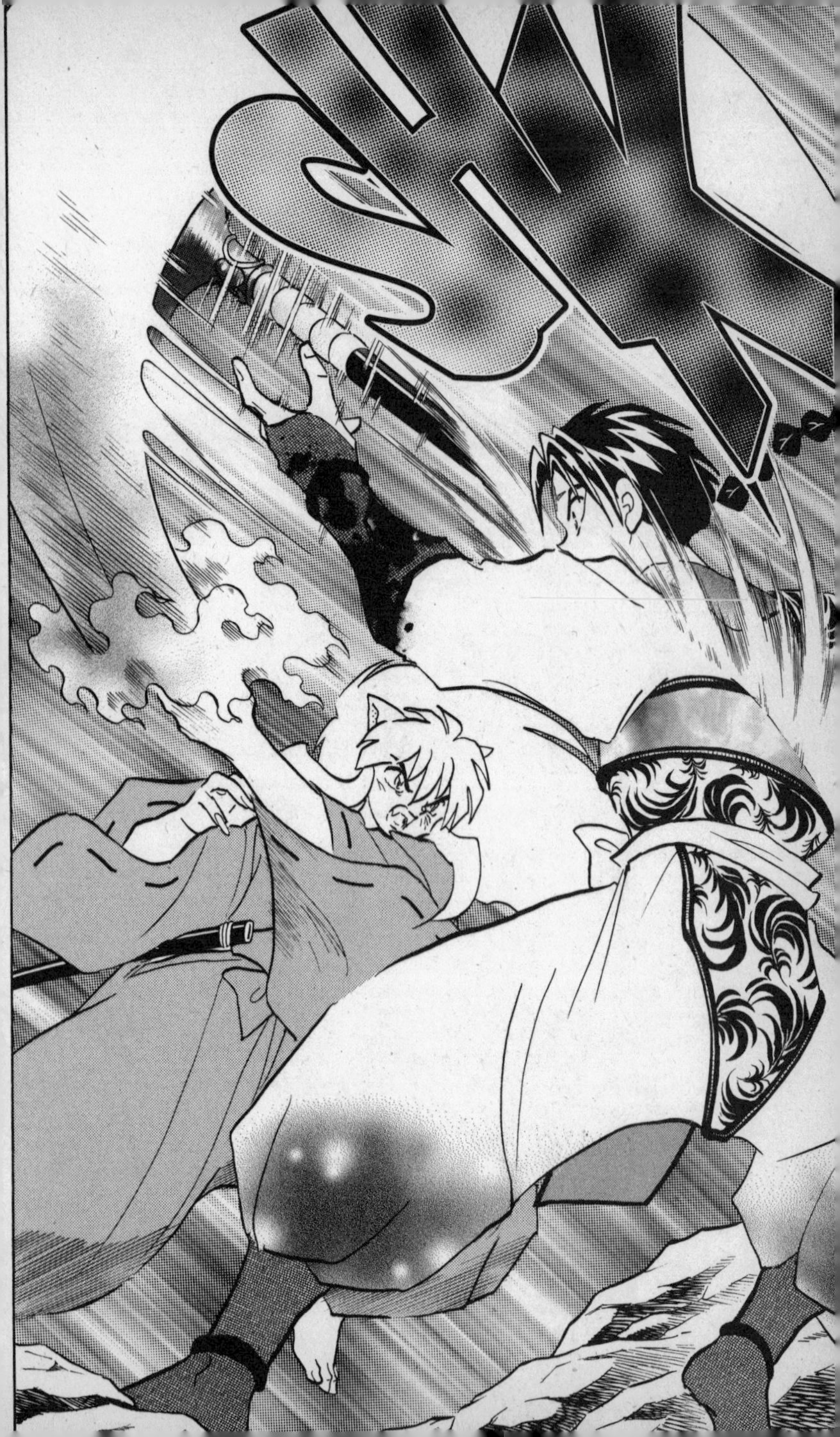

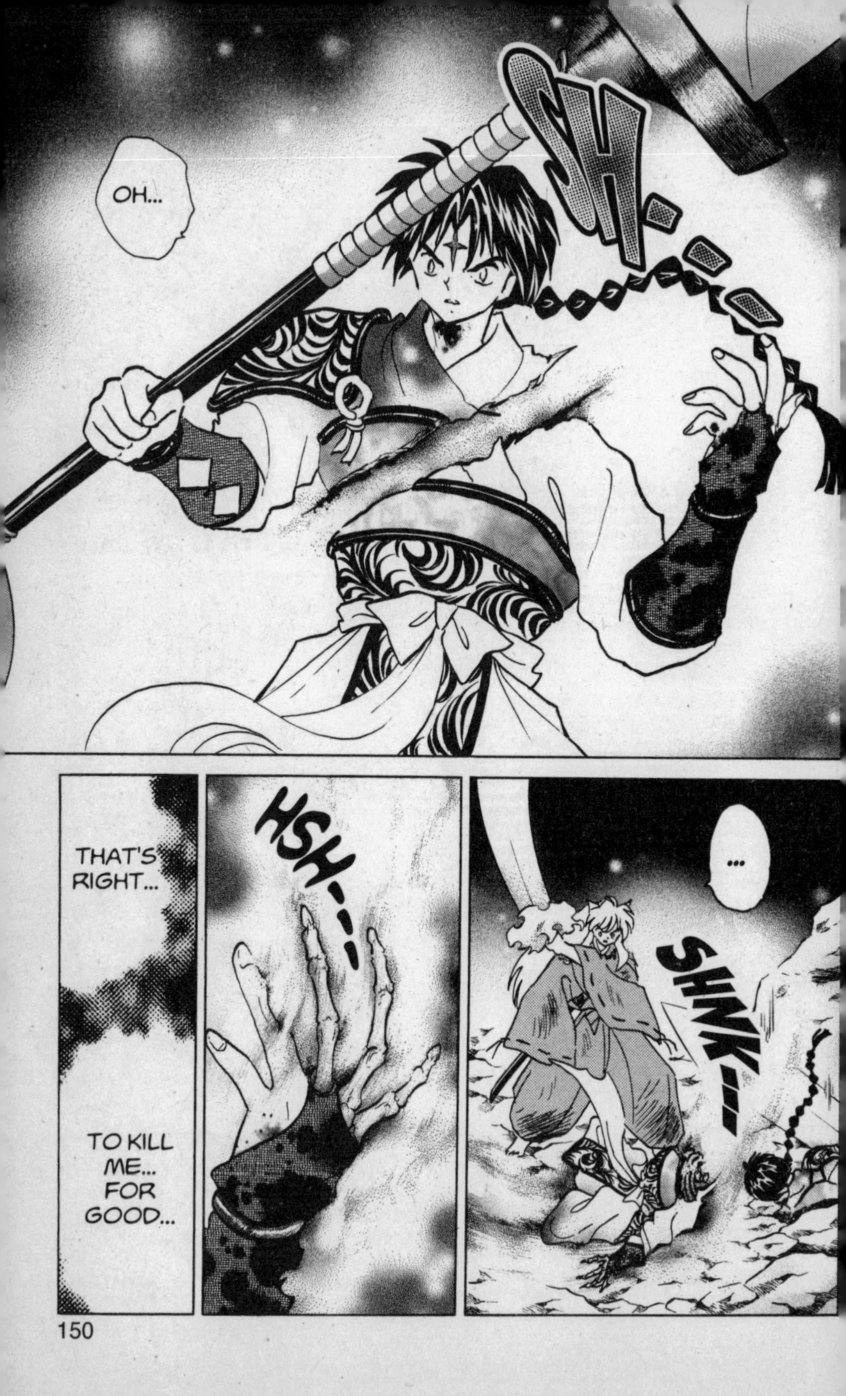
OH...
SH...
THAT'S RIGHT...
TO KILL ME... FOR GOOD...
HSH...
...
SHNK...

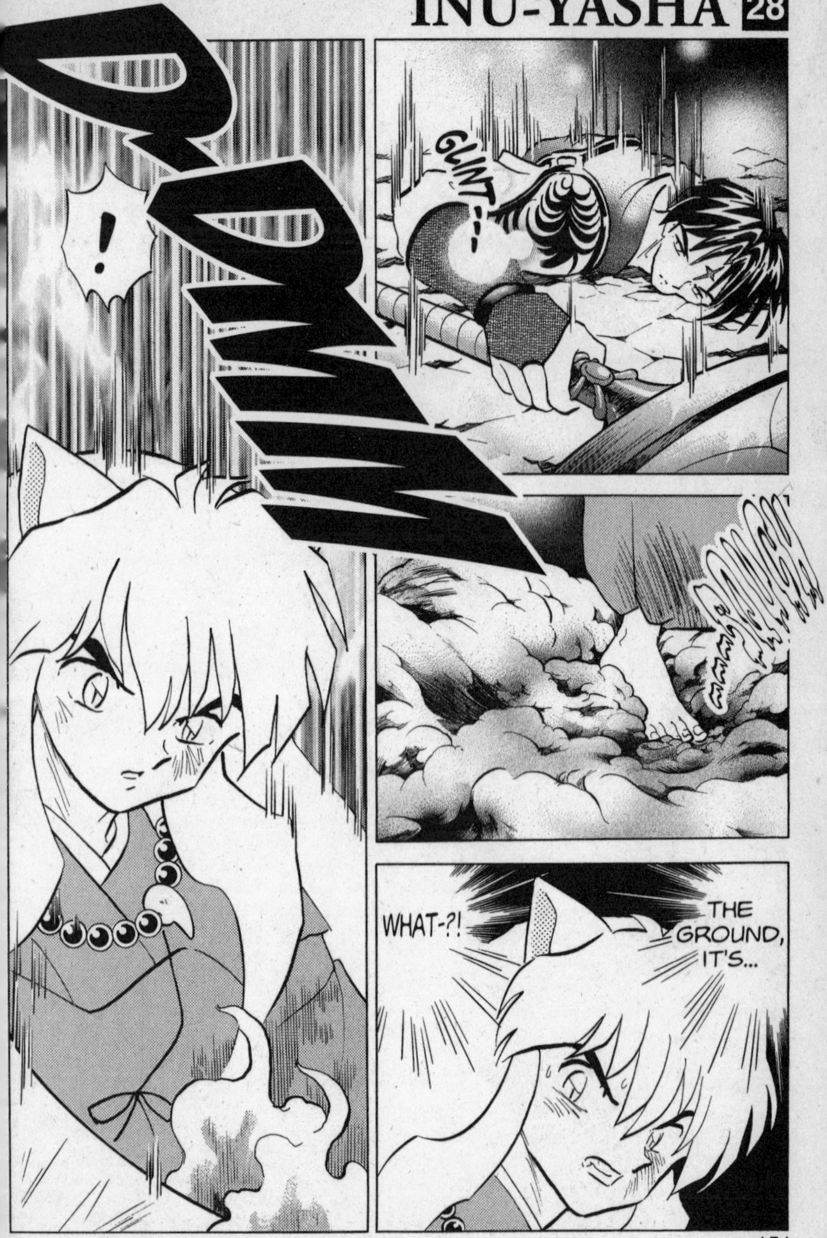
!
GLINT--
WHAT-?!
THE GROUND, IT'S...

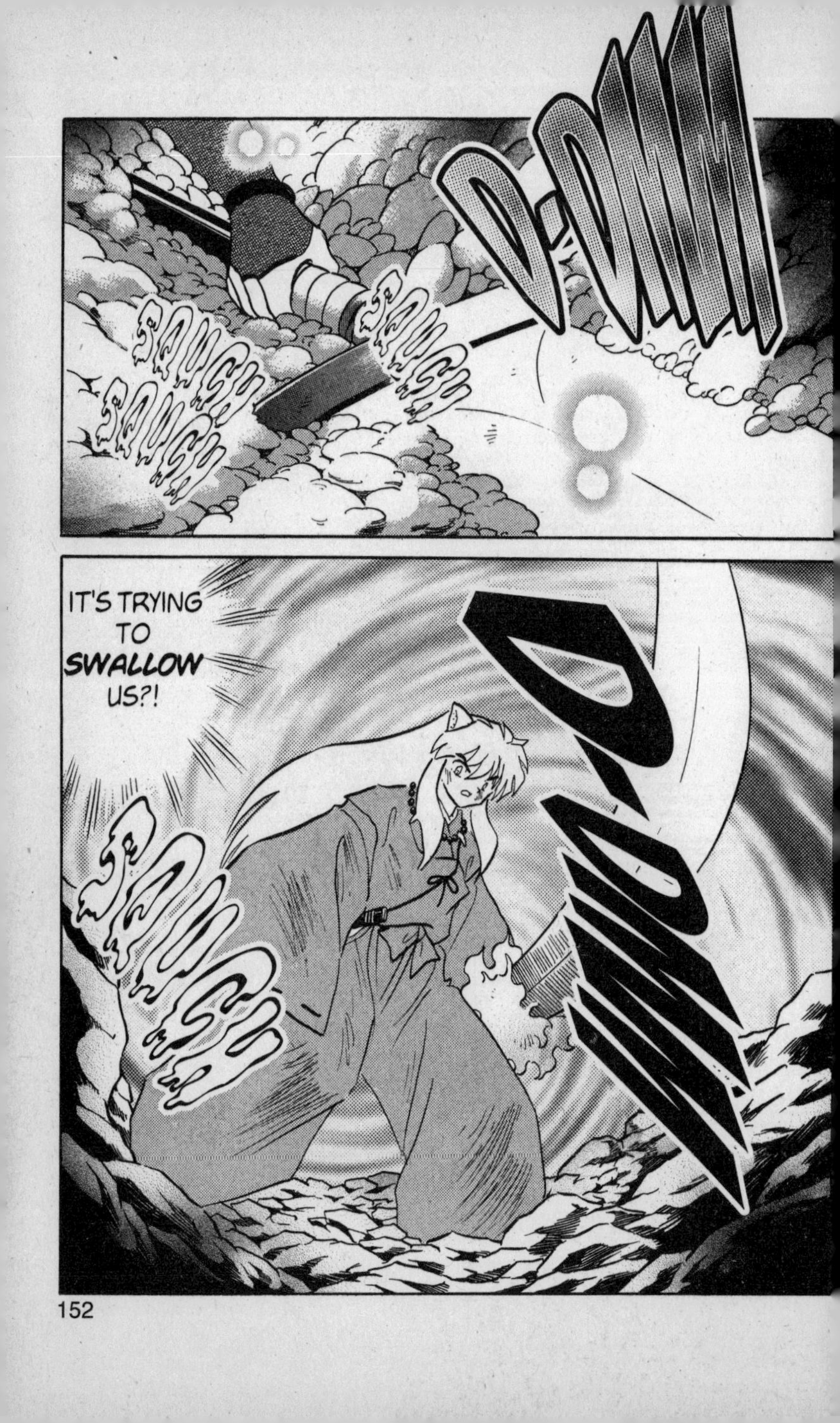
D-DOMM
SQUICH
SQUICH
SQUICH
IT'S TRYING TO SWALLOW US?!
DOOMMM
SQUICH

SCROLL 9
THE WALL OF FLESH

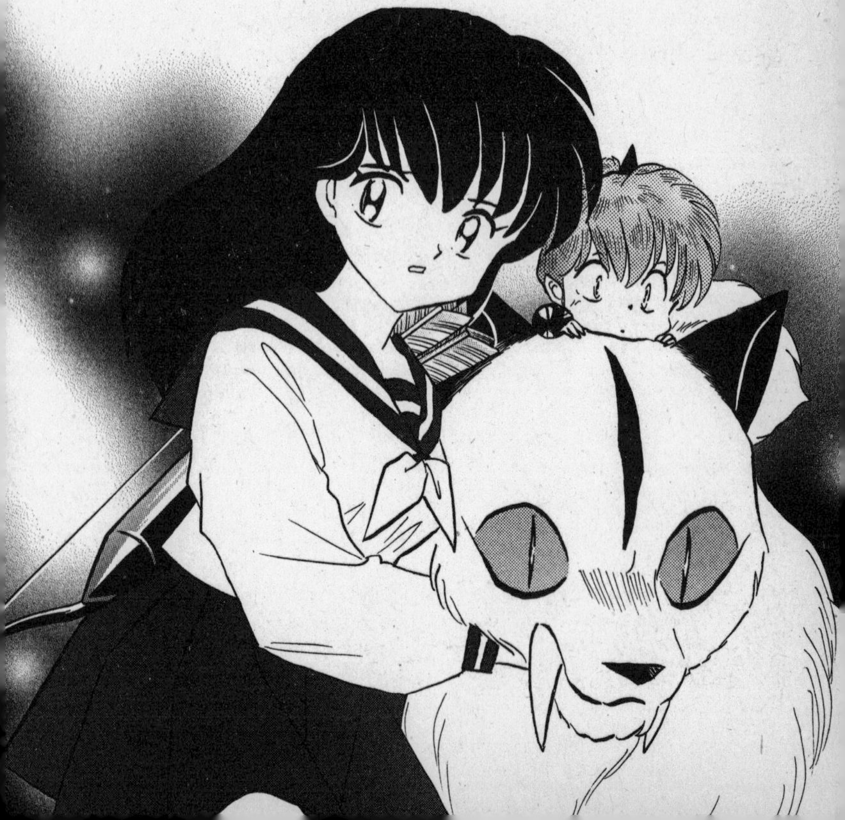

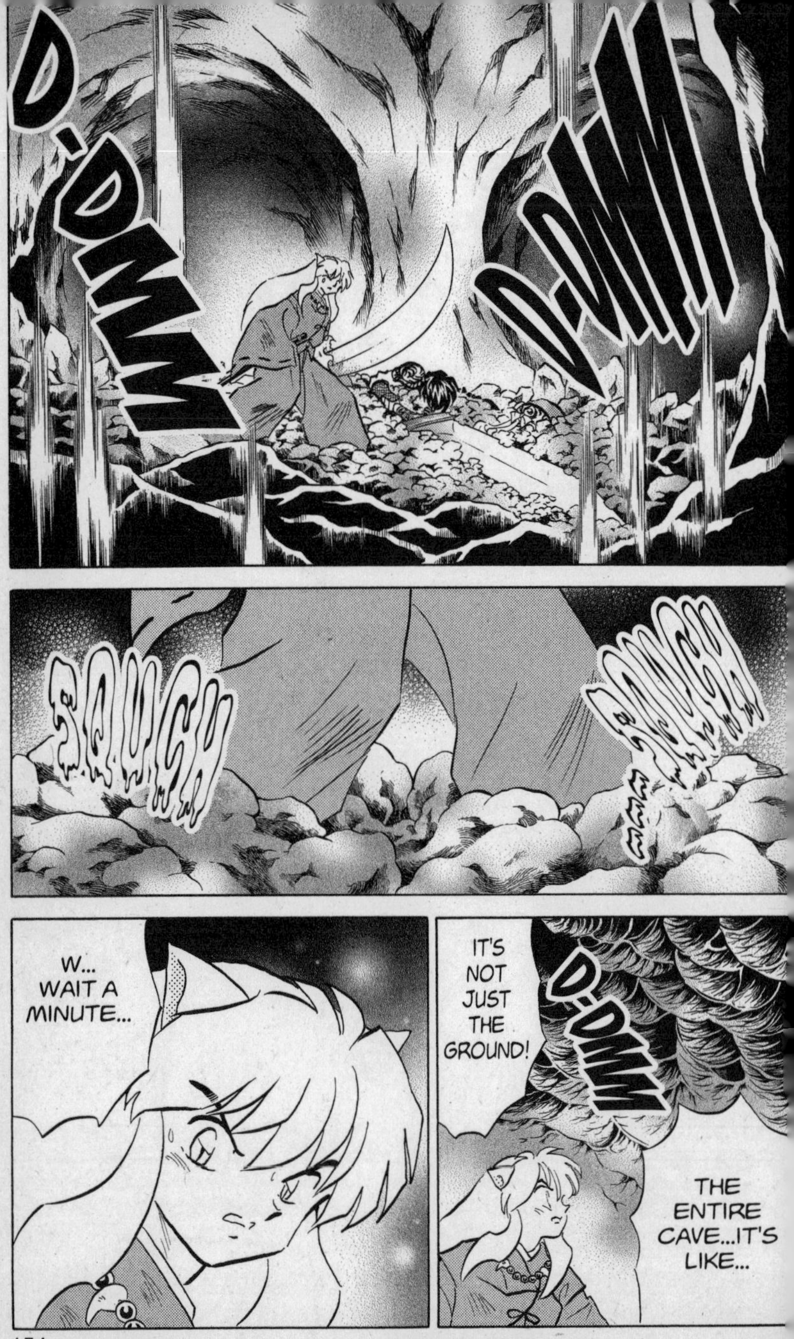
D-DMM
D-DMM
SQUCH
W... WAIT A MINUTE...
IT'S NOT JUST THE GROUND!
D-DMM
THE ENTIRE CAVE...IT'S LIKE...

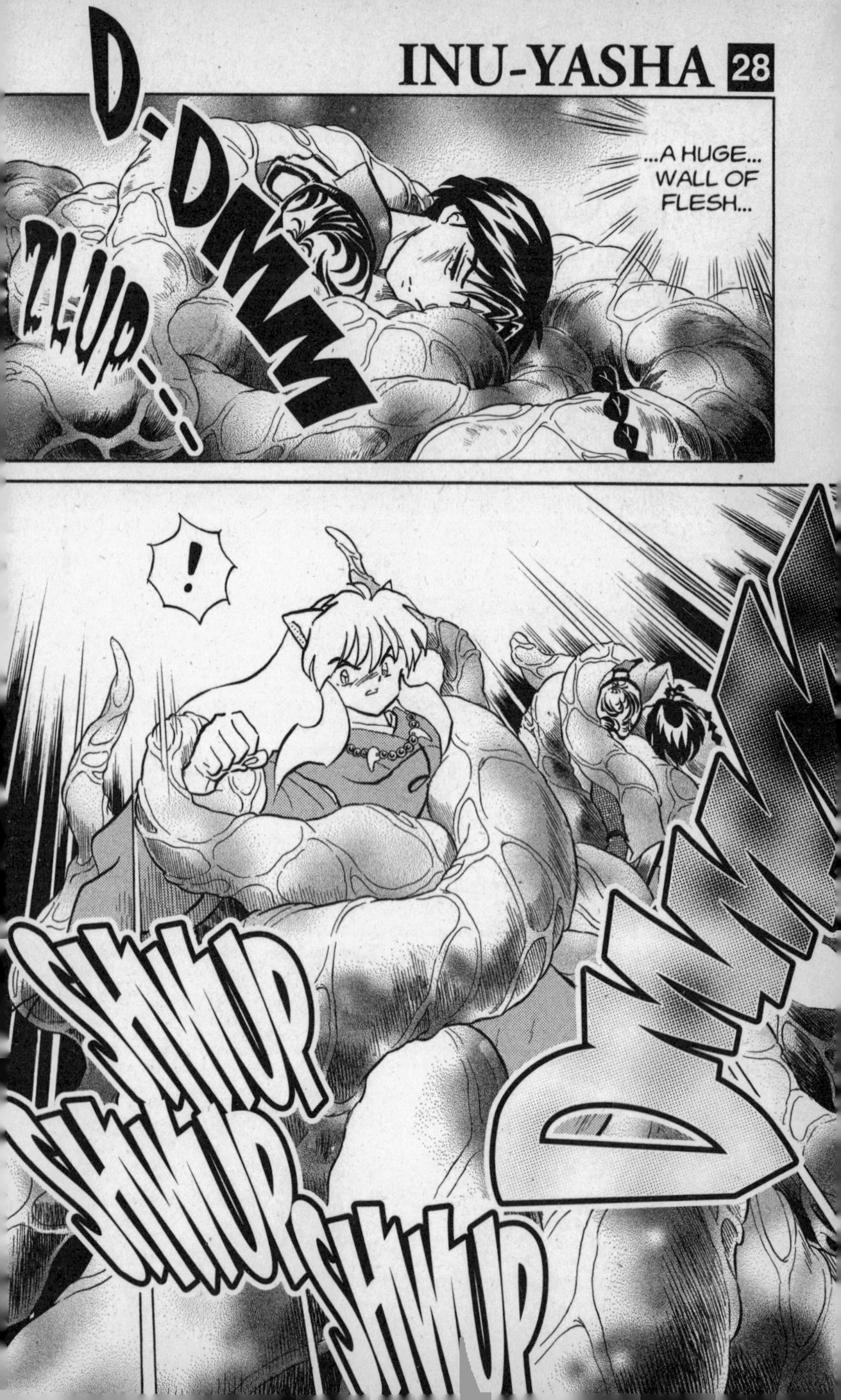
D-DMMM
ZLUP...
...A HUGE... WALL OF FLESH...
!
SHMUP
SHMUP
SHMUP
DMMM

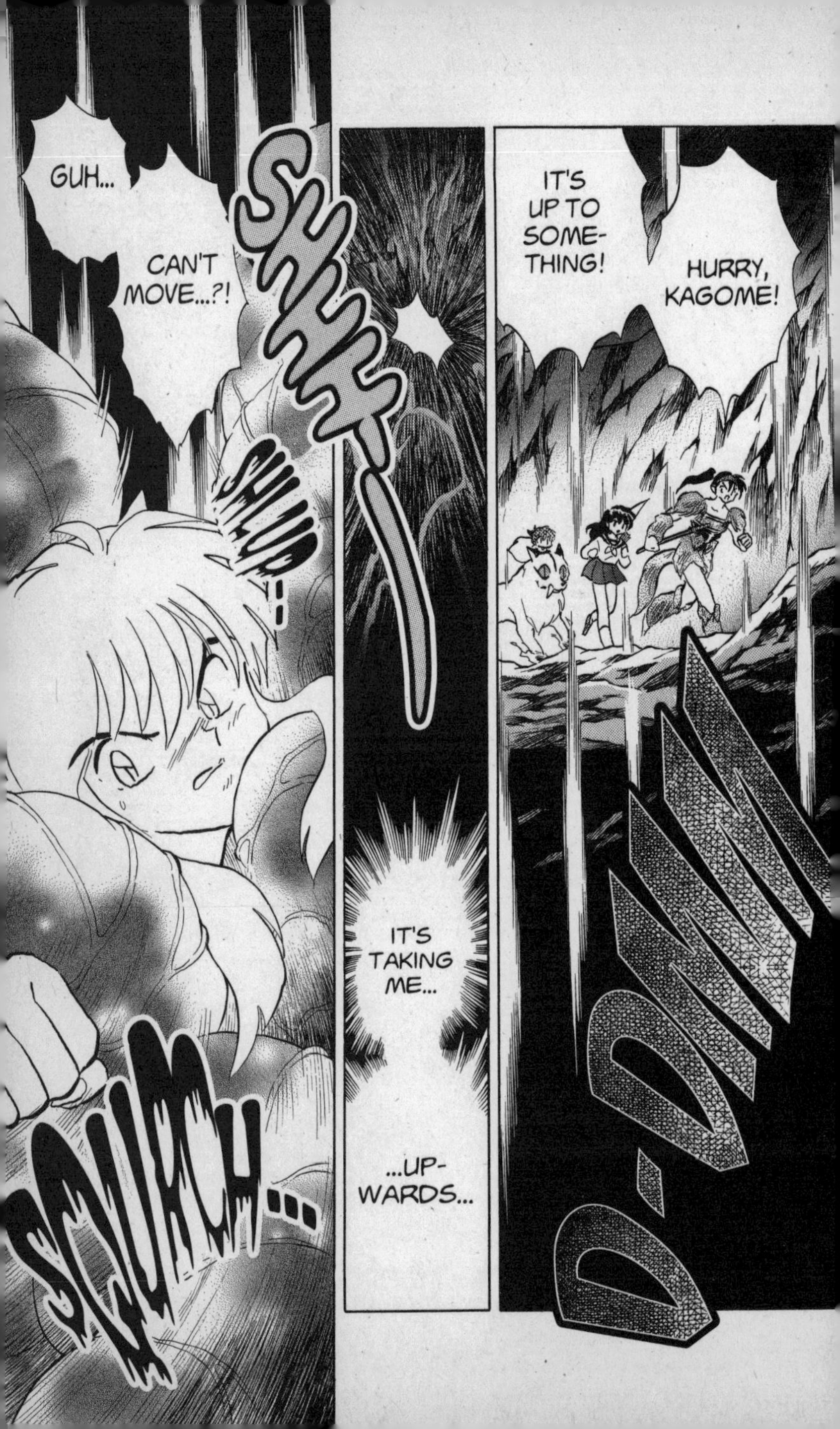
GUH...
CAN'T MOVE...?!
SHLUP!!
IT'S TAKING ME...
...UP-WARDS...
IT'S UP TO SOME-THING!
HURRY, KAGOME!
D-DMM

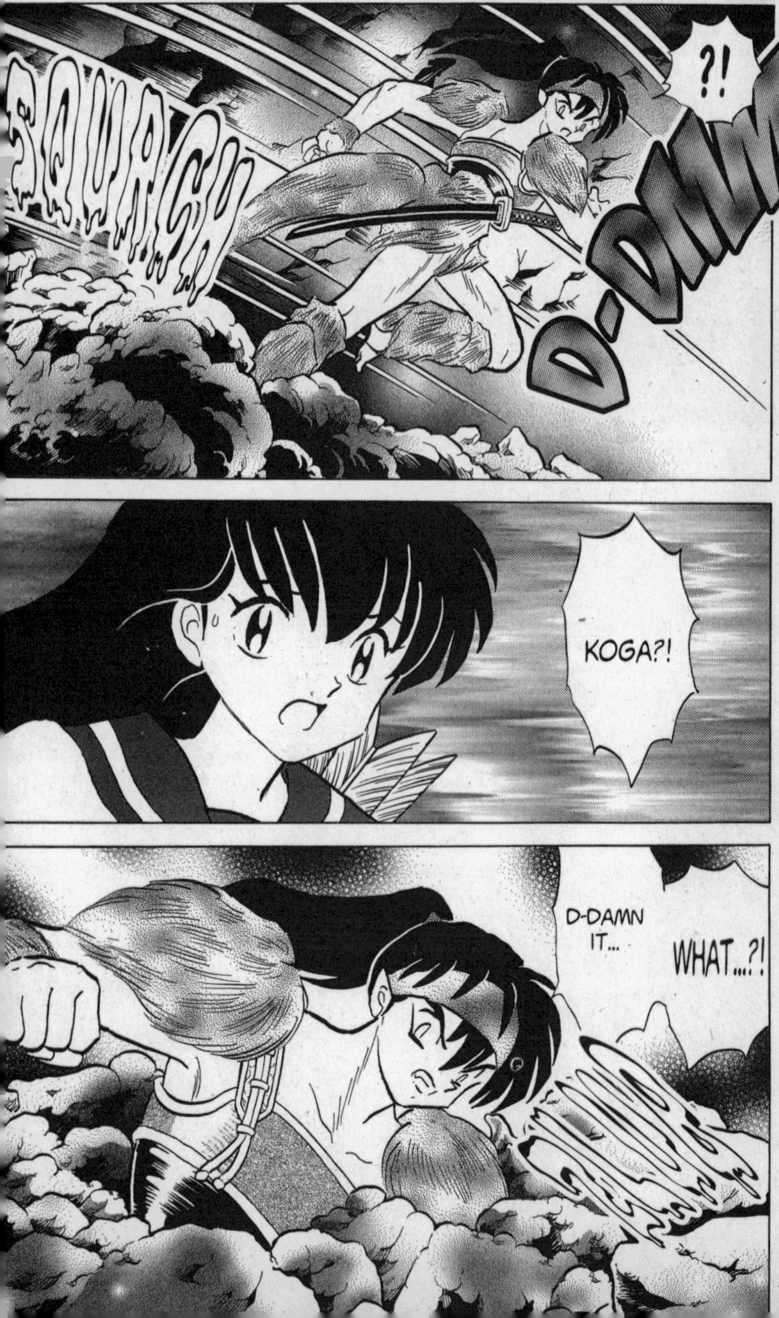
SQUACH
?!
D-DHUM
KOGA?!
D-DAMN IT...
WHAT...?!

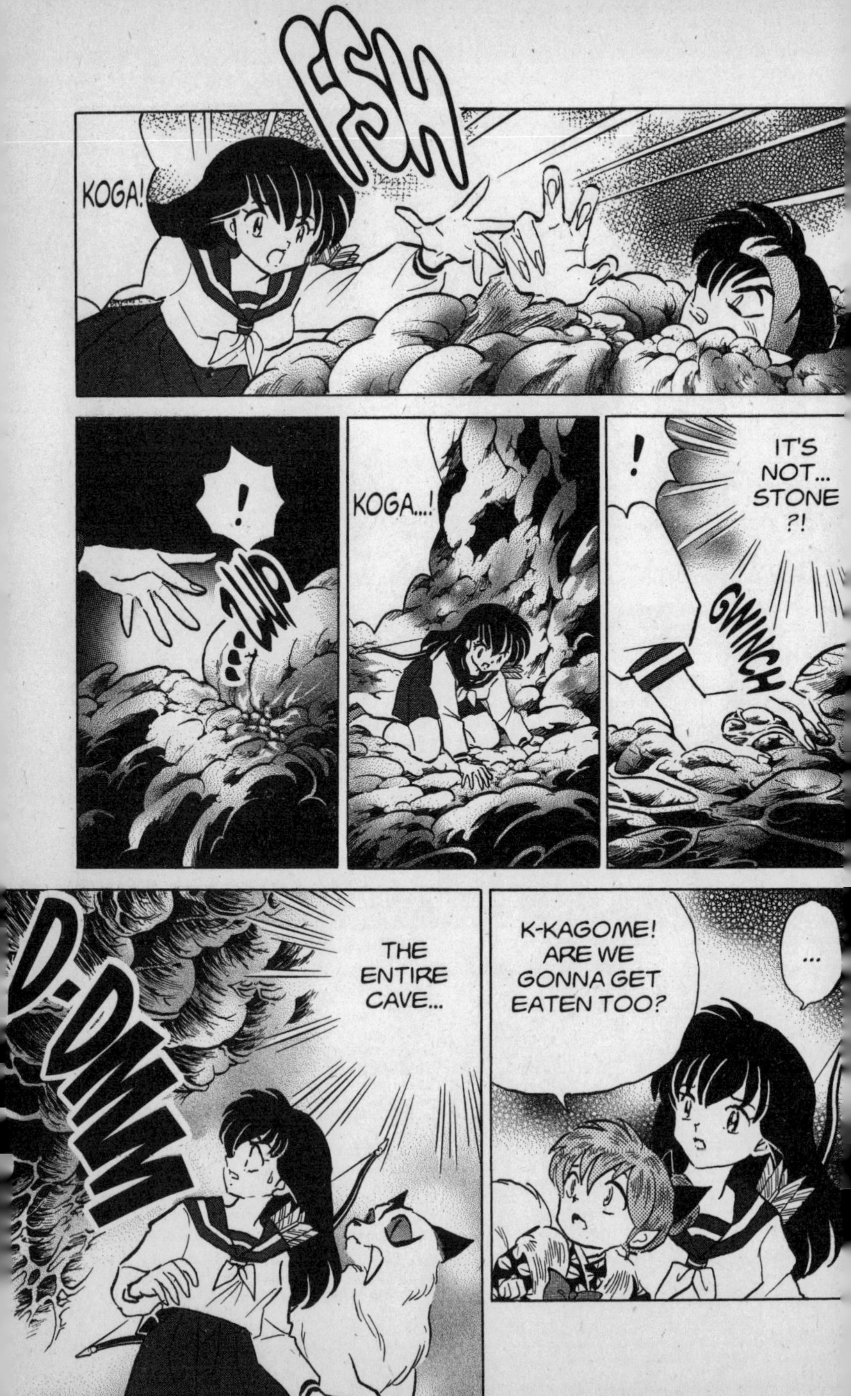
FSSH
KOGA!
!
ZWIP
KOGA...!
!
IT'S NOT... STONE ?!
GWINCH
D-DMM
THE ENTIRE CAVE...
K-KAGOME! ARE WE GONNA GET EATEN TOO?
...

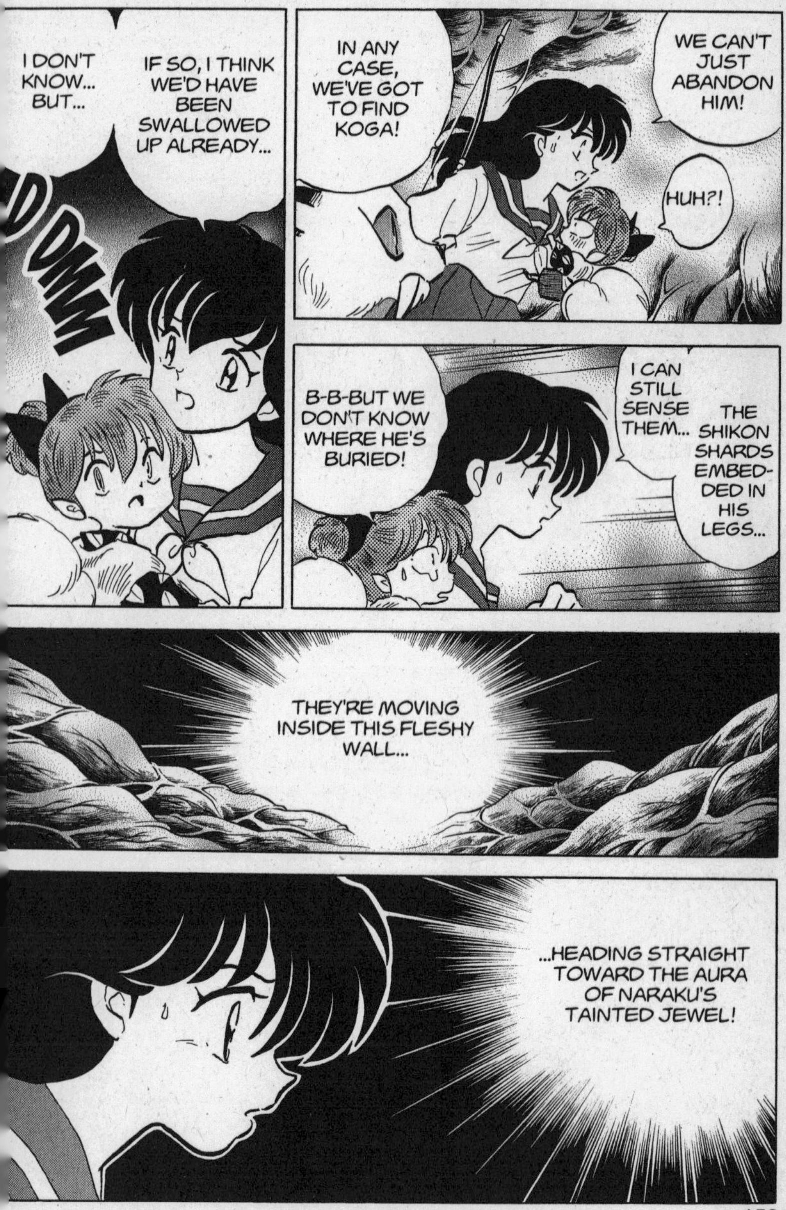

I DON'T KNOW... BUT...
IF SO, I THINK WE'D HAVE BEEN SWALLOWED UP ALREADY...
IN ANY CASE, WE'VE GOT TO FIND KOGA!
WE CAN'T JUST ABANDON HIM!
HUH?!
B-B-BUT WE DON'T KNOW WHERE HE'S BURIED!
I CAN STILL SENSE THEM...
THE SHIKON SHARDS EMBEDDED IN HIS LEGS...
THEY'RE MOVING INSIDE THIS FLESHY WALL...
...HEADING STRAIGHT TOWARD THE AURA OF NARAKU'S TAINTED JEWEL!

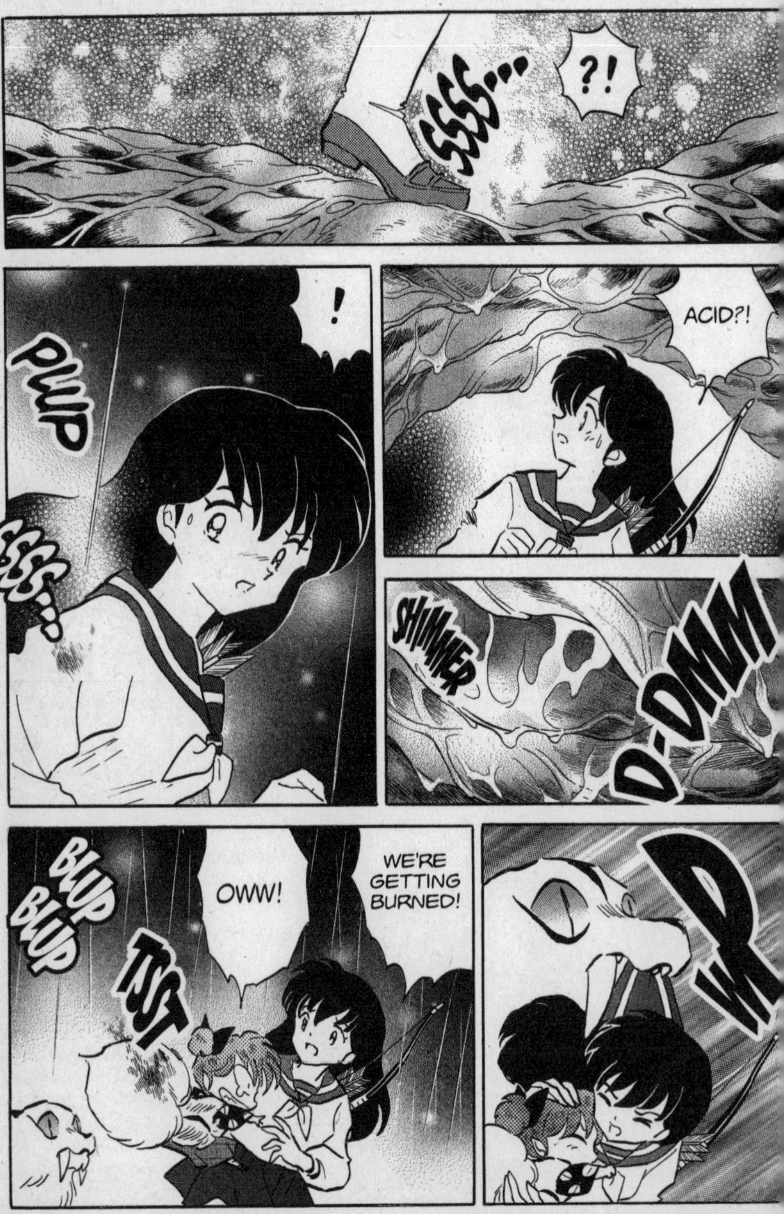
SSSS...
?!
!
PLUP
SSSS...
ACID?!
SHIMMER
D-DMM
BLUP BLUP
TSST
OWW!
WE'RE GETTING BURNED!
WMP

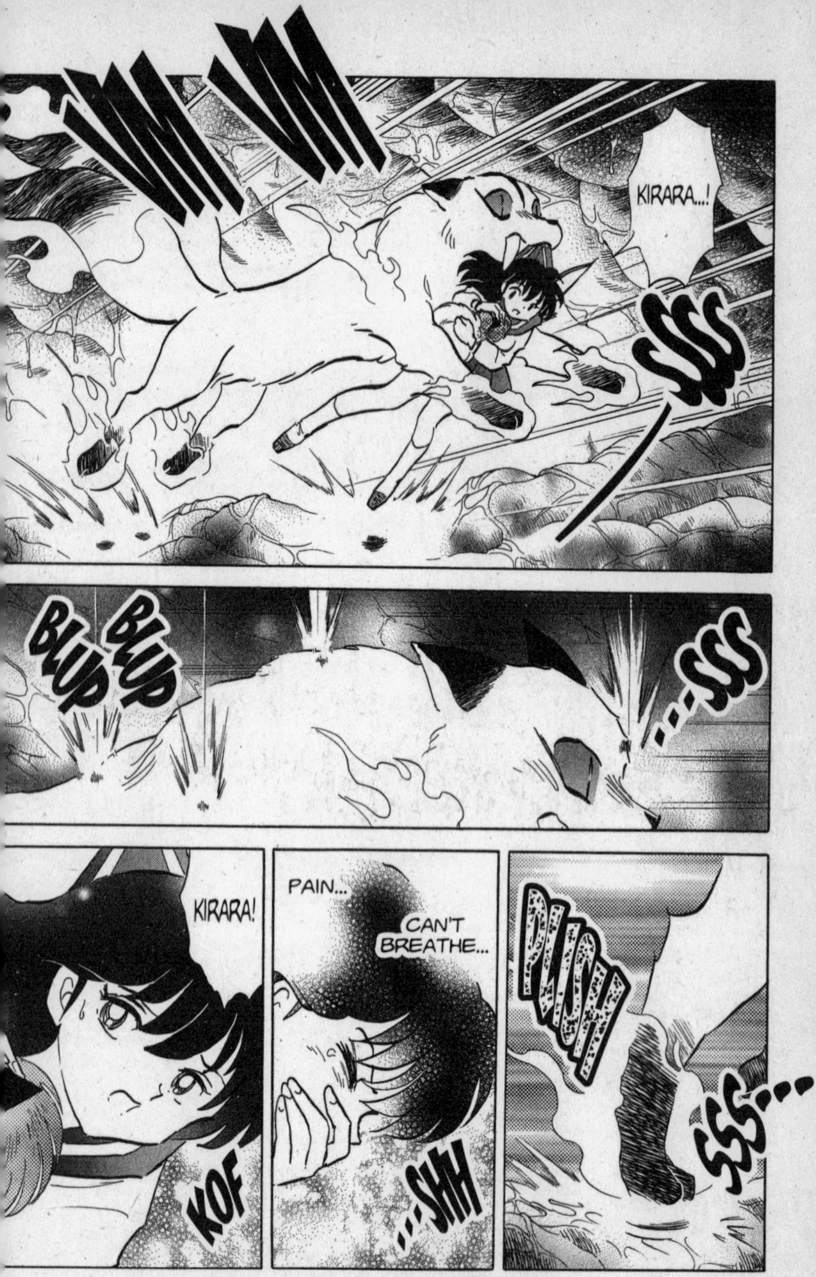

WMM
KIRARA...!
SSS
BLUP BLUP
...SSS
KIRARA!
KOF
PAIN...
CAN'T BREATHE...
...SHH
PLISH
SSS...

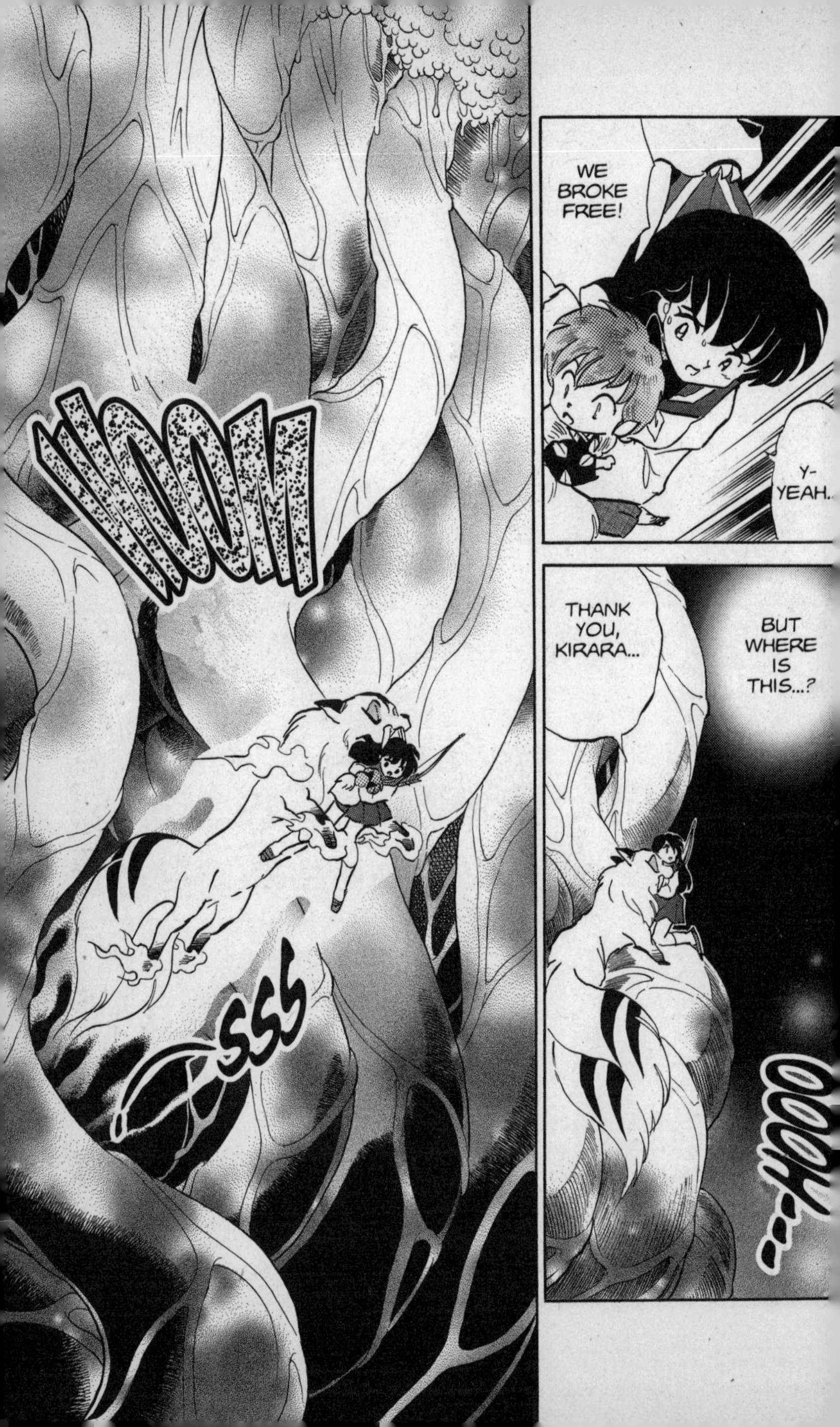
VROOM
SSS
WE BROKE FREE!
Y-YEAH...
THANK YOU, KIRARA...
BUT WHERE IS THIS...?
OOOOH...

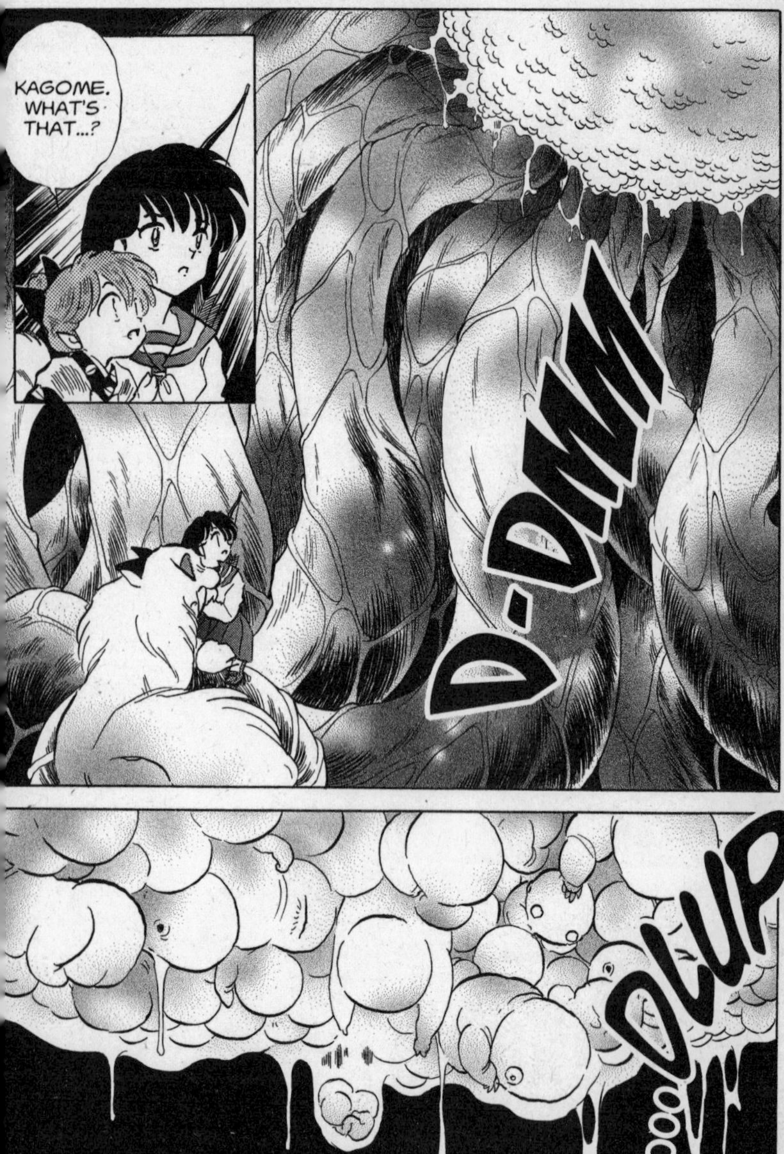
KAGOME. WHAT'S THAT...?
D-DMM
DLUP
OOO

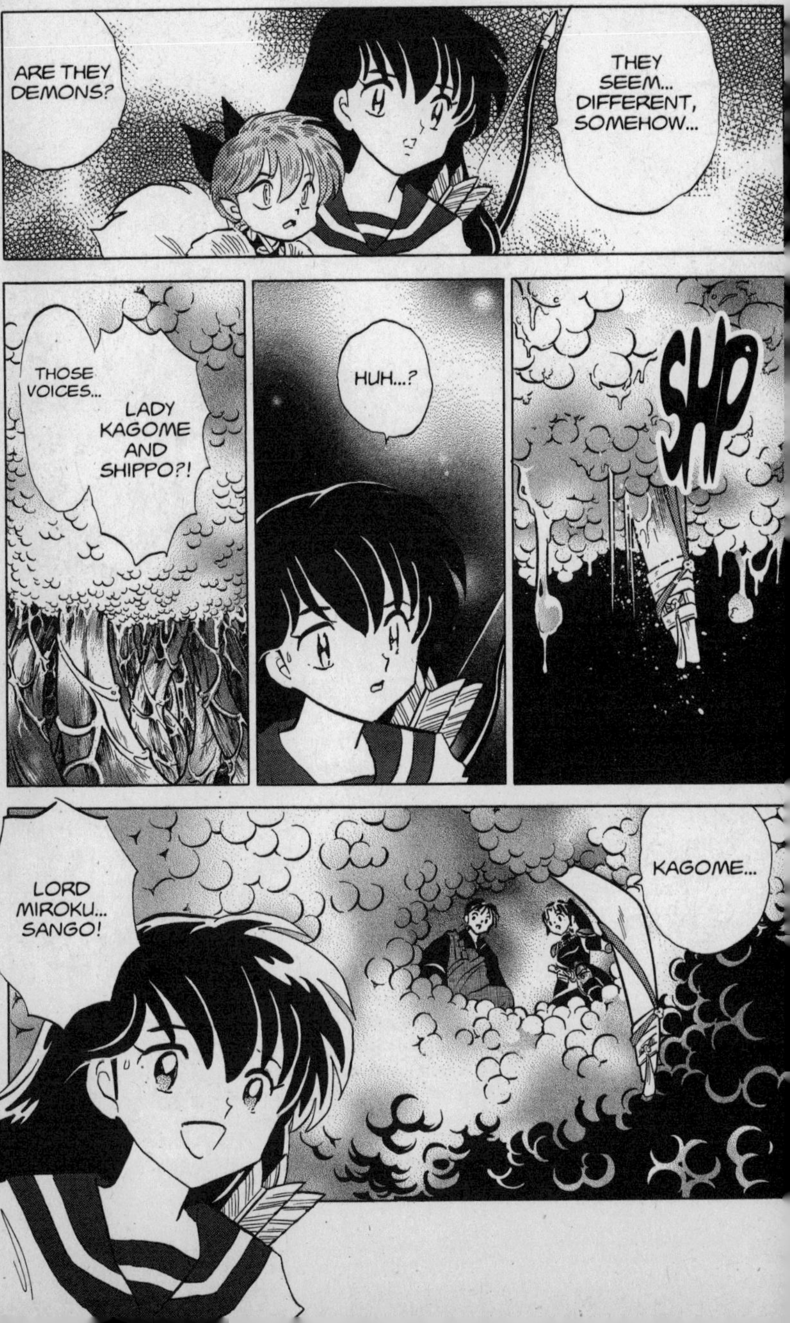
ARE THEY DEMONS?
THEY SEEM... DIFFERENT, SOMEHOW...
THOSE VOICES...
LADY KAGOME AND SHIPPO?!
HUH...?
SHP
LORD MIROKU... SANGO!
KAGOME...

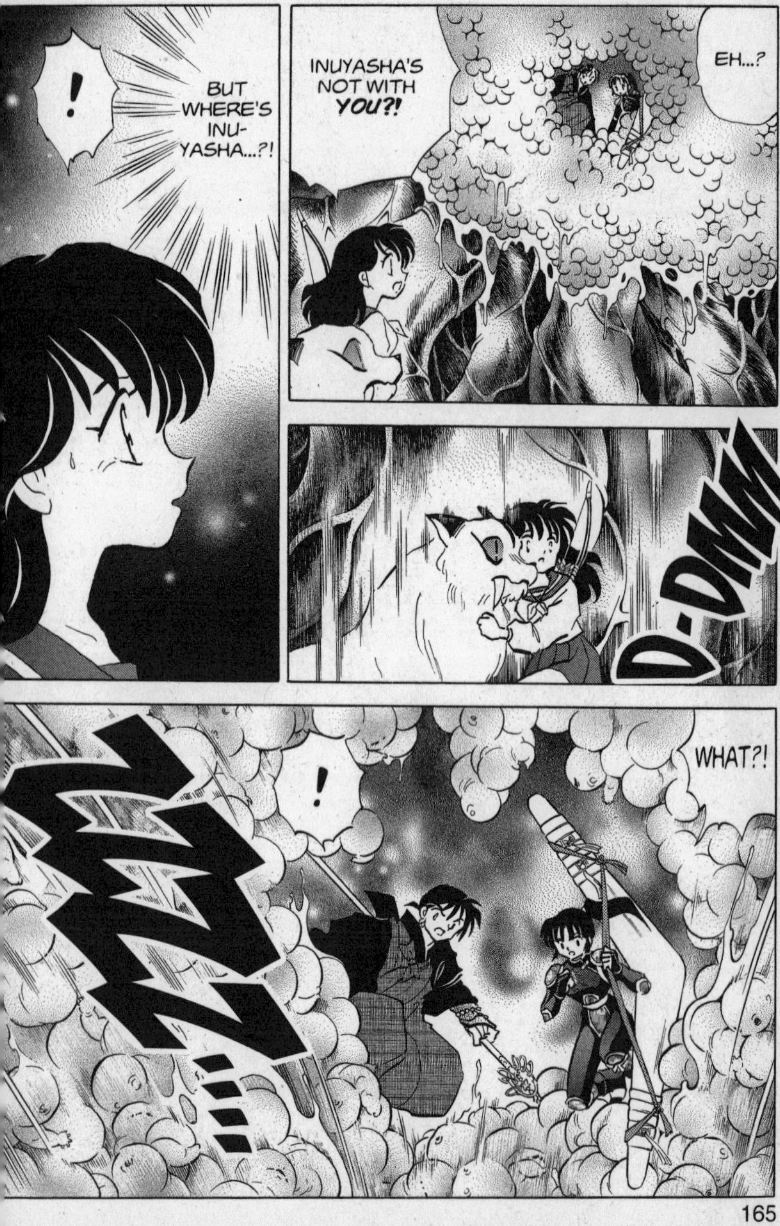
!
BUT WHERE'S INU-YASHA...?!
INUYASHA'S NOT WITH *YOU?!*
EH...?
D-DMM
ZMM...
!
WHAT?!

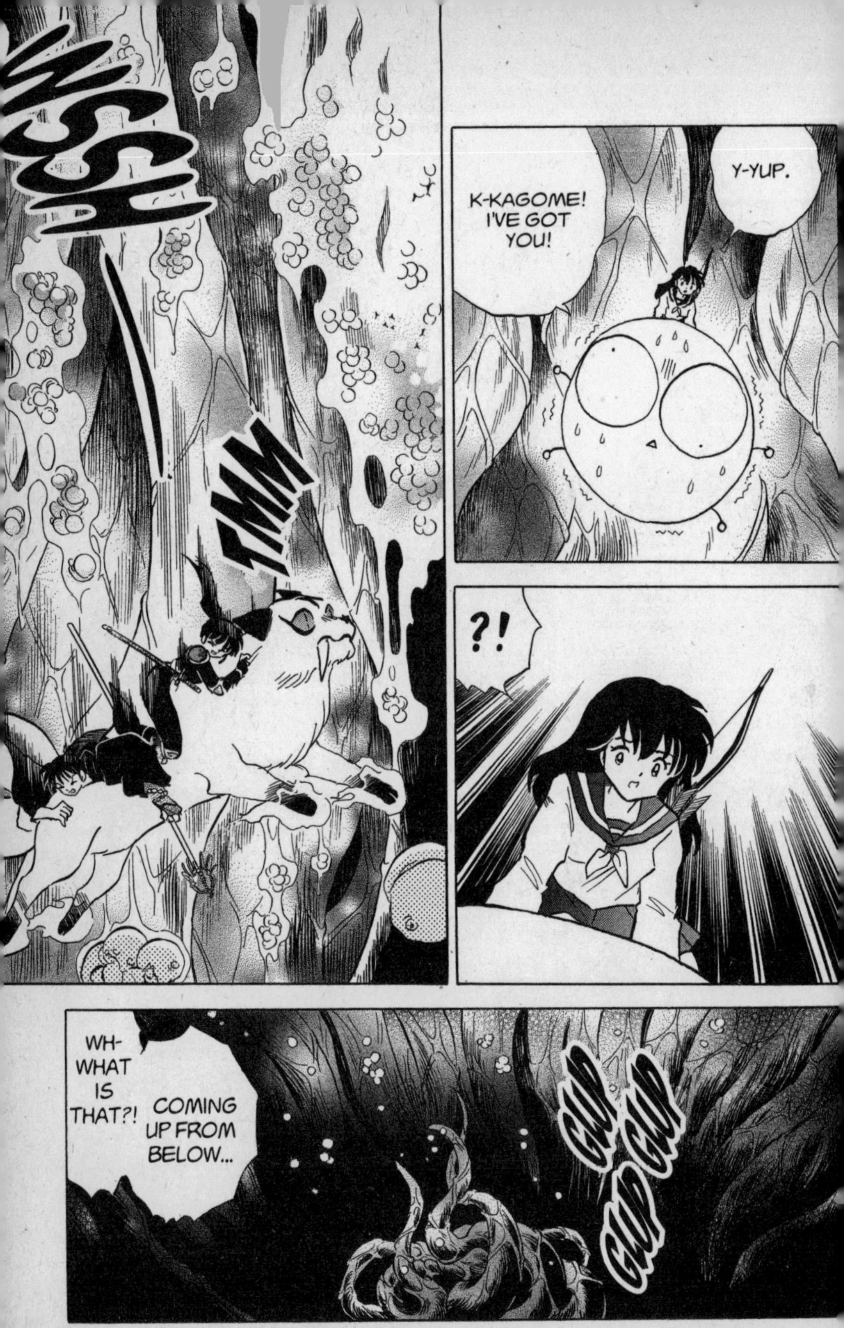
WHSSH
TMMM
K-KAGOME! I'VE GOT YOU!
Y-YUP.
?!
WH-WHAT IS THAT?!
COMING UP FROM BELOW...
GLOP GLOP GLOP

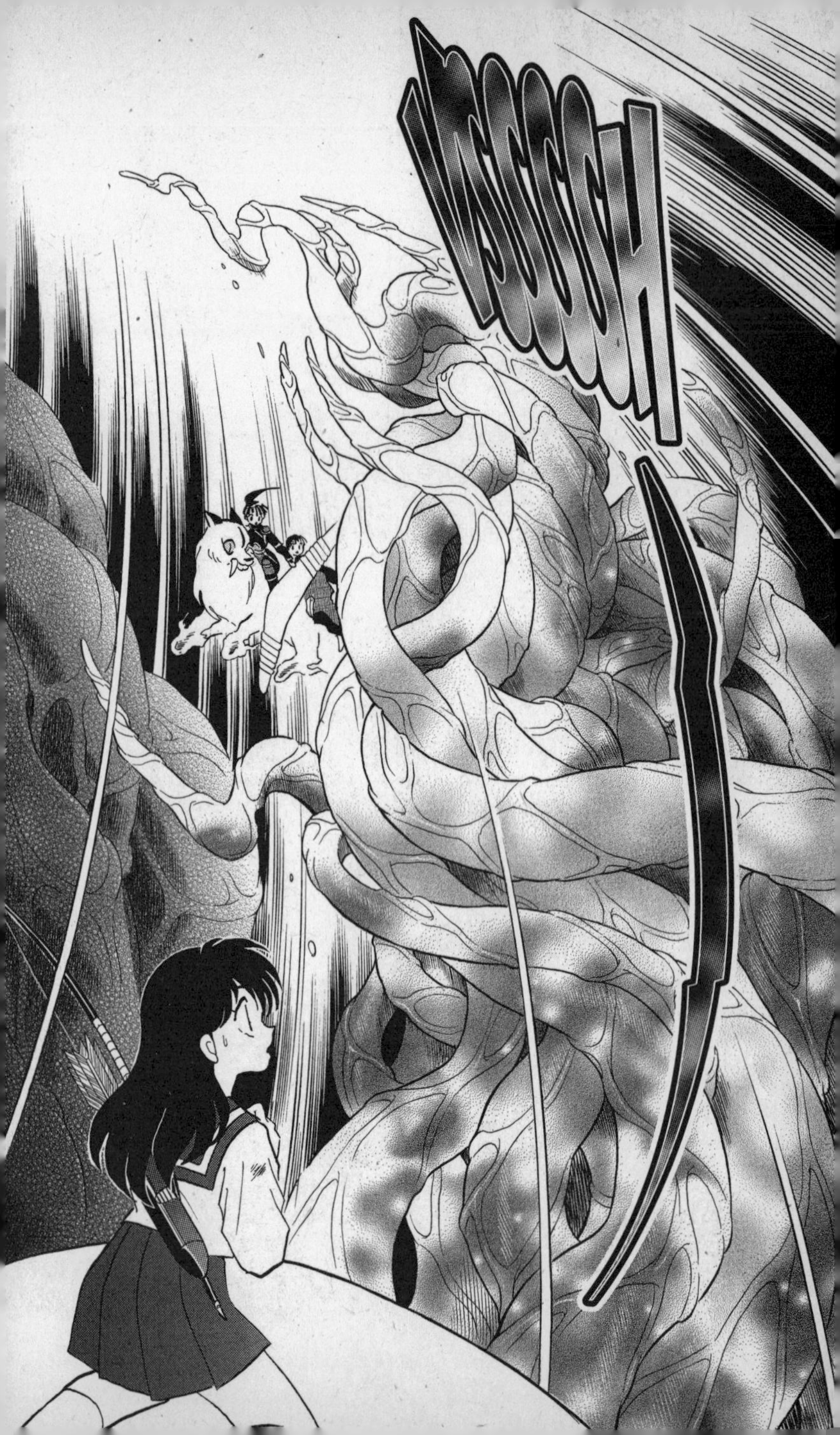
WSSSSH

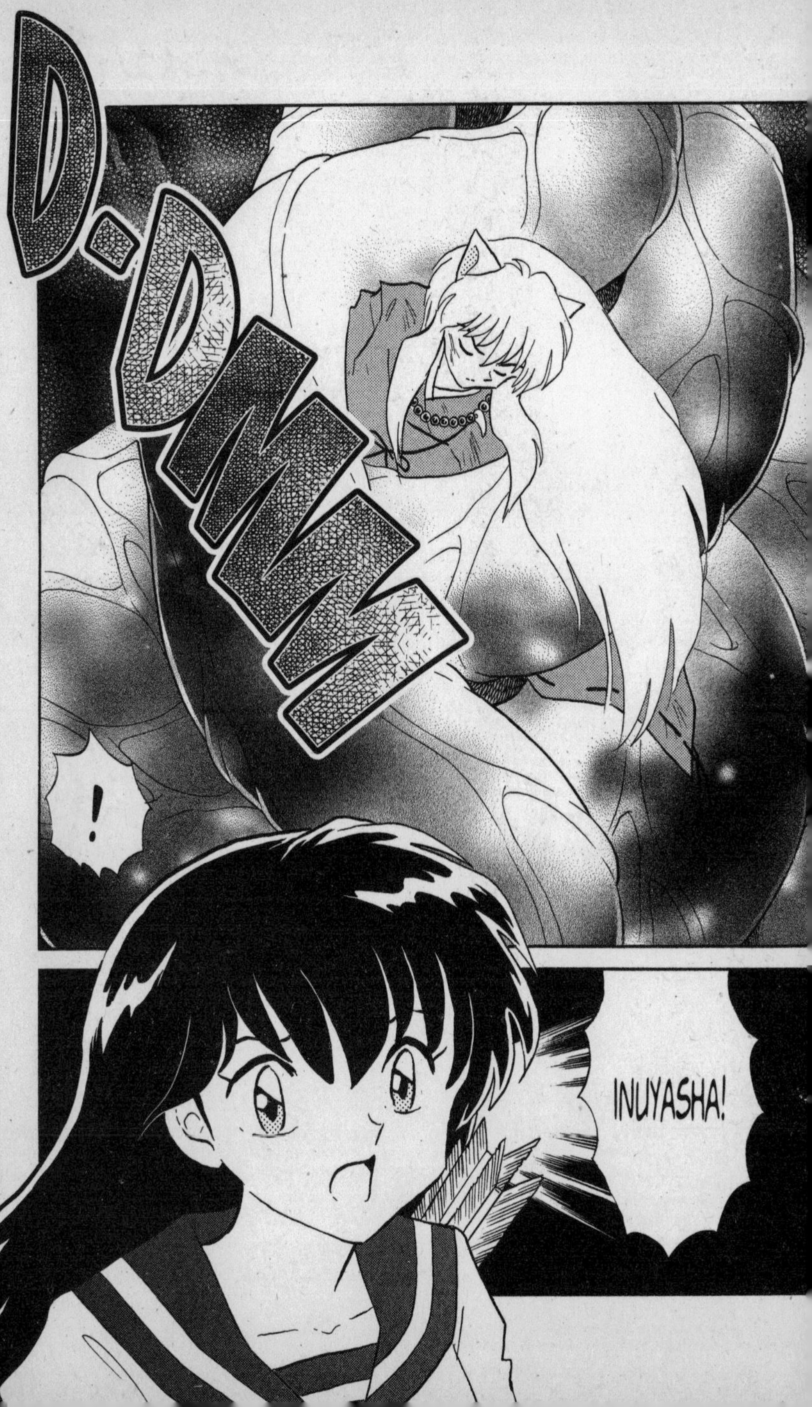
D-DMMM!
!
INUYASHA!

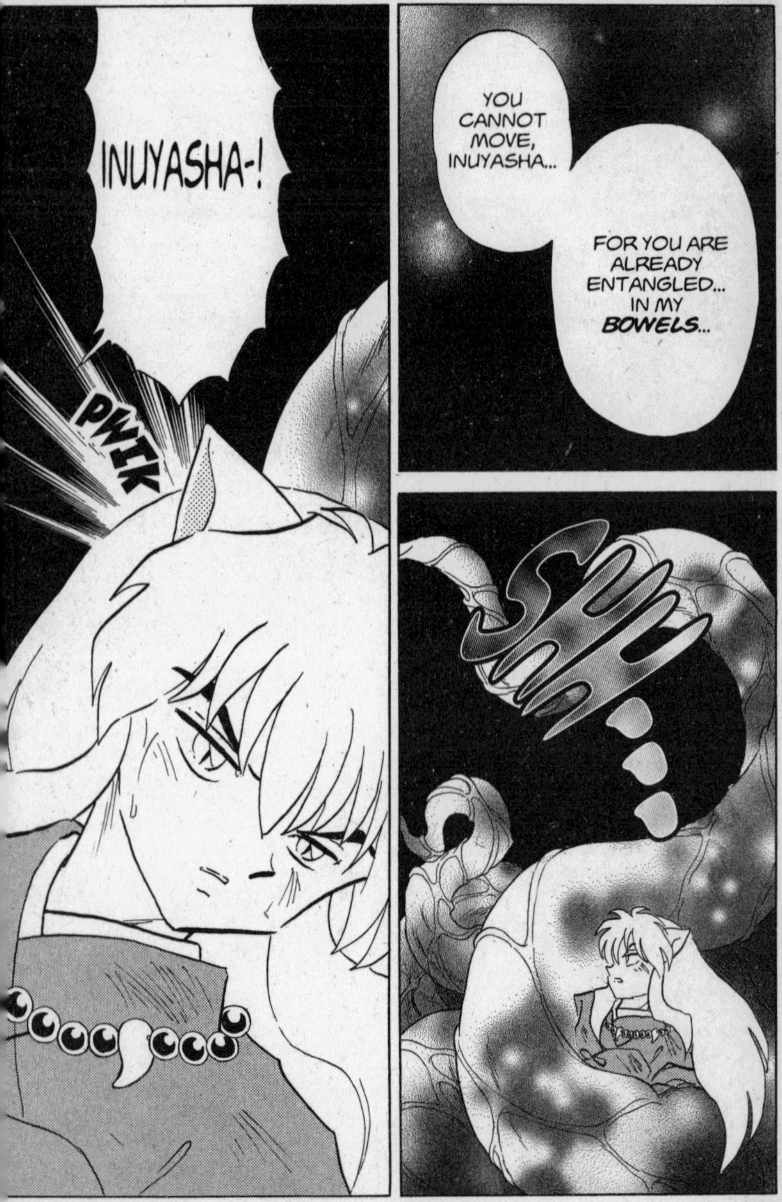
INUYASHA-!
PWIK
YOU CANNOT MOVE, INUYASHA...
FOR YOU ARE ALREADY ENTANGLED... IN MY BOWELS...
SHH

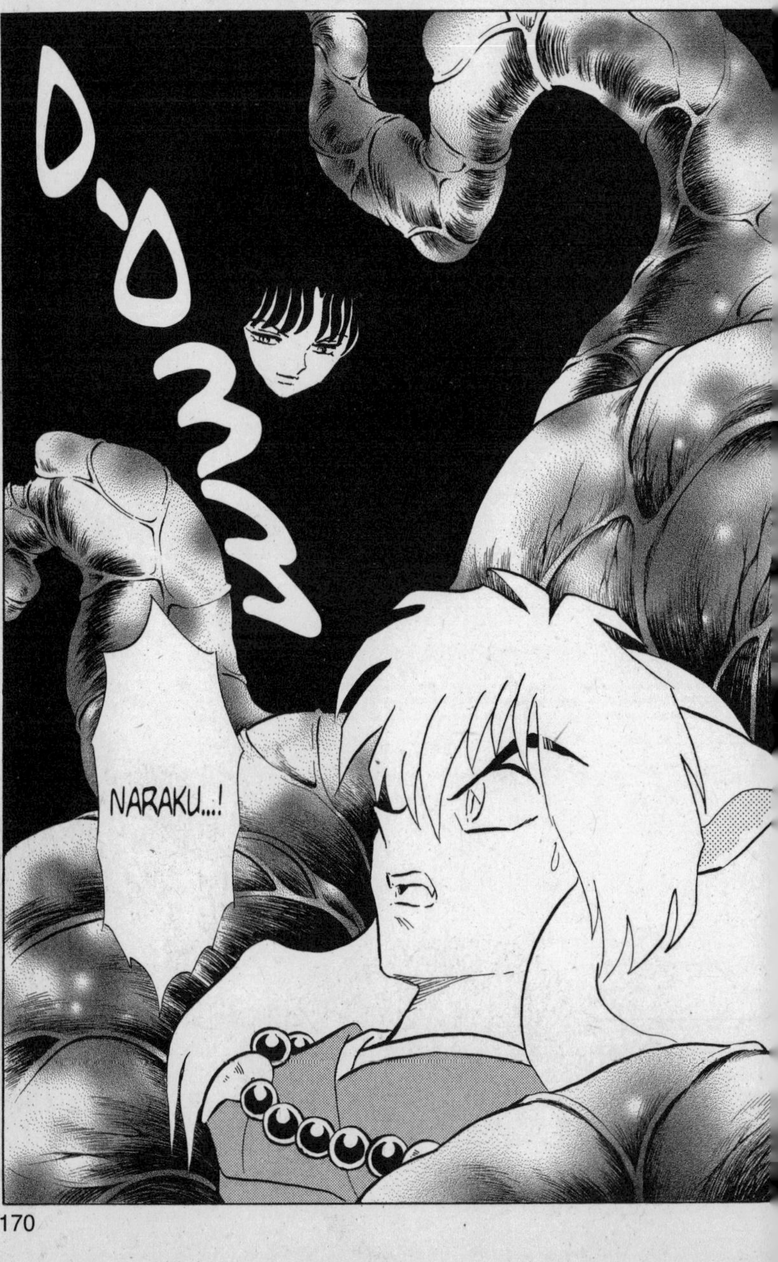
D-DOMMM
NARAKU...!

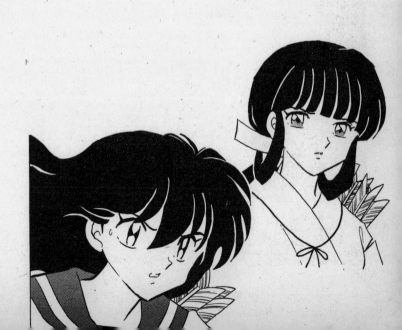

SCROLL 10

RESURRECTION

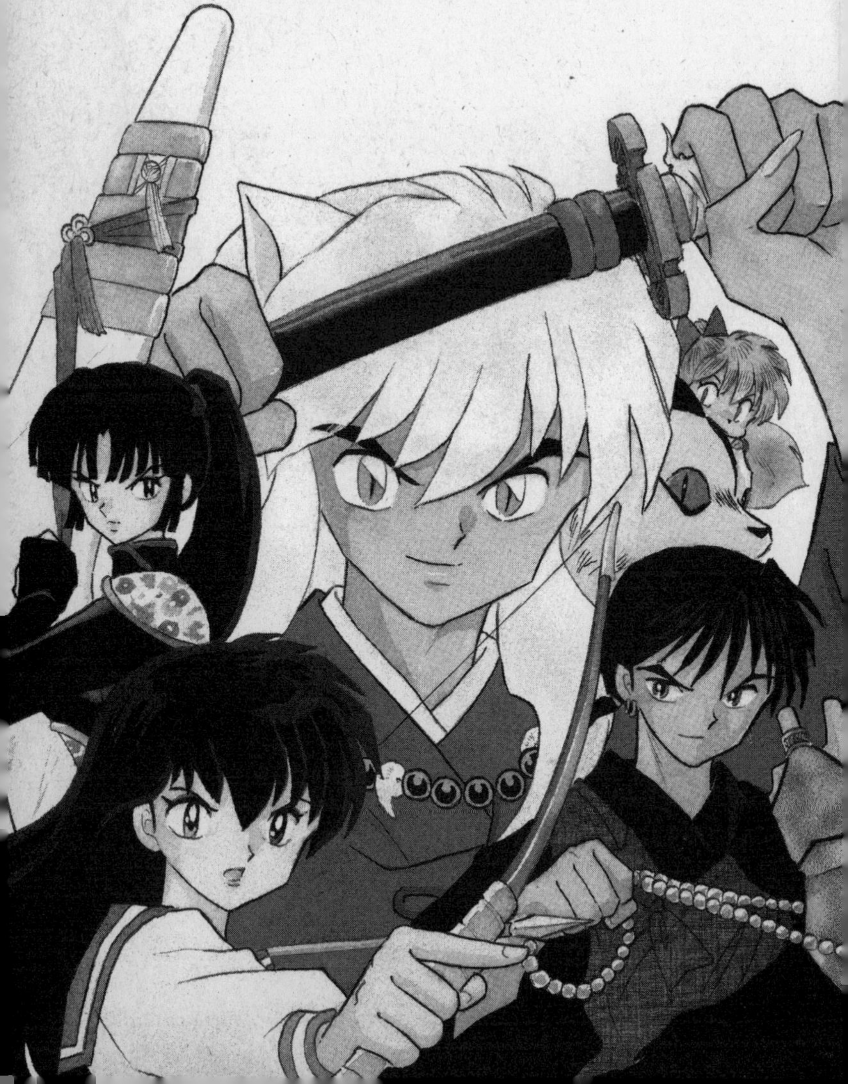

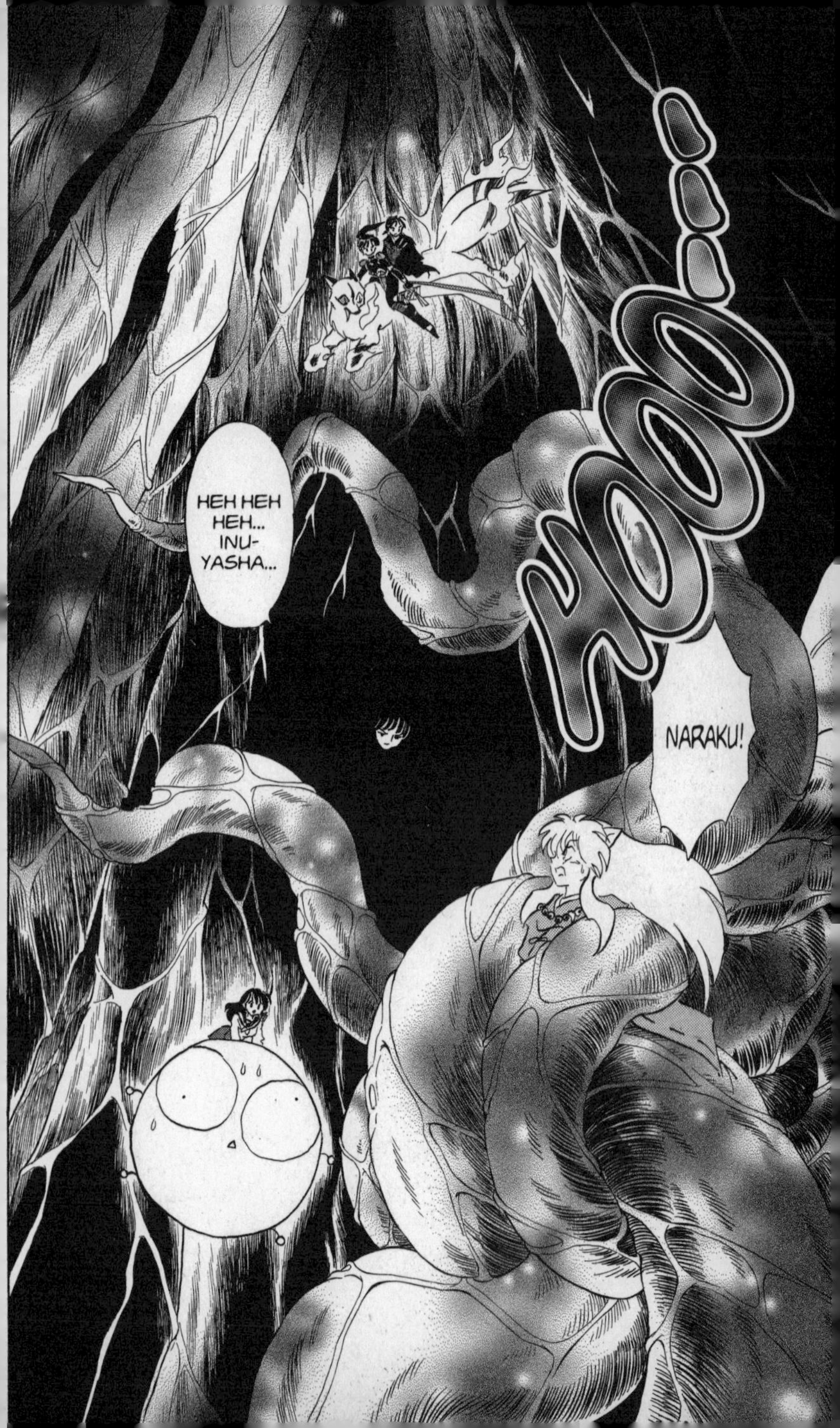
HOOOO...
HEH HEH HEH... INU-YASHA...
NARAKU!

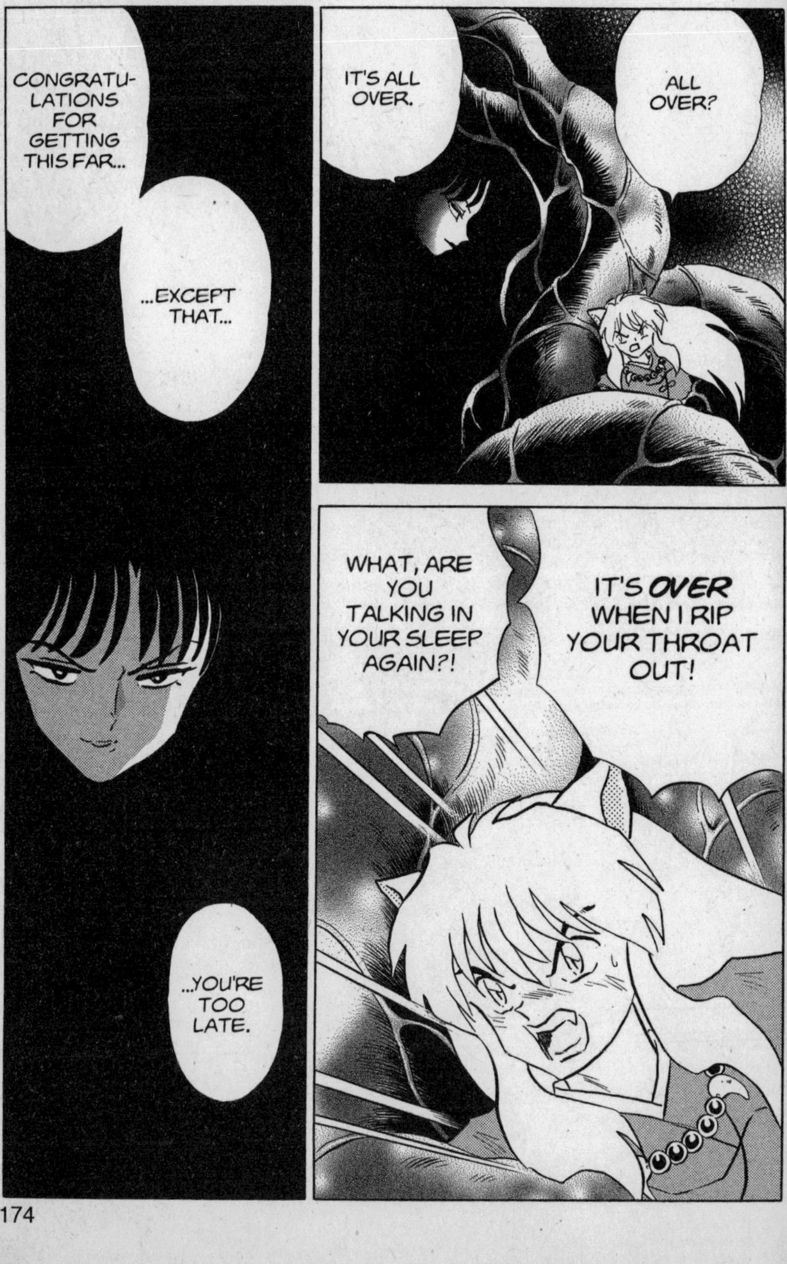
CONGRATU-LATIONS FOR GETTING THIS FAR...
...EXCEPT THAT...
...YOU'RE TOO LATE.
IT'S ALL OVER.
ALL OVER?
WHAT, ARE YOU TALKING IN YOUR SLEEP AGAIN?!
IT'S **OVER** WHEN I RIP YOUR THROAT OUT!

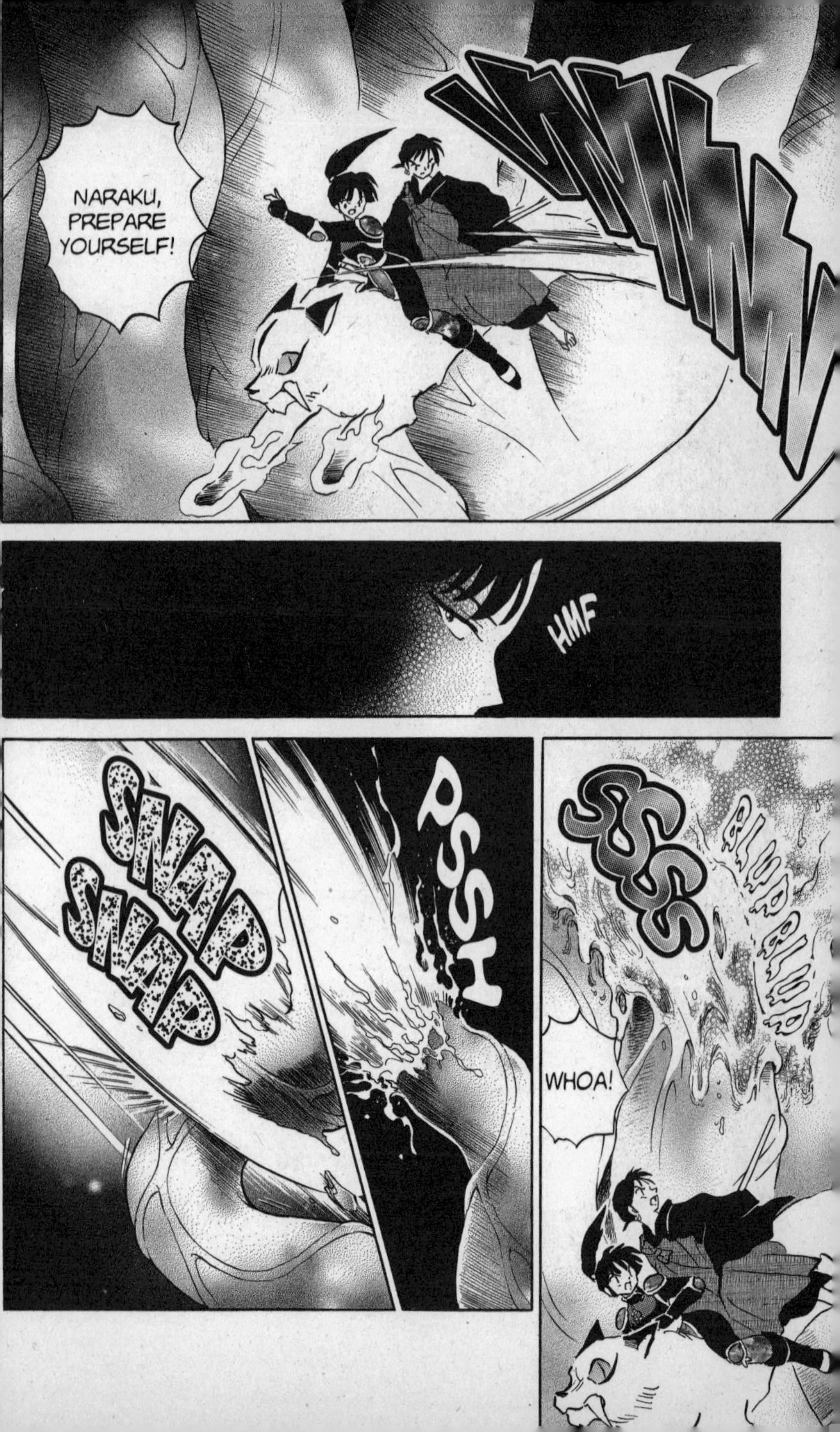
NARAKU, PREPARE YOURSELF!
HMF
SNAP SNAP
PSSH
BLUP BLUP
WHOA!

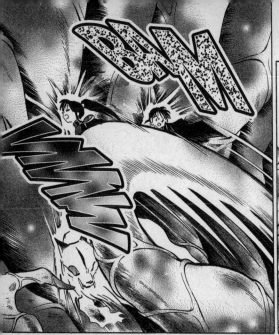

BAM

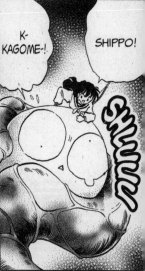

K-KAGOME-!

SHIPPO!

SHUUUU

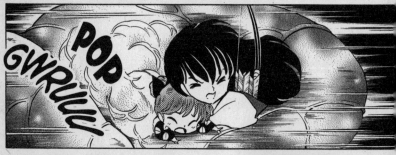

POP

GWRUUU

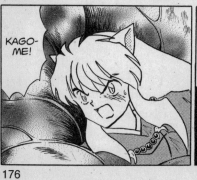

KAGO-ME!

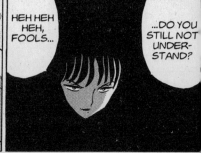

HEH HEH HEH, FOOLS...

...DO YOU STILL NOT UNDERSTAND?

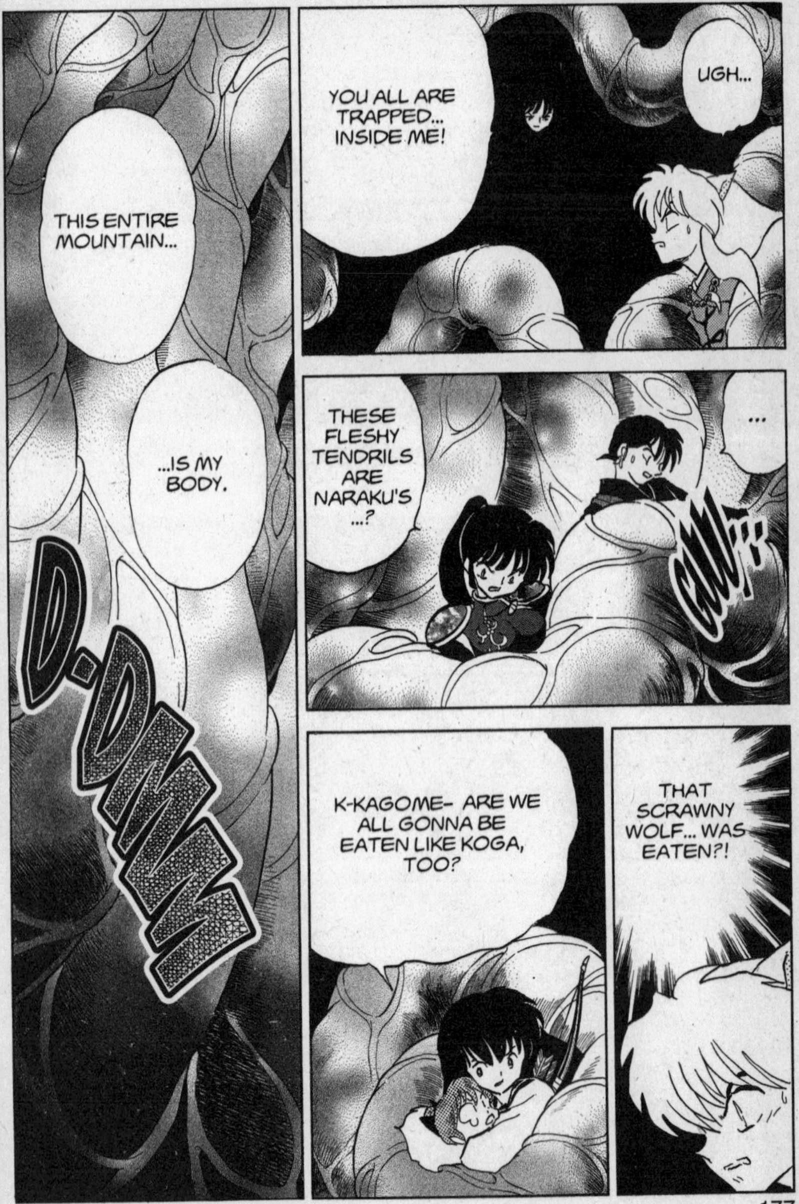
THIS ENTIRE MOUNTAIN...
...IS MY BODY.
YOU ALL ARE TRAPPED... INSIDE ME!
UGH...
THESE FLESHY TENDRILS ARE NARAKU'S ...?
...
K-KAGOME- ARE WE ALL GONNA BE EATEN LIKE KOGA, TOO?
THAT SCRAWNY WOLF... WAS EATEN?!

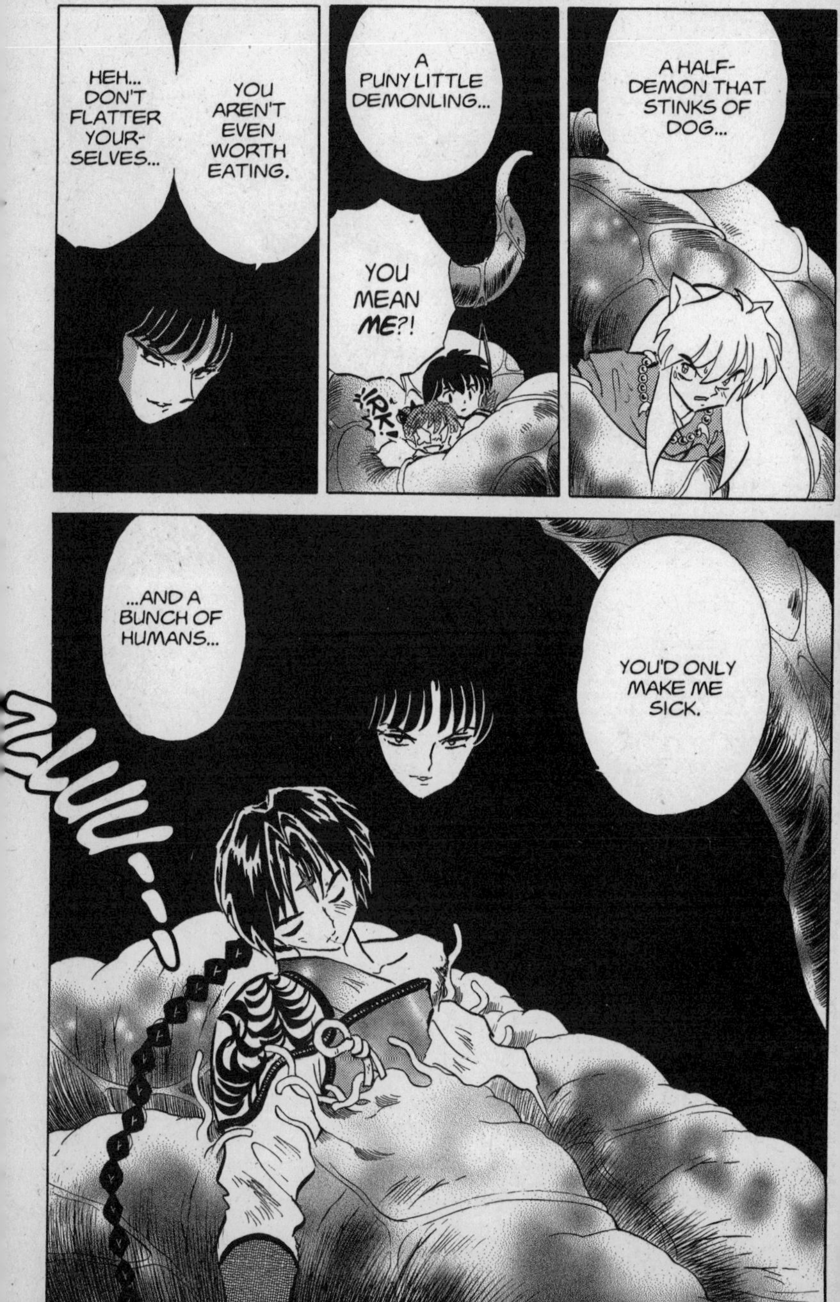
HEH... DON'T FLATTER YOUR-SELVES...
YOU AREN'T EVEN WORTH EATING.
A PUNY LITTLE DEMONLING...
YOU MEAN *ME*?!
RK!
A HALF-DEMON THAT STINKS OF DOG...
...AND A BUNCH OF HUMANS...
YOU'D ONLY MAKE ME SICK.

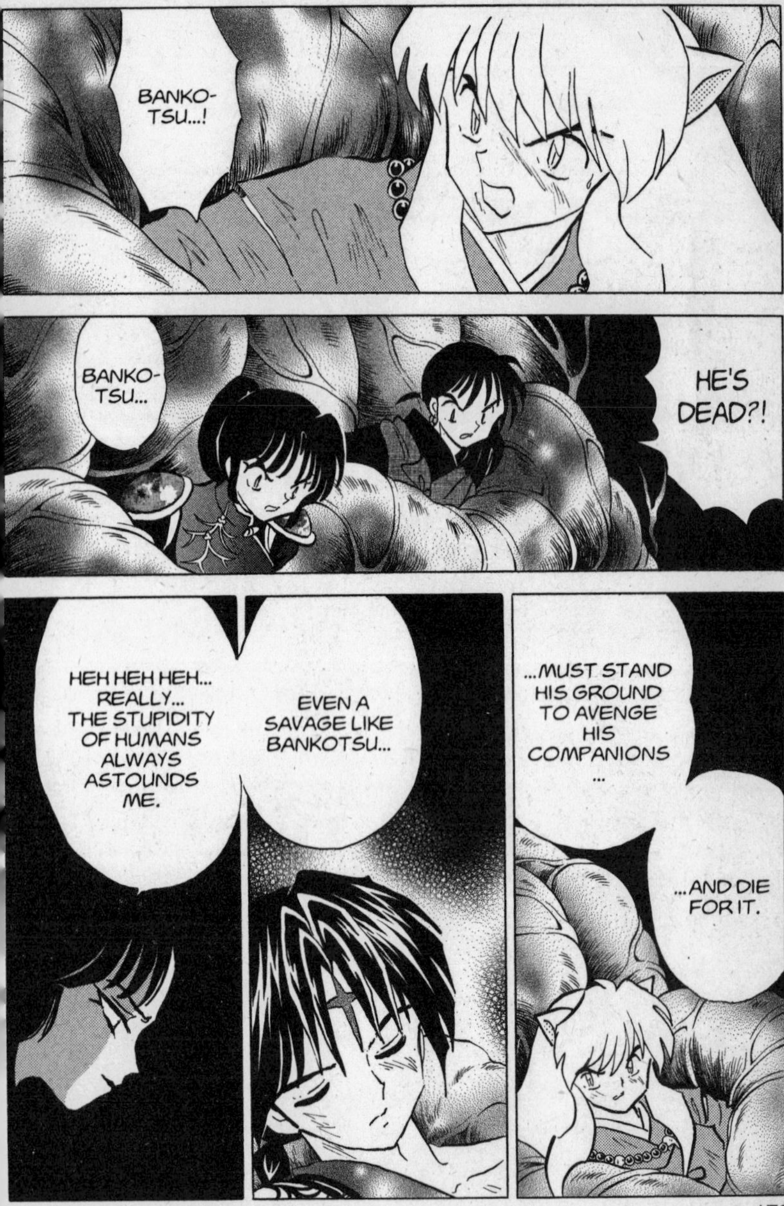
BANKO-TSU...!
BANKO-TSU...
HE'S DEAD?!
HEH HEH HEH... REALLY... THE STUPIDITY OF HUMANS ALWAYS ASTOUNDS ME.
EVEN A SAVAGE LIKE BANKOTSU...
...MUST STAND HIS GROUND TO AVENGE HIS COMPANIONS ...
...AND DIE FOR IT.

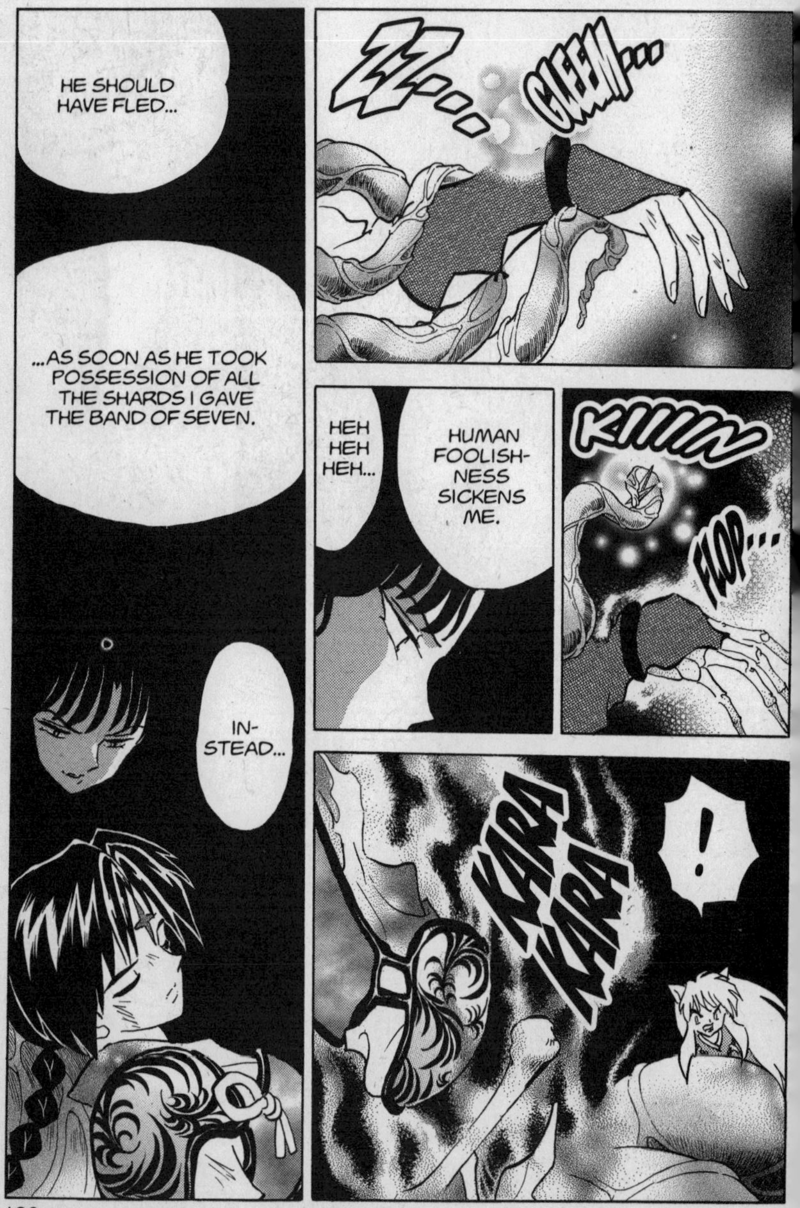

HE SHOULD HAVE FLED...
...AS SOON AS HE TOOK POSSESSION OF ALL THE SHARDS I GAVE THE BAND OF SEVEN.
IN-STEAD...
ZZ...
GIEEM...
HEH HEH HEH...
HUMAN FOOLISH-NESS SICKENS ME.
KIIIN
FLOP...
KARA KARA
!

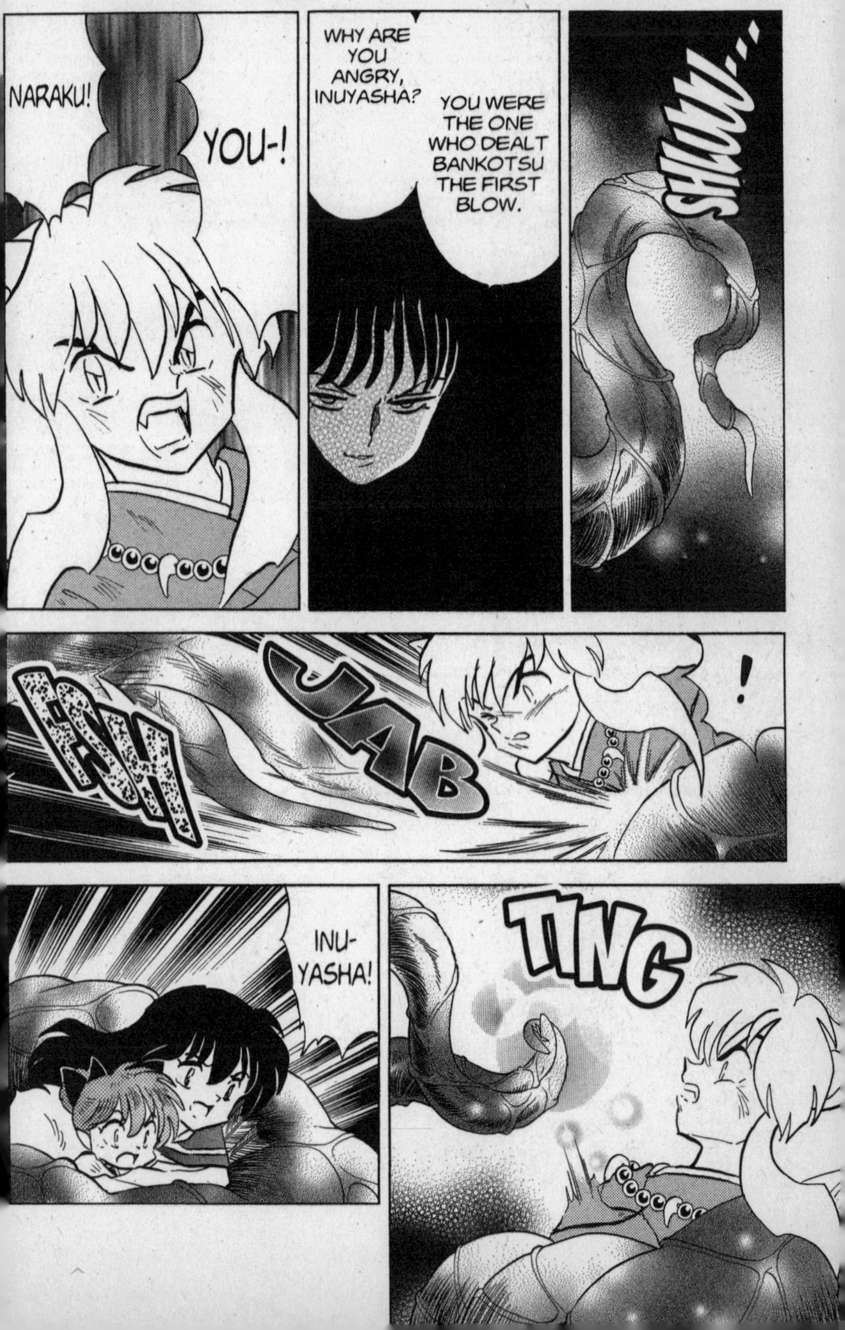
NARAKU!
YOU-!
WHY ARE YOU ANGRY, INUYASHA?
YOU WERE THE ONE WHO DEALT BANKOTSU THE FIRST BLOW.
SHWW...
FSH
JAB
!
INU-YASHA!
TING

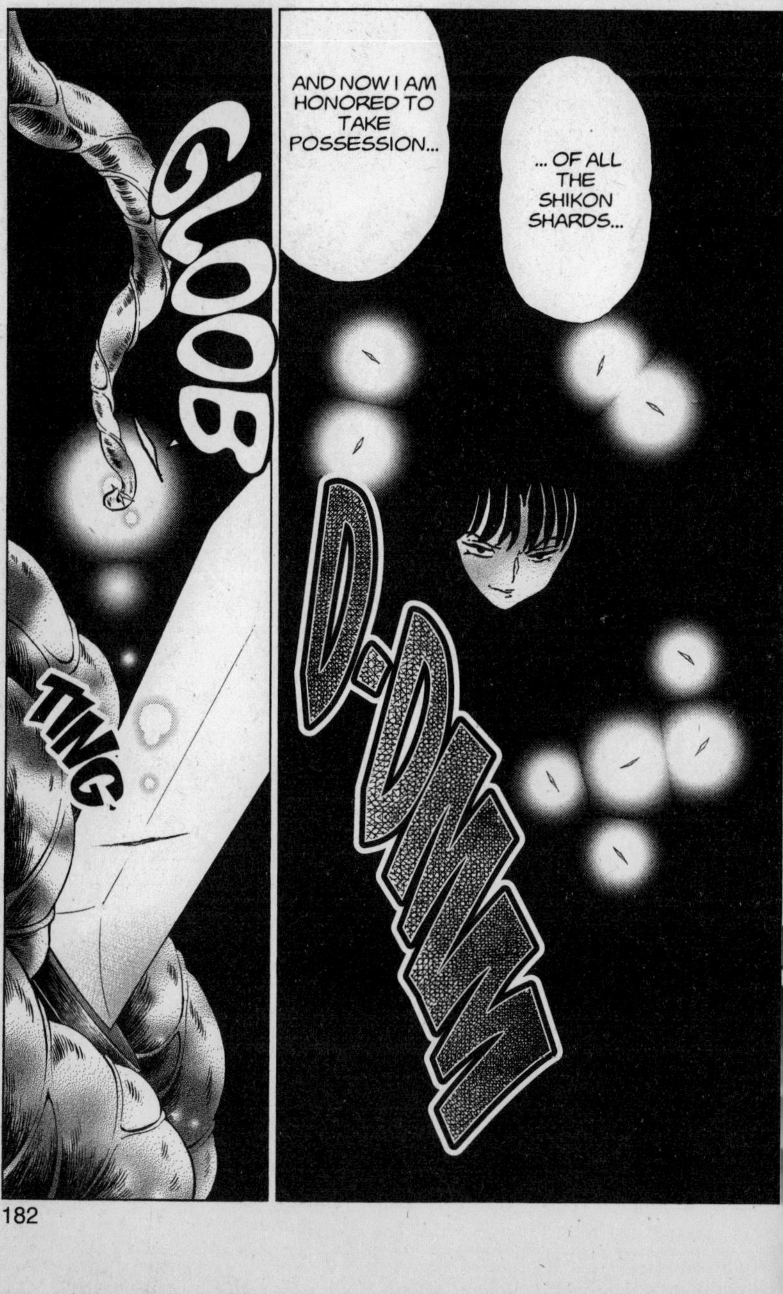
GLOOB
TING
AND NOW I AM HONORED TO TAKE POSSESSION...
... OF ALL THE SHIKON SHARDS...
D-DNNN

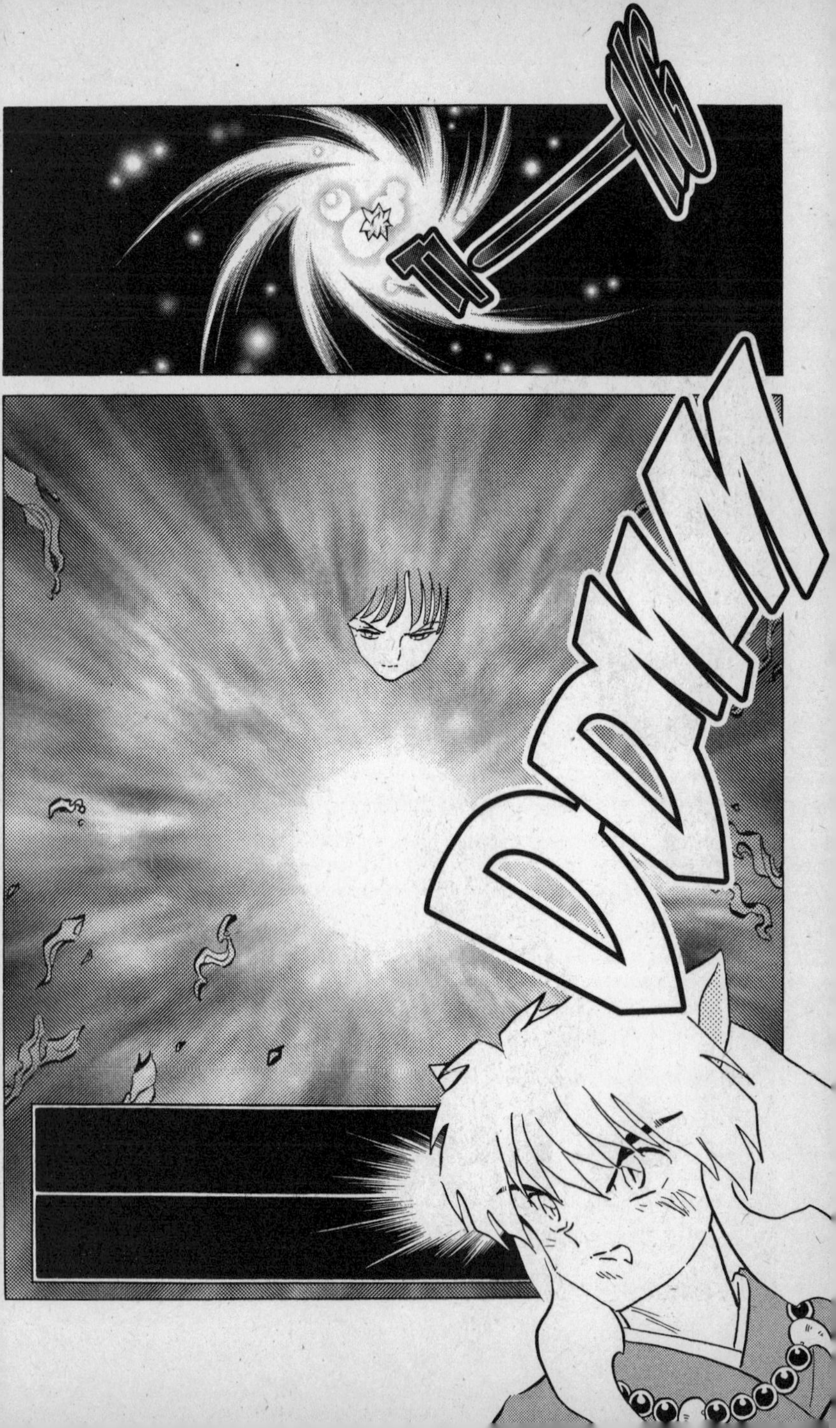

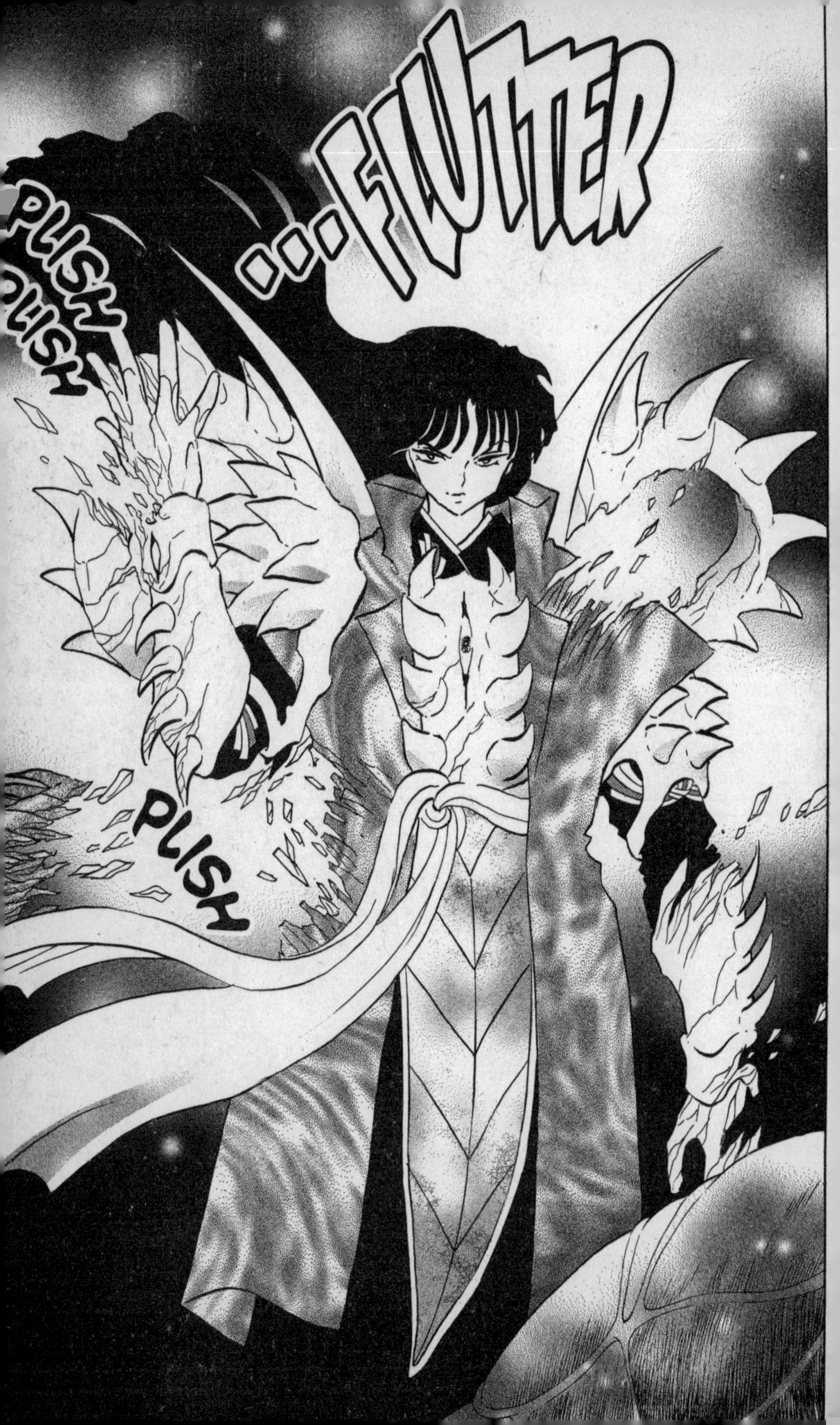
...FLUTTER
PLISH
PLISH
PLISH

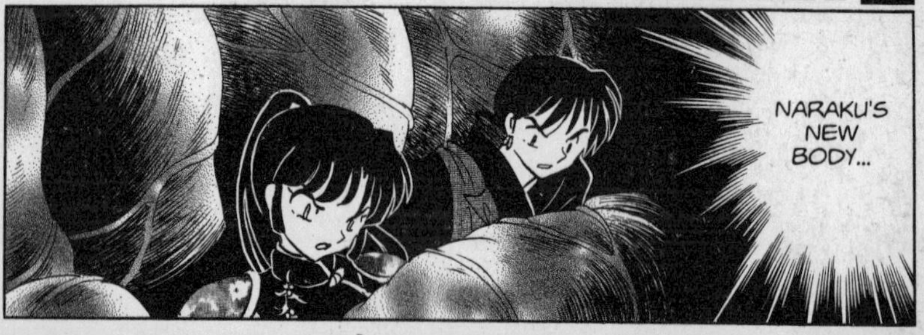
NARAKU'S NEW BODY...

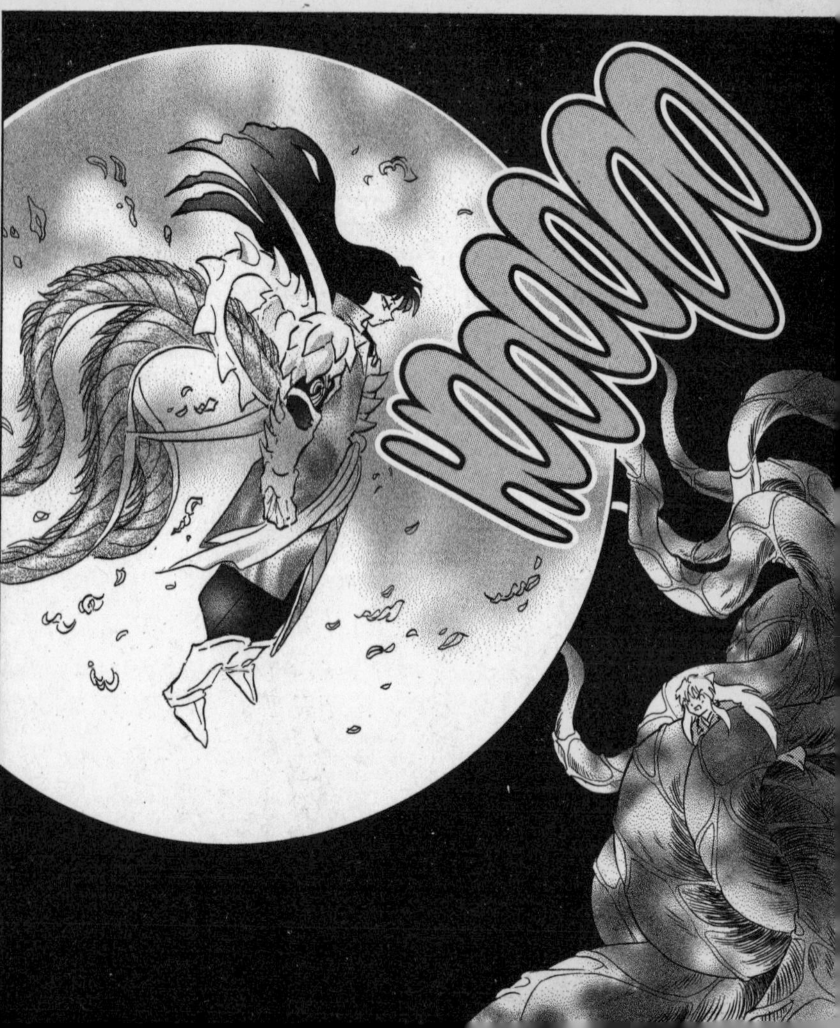

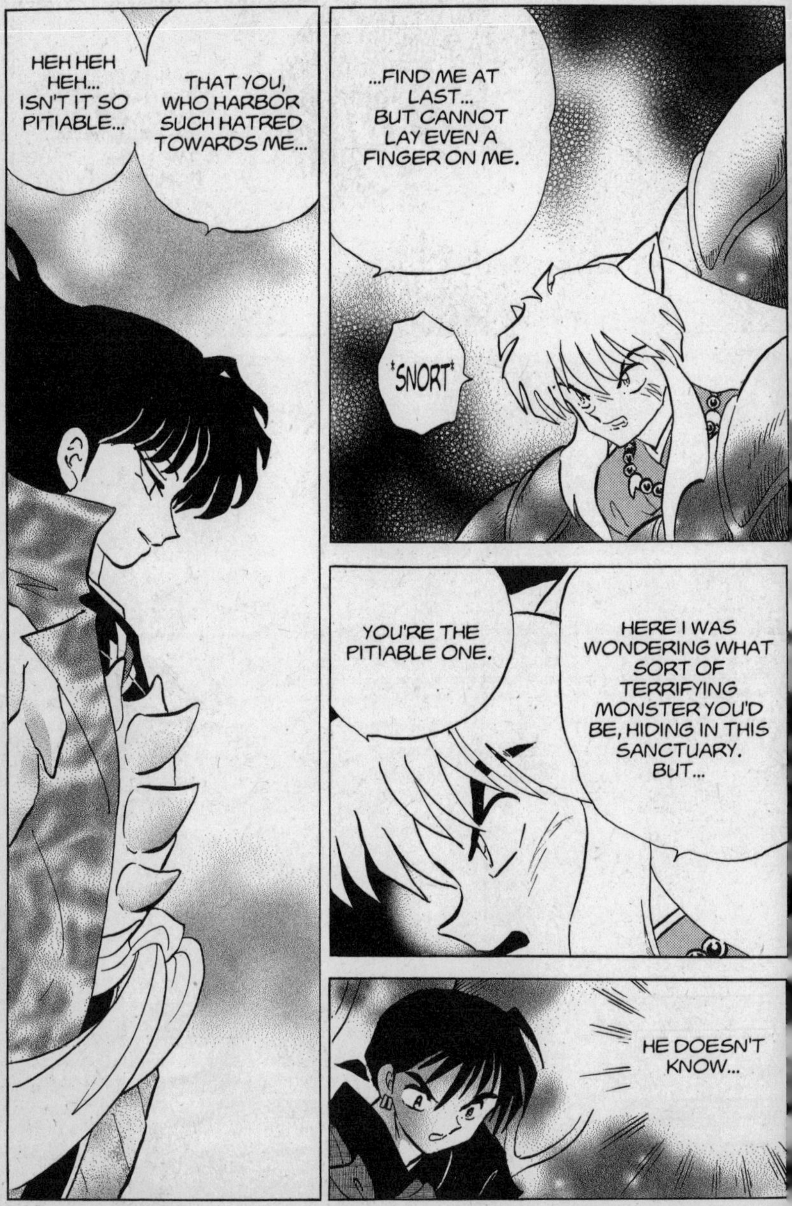
HEH HEH HEH... ISN'T IT SO PITIABLE...
THAT YOU, WHO HARBOR SUCH HATRED TOWARDS ME...
...FIND ME AT LAST... BUT CANNOT LAY EVEN A FINGER ON ME.
SNORT
YOU'RE THE PITIABLE ONE.
HERE I WAS WONDERING WHAT SORT OF TERRIFYING MONSTER YOU'D BE, HIDING IN THIS SANCTUARY. BUT...
HE DOESN'T KNOW...

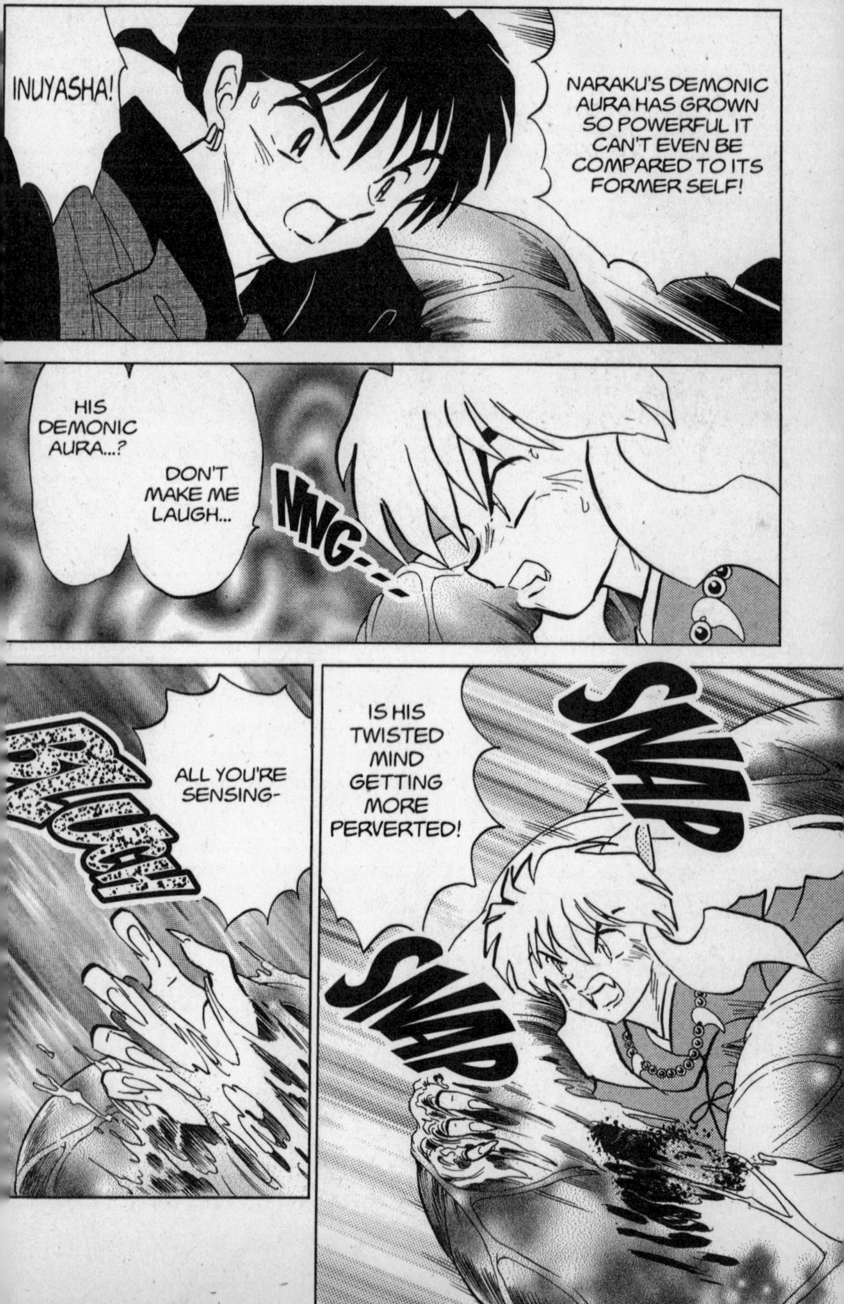
INUYASHA!
NARAKU'S DEMONIC AURA HAS GROWN SO POWERFUL IT CAN'T EVEN BE COMPARED TO ITS FORMER SELF!
HIS DEMONIC AURA...?
DON'T MAKE ME LAUGH...
MNG---
ALL YOU'RE SENSING-
IS HIS TWISTED MIND GETTING MORE PERVERTED!
SNAP
SNAP

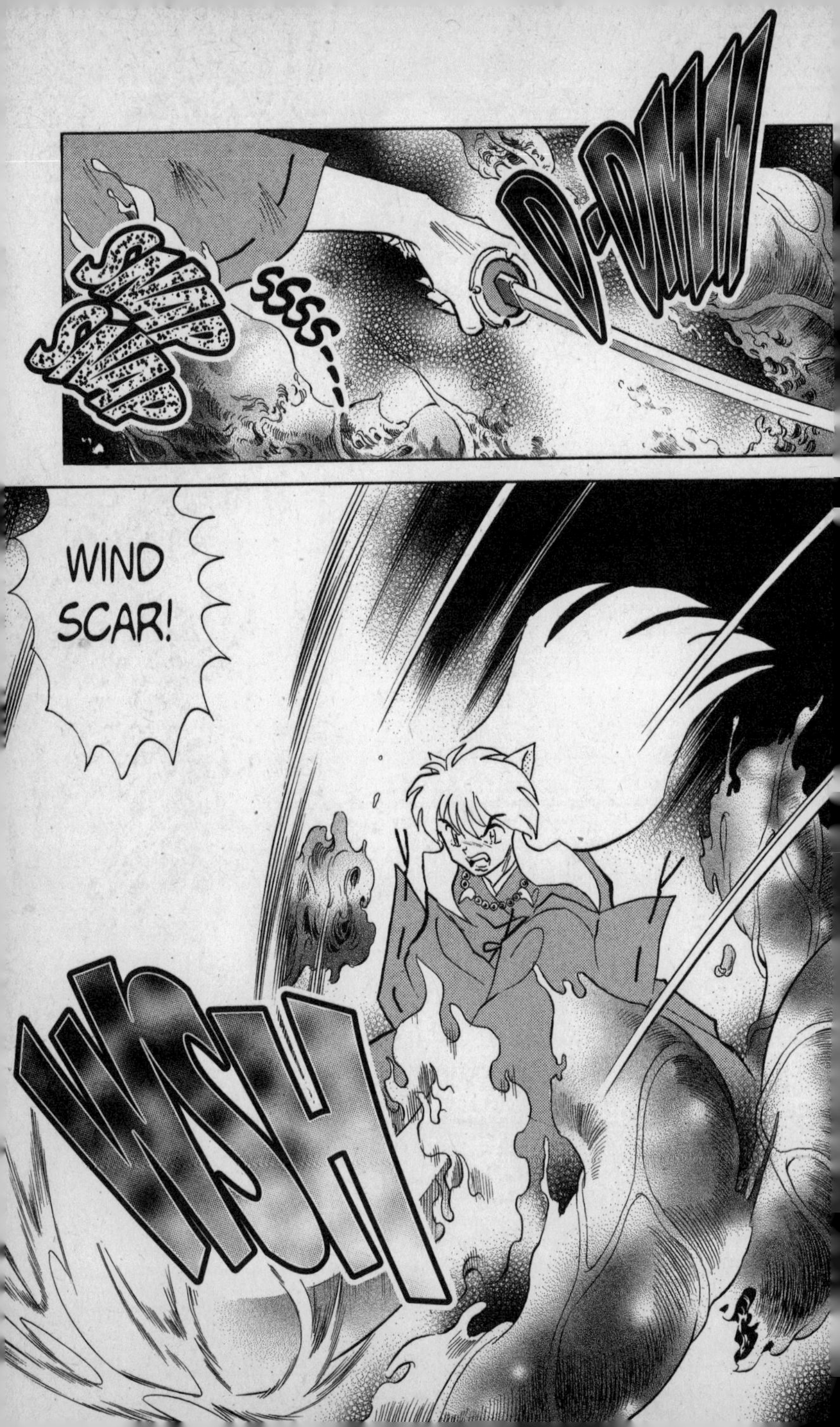
SSSS---
WIND SCAR!
WSSH!

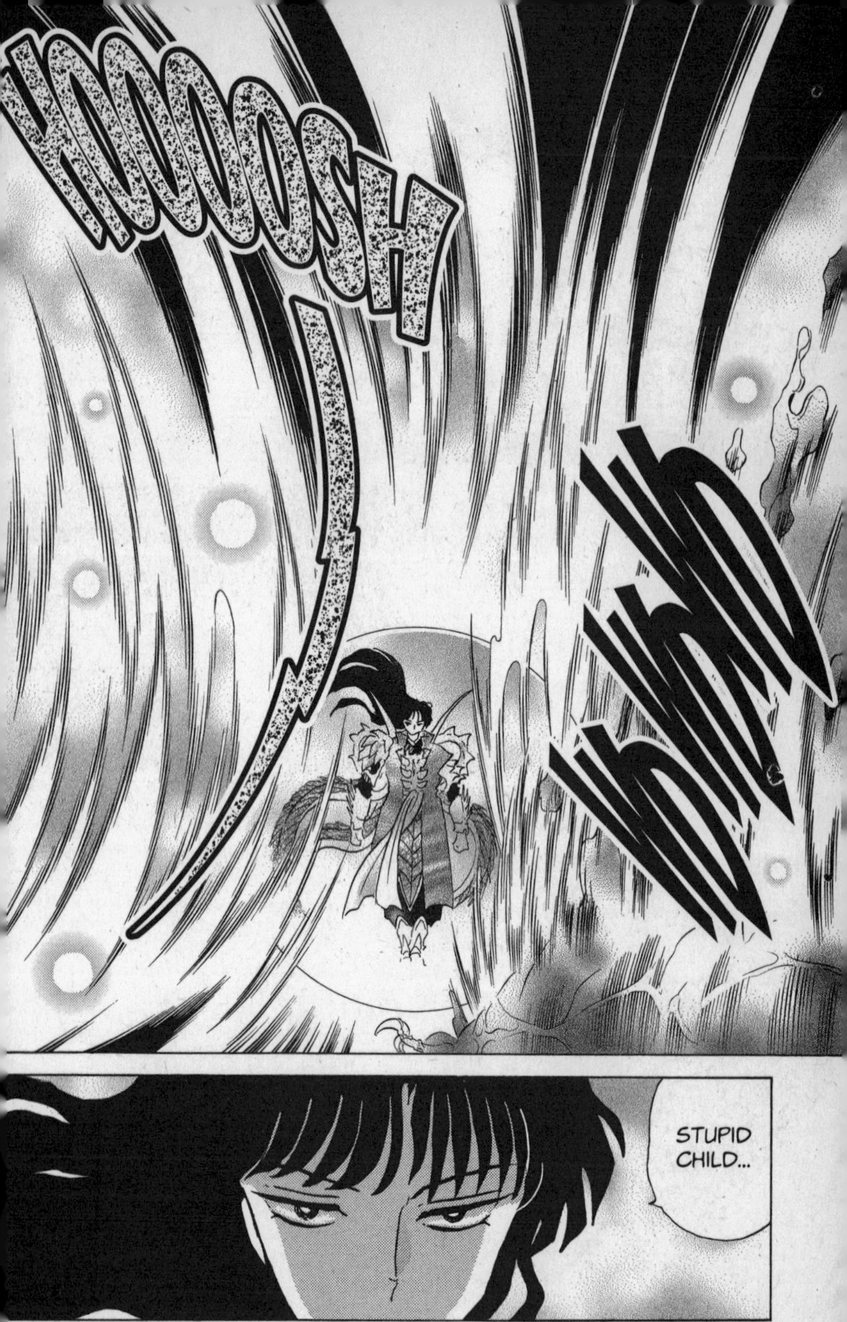
WHOOOSH
STUPID CHILD...

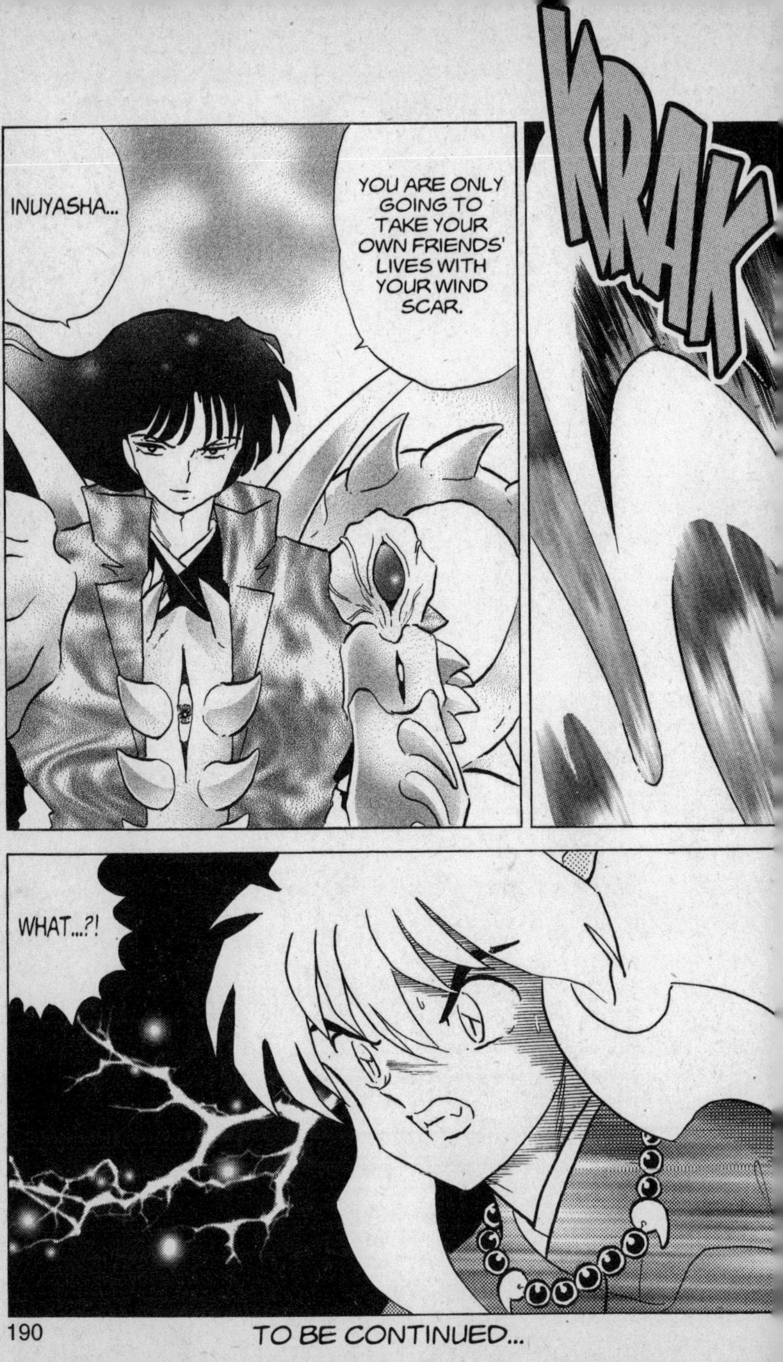
INUYASHA...
YOU ARE ONLY GOING TO TAKE YOUR OWN FRIENDS' LIVES WITH YOUR WIND SCAR.
KRAK
WHAT...?!

TO BE CONTINUED...

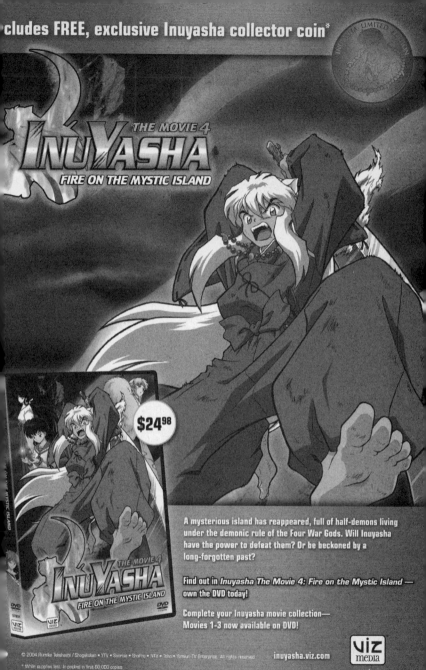

LOVE MANGA?
LET US KNOW WHAT YOU THINK!

W9-BJZ-009

OUR MANGA SURVEY IS NOW
AVAILABLE ONLINE. PLEASE VISIT:
VIZ.COM/MANGASURVEY

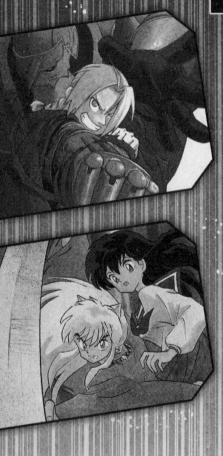

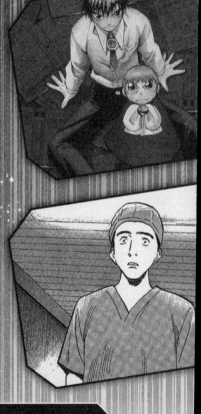

HELP US MAKE THE MANGA
YOU LOVE BETTER!

FULLMETAL ALCHEMIST © Hiromu Arakawa/SQUARE ENIX INUYASHA © 1997 Rumiko TAKAHASHI/Shogakukan Inc.
NAOKI URASAWA'S MONSTER © 1995 Naoki URASAWA Studio Nuts/Shogakukan Inc. ZATCH BELL! © 2001 Makoto RAIKU/Shogakukan Inc.